TRANSFORMING TI

STUDIES IN GOVERNMENT AND PUBLIC POLICY

TRANSFORMING THE CITY

Community Organizing and the Challenge of Political Change

Edited by
Marion Orr

 University Press of Kansas

Published by the University Press of Kansas (Lawrence, Kansas 66045), which was
organized by the Kansas Board of Regents and is operated and funded by Emporia State
University, Fort Hays State University, Kansas State University, Pittsburg State University,
the University of Kansas, and Wichita State University

Library of Congress Cataloging-in-Publication Data

Transforming the city : community organizing and the challenge of
political change / edited by Marion Orr.
      p. cm. — (Studies in government and public policy)
   Includes bibliographical references and index.
   ISBN 978-0-7006-1513-1 (cloth : alk. paper— ISBN 978-0-7006-1514-8
(pbk. : alk. paper)   1. Community organization—United States.
2. Community development, Urban—United States.   3. Social
participation—United States.   I. Orr, Marion, 1962–
   HN90.C6T684   2007
   307.3'4160973—dc22   2006038461

British Library Cataloguing-in-Publication Data is available.

Printed in the United States of America

10 9 8 7 6 5 4 3 2 1

The paper used in this publication meets the minimum requirements of the American
National Standard for Permanence of Paper for Printed Library Materials z39.48-1992.

To Professor Hanes Walton Jr.,
for inspiring me and his other students at
Savannah State College

CONTENTS

PREFACE AND ACKNOWLEDGMENTS

Many observers of contemporary American politics are concerned about the declining participation of citizens in public and civic life. Yet, in cities across the United States, community organizations like the ones covered in this collection are organizing, mobilizing, and empowering diverse groups of people around a wide range of issues. In Boston and Indianapolis, members of community organizations have partnered with local police and government social agencies to curb youth violence and improve police-community relations. In New York, Oakland, San Antonio, and Philadelphia, residents involved in community organizations worked to improve the quality of inner-city public schools and make schools more equitable. Community organizations in Baltimore and Memphis can claim responsibility for helping expand safe and affordable housing and making homeownership a reality for many low- and moderate-income city residents. Despite what some observers view as the continuing decline in the number of Americans who participate in civic and political affairs, there are community organizations in every major U.S. city working to empower residents to improve the quality of their lives and transform their communities.

Many of the individuals who are active in these organizations are low-income people of color who, according to the literature on political participation, are significantly less likely to be engaged in politics and civic life than are affluent citizens. Consider the story of Valerie Bell. When I met her in December 1999, Mrs. Bell was a widow, living in a small row house in West Baltimore. Born in Wilmington, Delaware, in 1941, Mrs. Bell moved to Baltimore in 1964 to live with her husband. Prior to 1994, Mrs. Bell, a high school graduate, had never joined a community organization or civic group. In 1994, she was earning $4.25 an hour as a custodian cleaning Southern High School. Although Southern High is a city school, Mrs. Bell was not a Baltimore municipal employee. She worked for a private firm, operating under a contract with the city. In recent decades, cities have tried to cut costs by outsourcing positions usually staffed by unionized municipal employees. In 1994, Mrs. Bell became part of an effort to fight what she described as "plain old city-sponsored poverty."* She became active in BUILD, a coalition of church-based community groups in Baltimore. BUILD was pushing the Baltimore

*Frederick N. Rasmussen, "Valerie M. Bell, 59, Wage Fight Leader," *Baltimore Sun*, October 3, 2000, 5B.

City Council to adopt an ordinance requiring companies with municipal contracts to pay their employees a "living wage."

Mrs. Bell was fired by the contractor after she tried to organize other custodians to join the living wage campaign. Mayor Kurt Schmoke would later intervene, helping her secure another custodian position as a municipal employee (at a higher wage and with fringe benefits). Nevertheless, Mrs. Bell remained active in BUILD's organizing effort, meeting with city hall officials, encouraging other custodians to join the campaign, appearing before the city council, and speaking at rallies. In December 1994, although he initially opposed it, Mayor Schmoke signed the nation's first "living wage" law. Mrs. Bell described her involvement in BUILD and the living wage campaign as an "eye-opener." "It was brought to my attention that I was being walked on up my back and down my chest." As Mrs. Bell recalled: "[BUILD] did open my eyes to political life, political standpoints; the fact that people can organize and move mountains. No matter who they are. No matter who it is they are against. They can organize against them. It's like the ant and the rubber tree. You think an ant can't move it, but the ants get organized and they can move the whole tree. And that's how I see BUILD. We the people are the ants, and we can move mountains if we're organized."*

In December 1999, when I interviewed her, Valerie Bell was still active in BUILD. She died in October 2000 of a heart attack at the age of fifty-nine. Shortly after Mrs. Bell's death, the *Baltimore Sun* published her obituary with a headline declaring her a "wage fight leader." The obituary, written by a *Sun* staff reporter, read like a news article; a photograph of Mrs. Bell accompanied it. Mayor Schmoke and other civic leaders were interviewed and quoted in the article. The dominant norm dictates that the placement and the format of Mrs. Bell's obituary in the *Sun* are usually reserved for bankers and top public officials, not someone who cleaned bathrooms, emptied trash, and straightened up offices. Valerie Bell's experience is similar to that of thousands of city residents who are engaged in community organizing and discover its potential for improving their quality of life. Their experiences challenge some dominant norms.

All the authors of the chapters in this book are sympathetic to the goals and aspirations represented in the work of community organizing. However, when we assess community organizing within the context of the changing cultural, political, social, and economic forces impacting U.S. cities, it is clear that as an avenue for progressive politics, community organizing faces certain challenges. The proliferation of low-wage jobs, for example, is associated with globalization and the restructuring of the U.S. economy. Unions, long an ally of community organizations, are experiencing historically low membership as global capital shifts more

*Interview with Valerie Bell, Baltimore, Maryland, December 4, 1999.

and more manufacturing jobs overseas. The formidable public culture of consumerism and hyperindividualism that squeezes families for time and keeps them on the go is a real constraint on community organizing. The frenetic pace of life— fueled by marketers operating in a competitive global economy—weakens families and communities, while the norm of radical individualism collides with the need for collective action. The increasing fragmentation and diffusion of local political and civic leadership in cities—where the center of local decision making is no longer lodged in city hall or found among a small group of local business leaders— make potential "targets" of the organizing effort less apparent. For example, mayors and city councillors increasingly share decision making in matters affecting their cities with governors and members of quasi-governmental boards and regional authorities, creating a strategic challenge for many community organizations. There are limits to what can be done locally. Many of the troubles facing the urban poor have roots in state and national politics and policies. Community organizing faces the challenge of developing the capacity to become translocal and part of something bigger. This volume addresses these issues and more.

This book grew out of two workshops organized at Brown University. I wish to thank Peter Burns, Peter Dreier, Michael Evans, Bob Fisher, Mark Santow, Dennis Shirley, Eric Shragge, Kathleen Staudt, Clarence Stone, Heidi Swarts, and Rich Wood for participating in the workshop and for their work on chapters contributed to this book. Janice Fine, who has done pioneering research on organizing immigrant workers, helped us think through some of the broader implications of the volume's conceptual framework on community organizing. Bringing this group of excellent scholars together helped me tremendously as I ventured into community organizing as an area of research.

This book has deep intellectual roots, reaching back to Savannah State College, a small college in my hometown, where I earned my undergraduate degree in political science. At Savannah State, Hanes Walton Jr. introduced me to the dominant paradigms and central concepts of political science. His well-known encyclopedic knowledge of the political science literature was freely shared in the classroom, during office hours, and in the hallways of Payne Hall. After I left Savannah for graduate school, Hanes continued to be a source of inspiration and support. Many years later I can still depend on him for a critical assessment of the latest "hot" research, inspiration for a new research idea, sage professional advice, a kind word, and a good laugh.

The conceptual approach of this volume is rooted in my graduate school training at the University of Maryland. Clarence N. Stone substantially enriched my understanding of urban politics. In *Regime Politics,* Clarence argued that the bedrock of urban power is the composition of the governing regime. In *Transforming the City,* we see community organizations working to gain positions in the governing regime in order to affect policy. In addition to contributing to this volume, Clarence has offered much useful advice. When I mentioned to him that I was considering editing a volume on community organizing, he warned me of the potential pitfalls of pulling together a collection of essays, chuckled, and told me that everybody ought to try editing a volume at least once in their career. Clarence has been a great friend and mentor.

I would be remiss if I did not thank those affiliated with Brown University for their support and assistance. Dean Mary Fennell and Provost Robert Zimmer provided critical institutional support for this project. Professor Darrell West has been a source of support and encouragement throughout this project. Ethan Horowitz, one of my former undergraduate students, who is now at Harvard Law School, helped organize the two workshops, facilitating the development of this book in several ways. Patricia Gardner of Brown's political science department also assisted in the logistics of the two meetings.

I also want to thank the external reviewers who evaluated the manuscript for the University Press of Kansas for their extraordinarily helpful comments. They provided useful criticisms and suggestions that improved the book. Fred Woodward, the Director of the University Press of Kansas, has been the consummate professional, providing good advice and feedback on many aspects of the project, overseeing it through to its end. Susan Schott, Larisa Martin, and other UPK staff treated the manuscript with great care and were a pleasure to work with.

Last, I am indebted to family and friends. My wife, Ramona L. Burton, read through parts of the manuscript, offering critical insights. An exceptionally well-trained political scientist, Ramona offered advice and ideas as I embarked on research on community organizing. Ramona is also a wonderful partner and friend, providing an enormous amount of emotional support and encouragement, always believing in my abilities even when I questioned them. My parents, Robert Lee Orr and Delores B. Orr, have always cheered me along. My brother and sister, Robert Orr and Rhonda Gale Orr, have been very supportive, as have my nephew Malcolm and niece, Katrina. Finally, I would like to thank the Reverend Barry Wright, a friend from our days at Duke University, for his support.

TRANSFORMING THE CITY

1. Community Organizing and the Changing Ecology of Civic Engagement

Marion Orr

There is considerable discussion and increasing concern about the declining levels of civic engagement in the United States. A recent study produced by a group of scholars affiliated with the American Political Science Association (APSA) proclaimed that "American democracy is at risk" because Americans have turned away from public and civic life.[1] Robert Putnam used the "bowling alone" metaphor to describe the decline in membership in civic organizations, fraternal groups, parent-teacher associations, Boy Scouts, and many other organizations.[2] Theda Skocpol attributes part of America's "diminished democracy" to the rise of "professional advocacy groups" (Common Cause, Sierra Club, Children's Defense Fund, AARP), political action committees, and professionally run nonprofit service delivery organizations. Skocpol calls them memberless organizations because the vast majority are connected to their "members" only through mailing lists.[3] A significant proportion of the American professional class that once dominated "local chapters of old-line membership federations" now support these staff-driven "advocacy" groups located in Washington, D.C., in state capitals, and in cities across the United States.[4] According to the study sponsored by the APSA, "Americans have turned away from politics and the public sphere in large numbers, leaving our civic life impoverished."[5]

Most observers agree that the decline of civic engagement and the hijacking of locally rooted organizations are not good news for the United States and that the problem is magnified and implications far-reaching in the country's central cities. Stephen Macedo and his colleagues point to metropolitan areas and their central cities as places "where the most serious challenges to healthy democratic life are also found." With higher concentrations of low-income and disadvantaged residents, cities are disproportionately hurt by civic disengagement.[6] The professionally operated and top-down advocacy organizations that now dominate the civic landscape are not targeting low-income, central city residents. Well-educated suburban communities are their targets, not central cities, where schools are disproportionately failing, unemployment is high, finding safe and affordable housing is

1

a challenge, and crime and drug use make daily headlines.[7] Is there a strategy that could address many of the social and economic challenges facing central cities and help reinvigorate civic engagement in urban communities? This book explores community organizing as such a strategy.

In general, the term *community organizing* refers to the process that engages people, organizations, and communities toward the goals of increased individual and community control, political efficacy, improved quality of life, and social justice. Community organizations operate at the local level—in cities, towns, and neighborhoods—confronting, negotiating and working with mayors, city councillors, appointed officials, civic and corporate leaders, and, increasingly, state-level officials. The central feature of community organizing is that it is a process and strategy designed to build political power.

It has been estimated that there are more than 6,000 community organizations working to organize, engage, and empower people in poor communities in the United States.[8] Typically, these groups employ professional organizers who identify committed community residents, assemble them for group actions, and instruct them in effective methods of community empowerment and improvement. Many of the people involved in these organizations live in low-income communities of color. These groups include local organizations affiliated with the leading national community organizing "networks," the Industrial Areas Foundation (IAF), Pacific Institute for Community Organization (PICO), the Gamaliel Foundation, and Direct Action and Research Training (DART). These organizations have a multi-issue organizing strategy and rely heavily on religious congregations as constituent members. There are also community organizations affiliated with networks like the Association of Community Organizations for Reform Now (ACORN) and the Center for Third World Organizing (CTWO) that enlist individuals, especially in poor communities, as dues-paying members.[9] There are hundreds of independent or "unaffiliated" local organizations like Boston's Dudley Street Neighborhood Initiative that are devoted to building power.[10]

A growing number of cases illustrate the promise of community organizing for empowering inner-city residents to bring tangible changes to their communities. In 1994, BUILD, a community organization in Baltimore, helped pass a city ordinance that increased the wages of approximately 4,000 to 5,000 low-wage workers, including janitors and cafeteria workers.[11] Today, more than 100 municipalities have adopted "living wage" laws, nearly all of them encouraged to do so by residents involved in community organizations.[12] Community organizations in New York City, Chicago, and Texas have organized residents to improve failing urban public schools.[13] Mothers on the Move, a community organization located in the Bronx, forced the superintendent to resign, exposed the disparity in achievement and resources between schools, transformed the school district's politics, and is credited

with helping students in once failing schools to improve their academic performance. In California, the Oakland Community Organization successfully organized
to win the endorsement of the school district for the creation of small, autonomous
schools. In Chicago, the Logan Square Neighborhood Association used traditional
organizing strategies and tactics to force the city to build two new middle schools
to address overcrowding. Community organizations have been successful at improving housing conditions in neighborhoods in New York City, Atlanta, Boston,
Chicago, Los Angeles, and other cities.[14] Von Hoffman argues that "the first and
essential ingredients" for successfully rebuilding urban neighborhoods were "good
grassroots organizations."[15]

Harry Boyte has long called attention to the "backyard revolution" fueled by
community organizing. Boyte considers organizing a mechanism through which
all Americans can do "public work."[16] "An organizing approach," he maintains,
"changes politics and empowers citizens."[17] Gregory Markus has shown that low-
income residents living in neighborhoods where a tradition of strong community
organization exists have higher levels of political and civic engagement than residents living in "more resourceful" communities.[18] The secret, writes Paul Osterman,
to "involving people in politics and mobilizing them is the development of strong
local organizations."[19] The implication is that community organizing could be an
antidote for the civic engagement paralysis prevalent in America's cities.

While acknowledging the benefits and potential of community organizing, a
theme of this volume is that as an avenue for progressive politics, community organizing faces certain challenges. This book assesses community organizing within the
context of the cultural, political, social, and economic forces that impact the local
ecology of civic engagement. By ecology of civic engagement, I mean the terms by
which major community and institutional sectors of a city relate to one another and
their role in the structure and function of local political regimes. I use the term ecology because it focuses on the interrelationship between community sectors and their
broader civic, cultural, economic, and political environment. Norton Long argues
that the politics of local communities could be thought of as "an ecology of games"
in which major institutional sectors of the city—including labor unions, business,
government, religious organizations, political parties—occupied a common "territorial field . . . interacting with one another" and "collaborating for different and
particular ends in the achievement of over-all social functions."[20] How the major
stakeholders in a community align themselves to respond to broad cultural, social,
economic, and political change, and how that alignment is shaped by the character
and history of interaction among and between them, informs our understanding of
the ecology of civic engagement. For community organizations, the challenge is to
develop a level of symbiosis with key institutional players in the face of broad
changes in the political, cultural, economic, and social environment of central cities.

Community organizing in the United States has a long history, tracing its roots to the settlement house movement of the late nineteenth century.[21] Although they are seldom identified as such, Ella Baker, Fannie Lou Hamer, Robert Moses, and other blacks who played central roles in the civil rights movement were effective community organizers.[22] Community organizing as we have come to know it today, however, was shaped and molded by Saul Alinsky. Alinsky's experience organizing in the white, ethnic Back of the Yards neighborhood in Chicago in the 1930s, and his later work in the predominantly African American Woodlawn neighborhood of Chicago in the 1960s, catapulted him into a national figure. In 1940, he formed the Industrial Areas Foundation (IAF) to train people to organize themselves and their communities into "people organizations." He directed the IAF until his death in 1972.[23] Alinsky's theories about community organizing and power have influenced the leaders of scores of community-based organizations.[24]

In this chapter, I use the early history of community organizing to help emphasize the importance of the local ecology of civic engagement. Using the experience of the Back of the Yards Neighborhood Council (Alinsky's first community organization, formed in 1939) as a starting point, I discuss the shift of the public culture away from a commonwealth to consumerism and hyperindividualism and how the shift impacted civic engagement and community organizing. The chapter employs an examination of the broad political, social, and economic changes that have occurred in the United States to describe and analyze the changes in the urban political economy and assess community organizing within the context of a changing ecology of civic engagement. I argue that the local ecology of civic engagement is much more diffused than when Alinsky was an organizer, creating major challenges for community organizing.

PUBLIC CULTURE, COMMUNITY ORGANIZING, AND THE ECOLOGY OF CIVIC ENGAGEMENT

Cultural theorists have long recognized the relationship between culture and political and social behavior.[25] Michael Denning's account of the "popular front" of the 1930s and 1940s provides an excellent example of how a public culture helped give birth to a coalition of millions of urban industrial workers and middle-class white urban professionals and shopkeepers.[26] The cornerstone of the Fordist and scientific management paradigms, mechanized production combined with mass consumption of standardized products, was fully institutionalized into American industry by the 1920s. While workers found the regularization of work demoralizing and dehumanizing, many others challenged the emphasis on market consumption and questioned its impact on families and communities. The popular front represented the resistance of workers and communities to Fordism and the negative externalities of the Fordist industrialist regime on the public culture.

According to Denning, the popular front was sustained by a "sense of class consciousness and a new rhetoric of class." Members of the popular front became the mass audience for the "cultural apparatus" (the new technologies of motion pictures, recorded sound, radio broadcasting, newsreels, and news magazines) of the period, and the rank-and-file "culture industry" workers largely responsible for running the "cultural apparatus" that influenced mass culture. The militancy and solidarity among workers were infused in the public culture through theatrical performances, small magazines, poems, songs, cartoons, and education. "Mass culture," Denning observed, "took on a distinctly plebian accent."[27] The popular front was successful because it touched the lives of millions of ordinary people. The public culture was such that an alternative vision of society and politics began to percolate. This vision translated into social movements and community organizing efforts in cities and factories.[28]

According to Denning, the popular front emerged in the late 1920s, "and it remained the central popular democratic movement over the following three decades."[29] Saul Alinsky "was most directly a child of the 1930s popular movements, when populist themes of older movements had come alive again on a massive scale, in new ways."[30] In 1939, when Alinsky organized Back of the Yards residents, Chicago's ecology of civic engagement was heavily influenced by the owners and managers of the meatpacking and slaughtering industry. Swift and Company and Armour and Company were industrial giants, headquartered in Chicago. As the city's largest private employers, the owners and managers of the meatpacking industry played a central role in its economic, civic, and political affairs. More than 60 percent of the workers in the Back of the Yards were employed in the stockyards. In his careful study of the Back of the Yards, Robert A. Slayton observes that "where one lived, what one ate, what one smelled were all determined, or at least influenced, by the meatpackers."[31] According to Slayton, "Decisions on every aspect of living came in response to what went on in the factories." He explains, "At any given time, a quarter of the work force might be out of work. The packers took men on as they needed them, and laid them off when they did not."[32] Advances in technology and expert ideas on how to increase productivity drove up profits while forcing work changes in the stockyards, decreasing pay for workers, increasing random layoffs, and causing a chaotic and unpredictable home and community life for the workers and their families.

Despite the divisions that existed among the various ethnic groups that constituted the Back of the Yards, the residents shared a culture that embraced community and valued the tradition of self-governance and concern for the general welfare, or "commonwealth."[33] Central to the public culture were institutions, social structures, values, and norms that allowed the Back of the Yards residents to frame an alternative vision of their community and lives. Slayton observes that the residents "sought and found pockets of experience they could call their own—areas where they could assume control, make decisions, and establish order."[34] When Saul Alinsky decided to organize Chicago's Back of the Yards neighborhood in 1939, he was able to tap into this public culture. As Boyte explains: "The loyalties of religion, ethnicity, neighborhood, craft, or simple day-to-day interaction forged in the ethnic and working-class communities of large cities or the small towns and countryside of rural areas produced the commitments that moved people to action when ways of life seemed threatened."[35]

In the parlance of community organizing, a "target" is "the person or people the organization must influence in order to make change."[36] Alinsky and other community leaders targeted Armour and Company and the other packinghouses, using the negotiations between the meatpackers and leaders of a stalled Congress of Industrial Organizations (CIO) labor organizing drive as the staging ground. Alinsky supported the unionization effort, believing that if it was successful, wages and benefits would increase and working conditions would improve, translating into stronger tax bases for the community, better schools, and improved public services. By the summer of 1939, with the help of local leaders in the neighborhood and a powerful Catholic bishop sympathetic to unionization, Alinsky brought together an array of existing local organizations—church societies, union locals, ethnic clubs, bowling leagues, business associations, card clubs, and the community's national Catholic parishes (whose priests had previously opposed unionization)—to form his first community organization, the Back of the Yards Neighborhood Council (BYNC).

In July 1939, the BYNC subsequently voted to support the CIO Packinghouse Workers Union. A few days later, the BYNC, labor organizers, and church leaders held a rally at the Chicago Coliseum attended by more than 30,000 people. The rally convinced the companies that they could not hold out against this coalition of neighborhood churches, residents, and workers. The companies agreed to recognize the labor union. The workers received better wages and increased benefits. In backing the victorious labor organizing drive, the BYNC demonstrated that a strong community organization could gain a victory against a corporate entity that had long dominated Chicago's local ecology of civic engagement. The BYNC would go on to target city government and public officials, gaining support for much-needed programs in the areas of health, education, housing, and hunger.

The formation of the BYNC realigned the civic and political ecology of the neighborhood. One observer suggested that the BYNC politically isolated Armour and the other packers "by changing their relationship with the Catholic Church. For nearly a half century in the Back of the Yards, church spires and packinghouse smokestacks had shared the skyline, each in their own place. After the July 14 weekend, the skyline somehow looked different. The spires and smokestacks now competed for space rather than shared it. As a political architect, Alinsky had done a masterful job."[37]

This historical account helps shed light on community organizing, public culture, and the changing ecology of civic engagement. Part of Alinsky's brilliance was his capacity to understand that the Back of the Yards could be organized by connecting with the uniqueness of the community and culture of the people. During the time that Alinsky organized the BYNC, the public culture in Chicago and other industrial cities was infused with a sense of resentment that powerful forces outside the community were threatening traditional ways of civic life. The residents of the Back of the Yards were shaped by a public culture that disliked and questioned the control experts, managers, and industrialists exerted over their lives. This public culture led the residents to draw on the tradition of citizen responsibility, to become engaged in "everyday politics" so that critical decisions about home life, schools, and community were not left in the hands of a few industrialists and the professional managers, experts, and technicians who sought and developed ways to increase their profit margins.

Nearly seventy years later, researchers and those closer to the action agree that the consumerism, materialism, and hyperindividualism of American public culture are draining the life out of contemporary civil society. For example, the professionally run, managerially oriented civic engagement prevalent today is not inconsistent with the consumerism, hypercommercialization, materialism, radical individualism, and frenetic pace of modern American life that are dominant features of contemporary public culture. The cultural industry machine of magazines, televisions, radio, cable channels, and Hollywood movies, fuels Americans' desires for more material goods. In 1999, QVC, the twenty-four-hour home television shopping network, with more than 111 million phone calls a year, had sales totaling $2.8 billion, making it more profitable than a host of traditional retailers. QVC, writes one author, "exemplifies a set of broader cultural impulses."[38] Edward Chambers, who succeeded Saul Alinsky as director of the IAF, argues that "television is a profoundly parochial, addictive medium with an almost universal range. It pumps out powerful images of what it is to be human, images frequently destructive of healthy family values."[39] The impact of television on the public culture of consumerism starts young, with logos and brand names dancing in the heads of children before they enter kindergarten. Designer clothing and the choice between $150.00 Nike or $160.00 Adidas sneakers are a part of the contemporary culture of consumption.

To keep the family money machine running, parents are working longer hours. Mothers scramble to transport children to after-school activities and part-time jobs.

Instead of "soccer moms," many mothers have become "strung-out chauffeurs."[40] To make it convenient for families to continue the frantic pace, marketers now encourage parents to dig a little deeper and invest in cellular telephones with special "family plans." Family dinnertime is no longer the routine for many Americans. Family traditions are eroding.

In addition to having significant staffing and funding problems, public schools are also suffering under the pressure of the contemporary public culture.[41] For instance, when educational researcher John Ogbu was invited to examine the causes of the black-white achievement gap in Shaker Heights, a suburb of Cleveland, Ohio, he found that part of the problem was "consumerism."[42] Although black parents had high academic expectations for their children, they were unable to show them how to succeed in school because household financial demands required them to work long hours, sometimes two jobs. As a consequence, many of Shaker Heights' African American parents were less likely to be involved in parent-teacher organizations or attend parent-teacher conferences. In addition, teachers and school personnel expressed concerns that high percentages of African American students allowed part-time jobs to compete with time spent on academics. According to Ogbu, while some students held jobs to supplement family income, others "did so to purchase material things or pay off credit card debts."[43]

Thomas Friedman and other observers have connected the contemporary public culture of consumerism to globalization.[44] Globalization helped spawn a public culture infused with a focus on materialism, heightening Americans' individualism and contributing to civic disengagement.[45] Americans are seeing civic life as one of many choices. A recent study found that young people do not view citizenship as accompanied by obligations to the wider community. According to the study, only 38 percent of young adults believe that civic life entails special obligations, and 58 percent say simply being a good person is enough.[46] As one study noted, "A form of individualism centered on unfettered choice has become a dominant cultural norm."[47]

Paradoxically, Americans are not happy and are alarmed by the public culture of consumption and materialism. According to a 1995 nationwide study by the Hardwood Group of attitudes toward the culture of consumerism, Americans from "all walks of life—rich and poor, men and women, all ages, all races, reach a remarkably similar conclusion: things are seriously out of whack," and the "culture of consumerism" robs "resources from future generations, generates too much waste, and undermines community and family."[48] People seem especially concerned about the influence of the consumer-oriented culture on America's children and youth. Eighty-six percent of those surveyed agreed that "today's youth are too focused on buying and consuming things."[49] African American respondents were nearly unanimous (94%) in their agreement.[50] The survey showed that the majority of the respondents yearned for a feeling of stability in their lives, "not to repudiate material gain, but to bring it more into proportion with the non-material rewards of life."[51]

Community organizers are returning their organizing work to culture. I say "returning" to culture, because by his later years, Alinsky had discounted culture and "even the older democratic language" used in the 1930s and 1940s.[52] When Alinsky organized black communities in Rochester and Chicago in the 1960s, he viewed organizing as a sort of interest group politics in which citizens would participate in community organizations to do battle with and achieve concessions from powerful institutions. For example, although African American churches were significant components of the organizations' membership, "Alinsky was not particularly interested in the culture and belief systems embedded in the churches he recruited."[53] Alinsky viewed the churches as essential for resource mobilization. Reflecting on the status of community organizing at the time of Alinsky's death in 1972, Harry Boyte observed that "on balance, Alinsky's style of community organization did much to keep alive and adapt older populist themes of organizing for power in the twentieth century. But it was not enough. While developing important methods for citizen empowerment, it nonetheless failed to address the wider democratic impoverishment of American political culture."[54]

By the 1980s, the modern IAF began to center its organizing more on the role culture and values played in citizens' daily lives.[55] This focus was originally laid out by Edward Chambers in a document entitled "Organizing for Family and Congregation," which articulated the belief that the public culture of consumerism and materialism had injured families and communities. Chambers characterized the challenge as fundamentally an issue of "who will shape the values of our society"— "the huge corporations, mass media, and 'benevolent' government" or families, congregations, "social groups like the Lions Club or the VFW, religious orders of men and women and perhaps a merchants association."[56] Since the early 1980s, the IAF has almost exclusively based its organizing around religious congregations, believing that their ideas and traditions might provide important values to sustain participatory politics. Michael Gecan, an IAF organizer, described organizing as "cultural work." "When you focus on culture, or cultures, you take into account habits, patterns, beliefs, symbols, heroes and heroines, including your own, not just legislation and policies, elections and appointments, current causes or party platforms."[57] The idea is that cultural work could lead to alternative visions of the world. This is akin to what Kristina Smock calls creating "transformative frames" that "provide residents with new lenses through which to make sense of their experiences— lenses that enable residents to perceive the connections between their own problems and broader economic and political arrangements."[58] Today, a significant portion of the national organizing networks focus their training and organizing on culture. PICO, for example, shifted its organizing focus to culture and values in the early

1980s. According to Richard Wood, "PICO's recent success has resulted in large measure from its religious cultural strategy."[59]

The focus on culture is not limited to congregation-based organizing. Formed in 1980, CTWO utilizes a "race-based organizing" model. CTWO appeals to "cultural elements identified with participants' racial, ethnic, or national traditions."[60] Rinku Sen, a former CTWO organizer, explained that developing local leaders is "culturally based, it has to resonate with people's lived experience but at the same time influence their understanding of their tradition. This process is best accomplished by grounding leadership development in the day-to-day realities that cause tiny shifts in cultural practice."[61] ACORN is not as explicit about its cultural work, but its culture of "direct action" is linked to the experiences many of its leaders had in the civil rights movement.[62]

The organizations covered in this volume are not like the Christian Coalition and the religious Right organizations, whose concerns about contemporary public culture have manifested into an issue agenda dominated by opposition to abortion, crackdowns on illegal immigration, bans of pornography, support for prayers in public schools, and restrictions on the rights of gays and lesbians.[63] The organizations discussed in this book are typically composed of multiple racial and ethnic groups and use their influence to improve public education, make housing affordable, address neighborhood crime, prevent predatory lending practices, and confront other issues faced by disadvantaged communities. The groups discussed here are not like the professionally managed advocacy groups without chapters or members that Theda Skocpol bemoans. Indeed, the community organizations covered in this volume are the antithesis of the advocacy groups that have been taken over by the specialists, experts, and professionals. Skocpol, in fact, singles out the kind of community organizing discussed in this volume as "innovative and effective" and "locally rooted."[64] Finally, the organizations discussed in the following chapters have not followed the lead of the citizen action groups criticized by Dana Fisher and others for their heavy use of the canvass, in which paid staff goes door-to-door collecting signatures on a petition or mobilizing residents.[65] Rather than "diminishing democracy," the organizations like the ones covered in this volume are attempting to replenish democracy.

ECOLOGY OF CIVIC ENGAGEMENT AND THE CHANGING URBAN POLITICAL ECONOMY

When Alinsky organized the BYNC in the late 1930s, a significant part of the community organizing strategy was to confront and negotiate with owners and managers of locally rooted companies. The BYNC did battle with Swift and Armour, two of the huge meatpacking firms headquartered in Chicago, over improved working conditions and better pay. In 1965, Rochester-based Eastman Kodak struggled with FIGHT over the latter's demand for a new jobs program designed to increase the number of African American employees. The belief was that locally owned corporations had a responsibility to help address the problems of local poverty and racial discrimination. Business owners and managers, who depended on local neighborhood residents for workers and consumers, became targets.[66]

Another strategy was to organize citizens to demand that city government provide high-quality public services such as schools, parks, and fire and police protection equitably. During much of the time that Alinsky was an organizer, municipal governments in many U.S. cities were controlled by political machines. Because machines were "rooted in the neighborhoods," ward-level politics and neighborhood politics were the areas of greatest activity in city affairs.[67] Political power was concentrated in the hands of precinct captains, block captains, ward committeemen, and city aldermen.[68] Neighborhood residents recognized machine politicians as men to go to to get streets paved, clean dirty alleys, have garbage collected, repair sidewalks, or install a new streetlight. They could also get people out of jail, assist in finding a job, lower a property tax assessment, and provide emergency food aid. Writing about Chicago in the 1930s, Slayton observed that "politics . . . meant reliance on individual politicians," especially those based at the district or ward levels. Even business interests acknowledged this basic fact of urban political life and worked closely with ward-level and district-level politicians when it came to building new homes, schools, sewer systems, and public transportation systems. The ecology of civic engagement centered on patronage and personal favors.[69]

For community organizations, the predominance of ward-level politics presented challenges and opportunities. Moving residents away from the pursuit of particular and personalistic opportunities toward a larger vision of how the community might be reformed was a considerable challenge. One of the problems with machine and patronage politics is that it undercut discussions of broad, community-wide issues. Approaching a ward leader to help bail out a son, for example, addresses a parent's immediate concern, but such an approach does not speak to the issue of the causes and prevention of juvenile delinquency. However, community organizing at the ward level provided organizers with a captive audience, often a mass of people with shared traditions, backgrounds, challenges, and interests. In addition, community organizers strategized that ward-level politicians were prime targets for addressing many of the issues facing poor communities. For example, Alinsky and the BYNC staged "sit-downs" in the offices of ward-level politicians who were rooted in the neighborhoods and strategically situated to move the municipal bureaucracy to affect their communities. "The officials snarled and made excuses but soon things began to improve—garbage was collected weekly, streets were repaired, police patrols were increased, vacant houses were boarded up."[70]

Since Alinsky began organizing in the late 1930s, and even after his death in 1972, there have been changes in the urban political economy that have impacted community organizing. According to a report from the Howard Samuels Center, "The city that community organizers and activists now inhabit is vastly different in many ways from the 'hog town' Alinsky found himself organizing in the late 1930s."[71] Globalization, for example, opened U.S. corporations to foreign competition, making them economically vulnerable. Corporate mergers and buyouts have left what were local companies in the hands of conglomerates based in other localities, sometimes in suburbs and often in distant cities or countries. Today, corporations like Eastman Kodak are more likely to eliminate jobs or outsource them overseas than to meet community organizers' demands to hire local residents.[72]

Globalization and economic restructuring have also led to the rise in the number of service sector and advanced corporate jobs and a dramatic decline in the number of manufacturing jobs. A study of seven northeastern and midwestern metropolitan areas found that between 1960 and 2000 the percentage of manufacturing jobs fell from 32 to 12 percent. During the same period, the percentage of service jobs rose from 15 to 36 percent.[73] In recent decades, large numbers of immigrants from Latin America have been drawn to the central city by opportunities created by globalization and economic restructuring, helping to create a bifurcated city workforce. There are many low-waged workers who clean office buildings and provide personal services to the professional class. These workers are often part-time or temporary, nonunionized, and largely African Americans and Latinos. The other workers are those whose skills and training put them in managerial and professional positions in the cities' new advanced corporate economy.[74]

Cities have responded to these changes in similar ways. For example, as the social and economic complexity of the postindustrial city increased and the competition between cities to attract capital investment expanded, the "structure of power" shifted away from ward-level and neighborhood politics toward citywide politics dominated by the mayor.[75] By the late 1950s, according to Robert Salisbury, a new "convergence of power" occurred in which city authority became more centralized, typically in the mayor's office. Mayors became the supreme political and civic tacticians. However, this too would change in the 1970s and 1980s, when political power in urban areas became much more diffuse. For example, mayors and other city officials share the local ecology with the professional staff and officials who operate the increasing number and range of local public authorities and special districts that are important to urban dwellers or directly impact their communities, including parks and recreation, housing, water service, highways, mass transit, libraries, hospitals, electric service, landfills, and airports.⁷⁶ These special districts and authorities have increased dramatically over the past thirty years. In addition, since the 1970s the number of quasi-public redevelopment corporations that play a significant role in central city land-use issues has increased significantly. Mark Levine shows that "in some cities, these corporations now wield extraordinary powers historically reserved for institutions of representative government: they can condemn and assemble land parcels, issue tax-exempt bonds, receive and administer grants and loans from other levels of government, and offer investment inducements such as tax abatements."⁷⁷

More than ever, mayors and city councillors increasingly share power with state officials and an array of local public authorities and special districts.⁷⁸ In Baltimore, for example, all the professional sport facilities, including Camden Yards (home to the city's professional baseball team) and the M and T Bank football stadium (home to the Baltimore Ravens professional football team) were constructed under the auspices of, and are currently operated by, the Maryland Stadium Authority (MSA). The MSA consists of seven members who serve four-year terms. Six are appointed by the governor with the advice and consent of the state senate. One is chosen by the mayor of Baltimore with senate advice and consent. The governor names the chair. With the governor's approval, the MSA appoints the executive director. In 1996 the MSA, which also has jurisdiction over Baltimore's downtown convention center, completed an expansion that tripled that facility's size.⁷⁹ State governments in recent years have exerted more involvement in central cities in an array of policy areas.

The diffused nature of the local ecology of civic engagement is also present at the community level. Consider, for example, El Paso and New Orleans, two cities covered in this volume. Prior to the 1970s, El Paso's leading political and civic force was lodged in a small white Anglo business community centered primarily in the banking industry. However, El Paso's ecology of civic engagement opened to new players, altering power relations. Today, business involvement is much more limited and selective. El Paso's business community is less cohesive. There is also a significant and growing Latino professional class. From about the middle 1940s through 1970, local ecology of civic engagement in New Orleans was dominated by a powerful group of small property holders and a social aristocracy. After the 1970s, the civic ecology of New Orleans was led by a concentration of oil and petrochemical executives. Today, it is much more diffuse, with nonprofit organizations, gaming industries, a regionally focused chamber of commerce, and hospitality and tourist organizations all having a significant place within the city's civic and political affairs. In short, in New Orleans and many other large cities, there is no longer a cohesive city structure or civic ecology.

The implications of these economic, demographic, and political changes for the local ecology of civic engagement and community organizing have been enormous.

For example, Saul Alinsky worked closely with John Lewis of the CIO and other labor unions, seeing the BYNC as sort of an extension of union organizing. With globalization and deindustrialization, labor unions declined as service sector jobs eclipsed the blue-collar unionized jobs that once dominated the urban industrial economy.[80] In 1954, more than 30 percent of wage and salary workers belonged to unions. In 2004, only 9 percent of private-sector wage and salary workers were union members.[81] Although labor unions and community organizers continue to work for shared goals ("living wage" campaigns, for example), the drop in union membership and the in-migration of nonunionized workers have weakened an early and important ally of community organizations.

Once local companies and businesses expanded into the global economy, their focus increasingly turned beyond the central city, weakening the level of attachment of corporate executives and senior managers to central cities and their residents. "Corporate delocalization," the decline in elite commitment to civic participation in city affairs, is one important result of globalization.[82] Now community organizations have to expend considerable resources and efforts convincing corporate leaders—whose loyalties may reside at corporate headquarters outside the city or state—that they have a special obligation to improve the life circumstances and opportunities of the inner-city poor. Consider BUILD's negotiations with the Greater Baltimore Committee (GBC), Baltimore's key business group, over a school compact proposal developed by the community organization. The school compact would have linked superior school performance for students enrolled in the city's schools with a guaranteed entry-level private-sector job. A number of GBC board members were reluctant to back the program, arguing that as a regional business group, with ties to the entire Baltimore metropolitan area, the business organization had to balance corporate donations across varied jurisdictions. As one top utility executive explained, "GBC must balance support between jurisdictions. They work with jurisdictions across the state. They can't give all the money to Baltimore."[83]

As corporate investment opportunities beyond the city became more attractive, mayors and city officials increasingly formed coalitions with corporate executives to entice capital investment in downtowns. The emphasis of the growth coalitions (often led by minority mayors elected on "progressive redistributive" agendas) on downtown redevelopment helped expand the number of low-wage, nonunionized service sector jobs.[84] City governments themselves—faced with declining revenues and a large poor population in need of government services—contributed to this employment sector by increasingly outsourcing "public" services to private contractors. As the experience of Valerie Bell covered in the preface of this volume shows, "These contractors generally paid their employees less, often not much more than the federal minimum. The end result was that many public services were being performed by workers left among the ranks of the working urban poor."[85] As mayors and other local officials increasingly provided public subsidies to corporations in order to spur private investment, and contracted with private companies to lower municipal expenditures, community organizations have had to push city hall to force those corporations to provide a "living wage" for their employees. Community organizers have also forcefully advocated municipal governments to require developers and businesses benefiting from public subsidies to hire a certain percentage of city residents. In other words, community organizations have attempted to indirectly pry concessions from the corporate sector by confronting and negotiating with local elected and appointed officials.

Downtown redevelopment as a response to globalization and economic restructuring also has the effect of exacerbating tensions between labor unions and African Americans, Latinos, and other members of community organizations with a stake in the inner city. According to Margaret Levi, "Stadium building, transportation programs, and downtown redevelopment confirm that unions and CBOs [community-based organizations] often possess competing issues of economic and community development. These public projects create jobs, but often at the expense of the current residents, who find themselves denied membership and apprenticeships in the unions whose members are razing their homes and neighborhoods. The distrust becomes mutual when protests and lobbying put at risk projects for which unions have won hard-fought battles to secure jobs for their members."[86] One way of mitigating potential tensions related to urban growth policy between unions and community organizing is for community organizations not to oppose development but, as noted earlier, to secure benefits from it.

The strong social networks among Latino immigrants provided organizers with easy access to large numbers of people. The resentment harbored by many immigrants who have been mistreated by powerful private corporations and public institutions allows organizers to "rub raw" the sores of discontent. On the other hand, for those immigrants unfamiliar with U.S. laws, fear of losing their jobs may make them hesitant to be actively involved in a community organization.[87] For undocumented immigrants, the risk of deportation looms large, putting considerable restrictions on their capacity to participate. Moreover, part-time and temporary workers "are difficult to organize because they are not a cohesive workforce with a single identity . . . and they are scattered throughout multiple workplaces. The result is that we cannot continue to organize in neat industrial sectors—people are jumping around from job to job."[88] There are also cultural differences in the approaches to community organizing brought on by immigration.[89] For example, many of the Latino community organizations in Los Angeles adopt the teachings of Paulo Freire that emphasize interplay between education and social change and developing a critical consciousness.[90] Community organizing in many African

American communities has had strong linkages to religious traditions and/or Black Nationalism. Organizers working in communities with huge percentages of immigrants are also constrained because they are working with large numbers of nonvoters. The influx of immigrants who are willing to work for cheap wages often triggered competition and tension between Latinos and other American minority groups.[91] In Los Angeles, African American leaders have expressed concerns about the large migration of Latinos into traditionally black neighborhoods and its impact on housing and jobs.[92] As one study noted, "The makeup of constituencies presents organizers with the dilemma of whether they should use models that stress universalism or difference."[93]

Finally, as poor residents are disproportionately negatively impacted by globalization and economic restructuring, community organizations have increasingly directed their attention toward social service provision. ACORN provides housing loan counseling, free tax preparation, and information campaigns on the federal Earned Income Tax Credit for its members. In San Antonio, Texas, the leaders of the IAF affiliate played an important role in designing, securing funding for, staffing, and recruiting candidates for Project Quest, a major job training program.[94] EPISO, the IAF affiliate in El Paso, operates a similar program. East Brooklyn Congregations (EBC), another IAF affiliate, runs one of the largest affordable housing programs in New York.[95] Community organizers in the Alinsky tradition have long warned that community organizations should limit their involvement in service provision. They argue that "it is difficult to integrate organizing into a service organization."[96] For example, community development corporations (CDCs) provide an important service in the areas of inner-city commercial development, economic development, and neighborhood planning. Many CDCs were spawned from the activism and mobilization of community organizations and are operated by them.[97] Randy Stoecker, however, argues that CDCs and community organizing "are based on potentially contradictory worldviews" and that it is difficult to do both effectively.[98] Nevertheless, because of the challenges poor communities face, many community organizations find themselves having to take on service provisions. Globalization and economic restructuring have the potential to further exacerbate the tensions within the community organizing field between service provision and community empowerment.

Community organizing is about engaging disadvantaged communities in order to achieve power. Beginning in the late 1930s, Saul Alinsky's BYNC gained a reputation for helping to unionize the packinghouses, beating city hall, and gaining and expanding important public services to the community. In the 1960s, Alinsky achieved national acclaim when he formed The Woodlawn Organization (TWO).

TWO became a major influence in Chicago's political life, leading one author to declare it the "most important and the most impressive experiment affecting Negroes anywhere in the United States."[99] In 1965, Alinsky formed FIGHT in Rochester, which focused its organizing on winning concessions for the African American community for a larger share of jobs at Eastman Kodak.

Today, organizing for the purpose of empowering disadvantaged communities is no less urgent (indeed it may be even more urgent), but the challenge is different. A central challenge is overcoming the strong influences of contemporary public culture. Mike Gecan criticizes the perspective pushed by the market culture that "society is best served when each isolated individual has the opportunity to make independent and free decisions in his or her own interest—billions and billions of such decisions."[100] Thomas Friedman observed that such a paradigm brings to light the tensions that exist in our "multiple identities" as "consumers, employees, citizens, taxpayers, and shareholders."[101] Community organizations must help resolve these tensions in favor of the citizens and on the side of the "commonwealth." Given how the public culture of consumerism and materialism has shaped the ecology of civic engagement, this is no easy task. The national survey cited earlier showed that Americans were "yearning for balance" and believed that materialism and consumerism were hurting their families and communities. However, they are extremely ambivalent about what to do. They "decry the crass materialism of our society and its consequences" but also "want 'success' for themselves and their children. . . . Thus, while people may want to act on their concerns, they are paralyzed by the tensions and contradictions embedded in their own beliefs." Thomas Friedman uses Wal-Mart to illustrate how—in the contemporary public culture—the individual's consumer identity typically wins. We want more for less, says Friedman.

> The Wal-Mart shopper in all of us wants the lowest price possible, with all the middlemen, fat, and friction removed. And the Wal-Mart shareholder in us wants Wal-Mart to be relentless about removing the fat and friction in its supply chain and in its employee benefits packages, in order to fatten the company's profits. But the Wal-Mart worker in us hates the benefits and pay packages that Wal-Mart offers its starting employees. And the Wal-Mart citizen in us knows that because Wal-Mart, the biggest company in America, doesn't cover all its employees with health care, some of them will just go to the emergency ward of the local hospital and the taxpayers will end up picking up the tab.[102]

The recent spate of studies on civic engagement paints a dismal picture of American democracy. Americans are less engaged in civic and political life. "Globalization grows individuals focused on private lives, not citizens concerned with the commonwealth," writes Boyte.[103] Jonathan Sacks makes a similar observation, noting that "it is difficult to talk about the common good when we lose the ability to speak about duty, obligation and restraint, and find ourselves only with desires clamoring for satisfaction."[104] The contemporary public culture of materialism and consumerism directs our attention inward and toward our individual wants. As the focus moves too far toward the individual and away from identity with the general welfare, engagement in public and civic affairs declines. In order to overcome the influences of contemporary public culture, community organizations have increasingly engaged in "cultural work," attempting to reorient the meanings, self-understandings, and narratives whereby Americans make sense of their lives.

Kristina Smock's research on various community organizing models, however, cautions that there are tensions between this kind of cultural/structural work and local organizing, especially among nonaffluent urban residents. Smock argues that low-income participants in community organizations are primarily interested in addressing their immediate problems and needs: "In the context of this individualistic struggle for survival, the linkages between individual interests and broader social structures tend to be far less tangible or straightforward. Consequently, abstract reflection and the pursuit of long-term systemic change can seem like a luxury compared to the more immediate struggle to meet basic needs."[105]

The kinds of tension discussed by Smock have strategic ramifications. While the world is increasingly flat and globalization an everyday reality, it is the community level that is of central concern to most citizens. As Smock puts it, "People experience contemporary social problems as they are manifested at a local level."[106] Urban residents function within a local ecology of civic engagement. For many community organizations, engaging these residents will mean hitting targets at the local level. Smock maintains that "the most effective way to get people involved in social action of any kind is by engaging them in struggles that relate directly to their everyday experiences in the neighborhood. Locally based organizing thus provides an essential mechanism for getting ordinary people—particularly America's most disenfranchised residents—involved in public life."[107]

During the forty-year period that Saul Alinsky worked as a professional organizer, targets were clear, well-defined, and easier to confront. Today, globalization, central-city economic restructuring, and urban political diffusion have created an ecology of civic engagement that is much more complex. Earlier community organizing was about confronting and negotiating with established centers of powers. Today, the centers of power within the local ecology of civic engagement may not be so readily apparent. This has led some to argue that long-term change is likely to occur when community organizations develop the capacities to become part of a broad social movement.[108] Smock reminds us that the creation of a broad-based social movement "is possible only if we start by organizing people at a local level around the issues of immediate concern in their daily lives."[109] This volume, using the ecology of civic engagement as a conceptual framework, sheds light on some of the issues community organizations face as they attempt to engage urban residents in the political and civic life of America's twenty-first-century cities and empower them to bring tangible changes to their families and communities.

OVERVIEW

These issues were discussed in two working group meetings held at and sponsored by Brown University. In the first meeting, the contributors convened as a working group guided by a "background paper" focused on the "ecology of civic engagement" concept. Prior to the working group meeting, each contributor shared outlines and abstracts for his or her essay. Through a wide-ranging discussion, the working group identified themes in the outlines and abstracts connected to the ecology of civic engagement concept. We used the discussion to guide the authors in revising the theme, focus, and emphasis of each essay. The authors reconvened to discuss, critique, and further develop the essays. These discussions, in turn, guided the authors in the final revisions of their chapters.

Mark Santow examines the intersection of race and geography in South Side Chicago during the 1960s. In 1960, Saul Alinsky formed the Organization for the Southwest Community (OSC), a community-wide, interracial group whose principal goal was to halt white flight that was occurring in Chicago's Southside neighborhoods at lightning speed. A major organizing task was to train white and black home owners on how panic peddling and blockbusting occurred, who was behind it and benefited from it, and how to stop it. While dealing with the issue of race in pre–World War II community organizations may have been a moral imperative, in no metropolitan area did community organizations working in urban white neighborhoods face race as part of the ecology of civic engagement in the same way that they would after World War II. The role of the federal government in racializing metropolitan space helped to create tight linkages between place, race, identities, and political interests.

While OSC was able to slow down racial transition, by 1970 the neighborhood had become completely African American. As the suburbs opened, more and more whites moved beyond Chicago's city limits. Meanwhile, pent-up black demands for better housing in the city made housing in Chicago worth more to blacks than it was to whites. This experience helped Alinsky see the limits of place-based organizing.[110] Santow builds on this point, making the case that community organizing must move beyond the central city and toward regional and metropolitan efforts.

Peter Burns's analysis of New Orleans describes what happens to community organizing when the local ecology is nearly depleted of resource-rich targets and lacks an identifiable ruling regime. Burns examines the evolution and changes in the city's economic, political, and civic life from the 1940s to the present. He explains how three local organizations in New Orleans were affected by these changes. ACORN has had a presence in New Orleans since 1976. All Congregations Together (ACT), a PICO affiliate, was formed in the late 1980s. Jeremiah, an IAF affiliate, was formed in the late 1990s. Because each of these community organizations came on the scene during a different period, they had to develop different strategies. Burns's analysis shows that during New Orleans's transition from a pro-growth regime to a "non-regime," public officials have found community organizing a substantial support and help to the city. Burns's chapter also includes some discussion of how these organizations have responded to the aftermath of Hurricane Katrina. The New Orleans case provides good evidence for the need for community organizations to forge linkages for a more concerted national effort.

Kathleen Staudt and Clarence Stone's chapter on El Paso illustrates that globalization has cultural and economic results. One cultural consequence is the brutality and family dissolution that impact poor workers on both sides of the U.S.-Mexican border. Ciudad Juárez, directly across the border from El Paso, is a cheap-labor mecca. Its *maquiladora* zone for foreign, mainly American-owned factories thrives on low-wage workers and lax enforcement of Mexico's weak labor and environmental standards. Impoverished workers from southern Mexican cities and neighboring Latin American countries migrate there frantically seeking cash income. On the U.S. side of the border, women in El Paso desperately look to find work when American garment factories relocate across the border. Staudt and Stone also examine El Paso's transformation from a city with an ecology of civic engagement that was once dominated by a small but powerful Anglo business sector into one characterized by fragmentation. Staudt and Stone argue that many players now occupy El Paso's civic and political ecology. They focus on EPISO, the local IAF affiliate, and describe the constraints IAF's organizing strategy has in a fragmented community geographically located at the epicenter of globalization.

Since the publication of the *Nation at Risk* report in the early 1980s, politicians, policymakers, educators, and business leaders have advocated education policies that would improve the quality of the nation's public schools. Although many of these actors may disagree on policy issues, all agree that globalization has little mercy on those with few skills and little training. In response to the pressures and changes in the new global economy, education officials are adopting policies designed to ratchet up standards. The passage in 2002 of the federal No Child Left Behind Act (NCLB) expanded federal involvement in local education policy and influenced the way community organizations focus on schools. National political factors and federal-level decision makers can impact local policy. Dennis Shirley and Michael Evans examine the responses of community organizations to NCLB and the varied impact the federal legislation has had on community organizations in Chicago, Miami, and Texas. In Chicago, ACORN has selectively used NCLB to support its education organizing, while at the same time protesting those provisions (like those pertaining to teacher qualifications) it believes constrain the community's efforts to improve public education. In Miami, People Acting for Community Together (PACT) has been less critical of NCLB. Since the middle 1990s, PACT has organized Miami parents and educators to improve student literacy and has worked directly with schools to implement a heavily phonics-based approach to reading. Those schools that have collaborated with PACT have shown the greatest gains on standardized reading examinations. PACT's organizing efforts seem to fit well with NCLB. In Texas, however, Shirley and Evans found that IAF's organizing in support of education has been significantly hampered by NCLB, especially the law's accountability provisions. Community organizers in Texas report that since the passage of NCLB, they have had difficulty engaging teachers and principals as the pressure to have students perform proficiently on standardized tests looms large, leaving little time for educators to work with communities on broader school-related issues.

Heidi Swarts's chapter on ACORN speaks to continuity within an environment of change. Swarts examines ACORN's longtime efforts to organize at the national level. Of all the major national organizing networks, ACORN is almost alone in its attempt to shape and influence federal policies that impact its poor, working-class members. ACORN has a strategy that, in some cases, is ahead of its time (and other community organizations). All community organizations are not alike. The point about combining national and local strategies is that it has enabled ACORN to survive and grow. Collective-action theory would predict that a grassroots organization, relying on individual memberships, would have limited sustainability. ACORN runs counter to that bit of conventional wisdom. Why has ACORN, unlike the IAF, PICO, DART, and other community organizing networks, been more willing to engage at the national level? Swarts emphasizes ACORN's centralized leadership structure, its penchant for experimentation, and its willingness to inject itself into an organizing effort when the political opportunity structure opens at the local, state, or national level.

Richard Wood's chapter provides an analysis of PICO's capacity to launch national-level organizing. As Wood shows, since 1996 PICO has organized statewide in California with some success, primarily on public education, health care, and affordable housing. If PICO has been able to affect policy in the nation's largest state, how does it go about scaling up to the national level? Since 2002, PICO has attempted to garner the "strategic capacity" to organize at the national level. Wood's chapter analyzes PICO's leadership meetings, describing and explaining the actions of PICO leaders as they fan out on Capitol Hill to test their capacity to influence national policies that directly impact their members back home. Wood's chapter also reminds us of the important "cultural work" that is a part of PICO's organizing strategy.

Robert Fisher and Eric Shragge provide a historical overview of community organizing, pointing out the tensions that have existed within the community organizing field concerning "community development" versus "social action." While acknowledging that a healthy debate exists in the literature about whether community development corporations and community organizing can be mentioned in the same breath, Fisher and Shragge show how community organizations have responded to national political and economic conservatism by moderating toward an emphasis on community building, collaboration, self-help, or service-oriented programs and away from social action. Fisher and Shragge's chapter calls for community organizations to move more closely to an oppositional and direct action orientation, and it describes the challenges community organizations must overcome to make direct action more effective.

In chapter 9, Peter Dreier reflects on the previous chapters and examines the role of community organizing in a progressive movement. Dreier describes the fragmentation that exists among "progressive" organizations. Community organizations, he argues, must join in a coalition with labor unions and other progressive groups; they need engagement both inside and outside electoral politics and must overcome problems related to excessive localism, funding, and division within the community organizing field. Community organizations need to be part of a broader social movement. Dreier asks how viable is such a strategy, especially in a national political environment dominated by conservatives? How might progressive forces like ACORN, IAF, PICO, and other community organizations compete at the national level with the kind of right-centered movement politics best exemplified by the Christian Coalition? What kind of evidence exists that suggests community organizations are able to pull this off?

In chapter 10, I return to some of the issues raised here, synthesize and assess the prior chapters, and reflect on broad implications for the understanding of community organizing.

NOTES

1. Stephen Macedo et al., *Democracy at Risk* (Washington, DC: Brookings Institution, 2005).
2. Robert D. Putnam, *Bowling Alone: The Collapse and Revival of American Community* (New York: Simon and Schuster, 2000).
3. Theda Skocpol, "Advocates without Members: The Recent Transformation of American Civic Life," in *Civic Engagement in American Democracy,* ed. Theda Skocpol and Morris Fiorina (Washington, DC: Brookings Institution, 1999), 498.
4. Theda Skocpol, *Diminished Democracy: From Membership to Management in American Civic Life* (Norman: University of Oklahoma Press, 2003); see also Skocpol, "Advocates without Members."
5. Macedo et al., *Democracy at Risk,* 1.

6. Putnam, *Bowling Alone*, 185.

7. Ibid., 318. Cathy Cohen and Michael Dawson found that people in high-poverty neighborhoods feel cut off from their political representatives and see political and community engagement as futile. Residents in high-poverty communities are less likely to believe that they had any direct influence over decisions of importance to their community. Civic engagement in poor central city communities is low, limiting inner-city residents' capacity to influence policies affecting their families and community. See Cathy Cohen and Michael Dawson, "Neighborhood Poverty and African American Politics," *American Political Science Review* 87 (1993): 286–302.

8. Mark Warren and Richard L. Wood, *Faith-Based Community Organizing: The State of the Field* (Jericho, NY: Interfaith Funders, 2001).

9. On the differences between ACORN and IAF, see John Atlas and Peter Dreier, "Enraging the Right," *Shelterforce Online*, no. 129 (May/June 2003).

10. Peter Medoff and Holly Sklar, *Streets of Hope: The Fall and Rise of an Urban Neighborhood* (Cambridge, MA: South End Press, 1994).

11. On BUILD and Baltimore's living wage ordinance, see Marion Orr, "Baltimoreans United in Leadership Development: Exploring the Role of Governing Nonprofits," in *Nonprofits in Urban America*, ed. Richard Hula and Cynthia Jackson-Elmoore (Westport, CT: Quorum Books, 2000), 151–167; and Janice Fine, "Community Unions and the Revival of the American Labor Movement," *Politics and Society* 33 (March 2005): 153–199.

12. Oren M. Levin-Waldman, *The Political Economy of the Living Wage: A Study of Four Cities* (New York: M. E. Sharpe, 2005).

13. Dennis Shirley, *Community Organizing for Urban School Reform* (Austin: University of Texas Press, 1997); Mark R. Warren, "Communities and Schools: A New View of Urban Education Reform," *Harvard Educational Review* 75 (2005): 133–175.

14. Alexander Von Hoffman, *House by House, Block by Block: The Rebirth of America's Urban Neighborhoods* (New York: Oxford University Press, 2003), 3.

15. Ibid.

16. Harry C. Boyte, *The Backyard Revolution: Understanding the New Citizen Movement* (Philadelphia: Temple University Press, 1980).

17. Harry C. Boyte, *Everyday Politics* (Philadelphia: University of Pennsylvania Press, 2004), 35.

18. Gregory B. Markus, "Civic Participation in American Cities," Institute for Social Research, University of Michigan, 2002, 13.

19. Paul Osterman, *Gathering Power* (Boston: Beacon Press, 2004), 21.

20. Norton Long, "The Local Community as an Ecology of Games," *American Journal of Sociology* 64 (November 1958): 251.

21. Robert Fisher, *Let the People Decide: Neighborhood Organizing in America* (New York: Twayne, 1994); Neil Betten and Michael J. Austin, *The Roots of Community Organizing, 1917–1939* (Philadelphia: Temple University Press, 1990).

22. See especially Barbara Ransby, *Ella Baker and the Black Freedom Movement: A Radical Democratic Vision* (Chapel Hill: University of North Carolina Press, 2003); Chana Kai Lee, *For Freedom's Sake: The Life of Fannie Lou Hamer* (Urbana: University of Illinois Press, 1999); Charles Payne, *I've Got the Light of Freedom: Organizing Tradition and the Mississippi Freedom Movement* (Berkeley: University of California Press, 1994); John Dittmer, *Local People: The Struggle for Civil Rights in Mississippi* (New York: Oxford University Press, 1994).

23. Sanford Horwitt, *Let Them Call Me Rebel* (New York: Vintage, 1998).

24. Donald Reitzes and Dietrich Reitzes, *The Alinsky Legacy: Alive and Kicking* (Greenwich, CT: JAI Press, 1987).

25. Herbert Gutman used the cultural lens to explain the behavior of industrial-era workers, to understand black resistance to slavery, showing the relation of culture to politics. See Ira Berlin, ed., *Power and Culture: Essays on the American Working Class* (New York: Pantheon, 1987).

26. See Michael Denning, *The Cultural Front: The Laboring of American Culture in the Twentieth Century* (New York: Verso, 1996).

27. Ibid., xx.

28. Ibid., 9.

29. Ibid., xvii.

30. Harry C. Boyte, *Commonwealth: A Return to Citizen Politics* (New York: Free Press, 1989), 52.

31. Robert A. Slayton, *Back of the Yards: The Making of a Local Democracy* (Chicago: University of Chicago Press, 1986), 15.

32. Ibid., 15, 89.

33. Boyte, *Commonwealth*.

34. Slayton, *Back of the Yards*, 225.

35. Boyte, *Commonwealth*, 52.

36. Jacqueline B. Mondros and Scott M. Wilson, *Organizing for Power and Empowerment* (New York: Columbia University Press, 1994), 142.

37. Horwitt, *Let Them Call Me Rebel*, 75.

38. David Gudelunas, "QVC: Television Retail and Ritual," *Journal of American and Comparative Culture* 25 (2002): 110.

39. Edward T. Chambers, *Roots for Radicals: Organizing for Power, Action, and Justice* (New York: Continuum Press, 2003), 134–135.

40. Ibid., 135.

41. Over the last decade commercial activities in public schools have increased in visibility and taken unprecedented forms. Businesses are eager to tap into the growing youth market, while schools are turning to businesses for resources such as cash and technology-related equipment and services. The variety and frequency of school-based commercial activities exceed the scope of most state laws and district policies. Some observers worry that students' behavior may be affected by the advertising, product sales, and other commercial activities taking place in schools.

42. John U. Ogbu, *Black American Students in an Affluent Suburb: A Study of Academic Disengagement* (Mahwah, NJ: Erlbaum, 2003), 215.

43. Ibid., 29.

44. Thomas L. Friedman, *The World Is Flat: A Brief History of the Twenty-first Century* (New York: Farrar, Straus, and Giroux, 2005). For example, Friedman (p. 213) describes how globalization changed work and work schedules. The proliferation of communication technology, much of it produced by foreign and multinational corporations, has made computers, PDAs, and especially cellular telephones available to many. At the same time, such technology has contributed to overscheduling and expanded work hours. "Even while on 'vacation,' you are always in. Therefore you are always on."

45. Robert N. Bellah et al., *Habits of the Heart: Individualism and Commitment in American Life* (Berkeley: University of California Press, 1996).

46. See Macedo et al., *Democracy at Risk*, 51.

47. Ibid.

48. "Yearning for Balance: Views of Americans on Consumption, Materialism, and the Environment" (prepared for the Merck Family Fund by The Hardwood Group, July 1995), 1.

49. Ibid., 4.

50. Ibid., 2.

51. Ibid., 1.

52. Boyte, *Commonwealth*, 60.

53. Mark R. Warren, *Dry Bones Rattling: Community Building to Revitalize American Democracy* (Princeton, NJ: Princeton University Press, 2001), 45.

54. Boyte, *Commonwealth*, 61.

55. For an insightful comparison of the influence of political culture on community organizing in Canada and the United States, see Randy Stoecker and Anna C. Vakil, "States, Culture, and Community Organizing: Two Tales of Two Neighborhoods," *Journal of Urban Affairs* 22 (2000): 439–458.

56. Industrial Areas Foundation, *Organizing for Family and Congregation* (Chicago: Author, 1978), 3, 18.

57. Michael Gecan, *Going Public* (Boston: Beacon Press, 2004), 152.

58. Kristina Smock, *Democracy in Action: Community Organizing and Urban Change* (New York: Columbia University Press, 2004), 231–232.

59. Richard L. Wood, *Faith in Action: Religion, Race, and Democratic Organizing in America* (Chicago: University of Chicago Press, 2002), 138.

60. Ibid., 7.

61. Rinku Sen, *Stir It Up: Lessons in Community Organizing and Advocacy* (San Francisco: Jossey-Bass, 2003), 109.

62. Gary Delgado, *Organizing the Movement: The Roots and Growth of ACORN* (Philadelphia: Temple University Press, 1986).

63. Ralph Reed, *Politically Incorrect* (Dallas: Word, 1994), 225; Thomas Frank, *What's the Matter with Kansas?* (New York: Henry Holt, 2004).

64. Skocpol, *Diminished Democracy*, 271–273.

65. Dana R. Fisher, *Activism: How the Outsourcing of Grassroots Campaigns Is Strangling Progressive Politics in America* (Stanford, CA: Stanford University Press, 2006); Boyte, *Everyday Politics*, 24–25.

66. See Alinsky's description of BYNC's boycott of the "Tycoon Department Store" in *Reveille for Radicals* (New York: Vintage Books, 1946), 135–146.

67. Dennis R. Judd and Todd Swanstrom, *City Politics: Private Power and Public Policy* (New York: Longman, 2004), 50.

68. Adam Cohen and Elizabeth Taylor, *American Pharaoh: Mayor Richard J. Daley* (Boston: Back Bay Books, 2000), 43.

69. Steven P. Erie, *Rainbow's End: Irish-Americans and the Dilemmas of Urban Machine Politics, 1840–1985* (Berkeley: University of California Press, 1988).

70. P. David Finks, *The Radical Vision of Saul Alinsky* (New York: Paulist Press, 1984), 21.

71. Howard Samuels Center, "Assessing Community Change: An Evaluation of the Ford Foundation's Community Organizing Initiative, 2000–2004" (The Graduate Center, City University of New York, April 2006).

72. In July 2005, Eastman Kodak announced that it would lay off up to 10,000 people because of declines in the film business. This in addition to the company's announcement in 2004 that it planned to eliminate 15,000 positions. See Vikas Bajaj, "Kodak Expands Layoffs to 10, 000," *New York Times*, July 21, 2005, C1.

73. Judd and Swanstrom, *City Politics*, 364.

74. William J. Wilson, *When Work Disappears* (New York: Vintage, 1996).

75. Robert H. Salisbury, "Urban Politics: The New Convergence of Power," *Journal of Politics* 26 (1964): 783.

76. Nancy Burns, *The Formation of American Local Governments: Private Values in Public Institutions* (New York: Oxford University Press, 1994).

77. Marc V. Levine, "The Politics of Partnership: Urban Redevelopment since 1945," in *Unequal Partnerships: The Political Economy of Urban Redevelopment in Postwar America*, ed. Gregory Squires (Newark, NJ: Rutgers University Press, 1989), 23.

78. Michael N. Danielson and Paul G. Lewis, "City Bound: Political Science and the American Metropolis," *Political Research Quarterly* 49 (1996): 213.

79. See, for example, Robert A. Caro, *The Power Broker: Robert Moses and the Fall of New York* (New York: Vintage, 1975).

80. Michael Goldfield, *The Decline of Organized Labor in the United States* (Chicago: University of Chicago Press, 1987).

81. Margaret Levi, "Organizing Power: The Prospects of an American Labor Movement," *Perspectives on Politics* 1 (2003): 47.

82. Charles H. Heying, "Civic Elites and Corporate Delocalization," *American Behavioral Scientist* 40 (1997): 657–668.

83. Marion Orr, *Black Social Capital: The Politics of School Reform in Baltimore* (Lawrence: University Press of Kansas, 1999), 128.

84. Dennis R. Judd and Susan Fainstein, eds., *The Tourist City* (New Haven, CT: Yale University Press, 1999).

85. Levin-Waldman, *The Political Economy of the Living Wage*, 28.

86. Levi, "Organizing Power," 55.

87. Michael Jones-Correa, *Between Two Nations: The Predicament of Latinos in New York City* (Ithaca, NY: Cornell University Press, 1998).

88. Sen, *Stir It Up*, 9.

89. Howard Samuels Center, "Assessing Community Change."

90. Paulo Freire, *Pedagogy of the Oppressed* (New York: Herder and Herder, 1970).

91. A number of reports have documented that employers have sometimes intentionally replaced American workers with immigrants to have a cheaper, perhaps more easily exploited workforce. For example, during much of the post–World War II period, African American workers dominated janitorial work in the high-rise districts of Los Angeles and were able to win "excellent wages and working conditions under the leadership of the Service Employees International Union." See General Accounting Office, *Illegal Aliens: Influence of Illegal Workers on Wages and Working Conditions of Legal Workers* (Washington, DC: U.S. Government Printing Office, March 1988), 39.

92. Nicolas C. Vaca, *The Presumed Alliance: The Unspoken Conflict between Latinos and Blacks and What It Means for America* (New York: HarperCollins, 2005).

93. Howard Samuels Center, "Assessing Community Change," 101.

94. Mark R. Warren, *Dry Bones Rattling*, 174.

95. Michael Gecan, *Going Public* (Boston: Beacon Press, 2002), 13.

96. Rinku Sen, *Stir It Up*, 45.

97. Avis C. Vidal, *Rebuilding Communities: A National Study of Urban Community Development Corporations* (New York: Community Development Research Center, New School for Social Research, 1992).

98. Randy Stoecker, "Understanding the Development-Organizing Dialectic," *Journal of Urban Affairs* 25 (2003): 493–512.

99. Charles E. Silberman, *Crisis in Black and White* (New York: Random House, 1964), 318. For a more detailed and critical analysis of TWO, see John Hall Fish, *Black Power, White Control: The Struggle of the Woodlawn Organization in Chicago* (Princeton, NJ: Princeton University Press, 1973).

100. Gecan, *Going Public,* 155.

101. Friedman, *The World Is Flat,* 214.

102. Ibid., 215.

103. Harry C. Boyte, "Breaking the Silence," *Kettering Review* 24 (Spring 2006): 33–45.

104. Jonathan Sacks, *The Dignity of Difference: How to Avoid the Clash of Civilizations* (New York: Continuum Press, 2002), 32.

105. Smock, *Democracy in Action,* 55.

106. Ibid., 226.

107. Ibid.

108. See, for example, Jean Anyon, *Radical Possibilities: Public Policy, Urban Education, and a New Social Movement* (New York: Routledge, 2005).

109. Smock, *Democracy in Action,* 242.

110. The limitation of local organizing is discussed in Delgado, *Organizing the Movement,* 91–122; and Boyte, *Backyard Revolution.*

2. Running in Place
Saul Alinsky, Race, and Community Organizing
Mark Santow

President Lyndon Johnson formed the National Advisory Commission on Civil Disorders in July 1967, to investigate the causes of the riots that had erupted in dozens of American cities since 1964 and to offer recommendations for reform. In its March 1968 report the Kerner Commission, as it was informally called, famously warned that if conditions were not remedied the nation was "moving toward two societies, one black, one white—separate and unequal." Perhaps the most comprehensive study of American racial and urban problems ever undertaken, the report laid out a complex and quite radical framework for dealing with the consequences of this "system of apartheid."

The nation faced three choices, according to the commission: the status quo, a policy of "enrichment aimed at improving dramatically the quality of ghetto life while abandoning integration as a goal," and a combination of inner-city improvement and residential integration policies. The first two approaches, the report argued, would have "ominous consequences for our society" because they involved "choosing a permanently divided country" while doing little to "arrest the deterioration of life in central city ghettos." While "large-scale improvement in the quality of ghetto life" was essential, this could only be an "interim strategy." If the primary goal was to create a "single society, in which every citizen will be free to live and work according to his capabilities and desires, not his color," the report concluded, both integration and ghetto enrichment were essential. Lyndon Johnson made his choice when he rejected the commission's recommendations. Through acts of omission as well as commission, we as a nation have made our choice as well.[1]

What have we chosen? Despite the recent passing of the fiftieth anniversary of the landmark *Brown v. Board of Education* (1954) decision, the ideal of residential integration seems to have been largely abandoned by our politicians, our courts, and many of the constituencies with a deep interest in reviving it. Writers and policymakers on both the right and the left differ about how we should address the problems of concentrated urban black poverty, but they generally agree that the solutions lie in a privatized version of the second option proposed by the Kerner Commission: fixing, repairing, or enabling inner-city communities (or their residents). For the Right, welfare reform, faith-based initiatives, and the right market incentives will solve the problems; for the Left, community development, local asset management, and the construction of social capital will uplift the urban minority poor. In an age of greatly diminished expectations—the "twilight of common dreams," as Todd Gitlin once put it—residential integration is seen as unrealistic, unnecessary, or paternalistic.[2]

It is not because racial segregation no longer exists. The 2000 U.S. census makes clear that despite real progress, the color line is still very much with us, particularly in the older metropolitan areas of the Northeast and the Midwest. Segregation remains a fundamental fact of life in the nation's cities and suburbs. Even a brief journey through America's largest metropolitan areas reveals an unmistakable connection between where (and how) people live, and who they are. I have taught American urban history in universities across the country. My students can quickly identify what groups of people live where in their home city. How they "map" the surrounding geography—how they see it, understand it, and place themselves within it—is profoundly shaped by race, as well as class. The "other side of the tracks," the "inner" city, "white flight," the "Black Belt," the "lily-white suburbs"—all these designations are geographic in nature, at once describing places, people, social processes, and history. Urban scholars generally refer to this relationship between place, identity, and social structure as "social geography." It has been said that one of the best ways to understand a society is to look at what it takes for granted. Social geography is taken for granted. It is like air, natural, immutable. Or so it seems. It took a long time and much effort to create the pattern of segregation by class and race that we see around us today. It will take a long time and much effort to reverse it, if we wish to do so.

More than almost any other urbanist of the past half century, community organizer Saul Alinsky was keenly aware of the intersection between race, place, and social belonging. Alinsky and his Industrial Areas Foundation (IAF) had a vision of the democratic city that relied heavily upon the creation and nurturing of territorial identities: connecting people to one another through—literally—common ground. His organizing work in Chicago and elsewhere in the first few decades after World War II reflected this belief. He helped to build large and influential neighborhood groups, with local leaders and organizations fighting for local needs.

In particular, Alinsky searched for local solutions to perhaps the most intractable problem faced by his native Chicago in the years following the war: racial segregation and the pattern of ghetto expansion, racial violence, and white flight that caused neighborhood after neighborhood on the city's South Side to be transformed virtually overnight from white to black residency. After his first community organization, the Back of the Yards Neighborhood Council (BYNC), became increasingly focused on racial exclusion in the 1950s, Alinsky began to concentrate his energies on creating a grassroots alternative to the segregation, racial conflict, and white flight that plagued Chicago and other cities in the postwar era. He helped to build an interracial community organization on Chicago's racially changing Southwest Side in the early 1960s and a black one in Woodlawn, which had recently experienced a rapid turnover from white to black. Alinsky attempted to create an "alternative racial geography"—a new vision of an integrated city—that could overcome the close connections between race, security, and property that characterized many of Chicago's white neighborhoods, and the poverty and powerlessness that seemed endemic to black ghetto areas. While Alinsky is often referred to as an essential part of the history of community organizing, his ideas and experiences with race are rarely examined.

Alinsky's story raises some important cautions for those seeking progressive change today. Since the 1960s, public and private efforts have mostly followed Alinsky in their neighborhood-based approaches to the problems of the American city. Frustrated by devolution and retrenchment at the federal level and the persistence of jurisdictional fragmentation in metropolitan areas, and disillusioned by the structural limitations of the American welfare state, progressives have increasingly looked to local grassroots organizing as a necessary site for sustaining social justice and furthering change in a way that is compatible with their democratic instincts. Their successes, while notable, have had a limited effect on the larger structures of racial geography, uneven development, and political economy that continue to impoverish cities and hamper the pursuit of social justice.[3] Indeed, Alinsky's story urges some caution: the use of place-based strategies alone to attack poverty, segregation, inequality, and uneven development—whether undertaken by government or by private entities—can exacerbate the very ways of thinking, acting, and living that have caused these problems in the first place if it is not accompanied by analysis and organizing strategy that operate at the metropolitan level. While conditions have changed somewhat since Alinsky's day, race remains heavily embedded in the contours of the American state and the social geography of our metropolitan areas. It is thus a constitutive element of the political ecology in which community organizing and metropolitan politics take place.

SAUL ALINSKY AND THE POLITICS OF RACIAL GEOGRAPHY

In a 1959 series entitled "The Panic Peddlers," the *Chicago Daily News* reported on the early stages of racial turnover in the middle-class neighborhood of East Chatham, where white residents were described as "jittery, confused, and generally unwilling to accept Negroes." Chatham and other Southwest Side communities were in the midst of an extraordinarily rapid transition of their populations from white to black. Real estate speculators were spreading fear, and banks were refusing to lend money for home improvements. While blacks still constituted less than 10 percent of the local population, approximately forty black families were moving into the Southwest Side each month.[4] The result was a growing sense of panic among local white homeowners as the Black Belt approached from the north and east, block by block. Blacks had crossed Cottage Grove Avenue and Seventy-ninth Street, a long-maintained racial boundary, and local whites were scared: as one elderly white housewife put it, "We can't afford to move again. We've been driven out twice before. The Negroes are coming. They'll run us off the streets. What are we to do?" Even those sympathetic to the black need for housing feared being "flooded." Homeowners often received dozens of phone calls a night informing them that nearby houses had already been sold to black families and encouraging them to sell now and "get their price." Vacancies and For Sale signs had begun to appear well before blacks began to move in, and by the fall of 1959 white housing demand in the area had evaporated. None of the whites interviewed for the series expressed hope in the possibility of stable racial integration.[5]

To many black newcomers the flight of white homeowners from Chicago's middle-class South Side neighborhoods, often at a financial loss, was a mystery. Reporters M. W. Newman and Harry Swegle, who found the increasingly black sections of the community to be "as respectable and law-abiding as most white sections, if not more so," were also baffled. Apparently, they concluded, this was "not the yardstick by which the average white person judges Negroes." Most whites in Chatham did not want to leave, Newman and Swegle argued, but they seemed to fear that even middle-class blacks would "bring with them problems often associated with the Negro 'ghetto': slums, overcrowding, skidding property values, unemployment, crime, dope"—in spite of the fact that, as one black newcomer, a lawyer, informed the *Daily News,* "that's what I'm running from myself." Despite the unfair payment burdens thrust upon them by racial discrimination in the housing and home finance markets, many black newcomers to Chatham were organizing block clubs and trying to improve their properties. As one black resident of the 8200 block of Maryland Avenue put it, "Negroes are getting better buildings and are keeping them better. It makes you think different if you can get out of the jam [of the Black Belt]."[6]

The resumption of housing construction in outlying city areas and in the suburbs in the late forties, long bottled up during the Depression and the Second World War, had opened up Chicago's housing market for the first time in a generation. Those whites who could move to the urban fringe, or leave the city altogether, did so at an extraordinary rate: aided by the Federal Housing Administration (FHA) and the Veterans Administration (VA), as well as friendly tax policies, more than

270,000 whites left the city from 1950 to 1956 alone. The population of Chicago's suburbs—from which black families were almost completely excluded—grew by a remarkable 71.5 percent during the fifties.[7] At the same time, the area of black settlement on the South Side of Chicago expanded rapidly. After decades of in-migration and racial discrimination, housing within the boundaries of the traditional Black Belt had become substandard and overcrowded, providing a strong incentive for upwardly mobile black families to move out. By the late forties there was actually somewhere for them to go. The enormous growth in the white suburban housing market, as well as the *Shelley v. Kraemer* (1948) Supreme Court decision invalidating state enforcement of racially restrictive covenants, which had formerly restricted black movement, greatly expanded the amount of housing available to black families. The rapid expansion of the white housing market initiated a filtering process in which upwardly mobile blacks began to move into the older and formerly white neighborhoods surrounding the traditional Black Belt. The pace of racial transition accelerated throughout the postwar decades, from nearly 4,000 dwelling units per year in the late forties to 7,800 in the late fifties. The tragic result was a wave of contested and often violent racial change in Chicago's neighborhoods in the first two postwar decades.[8]

The process of black "invasion" and white flight—what M. W. Newman referred to in 1960 as "Chicago's 'Great Question' "—was (and is) of vital importance for understanding the racial and political dynamics of metropolitan areas in postwar America. It altered forever both the nature and the spatial expression of American race relations. Even a brief perusal of city newspapers from the late fifties and early sixties reveals that the "Great Question" was hardly specific to Chicago, in either its existence or its importance. Racial transition and flight has been a common multigenerational experience for millions of Americans, white and black. These experiences, and the structural inequalities to which they are recursively related, serve as both the foundation of modern American urban and suburban politics, and the prism through which many whites and blacks map metropolitan space, create racial and territorial identities, and consider the possibilities and probabilities of social change. They are part of that "taken for granted" social geography, which makes racial integration even now seem impossible, or unimportant.[9]

Saul Alinsky's introduction to the subject of race and segregation came through the somewhat humbling experience of having his first successful community organization, the Back of the Yards Neighborhood Council, on Chicago's South Side, become a deliberately and effectively segregationist group in the 1950s. Organized initially to provide community support across ethnic lines for a union campaign in the nearby meatpacking plants, the BYNC shifted its efforts toward keeping the neighborhood all white as black families moved into adjacent areas after the war.

Alinsky was embarrassed by the association of the BYNC with segregation and began to think deeply about why whites in Chicago seemed to resist the idea of black neighbors so strongly. He gave a lot of thought to the relationship between identity and place, and how segregation is reproduced on the ground, house by house, block by block. For decades, realtors, banks, and the government had emphasized two important—and seemingly irrefutable—facts: homeownership in a stable community was the American dream, and black neighbors threatened that stability by decreasing property values, increasing crime, weakening tightly knit Catholic parishes, and overwhelming local public schools. Licensed realtors were bound by their professional code of ethics not to sell or rent property to blacks in an all-white neighborhood. Through 1948, racially restrictive covenants, generally drawn up by realtors in consultation with local white homeowner associations, threatened white owners with legal action if they transferred their property to blacks. Financial institutions rarely gave mortgage loans to black families for homes in white neighborhoods, or to whites living in areas close to the black ghetto.

After World War II, the federal government made loans and mortgage insurance increasingly available, but rarely for the purchase or construction of homes in urban areas. Through the advocacy of restrictive covenants and neighborhood homogeneity, government housing programs joined locally organized efforts to resist integration to both the law and the national purpose with regard to housing. These policies, in effect, punished whites who lived in racially diverse neighborhoods by devaluing their homes and raising the opportunity costs of denying the racial privileges upheld by segregation.[10]

This placed the American state decidedly in support of racial segregation on a metropolitan scale. Urban whites were encouraged to believe that black neighbors threatened their economic and social security and were given the tools to preserve their racial capital by signing restrictive covenants or by fleeing to the suburbs. The rules and assumptions embedded in government policies and the practices of housing market actors, when combined with the impressions presented to many white urbanites by the concentrated poverty of nearby black settlements and the racist images that permeated politics and the culture generally, were clear: blacks moving into white neighborhoods were a financial and social threat. The state-structured housing market established clear and unmistakable incentives for white homeowners to resist integrated living.

Alinsky took two approaches: he organized an interracial group on the rapidly changing Southwest Side, and he put together a black community organization in Woodlawn, a poor and recently turned-over neighborhood near the University of Chicago. Once the groups were organized, he hoped they could work together to control the housing market on the South Side and intentionally foster integration on the basis of mutual self-interest. The city's problems could not be overcome, Alinsky argued, until "the walls of racial partition have been at least partly dissolved." He presented his local approach as a more effective means for breaking down racial segregation than the methods proposed by racial liberals in the late fifties and early sixties, which tended to stress the passage of fair housing laws and the use of education and moral suasion. Anticipating a white backlash against such efforts, Alinsky insisted that only intensely local, place-based approaches that brought the races together as bargaining equals could succeed in convincing white homeowners that racial integration was not a profound threat to their social and economic security.

THE ORGANIZATION FOR THE SOUTHWEST COMMUNITY

Alinsky launched his Southwest organizing campaign in 1959. At the time, black families were beginning to move into upper reaches of the area. Most white residents in the community did not want to leave, but they did not know an alternative. By the late 1950s, many urban whites—encouraged by realtors, the home finance industry, the federal government, and many others—had come to associate black neighbors with danger and risk. As Tom Sugrue has argued, whites had come to believe that they had a right to avoid black neighbors. Those whites who did not mind some degree of integration, as well as those few who actively desired it, faced strong cultural and economic disincentives.[11] Alinsky hoped to acknowledge this and then utilize community organizing to gradually broaden the interests, identities, and perspectives of white homeowners in order to break their fears of interracial living. While racism and segregation are wrong and destructive, Alinsky insisted, "unless we can develop a program which recognizes the legitimate self-interest of white communities, we have no right to condemn them morally because they refuse to commit hara-kiri."[12]

The Southwest side had long been a haven for organized and violent resistance to black newcomers, largely initiated by property owner associations of various kinds, which began to emerge in the twenties and thirties with the encouragement of the Chicago Real Estate Board. "Keep-em-out groups" that policed the borders of racial segregation were scattered throughout the area; as Alinsky wrote to the IAF board in 1960, the Southwest side was "honeycombed with a dozen varieties of segregation conspiracies, some brutal and stupidly ineffectual, some intelligent and quite effective in their own way." Violence and intimidation remained primary weapons, especially in the areas closest to the advancing Black Belt.[13]

Through local churches, homeowner associations, and business and social groups, black newcomers and white residents formed the Organization for the Southwest Community (OSC) in 1959. The organizing strategy blended a large dose of pragmatism with a slightly smaller amount of subterfuge. Alinsky believed that only a community-wide, interracial, and interdenominational group could stabilize the area, preserve Catholic parishes, and prevent racial violence. The community organization that would result from such an effort would approach racial integration in a strictly utilitarian manner, emphasizing the "analogy of vaccination," or "the idea of being inoculated with a certain quota of Negroes for white immunity." Alinsky knew how explosive the issue of integration was on the Southwest Side, and he hoped to sell the new organization as a force for stability, not for integration. Even while Alinsky hoped that the new community group would be integrationist, he also knew that before it could even attempt to control the local housing market, it would have to accumulate broad-based local power and support. Alinsky believed this could only be done by focusing on a variety of relatively noncontroversial issues that directly addressed the interests of local institutional players.[14]

Though race inevitably came up as an issue, Alinsky's organizers promised neither integration nor segregation. As one organizer recounted to John Fish, they would talk to potential recruits about the problems of the expanding ghetto and ask for suggestions; the general sentiment was "to keep the community white, but they would accept half a loaf. We would say, 'there is no way to keep it white but maybe we can keep it stable and healthy.'" Bringing panic peddling and blockbusting to a halt became a useful issue for the organizers: as Alinsky preferred, it was dramatic, it was a part of many residents' immediate experience, and it focused on easily identified villains.[15] OSC staffers sought to teach member organizations about the structural roots of neighborhood transition, blockbusting, real estate practices, and the dual housing market. Organizers and staff repeatedly stressed issues that would prevent white flight and that might form the basis for an alliance of mutual self-interest between longtime residents and their new black neighbors.

In the month before the OSC's second annual congress in 1960, *Chicago Daily News* reporter M. W. Newman evaluated conditions on the Southwest Side in a three-part series on the group. The area had no socially integrated blocks, Newman observed, and several of the OSC's member organizations were of the " 'keep 'em out' school of thought." Many local residents—including members of the OSC—did not agree with the official organizational policy of accepting the right of blacks to move into the area. These sentiments were especially strong in those parts of the Southwest that as yet had few black families. Others—perhaps the majority—seemed to walk the same delicate line with regard to race relations that the OSC was attempting to maintain. In this respect, Newman apparently came to the same conclusion as Alinsky's organizers: although the Southwest Side had a small number of integrationists and segregationists, the majority of local residents preferred to avoid violence, flight, and the delicate moral implications of racial issues. The OSC, Newman wrote, "has already eased panic somewhat," and by opening "the Great Question" for public debate, it had "made it harder for whispers and sneaky rumors to have their way." While the organization "is still divided among itself as to just where it is going . . . it is trying." "On that somewhat slippery rock," he concluded, "the OSC stands."[16]

Early and broad support for the OSC in the community was built on its dedication to and success in stopping white attacks against the property and persons of black families moving into the area. By attempting to bring segregationist clergy and local homeowner associations into the organization, Alinsky and his staff succeeded in neutralizing the more violent of the Southwest Side's racists and convincing them that their attacks would simply accelerate white flight and the decline of the area. The OSC established a system of block captains, who reported criminal activity both to the organization and to the local police. Through its member associations, the OSC also established regular meetings between street cops and interracial committees of homeowners in transitional areas, in order to curb the youth violence that threatened racial peace. The organization's office had colored maps on its walls, pinpointing trouble spots; when one appeared to be critical, the OSC staff would organize block meetings between whites and blacks to open lines of communication and talk about their common interest in stability. As an OSC publication put it, they engaged in "hours of 'hand holding' with frightened people, informal meetings on threatened blocks, education through parish bulletins, brochures and flyers, conferences with ministers, priests, and civic leaders," in order to halt the violence and stem the tide of white panic and flight. By 1963, most local and outside observers claimed (prematurely) that through the efforts of the OSC "elimination of panic by homeowners appears almost complete."[17]

The effort to bring white and black neighbors together around law-and-order issues was part of a larger organizational campaign to encourage interracial cooperation, develop local black leadership, and increase the organized power of black newcomers within the OSC and the community at large. Blacks increasingly ran for and won leadership positions, and the OSC organized interracial block clubs on the edge of transition areas. As OSC staffer Barry Menuez put it, these clubs were able to "provide a forum and clearinghouse for all the complexities of the problems so that Negroes and whites can hammer out differences face to face." As a result, "grievances were aired," and "lines of communication and cooperation developed." By 1965, both the staff and many of the delegations to that year's congress were fully integrated. The size of the black community within the OSC's boundaries tripled from 1959 to 1965, and the group responded by taking stronger pro–civil rights positions and focusing more of its efforts on the immediate needs of the newcomers.[18]

The OSC also made a variety of attempts to try to convince whites to stay in the neighborhood. In 1963, it published 10,000 copies of the short play *How to Use Facts to Change Your Husband's Mind*—a suggested role-play for local wives to convince their spouses that the Southwest Side had the lonely suburbs beat. A home loan program was established to help creditworthy black families move into the area and enable whites to stay.

Finally, by attempting to gain control of the local housing market, the OSC dispelled some of the resignation and apathy that accelerated the flight of whites out of the area. Through its Real Estate Practices Committee and Housing and Zoning Committee, the OSC took a variety of actions to get zoning and housing codes enforced, to stop real estate speculation and "blockbusting," and to assuage white fears of property value losses in integrated blocks. The organization also tried to effect change in the housing market on a larger scale, though without much success: as early as 1961, it endorsed a Chicago open occupancy ordinance, and beginning in 1962, it sent interracial delegations to developments in nearby suburbs to convince them to integrate. Hearings on race and housing that were organized in preparation for the OSC Community Congress each fall were televised and brought citywide attention to local issues.[19]

Although in many ways the OSC was successful, its accomplishments were relatively short-lived. By stemming local violence and affecting the real estate market sufficiently to allow both whites and blacks a shot at fair value in both the housing and credit markets, the OSC succeeded in slowing down racial transition, stabilizing the quality and economic status of the community, and allowing some interracial cooperation to emerge. As sometime Alinsky organizer Msgr. John Egan observed in 1965, in those Catholic parishes that were strongly affiliated with the OSC—Saint Leo's and Saint Sabina's, in particular—racial turnover was peaceful and took more than six years. Neighboring churches that opposed or avoided the organization changed in less than two years. By the mid-1960s, IAF staffers came to believe that the OSC's signal accomplishment was preventing the area from becoming a slum in the wake of racial change.[20]

Nonetheless, the upper reaches of the Southwest Side continued to change over from white to black. Given the OSC's lack of widespread support in the larger community, and the withdrawal of the Southwest's more racially conservative groups from the organization, its attempts to curb crime and violence ultimately failed. Nicholas Von Hoffman wrote Alinsky that "the miraculous thing about OSC is that it has gotten as far as it has gotten against this ocean of anti-Negro sentiment."[21] A series of well-publicized racial confrontations along advancing racial boundaries— some of them within the heart of the OSC's territory—furthered weakened white housing demand. Already frightened by increases in car theft, purse snatching, and juvenile offenses, as well as by the appearance of panic peddlers in 1964, the OSC's white base quickly collapsed. One thousand families left the parish in 1965, and another thousand fled in 1966—an extraordinary demographic event, given the relatively small geographic size of the area. By 1966, whites in even the most heavily organized parts of the Southwest Side began to leave more rapidly; with the 1968 riots in the wake of the assassination of Dr. Martin Luther King, the trickle became a flood. By 1970, the area surrounding Saint Sabina—a neighborhood called Auburn Gresham—was almost entirely black.[22]

Time was an enormous issue. Small victories would not build the OSC, when all participants could see the larger battle ahead. The closer the expanding ghetto moved to the Southwest, the stronger white homeowners felt the deep connections between race, property, and their economic and social security. The effort of OSC staffers to frame local issues as nonracial—as simply a matter of community improvement and conservation—fooled no one, at least not for long. The intricate relationships between race, community, property, and geography were continually reproduced by the movements of Chicago's housing market and by the strongly held sense of interest and identity that the Southwest Side's white homeowners had formed in response. The OSC not only had to formulate a convincing alternative racial geography; it had to do so under severe time constraints.

Given the impending sense of crisis on the part of even the most racially liberal whites, it was virtually impossible for the OSC to stake out a position on Chicago's "Great Question" that would allow it to serve as a representative public forum. Delegates from the southern end of the community were especially hopeful that the OSC would play the role of racial gatekeeper and draw a line in the sand a good distance away from their homes and neighborhoods. When it became clear that the OSC would not (and could not) keep black families out of the area, racially conservative groups left the organization for federations that promised to do so. Many individuals moved to the suburbs or became resigned to the inevitability of racial change.

The group also struggled to develop a strong black organizational presence. Alinsky himself was well aware that his desire to make the OSC a force for racial integration was not widely shared in the neighborhoods, but he believed that pressure from strongly organized blacks was essential if the Southwest Side was to be integrated. Entire neighborhoods on the South Side frequently experienced almost complete racial turnover within just a few years, leaving an extremely small window of time for organizers to bring the races together on an equal basis. In a community as deeply organized as the Southwest, and as closely tied to geography and property as an expression of religious identity, social belonging, and financial security, the task of bringing black newcomers into the OSC with local whites and expecting them to negotiate as equals was almost hopelessly difficult. With sufficient resources and, most important, time, this would have been a formidable project; without either, the OSC could hope to do little other than help to facilitate the transition of the Southwest from a community of white middle-class homeowners to one of black middle-class homeowners.

The OSC was also limited in its ability to gain control over the local housing market, and its organizers and leaders underestimated the importance of sustaining white housing demand for creating racial balance. The viability of racial integration on the Southwest Side was heavily dependent on the ability of the group to deflect a substantial portion of black housing demand away from the white neighborhoods adjacent to the ghetto, and toward the area's broader housing market. As long as white homeowners in the southern (and wealthier) end of the area refused to open their neighborhoods up to limited black occupancy, and as long as the OSC's staff was unable to bring them into the group and convince them of the self-interested wisdom of such an approach, the limited base of the organization would prevent it from maintaining integration.

Alinsky believed that the only way to prevent the flight of white families from transition neighborhoods was to give them some reassurance that their communities would remain predominantly white and middle-class, both culturally and economically. Efforts at total exclusion of blacks were ineffective and morally wrong, he insisted, and the interests resistant whites were trying to protect could be better served by allowing a small influx of black families dispersed throughout the city. The OSC's racial moderates essentially bought this alternative racial geography as a form of racial retreat. Few shared the views of Alinsky, his staff, and the group's racial liberals that racial integration and dispersion were desirable in and of themselves.

Alinsky's intensely local organizing focus, driven in part by the institutional demands of the OSC's core funders and constituency groups, led him and his staff to concentrate on keeping whites from leaving. Targeting villains (blockbusters, panic peddlers, and, to a lesser extent, those white families considering flight) attracted local residents to the group and helped them to believe that their individual actions could make a difference, but it also interpreted the choice to stay or leave as a moral and social one, rather than as a decision situated within a much larger set of options that included nonracial factors. This approach was based on an incomplete analysis of the obstacles to local integration. The problem of sustaining white demand in racially mixed urban neighborhoods required approaches that encompassed both the city and the suburbs, but Alinsky was neither willing nor able to address it at that level. This parochial approach made the *exit* of whites the locus of organizing, while ignoring the other half of sustaining a strong local housing market for whites—namely, external demand.

While this local focus may have provided a pedagogical means for drawing connections between housing prices, population movements, and racial discrimination in the larger housing market for residents who were largely unaware of why racial transition occurred so rapidly, it was ultimately a faulty analysis of why white neighborhoods on the edge of the ghetto tended to turn over. Speculators certainly could drum up panic, but racial transition was dependent on a simple economic fact: real estate on the market on the white Southwest Side was worth more to blacks than it was to whites, given black demand, white supply, the quality of local housing, the proximity of the area to the expanding black ghetto, and the nature of housing conditions in the metropolitan area as a whole. And whites were unlikely to move into Southwest Side neighborhoods without some reassurance that the local black population was going to remain stable.

Ultimately, white homeowners seeking comparable housing standards and amenities in the Chicago area could find neighborhoods farther from the South Side ghetto that were under no imminent threat of racial turnover. This was part of what made integration in one community so difficult. As long as most urban and suburban neighborhoods remained closed to black families, whites could always find somewhere else in the metropolitan area where there was no black influx. If the OSC could not disperse black families into neighborhoods beyond the edge of the ghetto, or price most blacks out of the local market while sustaining white demand within it, as was occurring in Hyde Park, a solely inward-looking approach was bound to fail. Improvements to the area would continue to attract black families; unwilling to exclude them, the OSC was powerless.

Integration on the Southwest Side simply was not viable without at least a partial end to racial containment elsewhere in the city, and in its suburbs. To bring this about, Alinsky and his organizers needed to broaden the territorial interests and identities of white homeowners in the Southwest and make it clear to them that the viability of their neighborhoods was heavily dependent on what occurred elsewhere. Urban neighborhoods (and suburbs) are all specialized parts of the same political economy and the same social geography. To assert or attempt to establish the autonomy of any one part from the rest was thus impossible.

For integration to work, Alinsky needed to do more than just plead with local white homeowners not to leave, especially when decades of participating in and observing Chicago's housing markets encouraged them to do the opposite. A territorially based group would only reinforce these messages, if it did not seek to quickly educate and organize around the larger structural issues that made local integration seem so threatening. In 1961, John McDermott of the Chicago Catholic Interracial Council had warned that the Southwest Side would find it increasingly difficult to be "an island of sanity in a sea of confusion; an island of stable, normal integration in a sea of racial segregation." He was correct.[23]

Alinsky, of course, had hoped from the beginning to facilitate racial integration on the Southwest Side by simultaneously organizing a black community group, which would then work closely with the OSC to stabilize the housing market. The group he helped to create in 1960, The Woodlawn Organization (TWO), was arguably his greatest organizing success. TWO was organized on the South Side of

Chicago in the wake of white flight in Woodlawn. Local clergy, according to Arthur Brazier, believed that "within two or three years Woodlawn would become a major slum, unless a vigorous community organization was developed to stem the deterioration that was spreading across the community."[24] The population was not only rapidly turning over from white to black; it was also becoming younger and poorer.[25] Overwhelmed by the rapidity of change, the draining of resources, and the turnover of community residents, local organizations seemed powerless.[26] A coalition of churches invited Alinsky to help them.

TWO's story weaves through many of the larger events, ideas, and mobilizations of the turbulent sixties—from the Freedom Rides, to the Chicago Freedom Movement, to the War on Poverty, to Black Nationalism and community control. TWO and its members sought to define and institutionalize the organization's philosophy of self-determination. In the process, they struggled to articulate a relationship between race and place that moved beyond both integration and separatism. By the mid-1960s, its membership included nearly 150 local groups representing 40,000 of Woodlawn's 100,000 citizens. Despite its active participation in Chicago's larger civil rights movement, TWO's organizing efforts became increasingly local as the decade progressed. Guided by its belief in self-determination, and encouraged by the federal War on Poverty, TWO began to concentrate on the construction of low-income housing, greater accountability of social service agencies, and the nurturing of a mass base in the mid-1960s. Community development and control, rather than residential integration, came to define its agenda—and limit its ultimate success.

TWO AND THE WAR ON POVERTY

President Johnson envisioned the War on Poverty as a program to help communities more effectively mobilize their own local resources in order to improve the capacities of the poor. This improvement would come through better coordination of social services at the local level, and "maximum feasible participation" of the poor in the management and distribution of those services. The 1964 Equal Opportunity Act created a new federal agency, the Office of Economic Opportunity (OEO), which implemented a Community Action Program to bring this vision to life in cities around the country. Community Action Agencies (CAAs) were created at the local level, with representation from the poor (at least officially) welcomed.

In "Open Letter to Sargent Shriver," published in the *TWO Newsletter* in October 1964, TWO president Lynward Stevenson outlined the organization's plans with regard to the federal War on Poverty. The promise of maximum feasible participation, Stevenson argued, will allow TWO "to back up our program of self-determination with deeds." The TWO president proposed a comprehensive community-run job training program, complete with health and day care programs.[27] TWO forwarded the plan to Deton Brooks, the Richard Daley–appointed head of Chicago's CAA, for approval. Brooks and the city stonewalled: Mayor Daley had no intention of allowing the federal government to fund any organizations that were politically independent of city hall.[28] Brooks publicly questioned TWO's competence to run poverty programs, arguing that city experts and agencies could more efficiently and effectively spend federal money.[29]

Empowered by the participatory language of federal legislation, and the OEO's early willingness to enforce it, TWO launched a public attack on Daley's interpretation of the poverty program. Stevenson issued scathing criticisms of both Daley and Brooks, accusing them of subverting the War on Poverty by using it to maintain control of the black poor and feed the patronage system. The charges were certainly accurate: Chicago's CAA had fifty-four members, none of whom represented the poor, while applications for jobs in the poverty bureaucracy were funneled through ward committeemen.[30] Alinsky publicly criticized Daley's poverty program as a "prize piece of political pornography."[31] Stevenson testified before the House Committee on Labor and Education in April 1965, holding Daley up to national ridicule. In Chicago, Stevenson testified, the War on Poverty involved maximum feasible participation of the rich, the precinct captains, and the ward committeemen, not the poor. Under Daley's rule, he argued, "there is no War on Poverty. There is only more of the ancient, galling war against the poor."[32]

Throughout the fall and winter of 1965, TWO tried to use solid-bloc voting and large turnouts at meetings to gain influence on the local board, but without success. Daley was determined to shut TWO out of the poverty program. In December 1965, TWO published a "black paper" entitled "Poverty, Power and Race in Chicago" discussing its recent experiences. Federal poverty money, TWO argued, was being used to "buy off our rage against being confined in the ghetto" and to "distract black people from building enough power to break out of the ghetto." The root issue, according to the Black Paper, was "citizen participation . . . we insist that we be in on the decision-making of the War on Poverty. . . . That is what we mean by self-determination."[33]

Daley had succeeded in blocking TWO's participation in Chicago's poverty program, but with the creation of the federal Model Cities program in 1966 (which also mandated citizen participation), TWO had another opportunity. At its March 1967 Community Congress, TWO passed a series of resolutions empowering President Stevenson to hire technical consultants to help Woodlawn residents put together the programs and ideas for reform and renewal that had emerged over the course of the decade. Model Cities appeared to present an opportunity for TWO to implement its vision, while solidifying its status as bargaining agent for Woodlawn. Designed to give cities an opportunity to experiment in limited target areas, its focus was on "community development," unlike the Community Action Program.[34] While inherently limited in a number of ways, Model Cities encouraged municipalities to use existing community organizations and institutions to coordinate and implement programs.

The problem, of course, was that Model Cities plans had to be approved by municipal authorities—and Daley was not about to sign off on something that would render TWO the strongest independent political force in the city. Further, his disdain for citizen participation of any kind was made abundantly clear in the Model Cities plan Daley submitted to the Department of Housing and Urban Development (HUD) in spring 1968. Daley was to appoint all persons serving on citizen committees, and the city plan had no provision for technical assistance to local citizen committees. The city had chosen four target areas—including Woodlawn—but had not sought out any organized constituencies in any of the four in putting the plan together.[35]

TWO girded itself for a battle. The steering committee decided that TWO needed to quickly form a community planning council, get technical help, and put together its own Model Cities plan—one that would adhere to the legislative requirement of citizen participation. TWO would then have to use all its political and persuasive powers in Chicago and Washington to argue that its plan fit federal guidelines and promised greater success than Daley's.

TWO's ongoing relationship with a number of University of Chicago professors provided the planning framework. Chicago faculty, working alongside TWO members and staff, had created an experimental school district, a mental health center, a child health clinic, a legal aid facility, and a social service center in Woodlawn. Each facility had a TWO Citizen's Advisory Board that met frequently with professional staff and used citizens as subprofessionals and community agents. TWO leaders and Chicago faculty decided to use the existing TWO committee structure to put together a Model Cities plan, aided by a faculty task force affiliated with each committee.

The planning process kicked off with an all-day community conference at Saint Cyril's parish hall in late June 1968. More than 250 TWO members met with Chicago faculty and graduate students in plenary sessions and workshops to outline local problems and assemble the political machinery for running the planning process.[36] Proposals were often "criticized mercilessly," and more often than not, according to faculty participant William Swenson, "the suggestions of the Task Force members were completely revamped by the community members."[37] Faculty knew how to speak bureaucratic lingo and fix community-driven goals and programs to HUD requirements, but the community "continued to provide the substantive ingredi-ents."[38] TWO's Model Cities plan was presented to the Community Planning Coun-cil in November, and then to a series of community hearings with a total attendance of more than 1,400. Revisions based on these hearings were made and approved before 300 TWO members in December.

The TWO plan was organized around three concepts: citizen responsibility, the "whole man," and "decentralized centralization." Citizen responsibility for TWO meant more than just participation in planning, as mandated by federal guidelines. It also meant the creation of a structure that would allow the community and its cit-izens to exercise primary responsibility for implementing and administering pro-grams. Critics of poverty programs, TWO argued, often emphasize the lack of responsibility demanded from and exercised by the poor—but citizen responsibility ultimately must rest upon some degree of power and control, through community-based organizations. Only in this way, TWO concluded, can social and urban pol-icy improve lives and develop citizens. The second concept—treating inner-city citizens as "whole people"—was connected to the first. Community and personal problems are interrelated, and cannot be split up "in terms of conventional cate-gories of educational, medical, social welfare, or legal approaches." Poverty is expe-rienced both individually and collectively, its causes are structural and community-wide, and thus solutions must be located at this social level as well.[39]

The structure TWO proposed to implement such programs—"decentralized centralization"—called for the creation of neighborhood government, in which programs were to be carried out through community-based agencies with citizen boards. Such a localized structure would allow programs to adhere closely to local needs in a nonintrusive way, while embedding them into local civil society and respecting the dignity of citizens and communities.[40]

Overall, citizen participation in TWO's planning process was widespread, espe-cially when compared with that of the city. Daley continued to dominate the local Model Area Planning Councils, including the one in Woodlawn. By December, community organizations around the city were in an uproar over the lack of citi-zen participation in local councils, and TWO leaders were optimistic that HUD would throw Daley's plan out because of it.[41]

Their optimism was not rewarded, however. By early 1969, it became apparent that the new Nixon administration was not as interested in pressing HUD's citizen participation requirement as its predecessor had been. Local politicians friendly to TWO successfully urged the organization to participate in the local Model Area Planning Council, in exchange for a promise from the city that TWO's plan would get a fair hearing there. Daley had gotten the better of TWO again, because the "fair hearing" never took place. HUD adopted Daley's Model Cities plan in the summer of 1969.

TWO, SELF-DETERMINATION, AND THE POLITICS OF
RACIAL GEOGRAPHY

In his survey of northern black social movements in the civil rights era, Tom Jackson argues that TWO and other "black empowerment" groups shared both a community-centered focus and a particular historical interpretation of the origin and persistence of the northern ghetto. They sought to strengthen the black community institutionally, rather than just focusing on public policies that primarily benefited individuals or improved individual black mobility in the economic system. "Empowerment" referred both to the potential of black political power to bring in resources from the outside and to the beneficial effects of community organizing on the transformation of the community from within.[42] At the same time, they put forward the argument that concentrated urban black poverty in places like Woodlawn had deep roots in the nation's racial history, both north and south. After centuries of southern racism and economic deprivation, millions of blacks moved to the North just when manufacturing jobs were beginning to dry up. At the same time, racial codes—both formal and informal—excluded blacks from housing, unions, and job and educational opportunities. In cities like Chicago, growing but geographically concentrated black populations also had difficulty translating their growing numbers into real mass political power.[43]

The Great Society failed because it did too little to overcome this history. The agenda developed by TWO and other groups by the mid-1960s—employment programs (both job creation and training), income support, and black political empowerment—was (and has been) largely ignored. To Jackson, TWO stands as an example of both the potential and the limits of independent black community organizing as an antipoverty strategy. Although it was "the most sustained and successful community organization of the inner city poor in the 1960's" and a model of "indigenous community organizing," it was ultimately unable to stop the economic decline of Woodlawn.[44]

War on Poverty programs dealt with growing black challenges to the politics of racial geography by essentially ignoring both race and geography—and pulled black community groups like TWO into doing the same. TWO and other black community groups generally emerged in the early sixties with a focus on local issues. The almost complete exclusion of blacks as an organized force in urban politics—particularly in Chicago—virtually assured that any kind of community mobilization would take place outside of the conventional electoral system. Often, black community groups were first formed in opposition to urban renewal, or to the policies of local public service bureaucracies. These grievances, while reflective of important issues of social justice and often generative of popular mobilization, had a limited analytical reach. They provided little intellectual or political traction with regard to the economic sources of neighborhood decline.[45] Because of these issues and Alinsky's place-based organizing philosophy, TWO would struggle to move beyond the "gilding the ghetto" approach. The politics of race and community—of self-determination, in TWO's parlance—was too limited to attack the political economy and racial geography of Chicago. Both CAP and Model Cities would reinforce this localism, leaving the larger processes of neighborhood deterioration untouched.[46]

In the early 1970s TWO shifted to an emphasis on community development, launching housing and commercial projects in Woodlawn. It was a natural progression from the organization's increasingly exclusive focus on—and eventual disillusion with—federal poverty programs. Federal urban policy followed a similar path, from "community action" to community development. The War on Poverty, Model Cities, and community development all appeared to offer a way for Democrats in particular to do something about ghettos, but without engaging the issues of labor market discrimination, open occupancy, and residential integration that by the mid-1960s were dividing the party at the local level.[47]

Although this approach may have been politically palatable to conservatives who disliked big government programs, white voters who feared residential integration, job competition, and the redistribution of wealth, and black voters who valued the empowerment, patronage, and political power that community development tended to bring, it failed to understand or address the structural roots of racial inequality and uneven metropolitan development. Community development assumed racial segregation as a given and sought to improve the lives of ghetto residents within the limits segregation imposed. Much like community action and Model Cities, it sought to heal ghettos from within.

Federal policy, and racial liberalism more generally, missed both the salience of racial segregation and the politics, identities, and interests that had grown up around it. Or, more accurately, for reasons of cost and political expediency, these issues were simply elided—replaced with the old and evocative American keywords of community, neighborhood, empowerment, and individual uplift. Groups like TWO took up the slack in the political system available to them, used the rhetorical and institutional tools at hand, and tried to build opportunities for individual mobility, patronage, and group political power. They were left with little alternative. The terrain has not changed much since. When the Vietnam conflict, the splintering of the New Deal coalition, and the economic problems of the 1970s shortened the horizons of federal urban and social policy, communities like Woodlawn were essentially left on their own. It remains so today. The situation would get much worse in Woodlawn, before improving somewhat in the 1990s.[48]

The causes of black poverty in Woodlawn lay in larger regional structures of racial geography and political economy. Reorganized social services, locally controlled job training programs, and nonprofit housing construction, no matter how brilliantly and democratically conceived, did little to make Woodlawn a more stable, safe, and livable community. Neither did gaining control over underfunded federal programs that were premised on the notion that concentrated black poverty in Woodlawn could be fixed by improving human and social capital. Living wage jobs left for the suburbs, and upwardly mobile residents generally followed when possible. At best, groups like TWO provided a means for some black families to run up the "down escalator" of opportunity in urban America. Although this is not inconsequential, it is a limited form of social justice. The ghetto remained in place. Alinsky had higher ambitions.

DISCUSSION

Does localism serve the interests of racial justice, when the larger structures that limit opportunity and access are far broader geographically and perhaps require coalitions that cross the boundaries of race, class, and community? The primary difficulty with Alinsky's approach was that he attempted to construct local solutions to problems that were increasingly metropolitan area–wide in scope. The changes Alinsky sought to pursue—and those that he sought to prevent—were beyond his ability to bring about, without a more concentrated attempt to connect his organizations to the broader political and economic issues that were affecting their communities. Alinsky's organizations were never able to assemble the power and authority to reach the point at which local action generates larger social reform—that kind of alchemical mixture of local power and social movement capable of fundamentally reorienting social priorities.

By the late 1960s, Alinsky had come to this conclusion himself. As he gruffly put it in 1969, "A political idiot knows that most major issues are national, and in some cases international in scope. They cannot be coped with on the local community level." He advocated alliances across the boundaries of race, class, and geography to deal with the broader issues that could not be addressed by neighborhood-based identities and organizing.

Alinsky and the IAF created the Citizens Action Program (CAP) in the late sixties, both as a laboratory school for training community organizers and as an experiment in citywide organizing. The group, originally named the Campaign Against Pollution, started in November 1969 in response to a weather inversion that caused a cloud of polluted air to hang over the Chicago area for almost a week. In its first two years, it focused mainly on environmental issues, becoming one of the first such groups in the nation. From the beginning, CAP focused on issues and interests that affected local communities, but that originated in broader structures and processes. In many ways its approach to organizing was not much different from previous Alinsky groups: it retained the organization-of-organizations format and used confrontational tactics to embarrass prominent political and economic institutions into action. Importantly, however, CAP sought to replicate the traditional Alinsky model on a broader geographic plane, and to do so using issues of regional scope.[49] "The most important issues which affect a neighborhood—property taxes, pollution, mortgage loans, etc.—are determined outside the neighborhood by major economic forces," CAP organizer Paul Booth told a reporter in 1973. "A citywide, militant organization was the only way people could begin to deal with these problems."[50]

Most important, CAP brought together people of different races, classes, and neighborhoods in the Chicago area to address redlining and neighborhood deterioration. It began a campaign to expose the decisions of private investors and panic peddlers, FHA abuses and bank lending policies, and the influence of all these groups on city government. CAP campaigned to get pledges from people to withdraw their money from banks and savings and loans that practiced redlining, and deposit them in banks that agreed to invest the money in city neighborhoods. More than $120 million in "greenlining" pledges was collected by April 1975. The group successfully pressured the governor of Illinois to investigate redlining and other FHA abuses; his report, along with community lobbying, led to the passage of a law—which became a national model—prohibiting redlining and requiring disclosure of mortgage loan information. After negotiations with and demonstrations against the Federal Home Loan Bank of Chicago, the bank confirmed the existence of redlining. This led to a city ordinance prohibiting redlining by any institution that accepted city deposits. By all accounts CAP succeeded in shifting the focus of white neighborhood anger away from blacks and toward the government and housing market institutions largely responsible for the racial geopolitics that continued to set the races against one another. Individuals and groups that spun off from CAP helped to lead the movement that resulted in the Community Reinvestment Act, which Congress passed in 1977 and which has helped to reverse at least some of damage done to inner cities by the politics of racial geography.[51]

The post-Alinsky IAF has attempted to build similar coalitions, including United Power for Action and Justice (UPAJ) in Chicago. The result of a decadelong crusade by Alinsky's friend and ally Msgr. John Egan, efforts to organize a regional federation of community, labor, and religious groups that crossed the boundaries of class, race, ethnicity, and jurisdiction began in the early nineties and culminated in a massive founding convention—with 10,000 people in attendance—at the University of Illinois–Chicago's auditorium in October 1997. UPAJ's purpose, according to its guidelines, "is to create a broad-based organization whose goal is to build relational power for collective actions in the name of justice and the common good. We are an organization of other organizations weaving together city and suburbs. We are inclusive, embracing the full diversity of metropolitan Chicago."

The issues that the UPAJ has decided to work on in the next few years— expanding health insurance for the uncovered in the Chicago area and increasing opportunities for homeownership for the working and middle classes—may be somewhat limited and have little directly to say about racial and economic segregation. But with a working coalition in place, the UPAJ has an unprecedented opportunity to construct a strong political constituency dedicated to an alternative racial geography.[52]

In a few places in recent years, political coalitions, government entities, and integrative housing policies have been built at the metropolitan level. Regional land-use planning, fair-share low- and moderate-income housing, and revenue sharing have been adopted in an effort to deal with sprawl, concentrations of poverty, fiscal disparity, and uneven development. As Myron Orfield, William Julius Wilson, and others have argued, only efforts like these that challenge jurisdictional fragmentation have any hope of diminishing the structural problems of the nation's cities and older inner-ring suburbs. Federal efforts like Moving to Opportunity and the Gautreaux experiment are based on the same kind of analysis.[53]

While their successes (and popular support) remain somewhat limited thus far, these efforts are praiseworthy: they seek to break the popular understanding that ghettos can be "uplifted" and cities "saved" with just the right combination of market incentives, bootstrap uplift, local assets and faith-based initiatives.[54] Because such initiatives are metropolitan area–wide in scope, they require participants (and opponents) to begin to draw connections between issues that the politics of racial geography have allowed us to keep separate for so long: the relationship between suburban wealth and urban squalor, private wealth and public squalor, white wealth and black squalor, sprawl and city disinvestment, and white middle-class anxiety and the "Robin Hood in reverse" economic and tax policies of the past two decades. Our racialized social geography not only distracts citizens and community groups from the atrophy of the nation's opportunity structure in the past three decades; it has contributed to the rising influence of conservative narratives of public obligation, desert, and private behavior that posit inequality as the natural and inevitable result of markets, individual choice, and merit. This narrative posits a truncated sociological imagination and an impoverished vision of the commonweal. It is an unsustainable "garrison impulse" that can only be broken when our social geography, and the interests and identities that have grown up around it, is broken. Limited by the political ecology in which he operated, as well as his own approach to organizing, Alinsky could not find a path around that impulse.[55]

CONCLUSION

It is a classic progressive dilemma to wonder and theorize about the proper level of focus, when there seems so much to do, and all problems seem connected. Alinsky's story does not tell us that local means for addressing the issues of segregation, concentrated poverty, racial inequality, and urban disinvestment are a dead end. What it may tell us, instead, is that neighborhood organizing must be ultimately directed toward changes in the law and in the distribution of political power, and toward the creation of multiracial geographically broad coalitions. To build effective democratic organizations capable of exercising power and mobilizing people, local action is a necessity, as Alinsky argued. Given the rightward tilt of American politics since 1968, the abandonment of residential integration in recent decades is more of a tactical retreat than a moral choice. This retreat is not without costs, however. Alinsky's experiences in Chicago point to some of the limitations of focusing exclusively on the "inside game," as David Rusk puts it, while ignoring the "outside game." Segregation remains a fundamental fact of life in the nation's cities and suburbs. Because that geography has been so deeply shaped by race, those who live within it have been as well. Place-based approaches alone will not challenge these connections, since they take that social geography as a given; they may even reinforce them.

Most public and private approaches to the problems of the American city today and in the past tend to be place-based. Of course, a wide variety of community organizing and development approaches exist today; many of them, at least in theory, have moved beyond being "place-based" in the way that the BYNC, OSC, and TWO were. I do not want to create a straw man about present-day community organizations. Many of them—including the IAF—do not operate like Alinsky groups did. For most, however, the basic focus remains local, in the sense that the issue of racial and economic segregation is put aside in favor of marshaling resources and political power to benefit some portion of a city (or in some cases a city as a whole).

Ultimately, however, government and civil society must focus on solutions to the problems of cities that are informed by the insight that place and the distribution of primary social goods have been and still are related, and that seek to break that connection by devising policies that take it seriously. Devising policies that take it seriously means assembling coalitions that do so as well. A neighborhood or community segregated by race or class is not just a place where poor and black people live (or rich and white people); it is a social structure that embeds injustice into our daily lives and that foments identities and politics that fragment efforts to overcome it.[56]

The community organizing and community development movements have had both tangible (improved schools, the construction of affordable housing, increased investment capital) and intangible (social capital and empowerment) effects on the lives of ordinary Americans. Naturally, we should continue to build and support ghetto organizations and institutions; we must continue to invest in social capital as well as human capital. However, the intractability of our social geography remains, creating social and political fragmentation, sedimenting inequality and injustice into the very bones of American life, and truncating our moral and political imaginations. The politics that has grown up around it persists as well. The atrophy of the "commons," so often lamented in recent years, can be attributed to many things. In the United States, at least, racial and economic segregation have greatly exacerbated the weakness of the public sphere by atomizing and privatizing experiences and interests that have their origins in broader structures and deeper historical patterns properly amenable to our common governance.

Alinsky's ideas and experiences—especially his failures—with regard to race must raise a few cautions for community organizing and for urban and social policy more generally. They demand a healthy, optimistic skepticism about the limits of place-based organizing and policy, particularly in urban areas that are predominantly poor and minority. Social justice demands that we break the politics and ways of thinking that have grown up in the past century around social geography. Although in-place strategies are a critical component of any democratic approach, they must be accompanied by broad coalitions and government policies aimed at this goal. Place-based groups in civil society have perhaps prevented a free fall in some places, allowing the disadvantaged to marshal resources and hope, laying the groundwork for a progressive political revival. But efforts by government and civil society will replicate the fragmentation that frustrated Alinsky, and which divides us today, without a conscious effort to reach beyond our present social geography.

NOTES

1. National Advisory Commission on Civil Disorders, *Report* (New York: Bantam Books, 1968), chap. 16.

2. Todd Gitlin, *The Twilight of Common Dreams: Why America Is Wracked by Culture Wars* (New York: Metropolitan Books, 1995).

3. Peter Dreier, John Mollenkopf, and Todd Swanstrom, *Place Matters: Metropolitics for the Twenty-first Century* (Lawrence: University Press of Kansas, 2001); David Rusk, *Inside Game/Outside Game: Winning Strategies for Saving Urban America* (Washington, DC: Brookings Institution Press, 2001); Peter Dreier et al., *Regions That Work* (Minneapolis: University of Minnesota Press, 2000); Randy Stoecker, "The CDC Model of Urban Development: A Critique and Alternative," *Journal of Urban Affairs* 19 (1997): 1–22; Nicholas Lemann, "The Myth of Community Development," *New York Times Magazine*, January 9, 1994.

4. M. W. Newman, "South Side Neighborhood Works for Racial Peace," three-part series, *Chicago Daily News*, September 1 through 3, 1960; Fr. John Egan, "The OSC—An Evaluation, October 1965," Egan papers, University of Notre Dame Archives, South Bend, Indiana.

5. M. W. Newman and Harry Swegle, "The Panic Peddlers," nine-part series, *Chicago Daily News*, October 13 through 22, 1959.

6. Newman and Swegle, "The Panic Peddlers," October 21, 1959.

7. Evelyn Kitagawa and Karl Taeuber, *Chicago Community Fact Book, Chicago Metropolitan Area, 1960* (Chicago: Chicago Community Inventory, 1963), 8–9; see also Beverly Duncan, *Population Growth in the Chicago SMA* (Chicago: Chicago Community Inventory, 1958), 12.

8. Karl Tauber and Alma Tauber, "The Negro as an Immigrant Group: Trends in Economic and Racial Segregation in Chicago," *American Journal of Sociology* 69 (1964): 374–382.

9. The phrase "Chicago's Great Question" comes from Newman, "South Side Neighborhood Works for Racial Peace." For works that examine the transition and disappearance of white ethnic city neighborhoods, and their effects on identity and politics, see Ray Suarez, *The Old Neighborhood* (New York: Free Press, 1999); Gerald Gamm, *Urban Exodus: Why the Jews Left Boston and the Catholics Stayed* (Cambridge, MA: Harvard University Press, 1999); Louis Rosen, *South Side: The Racial Transformation of an American Neighborhood* (New York: Ivan Dee, 1998); Tom Sugrue, *Origins of the Urban Crisis: Race and Inequality in Postwar Detroit* (Princeton, NJ: Princeton University Press, 1996); Alan Ehrenhalt, *Lost City: Discovering the Forgotten Virtues of Community in the Chicago of the 1950's* (New York: HarperCollins, 1995); Alexander Von Hoffman, *Local Attachments: The Making of an American Neighborhood 1850–1920* (Baltimore: Johns Hopkins University Press, 1994); Hillel Levine and Lawrence Harmon, *The Death of an American Jewish Community: A Tragedy of Good Intentions* (New York: Free Press, 1992); J. Anthony Lukas, *Common Ground: A Turbulent Decade in the Lives of Three American Families* (New York: Vintage Books, 1986); Jonathan Reider, *Canarsie: The Jews and Italians of Brooklyn against Liberalism* (Cambridge, MA: Harvard University Press, 1985); Eleanor Wolf, Charles LeBeaux, Shirley Terreberry, and Harriet Saperstein, *Change and Renewal in an Urban Community: Five Case Studies of Detroit* (Westport, CT: Praeger, 1969); Vincent Giese, *Revolution in the City* (Chicago: Fides, 1961).

10. See U.S. Federal Housing Administration, *Underwriting Manual* (Washington, DC: U.S. Government Printing Office, 1938), par. 937; U.S. Federal Housing Administration, *Underwriting Manual* (Washington, DC: U.S. Government Printing Office, 1947), pars. 1320(1), 1320(2).

11. Sugrue, *Origins of the Urban Crisis*.

12. Testimony of Saul Alinsky before the U.S. Commission on Civil Rights, Chicago, Illinois, May 5, 1959, 769–781, Alinsky papers, University of Illinois–Chicago, Special Collections.

13. Wendy Plotkin, "Neighbors and Boundaries: Racial Restrictive Covenants in Chicago, 1900–1948" (paper presented at the meeting of the Organization for American Historians, Indianapolis, April 2– 5, 1998, in author's possession); Arnold Hirsch, *Making the Second Ghetto* (Chicago: University of Chicago Press, 1983); Louis Washington, *A Study of Restrictive Covenants in Chicago* (M.A. thesis, University of Chicago, 1948); Chicago Council against Racial and Religious Discrimination, *Chicago's Neighborhood Improvement Associations* (Chicago: Chicago Council against Racial and Religious Discrimination, 1943); Zorita Mikva, "The Neighborhood Improvement Association: A Counter-force to the Expansion of Chicago's Negro Population" (M.A. thesis, University of Chicago, 1951); Isaac Groner, "Race Discrimination in Housing," *Yale Law Journal* 57 (1948): 426–458.

14. See Saul Alinsky, "The Urban Immigrant" (paper presented at the conference "Roman Catholicism and the American Way of Life," University of Notre Dame, South Bend, Indiana, February 13, 1959), for his version of the January meeting and the days that followed. File 292, Alinsky papers.

15. See quotations by future OSC staffer Peter Martinez in Eileen McMahon, *What Parish Are You From? A Chicago Irish Community and Race Relations* (Lexington: University Press of Ken-

tucky, 1995), 139; and by Rev. Robert Christ in John Fish et al., *The Edge of the Ghetto: A Study of Church Involvement in Community Organization* (Chicago: University of Chicago Divinity School, 1966), 12.

16. Newman, "South Side Neighborhood Works for Racial Peace."

17. "The Community That Lifted Itself by Its Own Boostraps," *Midwest Magazine*, December 4, 1960; Egan, "The OSC—An Evaluation"; "Program and Accomplishments of OSC," April 1961, box 38, OSC File, Egan papers; "OSC Progress Report" (1962), box 38, OSC file, Egan papers; "Negroes Branch Out—Mostly in Peace," *Chicago Daily News*, July 21, 1962; Barry Meneuz, "Notes for Address to Clergy," April 1, 1963, box 38, OSC file, Egan papers; memo from Nicholas Von Hoffman to Saul Alinsky, June 21, 1963, Alinsky papers; "OSC Progress Detailed for 5 Years," *Southtown Economist*, October 28, 1964; "OSC," in *Community Organization Notebook* (October 1968), Interreligious Council on Urban Affairs, Human Relations and Ecumenism file, box 10021.10, Archives of the Archdiocese of Chicago.

18. Community Relations Committee report (1962), file 307, Alinsky papers; Barry Menuez, "Stabilizing Neighborhoods in Racial Transition," *Church in Metropolis* (1965), 31.

19. The 1961 law was defeated in the state assembly. See Lynn Eley and Thomas Casstevens, eds., *The Politics of Fair-Housing Legislation: State and Local Case Studies* (San Francisco: Chandler, 1968); Resolution, Beverly Hills-Morgan Park Council on Human Relations, n.d., file 307 Alinsky papers; MPPO resolution to OSC Congress Regarding Race Relations, n.d., file 307 Alinsky papers; Fish et al., *Edge of the Ghetto*, 27; undated MPPO press release, box 35, Egan papers.

20. Egan, "The OSC—An Evaluation"; Menuez, "Stabilizing Neighborhoods in Racial Transition"; Von Hoffman to Alinsky, June 21, 1963, Alinsky papers.

21. On the polls, see *Southwest News-Herald*, March 16, 1967, 1; and James Ralph, *Northern Protest: Martin Luther King, Jr., Chicago, and the Civil Rights Movement* (Cambridge, MA: Harvard University Press, 1993), 116, 222; Von Hoffman to Alinsky, June 21, 1963, 2, Alinsky papers.

22. See McMahon, *What Parish Are You From?*; Chicago Fact Book Consortium, *Chicago Community Fact Book: 1970 and 1980* (Chicago: Chicago Review Press, 1984); Chicago Urban League, *Where Blacks Live: Race and Residence in Chicago in the 1970's* (Chicago: Chicago Urban League, 1978).

23. Statement by John McDermott, Executive Director, Catholic Interracial Council, to Public Hearing No. 3, OSC, September 14, 1961, Alinsky papers.

24. Arthur Brazier, *Black Self-Determination* (Grand Rapids, MI: Eerdmans, 1969), 24.

25. By 1960 more than 23 percent of local residents received some form of public assistance. Chicago Department of City Planning, "Statistics," December 27, 1961, Ruth Moore papers, box 8, Chicago Historical Society (CHS).

26. Floyd Mulkey, "Historical Sketches of Organizations in Woodlawn," October 8, 1962, TWO file, Chicago Historical Society; Hampton Price, "Christmas Letter from an Inner-City Pastor to His Friends," February 16, 1961, Emil Schwarzhaupt Foundation papers, box 29, folder 14, University of Chicago Special Collections.

27. "Open Letter to Sargent Shriver," *TWO Newsletter*, October 21, 1964.

28. Lois Wille, "TWO Wants to Know: Will We Share in Poverty Funds?" *Chicago Daily News*, April 5 through 9, 1965.

29. Ibid.

30. Ibid.

31. Saul Alinsky, "The War on Poverty: Political Pornography," *Journal of Social Issues* 11 (Summer 1965): 41–47.

32. Congressional testimony of Lynward Stevenson before the House Committee on Labor and Education, Examination of the War on Poverty, in *TWO Newsletter*, April 14, 1965.

33. "TWO Black Paper Number Two: Poverty, Power and Race in Chicago," *TWO Newsletter*, December 9, 1965, 14–16.

34. U.S. Department of Housing and Urban Development, Model Cities Administration, *Program Guide: Model Neighborhoods in Demonstration Cities*, HUD PG-47 (Washington, DC: U.S. Government Printing Office, 1967), 3.

35. Community Legal Council, "Citizen Participation in Chicago's Model Cities Program: A Critical Analysis" (Chicago: Community Legal Council, May 15, 1968).

36. William Swenson, "The Continuing Colloquium on University of Chicago Demonstration Projects in Woodlawn: Aspects of a Major University's Commitment to an Inner-City Ghetto" (Center for Urban Studies, University of Chicago, 1968), 248.

37. Ibid., 120.

38. Ibid., 119.

39. The Woodlawn Organization, *Woodlawn's Model Cities Plan* (Chicago: Whitehall, 1970), 26.

40. See ibid.; Eddie Williams, "The Model Cities Plan of TWO—An Abstract," in *Delivery Systems for Model Cities: New Concepts in Serving the Urban Community*, ed. Eddie Williams et al. (Chicago: University of Chicago Center for Policy Study, 1969), 79–102.

41. See "Ex–Model Cities Chief Tells Why He Quit," *Chicago Sun-Times*, December 13, 1968, 50; *Woodlawn Observer*, December 18, 1968, 1.

42. Tom Jackson, "The State, the Movement, and the Urban Poor: The War on Poverty and Political Mobilization in the 1960's," in *The Underclass Debate: Views from History*, ed. Michael Katz (Princeton, NJ: Princeton University Press, 1993), 405–406.

43. Ibid.

44. Ibid., 428.

45. Ibid., 424–425.

46. Ibid., 424–429.

47. Lemann, *The Promised Land*, 199.

48. On recent improvements in Woodlawn, see Celeste Garrett, "Woodlawn Has a Bold Vision: Renewal Already Making Its Mark," *Chicago Tribune*, December 22, 2002.

49. Derek Shearer, "CAP: New Breeze in the Windy City," *Ramparts*, October 1973, 12–16; Joan Lancourt, *Confront or Concede: The Alinsky Citizen-Action Organizations* (Lanham, MD: Lexington Books, 1979), 26–28; Don Rose and Richard Rothstein, "The CAP Story: Working Class Reformers," *Chicago Reader*, October 1974, 1, 16.

50. Shearer, "CAP," 14.

51. On CAP, see David Emmons, "Community Organizing and Urban Policy: Saul Alinsky and Chicago's Citizens Action Program" (Ph.D. thesis, University of Chicago, 1986); Henry Scheff, "Issues and Communities: The CAP Model of Organizing," *Focus/Midwest* 11, no. 69 (n.d.): 14–17; Ron Dorfman, "Greenlining Chicago: The Citizens Action Program," *Working Papers* 3 (Summer 1975); Lancourt, *Confront or Concede*; Gregory Squires, *Chicago: Race, Class, and the Response to Urban Decline* (Philadelphia: Temple University Press, 1987), 141–142; Shearer, "CAP."

52. On UPAJ, see Robert McClory, "Reviving the Energy for Action and Justice," *National Catholic Reporter*, January 15, 1999, 3–4; Thomas Lenz, "Building a Force for the Common Good," *Shelterforce*, September/October 1998; David Moberg, "New City-Suburban Coalition Tackles Shared Social Problems," *North Shore Magazine*, January 1998; Steve Kloehn, "Activists Powered by Faith, Not Plans," *Chicago Tribune*, October 20, 1997, 1; "Grassroots Organizing Coming to Suburbia," *Chicago Tribune*, July 15, 1996. For an optimistic view of today's IAF and the possibility for multiracial coalitions, see William Julius Wilson, *The Bridge over the Racial Divide: Rising Inequality and Coalition Politics* (Berkeley: University of California Press, 1999), especially chap. 3.

53. Xavier DeSousa Briggs, *The Geography of Opportunity: Race and Housing Choice in Metropolitan America* (Washington, DC: Brookings Institution Press, 2005); Michael T. Maly, *Beyond Segregation: Multiracial and Multiethnic Neighborhoods in the United States* (Philadelphia: Temple University Press, 2005); John Goering, *Choosing a Better Life? Evaluating the Moving to Opportunity Experiment* (Washington, DC: Urban Institute Press, 2003); Edward Goetz, *Clearing the Way: Deconcentrating the Poor in America* (Washington, DC: Urban Institute Press, 2003); Leonard Rubinowitz and James Rosenbaum, *Crossing the Class and Color Lines: From Public Housing to Suburbia* (Chicago: University of Chicago Press, 2002); Rusk, *Inside Game/Outside Game;* Dreier et al., *Regions That Work;* Myron Orfield, *American Metropolitics: The New Suburban Reality* (Washington, DC: Brookings Institution Press, 2002); Myron Orfield, *Metropolitics: A Regional Agenda for Community and Stability* (Washington, DC: Brookings Institution Press, 1997).

54. Alexander Polikoff, "Unlikely Times," and Owen Fiss, "A Task Unfinished," in *A Way Out* (Princeton, NJ: Princeton University Press, 2004), ed. Owen Fiss.

55. Sheryl Cashin, *The Failures of Integration* (New York: Public Affairs, 2004), 169–170, 179.

56. Fiss, *A Way Out,* 5, 116.

3. Community Organizing in a Nonregime City

The New Orleans Experience

Peter F. Burns

In his classic article on unconventional tactics, Michael Lipsky explained how the powerless, namely, African Americans and the poor, used protest to gain responsiveness to their concerns. "Protest activity is defined by the mode of political action oriented toward objection to one or more policies or conditions, characterized by showmanship or display of an unconventional nature, and undertaken to obtain rewards from political or economic systems while working within the systems."[1] According to Lipsky, the protest group lacks power, which includes access to government and financial resources. Therefore, it tries to attract the attention of those with power, whom Lipsky calls reference publics. The protest group aims to spur the reference publics to force action from the target group, which can satisfy the protesters' requests. In most instances, government and business constitute the target group because they possess the authority and financial rewards that protest groups seek.

Community groups and neighborhood-based organizations employ unconventional tactics, including protest, in attempts to secure rewards from the political and economic systems. They assume that the target group possesses the capacity to provide benefits to them. The civic ecology changed in urban settings over the last fifty years, however, leaving many cities without target groups capable of delivering political or economic rewards to protest groups on a regular basis.

What happens to community organizing when cities lack target groups with the capacity to meet the demands of these groups? To address this question, this chapter examines community organizing in New Orleans, a city whose corporate community diminished well before Hurricane Katrina struck in August 2005. This chapter employs urban regime analysis to describe the civic ecology in many cities. It explains the changes in the New Orleans regime and how a pro-growth regime no longer rules this city.[2] It includes a description of the role community organizations play in the aftermath of Hurricane Katrina. The central purpose of this chapter is to examine how this new civic ecology of scarce resources and a relatively weak corporate leadership affects the manner in which local affiliates of the Association of Community Organizations for Reform Now (ACORN), People Improving Communities through Organizing (PICO), and the Industrial Areas Foundation (IAF) approach community organizing.

URBAN REGIMES

Like other kinds of ecologies, those of the civic nature vary from place to place. Regimes make up an important and necessary part of the local ecology in many urban areas because cities operate with scarce resources. Urban regimes are informal but long-lasting partnerships among resource providers.[3] In many instances, city government creates partnerships with the private sector in order to execute public policy. Public and private actors establish regimes because the former possesses authority, whereas the latter controls financial decisions, and both of these resources are necessary for urban governance.[4]

Regime actors establish reciprocal relationships to meet their policy interests, and they exclude those who do not belong to the regime. Government and business tend to form pro-growth regimes through which economic interests provide financial and human capital to the public sphere; in exchange, they receive preferential zoning laws, reduced taxes, and other governmental benefits.[5] The poor are usually excluded from regimes because they lack resources.[6] African American mayors lead black urban regimes, which provide patronage positions to racial and ethnic minorities but pursue economic development with as much fervor as pro-growth regimes led by white mayors.[7]

According to regime theory, public officials lack *power over* governance.[8] Instead, they must create the *power to* govern with other resource providers. Lipsky's model assumes that public officials maintain *power over* cities. Protest groups infer that public officials possess the capacity to respond to their demands. Lipsky does not consider what happens to protest group demands when jurisdictions lack a regime. Likewise, community organizations' use of unconventional activities assumes that a regime rules each city.

Regimes do not form in every city. Reasons for nonregime cities include conflicts between government and business or a dearth of private actors necessary to form a regime. In Milwaukee, for example, public and private resource providers failed to agree on a common agenda during the period from 1948 to 1960.[9] Joel Rast concludes that the breakdown of public-private partnerships opens agenda setting to a wider set of interests than those incorporated in pro-growth regimes.[10] As I explain later, the flight of resource-providing corporations limits regime formation in present-day New Orleans.

A nonregime city may present obstacles or opportunities to community organizations, depending on the strategies groups employ. If community organizations assume that government or business maintains the capacity to respond to their
concerns, then their tactics may limit the extent to which they receive substantive
representation. By contrast, if they understand the limitations of government and
business, then they may apply pressure to target groups on a more strategic basis and
attempt to create partnerships to meet their policy concerns.

CHANGES IN THE NEW ORLEANS REGIME

From 1945 to 1970, a caretaker regime protected small property holders and members of the New Orleans social aristocracy by resisting large-scale economic development in this city.[11] After 1970, African American mayors and business organizations that represented large and medium-sized companies oversaw the New Orleans
pro-growth regime, largely financed by federal and state funds.[12] In the late 1980s, a
number of private entities planned and executed New Orleans' economic development strategies. Oil, the New Orleans port, and tourism drove the city's economy
during this period.[13]

A strong case can be made that New Orleans' leaders focused on the interest of
business and the central city to the exclusion of neighborhoods and issues that
affect African Americans and the poor. For example, the urban renewal programs
of the 1970s through the 1990s displaced the poor and many African Americans
while it concentrated on providing substantive benefits to the New Orleans corporate community.[14] Over the last thirty-five years, New Orleans' governmental and
business leaders focused on the economic development of the French Quarter and
the central business district. Economic development projects in these areas include
two malls, an aquarium, a multipurpose stadium, a basketball arena, the relocation
of a National Basketball Association (NBA) team to the city, a land-based casino,
the revitalization of one of the city's main streets (Poydras Street), and the construction of numerous hotels.[15] From the 1970s to the present time, public policy
provided symbolic benefits but not tangible rewards, such as jobs, to the poor and
African Americans in New Orleans.[16]

Tourism-related jobs increased dramatically in New Orleans over time. In 1999,
tourism jobs accounted for 16 percent of the jobs in New Orleans, whereas they
made up only 7 percent in the late 1980s.[17] In the last thirty-five years, the city hosted
a world's fair, the Republican National Convention, and nine Super Bowls.

As in other cities, a loss of many major businesses and decreases in federal aid
created a leadership and resource void in New Orleans. In the late 1980s, oil and gas

prices dropped significantly and the city lost business to ports in Miami and Houston. By 2000, the city's power company remained the only Fortune 500 company in New Orleans. These major changes removed financial resources and private leaders capable of sustaining and leading a pro-growth regime.

Despite significant losses to the city's petrochemical industry, a small set of business leaders persists. This group includes the president and chief executive officer of the Audubon Nature Institute, which runs the city's aquarium and zoo. The New Orleans Regional Chamber of Commerce, a group of more than 2,100 large and medium-sized businesses in the New Orleans metropolitan area, also makes up part of the city's business leadership. The Business Council, an organization that lobbies for business interests, maintained some power in the 1980s, but it became relatively inactive after its former leader took on other interests. In the post-Katrina period, however, it reenergized and helped initiate the mayoral campaign of prominent businessman Ron Forman. These businesses do not have the kinds of resources necessary to facilitate governance on a regular basis. African American mayors have controlled New Orleans' institutional resources, including patronage positions and authority over the city's bureaucracy. However, scarce resources limit the mayor's ability to accomplish public policy goals without significant assistance from others.

Does anyone rule New Orleans? No, says one longtime political actor. According to this person, in the era leading up to Hurricane Katrina, New Orleans lacked an establishment capable of getting things done.[18] A prominent and longtime business leader noted that the city's corporate community exerted much less influence than it wielded in the past.[19] This leader recalls when the chamber of commerce constituted an important element in New Orleans' policymaking, but he never heard about the chamber in the late 1990s or the early twenty-first century. According to this business leader, the city is much different politically than it was thirty years ago. New Orleans lacks identifiable leadership, whereas thirty to forty years ago a small group of business leaders got together and accomplished something. This leader notes that this kind of leadership nucleus is missing from present-day New Orleans.

A series of issue-based coalitions have governed New Orleans.[20] For example, the mayor, the police department, and community-based organizations initiated public safety reform in the mid-1990s. By contrast, the governor, the mayor, and the chamber of commerce formed the coalition that secured an NBA franchise for New Orleans.[21] State government allocated the financial resources necessary to attract an NBA franchise, whereas the corporate community provided these funds in other cities, such as Memphis.

How does this new ecology affect community organizing in New Orleans? Does it present a political opportunity structure for community organizations to assume a more prominent place in the city's civic ecology?[22] Faced with ever-decreasing resources, does government look for assistance from entities that can help it perform its job? Have community organizations filled the leadership and resource voids created by the loss of business and private and public finances? Do community organizations use their access to low- to moderate-income residents to collaborate with government to address heightened crime and poverty in addition to other areas of concern? I address these questions in this chapter and summarize my answers in the conclusion.

COMMUNITY ORGANIZING IN NEW ORLEANS

Even before Hurricane Katrina, New Orleans faced many challenges. A poor educational system, crime, poverty, and inadequate housing negatively affected this city. New Orleans schools finished at the bottom of the state in regard to academic performance. Many referred to New Orleans as the murder capital of the United States because of its high homicide rate. Murders increased each year in New Orleans from 1999 to 2003, from 159 in 1999 to 275 in 2003. In 2004, the number of murders in New Orleans totaled 236.

Like other cities, New Orleans operates with scarce resources.[23] New Orleans' poverty rate is nearly triple the national average. The city lost more than 50,000 jobs over the last twenty years, whereas employment increased in other southern cities, including Atlanta, Austin, and Orlando.[24] Mismanagement, corruption, and substandard facilities typified New Orleans' public housing in the last quarter of the twentieth century. In 2002, the federal government took control of the Housing Authority of New Orleans (HANO) because it believed the city misappropriated money designated for public housing.[25] The Department of Housing and Urban Development (HUD) also condemned HANO for failing to repair substandard and unlivable homes. The federal government used HOPE VI grants to transform public housing in New Orleans; as a consequence, the number of public housing units decreased from 1,510 to 296.

Over time, a number of community organizations formed to address these problems. New Orleans is home to the local, state, and national headquarters of ACORN. All Congregations Together (ACT) and the Jeremiah Group (Jeremiah) are faith-based organizations that derive their training from PICO and IAF, respectively. An examination of how these three organizations develop power for the less fortunate and bring the powerless into a relationship with those who govern provides a special opportunity to compare how community groups attempt to affect the local ecology of civic engagement in a nonregime city.

ACORN'S ACTIVITIES IN THE PRO-GROWTH REGIME PERIOD

The New Orleans civic ecology was different in 1976, when ACORN began in New Orleans, than in the late 1980s and early 1990s, when ACT and Jeremiah were founded. ACORN began when New Orleans possessed a regime that consisted of the oil and gas industry, government, and the wealthy and mainly white social aristocracy. ACORN started in New Orleans six years after it originated in Arkansas.[26] It expanded to New Orleans partly because this city and Little Rock experienced similar problems. Conservative, wealthy whites formed part of the regime in each city, and they wanted to maintain the political status quo.[27] Racial division and resistance to the interests of the poor and African Americans also characterized Little Rock and New Orleans during this period.[28]

Low- and moderate-income families and individuals, rather than institutions, make up ACORN's membership. ACORN, with monthly family dues of ten dollars, claims to be the "nation's largest community organization of low- and moderate-income families."[29] ACORN relies on individual as opposed to institutional members because it believes this method empowers the low- to moderate-income residents who make up the organization's membership.

Several neighborhood chapters make up ACORN's active membership in New Orleans. ACORN works primarily in Mid-City, Carrollton, the Upper and Lower Ninth Wards, Hollygrove, and various parts of New Orleans East (see map 1). Many low- to moderate-income residents and African Americans lived in each of these neighborhoods, which tend to receive scant government attention.[30] The presidents of these neighborhood chapters form ACORN's citywide board. Each neighborhood council determines the issues on which it wants to work, whereas the citywide council decides if the entire organization should pursue a subject. In the past fifteen years, New Orleans ACORN worked on homeownership, crime, fair housing and neighborhood revitalization, housing and mortgage discrimination, blight, and an increase to the minimum wage, also known as the living wage campaign.

ACORN makes a clear distinction between group members and organizers. Low- to moderate-income residents constitute the members of the organizations, and they decide the issues on which ACORN focuses. The paid staff aids the members in organizing campaigns, but it insists that the issues flow from the members. Because it is not a 501(c)(3) organization, ACORN pursues any issue chosen by its members.[31] Approximately thirty paid staffers work for ACORN. Some of the staff members organize, whereas others focus on voter registration drives or get-out-the-vote campaigns.

During New Orleans' corporate regime period, ACORN played an important but limited role in the city's civic ecology. It aimed to improve the quality of life for low- and moderate-income neighborhoods, families, and individuals and the

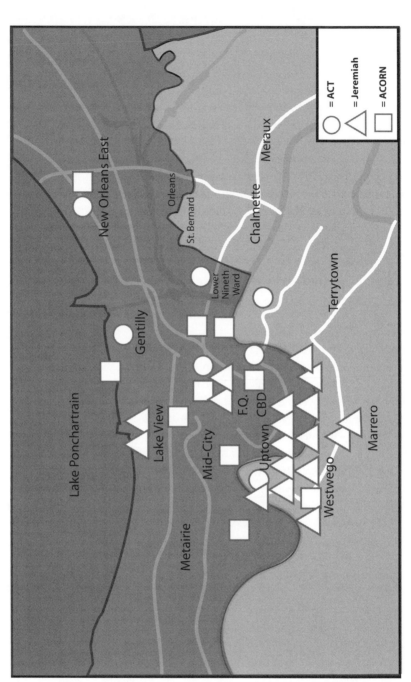

Map 1. Location of ACORN, ACT, and Jeremiah in the New Orleans Metropolitan Area.

underrepresented, and it targeted businesses and government in order to accomplish this goal. ACORN maintained largely adversarial relations with government and business during this time.

Because ACORN formed during a time in which an identifiable corporate regime ruled New Orleans, its tactics focused on winning concessions from government and business. ACORN relied on and continues to employ direct-action tactics, such as demonstrations, picketing, sit-ins, and taking abandoned property, to get target groups, such as government and business, to take action on its constituents' concerns. ACORN claims that "its long history proves that confronting decision-makers face-to-face brings the best results."[32] According to one person who has worked with the organization, "ACORN is mostly oppositional."[33]

The issues around which ACORN mobilized during this period included predatory lending, safer schools, increased access to affordable housing, and higher wages for the working poor.[34] The pursuit of these issues placed ACORN into direct conflict with the private sphere of the New Orleans pro-growth regime. During this period, ACORN targeted banks, lenders, hotels, and restaurants, among others, and it needed to direct the city government's attention toward either implementing or creating laws that aided poor and minority neighborhoods. To say the least, city government slowly reacted to issues that affected ACORN's constituents.

In the pro-growth regime era, ACORN did not concentrate on building relational power. Instead, it collaborated with a few groups on a regular basis. It worked most often with churches and organized labor in general, and with Service Employees International Union (SEIU) Local 100 in particular. Wade Rathke, ACORN's founder, established Local 100 in New Orleans in 1980, and he continues to serve as the union's chief organizer.

Whereas ACORN and Local 100 maintain separate boards, budgets, and leaders, they established a reciprocal relationship because the former organization addresses low- to moderate-income issues in the community, whereas the latter focuses on these topics in the workplace. In 1980, for example, Rathke, Hyatt Hotel housekeepers, and cafeteria, janitorial, and line staff at Tulane University organized an independent union, which affiliated with SEIU four years later.[35] The Hyatt remains the only unionized hotel in New Orleans.[36] Rathke helped establish Local 100 partly because union organizing did not address labor issues in the late 1970s, and workers in certain jobs, such as the hospitality and home health care industries, were not organized.

Historically, ACORN used electoral channels to supplement its unconventional tactics. In 1972, ACORN formed a political action committee (PAC). When local ACORN chapters want to support candidates, the ACORN PAC provides them with human resources to register voters and get out the vote. Rathke believes that ACORN needs direct involvement in political campaigns to realize its people power.

He says that the PAC allows ACORN to exercise power, whereas Saul Alinsky felt that numbers equaled power. According to Rathke, direct political action legitimates the strength of ACORN's large membership. The PAC and this philosophy make ACORN more outwardly political than ACT or Jeremiah. ACORN's PAC has secured electoral victories in New Orleans. Most recently, ACORN helped elect Marlin Gusman to criminal sheriff in 2004. The assumption underlying this overt political strategy is that government maintains the capacity to respond to ACORN's concerns.

ACORN AND CHANGES IN THE NEW ORLEANS CIVIC ECOLOGY

In New Orleans, ACORN continues to mobilize around issues that affect African Americans and the poor, and it still approaches business and government with the assumption that these entities control the economic and political resources it desires. ACORN targets business and government when it believes these institutions ignore or work against its constituents. In New Orleans and across the country, for example, ACORN demonstrated against H&R Block for allegedly overcharging for tax return preparation. ACORN members went into H&R Block offices and gave customers flyers that explained where people could receive free tax preparation. In 2000, after a federal court rejected its lawsuit, ACORN conducted what it called "a summer of protest" against an expansion of the Industrial Canal Lock Replacement Project, which it claimed would negatively affect Ninth Ward residents. These strategies are consistent with ACORN's philosophy of trying to win policy concessions from target groups.

ACORN continues to target government and business. Over a four-year period that began in 1999, ACORN worked to close a concrete crushing plant, which caused many health problems in Hollygrove, a working-class residential neighborhood.[37] The plant closed after years of ACORN-initiated pressure, which included meetings, protests, repeated contacts with local, state, and federal officials, and threats of a class-action lawsuit against the owner of the facility.[38]

In regard to ACORN's interactions with government, one of this organization's common tactics includes deluging government officials with calls when the public sector neglects a community or neighborhood. After months of unsuccessful attempts to get city government to clean up a blighted lot across from her house, for example, an ACORN member brought the issue to this organization.[39] The city cleared the lot after ACORN members made fifty calls to government officials in one day.

Even though most of ACORN's tactics assume that a regime continues to exist in New Orleans, they changed somewhat over time. As the corporate-centered regime began to break down in New Orleans, ACORN used direct-action strategies to create issue-oriented partnerships with its former adversaries. "Conflict produces a different kind of recognition and understanding," says one ACORN leader.[40] The new civic ecology encouraged ACORN to establish reciprocal relationships with business on a short-term or single-issue basis. ACORN used confrontation to educate its opponents about the benefits of aiding ACORN. After ACORN challenged Hibernia Bank's lending practices, the two groups and others worked together to provide funds for victims of predatory loans. ACORN and H&R Block, which were former adversaries, joined to educate people about the Earned Income Tax Credit (EITC). Local 100 and ACORN continue to collaborate on many issues, including the passage of a living wage ordinance and the defeat of the privatization of the sewage and water board in New Orleans.

ACORN formed an environmental coalition with Tulane and Xavier Universities and the city and state departments of health to reduce lead poisoning. To stop predatory lending, ACORN developed a partnership with churches, its housing corporation, HUD, the Louisiana attorney general's office, Whitney and Hibernia Banks, and the American Association of Retired Persons (AARP). Banks also work with ACORN on housing fairs. As Whitney Bank's vice president for community affairs explained, "ACORN finds the buyers and trains them. We provide permanent financing for the graduates of its home-buying program at below-market rates."[41] This example illustrates the reciprocal relationships that ACORN and business can form. ACORN provides the banks with access to customers, whereas the banks satisfy ACORN's demands for adequate and fair housing.

Despite changes in the civic ecology and its greater willingness to establish issue-based coalitions, ACORN still acts as if it can wrest policy concessions from government and business. It does not proceed as if public actors need to create the capacity to govern. For example, it used ballot initiatives to force the public and private sectors to increase wages.[42] New Orleans voters approved a one-dollar increase to the minimum wage by a two-to-one margin. ACORN also relied on lawsuits to gain responsiveness. In New Orleans, it sued landlords who it contended denied rental property to the disabled.

ACORN's approach resembles the Lipsky model. ACORN relies on "showmanship" and "displays of an unconventional nature" to secure policy victories. ACORN shows little to no interest in developing long-lasting and stable partnerships with government or business. Instead, it employs unconventional strategies to convince and even force government and business to respond to its constituents' interests. This continued reliance on unconventional activities is a likely by-product of ACORN's origins during a time in which cities possessed regimes capable of reacting to these strategies.

ACT AND JEREMIAH IN A NEW CIVIC ECOLOGY

The current ecology of civic engagement in New Orleans encouraged the newer community organizations to develop reciprocal relationships with business and government. Whereas ACORN began when the pro-growth regime existed, the other organizations started when the city regime was loosely held together and in dire need of resources. ACT formed in 1989 in response to violent crime and drug activity in New Orleans. It serves as the local affiliate of PICO and works with Louisiana Interfaiths Together (LIFT), the state affiliate of PICO. Initially, ACT's members included more than thirty churches.[43] In 2006, eighteen churches serve as core members of ACT and another ten churches support ACT's mission but have yet to join this organization.[44]

ACT's member institutions cover eight areas of New Orleans: Gentilly and Pontchartrain, Lower Ninth Ward area, Upper Ninth Ward, New Orleans East, West Bank, Uptown/Central City, the Sixth Ward, and the Seventh Ward (see map 1). The congregations of these churches include people from different races and of varying socioeconomic characteristics. White, wealthier, and better educated residents tend to live in Uptown New Orleans; poor African Americans tend to reside in the Lower Ninth Ward.

PICO sends professional organizers to train members of ACT. Normally, PICO allocates one full-time organizer to work with ACT, but after Katrina, it sent two organizers to New Orleans. ACT's organizers attend training conferences two times a year in Los Altos, California, and other sites that include New York City and Philadelphia.[45] ACT's professional organizer trains local leaders, who then teach others in New Orleans.

Jeremiah organized in 1990. Its initial membership included twelve churches, and it covered the region to the east and west of the Mississippi River and to the north of Lake Pontchartrain.[46] In 2003, about twenty churches and organizations constituted Jeremiah's membership (see map 1). As is the case with ACT, congregations of Jeremiah's member institutions run the socioeconomic gamut. By 2005, its strongest institutional members were the Saint Joseph the Worker Catholic Church in New Orleans and the Shiloh Missionary Baptist Church in Westwego, Louisiana, which is on the West Bank of New Orleans.[47] Middle-class African Americans make up a majority of these churches' congregations.

Jeremiah's leaders, who are volunteers, receive training in one of three ways: local training by local leaders, local training by regional leaders, or national training by IAF leaders.[48] At a typical IAF conference, Jeremiah's organizers get information regarding how to address various issues, including housing, education, and public safety.[49]

Three kinds of leaders work with Jeremiah.[50] Primary leaders think about the organization from a macro perspective. They concentrate on relationship building with political leaders, businesses, and others in the community. Secondary leaders work on a particular issue. The tertiary leader attends meetings and performs tasks, such as placing phone calls to other members. Jeremiah needs all three kinds of leaders, but it attempts to move tertiary leaders to secondary leaders and secondary leaders to the primary position.

In stark contrast to ACORN's more confrontational strategies, ACT and Jeremiah build relational power in New Orleans. This tactic indicates that these organizations understand that the political and economic leaders possess limited rewards and consequently need partners to facilitate governance. These organizations use confrontation as a final resort rather than a standard operating procedure. ACT and Jeremiah regard themselves as nonpolitical, and neither endorses candidates. ACT meets with the mayor on a quarterly basis and holds regular meetings with school board members. One of Jeremiah's leaders contends that the group can get a meeting with the mayor anytime it wishes.

ACT's primary issues of concern are blight, crime, drugs, and education reform. ACT conducts research actions once "an issue with energy moves to the forefront."[51] If public safety affects a congregation or the city, for instance, members of ACT interview various power holders, including the city attorney and police captains, to determine what the police are doing to attack the problem. After ACT members hear from government officials and other stakeholders, they create specific proposals to attack a particular problem. Then the organization gets government officials to commit to follow ACT's proposal.

ACT uses forums to keep the pressure on government. It measures government's actions, praising success and criticizing failure. At one accountability meeting, ACT gave straight As to the police department for drug enforcement, whereas the city's health department received Ds for a number of areas, including creating relationships with citizens.[52] In response to criticisms that ACT ambushes elected officials at accountability meetings, a member of ACT commented, "I wouldn't say that we're confrontational. All we ask is that they try to do something to respond to us. Relationships are the key."[53]

Government and ACT collaborate regularly. Elected and appointed officials, candidates, and public bureaucrats frequently attend ACT's public forums, accountability sessions, and private meetings. They provide information to ACT about how to improve city services, and they often agree to work with ACT to accomplish this goal.

Early in his administration, Mayor Marc Morial said, "We have a relationship with ACT, and we're going to do everything in our power to work with them, because their vision for the city is my vision for the city. I want to build a synergy between government and the people. Their people are on our task forces; they're on our advisory committees. Their people are involved in the confection of policy in this administration. And that's what ACT wants, to have a seat at the table."[54] The mayor and ACT established a mutually beneficial relationship. For the most part, Morial lived up to his promises to ACT. He worked with ACT to address blight in neighborhoods; he supported ACT's plan to create a state law to allow people in the neighborhood to take abandoned property.[55] Based on ACT's recommendation, Morial worked with banks to establish a lending pool so that low- to moderate-income people could purchase and fix blighted houses.[56] ACT, Morial, and the state legislature collaborated on the ongoing $5.1 million renovation and cleanup of Lincoln Beach.

Morial, the police department, and ACT worked together to address the crime rate. In exchange for his support for ACT's 1998 platform, Morial convinced ACT to form more than 100 neighborhood watch organizations.[57] Morial also presented his crime plan to a public forum hosted by ACT, which unanimously approved the proposal. Mayor Morial appointed ACT members to search committees for police chief and superintendent of schools.

According to one ACT leader, "Marc [Morial] and ACT formed a symbiotic relationship. Neither was a captive of the other but each recognized the importance of working together."[58] Morial supported ACT for a variety of reasons. First, he had a preexisting relationship with ACT's head organizer, who worked in the recreation department when Morial's father was mayor. Next, Sybil Morial, Marc's mother, has been an organizational mainstay in ACT. She helps raise funds for ACT. Finally and perhaps most important, ACT addressed issues of central concern to Morial's chief constituencies: African Americans and the working poor.

ACT possesses resources that government needs. It has information about community concerns that government lacks. Furthermore, ACT and other community organizations maintain access to and have the trust of neighborhoods, whereas this is not always the case for government. ACT also saves money and time for the resource-depleted government because it provides technical information about various problems that affect its constituents. In exchange for information, access to the poor, and assistance with service delivery, government often pays attention to and substantively represents ACT on these issue areas.

ACT's relationship with government continues under Marc Morial's successor, C. Ray Nagin. Like Morial, Nagin and his staff attended an ACT retreat. Mayor Nagin worked with ACT to create plans to deal with blight, housing, and safety.[59] ACT, District Attorney Eddie Jordan, and Mayor Nagin collaborated to establish additional civil penalties for violators of public nuisance laws.[60] ACT pushed for public nuisance laws at the state level because many businesses abetted drug dealers and prostitutes in its neighborhoods. Public nuisance laws enabled government to close down businesses that had been convicted for two or more crimes.[61]

Jeremiah also believes that relationships constitute the key ingredient to organizing. Jeremiah asks for private meetings with public officials at which time its organizers elicit cooperation.[62] If government does not respond, then Jeremiah employs more public tactics, including candidate accountability sessions, which resemble the ones used by ACT. In this nonregime civic ecology, Jeremiah opts for relationship building rather than more unconventional tactics because its leaders believe that government is more inclined to listen to and work with organizations that are less confrontational.

In the current civic ecology in New Orleans, Jeremiah uses its access to many people and its in-depth knowledge of community interests as resources to form mutually beneficial relationships with government and other power holders. Jeremiah's issues of concern have included job opportunities, crime, policing, and drugs. Jeremiah regards itself as a constructive force.[63] It is constructive because it does not rely on confrontation. It is a force because it connects people to government and business. For example, after Jeremiah completed its one-on-one sessions, house meetings, neighborhood walks, and research, it concluded that the Bienville Corridor section of the city needed after-school programs and a safe park.[64] It copyrighted a plan, which it presented to Mayor Morial. The mayor responded that it would take at least five years to establish a park, and this response dissatisfied Jeremiah's members. The mayor and Jeremiah reached an agreement for the city to supply a volunteer coordinator and $95,000 worth of playground equipment to a school in the area, whereas Jeremiah provides volunteers. In the meantime, the city worked to establish a permanent park in that area. When a new mayor and school superintendent entered office, Jeremiah met with each to ensure that the plans remained unchanged. In this context of scarce resources, government needs the kind of information, technical skills, and human resources that groups like Jeremiah provide.

Most recently, Jeremiah formed a coalition to gain employment for the unemployed and underemployed in the New Orleans area. Members of this Northrop Grumman Bridge Collaborative include the city of New Orleans' Workforce Development, the Jefferson Parish Workforce Investment Board, a regional economic development organization, Delgado Community College, Louisiana Technical Colleges, and the Catholic Charities Archdiocese of New Orleans.[65] The bridge "is a system-wide realignment and coordination of existing resources for efficiency, sustainability, and inclusiveness."[66] These groups are essential to the project because their "interests intersect in the design, construction, maintenance, and modification of the bridge."[67]

The Bridge Collaborative exemplifies the nature of reciprocal relationships among community organizations, business, government, and others in the non-regime period. Business, government, and others gain access to the community through Jeremiah, which tells congregations that business and government can be trusted because it is a founding partner in this program and it will hold others accountable. In return for this access, government substantively addresses the issue of greatest concern to Jeremiah.

ACORN, ACT, and Jeremiah rarely, if ever, work together even though they address some of the same issues. The differences in how these groups approach New Orleans' civic ecology make collaboration nearly impossible. One ACT leader believes partnerships among these community groups are difficult because each organization employs a different model and a distinct set of processes.[68] An ACORN leader agrees with this assertion. ACORN wants to move more quickly on issues than allowed for by ACT's more deliberate and timely issue selection process.[69] According to one ACORN leader, turfism does not negatively affect relationship building between ACORN and ACT. ACORN organizes individuals from ACT's churches and does not come into conflict with ACT because the two groups compete for different members. ACORN relies on individuals for membership, whereas churches constitute the primary members of Jeremiah or ACT. Jeremiah has difficulty working with ACORN because it does not believe that organizations should rely on public confrontation.

SUCCESSES

Over the past twenty years, each community organization achieved significant victories in New Orleans. The living wage campaign of 2002 represents ACORN's most significant victory and perhaps its greatest defeat.[70] In 1996, the New Orleans City Council rejected a petition to place a minimum-wage increase on the ballot. It invalidated the petition because ACT did not file the 10,000 signatures necessary to put an issue on the ballot at the same time. In 1997, the Louisiana Restaurant Association, the New Orleans Hotel-Motel Association, and other business organizations successfully lobbied the state legislature to pass a law to prohibit any municipality from raising its minimum wage to a level higher than the federal minimum wage.

After their first attempt to place the measure on the ballot failed, ACORN and others gathered the requisite 15,000 signatures, but the city council refused to place the issue on the ballot because the new state law prohibited a local increase to the minimum wage. Ultimately, a state appeals court ruled that New Orleans must place the living wage charter amendment on the ballot. Former New Orleans mayor Moon Landrieu, one of the three judges at the time, wrote, "Should the electorate reject the amendment, the question of its constitutionality will be moot. Should the electorate adopt the amendment, the opponents will have ample time to challenge its constitutionality in the courts before the amendment becomes effective."[71]

Voters decided whether to increase the minimum wage by one dollar in the February 2, 2002, mayoral election. At the beginning of the mayoral race, all but one candidate opposed the living wage amendment. By the end of the campaign, all but one candidate supported it. Nagin, the eventual winner, opposed the amendment on the grounds it violated state law.

New Orleans voters supported the living wage amendment by a 63 percent to 37 percent margin. The Small Business Coalition to Save Jobs, a group that included the Louisiana Restaurant Association, the New Orleans Regional Chamber of Commerce, and the New Orleans Business Council, filed suit to overturn the voters' decision. A civil district court judge ruled in favor of the living wage amendment, but, in a six-to-one decision, the state supreme court concluded that the amendment violated the state's police powers. Since that verdict, ACORN has worked to try to get the state legislature to change the state law on increasing the minimum wage.

ACORN's living wage campaign illustrates the limits of local civic ecologies. Despite the organization's decisive victory in New Orleans, the living wage's opponents brought the issue to a higher level of government. The opponents won because they convinced the state legislature to create a law to limit minimum-wage increases throughout the state. If ACORN wants to win the living wage campaign, it must do so on the state or even federal level. The living wage debate also highlights the tensions that continue to exist between ACORN and business.

In the past ten years alone, ACORN scored several other victories in the public and private sectors in New Orleans. In the early 2000s, ACORN worked with Tulane University and Xavier University to pass a city ordinance to prohibit dry sanding of lead-based paint. In 2003, ACORN, the city, and these two universities received $5 million from HUD to research, prevent, and remove lead contamination. Following the living wage campaign, ACORN helped stop the privatization of the city's sewage and water board. As a result of its protests, ACORN joined a coalition with H&R Block to educate low- to moderate-income residents about the EITC.

ACT achieved significant policy victories at the state and local levels. Crime and blighted housing represent policy areas over which ACT exerted influence. Mayors Barthelemy and Morial paid considerable attention to ACT's policy preferences in crime. Barthelemy listened to ACT after members of this organization took over his office for a few days.[72] Morial adopted ACT's platform to address crime. ACT provided technical information and popular support for a crime plan that Morial endorsed. This kind of reciprocity is more common in the new civic ecology in New Orleans.

Mayor Marc Morial worked with ACT and other leaders to address blighted housing in the city. Through the efforts of Morial, ACT, the New Orleans delegation to the state legislature, and other legislative leaders, the Louisiana legislature altered the laws governing blighted housing, changing the rules by which localities took property and enforced zoning codes.[73] Each of these legal changes decreased the time it took local government to confiscate blighted property.

Jeremiah provides job training and educational assistance to its members.[74] It collaborated with officials in Jefferson Parish, which borders New Orleans, to establish a drug court and a detoxification center. Jefferson Parish's education system and Jeremiah established an alternative school on the west bank of New Orleans. One Jeremiah organizer said that the group has no permanent enemies because it can work with anyone on any issue.[75]

DID THESE COMMUNITY ORGANIZATIONS OCCUPY A PROMINENT PLACE IN PRE-KATRINA NEW ORLEANS?

ACORN, ACT, and Jeremiah approach the New Orleans civic ecology in different ways, and each has scored policy victories. These organizations, which represent geographic and policy areas not addressed by government or business, illustrate how unaware and unresponsive government can be toward traditionally excluded groups. New Orleans' ecology limits the success of these groups. That is, the scarcity of resources in the city, the elite nature of New Orleans, and the fragmentation of leadership limit the extent to which a regime exists, thereby impairing the success of these groups.

The strategies of all three groups have significant limitations. The nonregime ecology limits community organizations no matter which tactics these groups pursue. Protest produces limited rewards because target groups either do not exist, lack the resources necessary to meet ACORN's demands, or outwardly resist this tactic. Relational power is productive but only on a limited basis. On many occasions, either community organizations have no one with whom to share power, or else public and private leaders do not want to partner with them.

ACORN showed little to no interest in creating long-lasting partnerships with government. Its tactics suggest that ACORN believes that public officials exert *power over* governance. ACORN attempts to win policy concessions from government, businesses, and other actors. It does not develop long-term or stable partnerships to take advantage of the diffusion of power in New Orleans. ACORN relies on confrontation and often employs outside strategies, including protests, lawsuits, and ballot initiatives, to secure policy victories. Despite the continued use of protest to gain responsiveness, ACORN established issue-based partnerships to a greater extent in the nonregime period than in the time in which a corporate regime ran New Orleans.

The problem with ACORN's tactics is that New Orleans possesses no identifiable regime from which to win policy concessions. Whereas business and political leadership formed a regime when ACORN started in 1976, these entities no longer make up a stable and long-lasting partnership. Part of the ACORN model is to demand policy changes from public and private leadership, but New Orleans' leaders maintain few resources to make the kinds of changes ACORN requests. ACORN's victories in New Orleans came mainly in the private sector against banks and lending institutions. Its wins in the public sphere occurred in areas where government could make a difference, as was the case when the city council passed an ordinance to protect citizens against lead poisoning. Overall, however, a confrontational style is limited in New Orleans because the city lacks a regime from which to secure policy victories.

Membership also limits ACORN's position in New Orleans' civic ecology. Well before Katrina hit, the city's social history was replete with examples of governmental ignorance and neglect of issues that affect African Americans and the poor. New Orleans' government is unlikely to understand or address ACORN's interests partly because it does not and has not actively pursued the concerns of poor residents. The focus on low- to moderate-income residents reduces ACORN's access to financial resources and prevents certain issues from receiving attention that could be gained with a citywide membership.

ACT's and Jeremiah's strategies also face serious obstacles in New Orleans. ACT and Jeremiah operate as if public officials and other actors need to create the *power to* govern. They use relationship building as their primary tactic. The problem these groups face is that the city lacks a regime with which they can partner. A regime requires a long-lasting and stable partnership among resource providers. Because a regime does not rule New Orleans, ACT and Jeremiah possess limited options for creating the power to govern.

On a number of issues, ACT and Jeremiah formed reciprocal relations with government. For instance, Mayor Morial supported ACT's agenda; in exchange, this organization established neighborhood watches. ACT and Jeremiah built relational power by working on the inside, with government. ACT and Jeremiah illustrate how community organizations provide valuable resources to government. These groups not only facilitate governance but also receive substantive representation of their policy concerns.[76]

Despite these strengths, ACT and Jeremiah do not hold a prominent position in the New Orleans civic ecology. They establish strong issue-based coalitions with government, but they are not partners in governance because no regime exists in the city. Issue-based coalitions run the city's public policy. These coalitions between ACT or Jeremiah and government stay together only when an issue affects both these community organizations and government. When government needs the support or resources of ACT or Jeremiah, issue-based coalitions develop. By contrast, government does not tend to consult with these community organizations on issues that do not affect ACT or Jeremiah. ACT and Jeremiah have little to no role in economic development, and they maintain a weak relationship with business.

The coalitions that ACT and Jeremiah form with government are not long-lasting. ACT and Jeremiah gain strength when their issues have energy, but they lose momentum when their members lack interest in an issue. ACT made great strides on crime because this matter dramatically affected its member institutions. As the crime rate decreased, ACT lost some of its ability to capture government and public attention. These issue-based coalitions also lack stability partly because ACT and Jeremiah must work to ensure that government delivers on its promises.

Broad-based membership increases ACT's and Jeremiah's access to financial and technical resources. It also adds legitimacy to issues. Government is more likely to gain awareness of an issue when it hears citywide, as opposed to neighborhood, concerns.[77] It pays attention to community organizations when resource providers, namely, citizens with wealth, collaborate with low- to moderate-income residents.

Another limitation ACT and Jeremiah face in New Orleans is the traditional nature of the city. These groups have great difficulty when they espouse issues that primarily affect low- to moderate-income residents. The New Orleans elite have been unlikely to respond to these issues over time.

ORGANIZING IN POST-KATRINA NEW ORLEANS

In the aftermath of Hurricane Katrina, ACORN, ACT, and Jeremiah face significant obstacles mainly because the storm struck many of the areas where they organize and displaced significant numbers of their members. ACORN has been the most visible organization in its response to Hurricane Katrina. Among other things, it created the ACORN Katrina Survivors Association, which, according to ACORN, is the "first nationwide organization of displaced New Orleans residents and other Katrina survivors."[78] "The ACORN Katrina Survivors Association uses public pressure, direct action, and dialogue with elected officials and public policy experts to win respect and a voice for survivors, the resources needed for families to survive, and a rebuilding plan that builds stronger communities for all."[79] The association calls for access to affordable housing, health care, and quality education, the right of displaced residents to return to the city, and an independent investigation to determine why the levees broke.[80]

The Katrina Survivors Association achieved several accomplishments and performed many activities in its first six months of operation. It secured transportation to health care facilities, extended benefits, and bilingual materials for Hurricane

Rita victims in Houston; it held rallies, conferences, and forums in New Orleans and Baton Rouge; and it won a court case that requires landlords to send eviction notices to tenants.[81]

On February 8 and 9, 2006, ACORN and its Katrina Survivors Association held rallies and conducted marches in Washington, D.C., to "press the Bush Administration and Congress to provide funds to rebuild New Orleans and the Gulf Coast."[82] During these two days, ACORN visited U.S. senators and representatives and members of the Bush administration. Its members testified at a special hearing on Hurricane Katrina that was organized by Democrats. ACORN's Katrina Survivors Association also conducted an evening rally and prayer vigil outside the White House.

In its message to Congress, the ACORN Katrina Survivors Association noted that it needed resources to rebuild New Orleans. It also made the following claims: after five months, the government had made no progress in rebuilding their neighborhoods; citizens wanted to return to a rebuilt New Orleans; the Small Business Administration denied home and disaster loans to many residents of devastated areas; displaced residents needed Disaster Medicaid, extended unemployment benefits, and a longer period of emergency food stamps; and government needed to pay greater attention to the housing needs of displaced citizens.[83]

ACORN established the Home Cleanout Demonstration Project, through which it vowed to rehabilitate 1,000 homes before March 31, 2006. According to ACORN, this project is the "first large-scale renovation activity in lower income neighborhoods," which "not only has a practical impact—but sends a message to policymakers that the people of New Orleans are coming home to rebuild. We can't save New Orleans on our own—but we can preserve the homes of many families, and show policymakers that the people of New Orleans will not let our communities be left behind."[84]

ACORN sued Louisiana to ensure that displaced residents maintained their right to vote.[85] Based on laws passed in a special legislative session, displaced residents could vote in one of three ways: early, in-person voting in satellite polling places established in ten parishes in Louisiana, via absentee ballot, or in New Orleans on election day. ACORN claimed that these provisions disadvantaged many poor African Americans who were displaced because these methods required voters to either travel great distances to ballot or made voting too complicated.[86] Furthermore, the first two options mandated that voters participate in advance because the early, in-person voting takes place twelve to six days before the election, whereas absentee ballots must be in by 4:30 P.M. on election day. ACORN sought satellite polling places in areas outside of Louisiana with the highest concentrations of displaced residents; it wanted the satellite voting to take place on election day; and it pushed for absentee ballots to be valid if they were postmarked on election day.

The suit claimed that displaced residents faced much different and far more difficult circumstances to vote than did people who live in New Orleans. A U.S. district court judge denied ACORN's requests on the grounds that Louisiana took appropriate steps to provide equal access to voting.

ACT and Jeremiah served as advocates for displaced residents, especially those from the Lower Ninth Ward. In early November, ACT cohosted a rally at New Orleans City Hall in order to receive status reports from public and private entities about the progress made in the Lower Ninth Ward.[87] Its executive director, Mary Fontenot, has attended meetings with community leaders, business leaders, and government officials to represent the interests of Lower Ninth Ward residents. According to Fontenot, ACT's "No. 1 effort is to see our people back in their homes."[88]

In early January 2006, the urban planning committee of the Bring New Orleans Back Commission, Mayor Nagin's advisory panel on rebuilding New Orleans, recommended that certain areas of the city, including parts of the Lower Ninth Ward, New Orleans East, Gentilly, Mid-City, and Hollygrove, be converted to green space or returned to natural barriers against hurricanes.[89] Based on water levels, flood maps, past hurricanes, and other data, the committee contended future storms would wreak the greatest havoc on these areas. The planning committee also recommended that the city "consolidate neighborhoods with insufficient population to support equitable and efficient service delivery."[90]

In response to this report, many of ACT's members conducted "Days of Declaration" on March 12, 2006.[91] Through this campaign, ACT's member-institutions affirmed that they have returned.[92] They wanted to show the city that these neighborhoods were already viable and should be rebuilt. Louisiana governor Kathleen Babineaux Blanco signed a rebuilding covenant, in which she pledged to work with PICO/LIFT ministers "to make sure that Louisianans get the jobs to rebuild the state, that host families receive assistance, and that displaced families be guaranteed the right to return to their homes."[93]

In the so-called Days of Declaration, ACT's members made several policy recommendations.[94] They requested affordable housing, and they wanted government to allocate money for homeowners to improve and rehabilitate homes. ACT members regarded Federal Emergency Management Agency trailers as insufficient means of housing. They asked for medical triage units in all areas of the city so that residents can receive emergency care. As of March 2006, residents in the Lower Ninth Ward and Treme, among other places, needed to travel great distances to other parishes to get medical treatment. ACT also urged the federal, state, and local governments to create a viable school system and educational plan by May, a month in which many displaced residents with children would decide whether to return to New Orleans.

Jeremiah joined with the Northern and Central Louisiana Interfaith organizations to create the Louisiana Industrial Areas Foundation (LIAFN), which is affiliated with the IAF.[95] These groups recognized that a broader-based coalition was essential to have their interests not only heard but also represented. Among other things, the LIAFN opposed the Urban Land Institute's (ULI) recommendation to shrink the footprint of New Orleans. One leader of the Jeremiah Group said the ULI plan would establish a "whiter, richer, and less populated New Orleans that excludes the very kinds of people that give New Orleans its character and culture. [The plan] excludes redevelopment of much of New Orleans East and much of the Lower 9th Ward and Gentilly, places where middle class, working families live of all colors, shapes, and sizes."[96] LIAFN wants displaced residents to have greater input into the rebuilding process.[97] It urged state and local officials to build more temporary housing so that displaced residents could move back to New Orleans.[98]

The LIAFN also pushed for greater voting access for displaced residents. The state legislature met some of LIAFN's requests by providing satellite voting places throughout Louisiana, and it lifted its requirement that first-time voters must ballot in person. It also enabled displaced residents to vote absentee as long as the state or the city received the ballot by 4:30 P.M. on election day.

COMMON GOOD?

At least one organizing effort recognizes the importance of working across sectors in order to facilitate governance in New Orleans. Created in early 2006 in part by one of Jeremiah's cofounders and the chair of New Orleans' Human Relations Commission, the Common Good Initiative includes institutions that represent religious groups, higher education, nonprofit agencies, civil rights groups, the arts and humanities, preservationists, civic groups, community organizations, and tourism, among others. It aims to discuss and overcome racial divisions that existed well before Hurricane Katrina struck New Orleans. It wants to work with the city's other centers of power, namely, business leadership, the mayor, and the city council, in order to hold government accountable, develop a multiyear plan for Level 5 hurricane protection, expand businesses in the city, increase the availability of jobs, diversify the tax base, and improve public education, among other things.[99]

In describing the creation of the organization, the cofounder recognizes the need for a regime to govern the city. He wants Common Good to create a power center for various underrepresented groups; this entity will interact with other decision makers to govern New Orleans.

The Common Good Initiative plans to hold structured, town hall meetings for mayoral and city council candidates, with each meeting focusing on a major topic, such as levee protection or education reform. At the final assembly, Common Good will ask candidates to pledge to attend bimonthly civic assemblies if they are elected.

The pledge also asks those candidates who are elected to report on the progress made toward Common Good's plans and to listen to specific concerns of the group's membership.[100]

ORGANIZING IN THE FUTURE

In this conclusion, I return to questions I posed earlier in this chapter about community organizing in a nonregime civic ecology. How does New Orleans' nonregime ecology affect community organizing? Community organizations adopt less confrontational strategies in order to create partnerships with government in this new ecology. ACT and Jeremiah build relationships with target groups in New Orleans. They employ more confrontational strategies only when relationship building breaks down. ACORN, which continues to rely on confrontational tactics, developed issue-based relationships with business and government to a much greater extent in this era.

The nonregime civic ecology presented a political opportunity structure for community organizations to assume a more prominent place in the city's civic ecology. Here, however, I am only discussing matters of degree. That is, community organizations occupy a more prominent place in decision making in New Orleans, but this position does not mean they hold an important location in the overall ecology. Instead, community organizations maintain significance when government and business need their assistance or when these aforementioned actors feel compelled to respond.

Government expressed greater willingness to enter into reciprocal relationships with community organizations in this new civic ecology because groups like ACT, Jeremiah, and ACORN control resources that government needs. Community organizations provide information, service delivery, and plans of action to government. In a context of scarce resources, these functions facilitate governance. In exchange for these resources, government substantively represents community organizations in certain policy areas. Government needed the technical assistance that these community organizations provided, and it depended on community organizations for vital information about crime.

In the transformation from a pro-growth regime to a nonregime city, business changed its stance toward community organizations. In the pro-growth period, most businesses pursued development to the exclusion of the poor, African Americans, and other constituents of community organizations. In this era, ACORN used direct-action tactics to force these institutions, including banks and hotels, to address the issues of the poor or stop outright discrimination against these groups. In the nonregime period, businesses like Northrop Grumman are more likely to establish relations with community organizations, such as Jeremiah, in order to gain access to the unemployed and underemployed in the city.

Tensions persist between community organizations and business. In particular, ACORN still feels that economic interests ignore or discriminate against its low-income constituents. The living wage campaign and ACORN's actions against H&R Block lend support to the assertion that business continues to neglect the needs of the poor. They also indicate that business and community organizations have yet to form a strong relationship even though economic resources and leadership greatly diminished over time in New Orleans.

Community organizations filled some of the leadership and resource voids created by changes in New Orleans over the last thirty-five years. They acted on behalf of the powerless and worked with government to address issues that affect low- to moderate-income communities in New Orleans. In spite of their work, ACORN, ACT, and Jeremiah faced great challenges in pre-Katrina New Orleans. Poor public schools, crime, poverty, inadequate housing, and discrimination plagued New Orleans, and the city's ecology paid little attention to these problems.

In the post-Katrina environment, these community organizations must overcome even greater obstacles partly because the storm exacerbated problems with housing, education, and other city services. Furthermore, a reduction in New Orleans' footprint means that a substantial number of displaced residents, many of whom belong to at least one of these three organizations, will not return. The opportunities for these groups may increase, however, because government and business are in greater need of the resources that these organizations allocate. Whether these community organizations have the capacity to get government, business, and other stakeholders to address these problems on a full-time basis is quite uncertain. In spite of significant victories by community organizations in New Orleans, the struggle continues.

NOTES

1. Michael Lipsky, "Protest as a Political Resource," *American Political Science Review* 62 (1968): 1144–1158, quotation on 1145.

2. In this chapter, corporate regime and pro-growth regime are the same.

3. Clarence N. Stone, *Regime Politics: Governing Atlanta, 1946–1988* (Lawrence: University Press of Kansas Press, 1989); C. N. Stone, "Urban Regimes and the Capacity to Govern: A Political Economy Approach," *Journal of Urban Affairs* 15 (1993): 1–28.

4. Stone, *Regime Politics*; Stephen L. Elkin, *City and Regime in the American Republic* (Chicago: University of Chicago Press, 1987); Karen Mossberger and Gerry Stoker, "The Evolution of Regime Theory: The Challenge of Conceptualization," *Urban Affairs Review* 36 (2001): 810–835.

5. Clarence N. Stone and Heywood T. Sanders, eds., *The Politics of Urban Development* (Lawrence: University Press of Kansas, 1987), 216–229.

6. Stone, "Urban Regimes and the Capacity to Govern."

7. Adolph Reed Jr., "The Black Urban Regime: Structural Origins and Constraints," *Comparative Urban and Community Research: An Annual Review* 1 (1988): 138–189.

8. Stone, *Regime Politics*.

9. Joel Rast, "Governing the Regimeless City: The Frank Zeidler Administration in Milwaukee, 1948–1960," *Urban Affairs Review* 42 (2006): 81–112.

10. Ibid., 23.

11. Robert K. Whelan, "New Orleans: Mayoral Politics and Economic-Development Policies in the Postwar Years, 1945–86," in *The Politics of Urban Development*, ed. Clarence N. Stone and Heywood T. Sanders (Lawrence: University Press of Kansas, 1987), 216–229.

12. Robert K. Whelan, Alma H. Young, and Mickey Lauria, "Urban Regimes and Racial Politics in New Orleans," *Journal of Urban Affairs* 16 (1994): 1–21.

13. Robert K. Whelan, "New Orleans: Public-Private Partnerships and Uneven Development," in *Unequal Partnerships*, ed. Gregory D. Squires (New Brunswick, NJ: Rutgers University Press, 1987), 222–239.

14. Oren M. Levin-Waldman, *The Political Economy of the Living Wage: A Study of Four Cities* (Armonk, NY: M. E. Sharpe, 2005), 170.

15. Peter F. Burns and Matthew O. Thomas, "State Government and the Development Regime in New Orleans," *Urban Affairs Review* 39 (2004): 791–812.

16. Whelan, Young, and Lauria, "Urban Regimes and Racial Politics in New Orleans."

17. Frédéric Dimanche and Alenna Lepetic, "New Orleans Tourism and Crime: A Case Study," *Journal of Travel Research* 38 (August 1999): 19–23.

18. Political leader 1, personal communication, January 13, 2005.

19. Business leader 1, personal communication, January 14, 2005.

20. Peter F. Burns and Matthew O. Thomas, "The Failure of the Nonregime: How Katrina Exposed New Orleans as a Regimeless City," *Urban Affairs Review* 41 (2006): 517–527.

21. Burns and Thomas, "State Government and the Development Regime in New Orleans."

22. Douglas McAdam, *Political Process and the Development of Black Insurgency, 1930–1970* (Chicago: University of Chicago Press, 1982); Sidney Tarrow, *Power in Movement: Social Movements, Collective Action, and Politics*, 2nd ed. (New York: Cambridge University Press, 1998).

23. A significant portion of the information on the context of New Orleans comes directly from Burns and Thomas, "State Government and the Development Regime in New Orleans."

24. Anthony Mumfrey and Karen Ann Pinell, "New Orleans and the Top 25 Cities: Central City and Metropolitan Dualities" (working paper no. 1, prepared for the College of Urban and Public Affairs, University of New Orleans, 1992); Angelos Angelou, The Techvision 2020 Assessments, Angelou Economics, 1992, http://www.techvision2020.org/AngelouFinalPres.PDF.

25. Gordon Russell, "Public Housing in Some Areas of New Orleans Is Almost Unrecognizable Today. So Is HANO, the Agency Overseeing the Transformation," *Times-Picayune*, November 14, 2004, 1.

26. Gary Delgado, *Organizing the Movement: The Roots and Growth of ACORN* (Philadelphia: Temple University Press, 1986).

27. Association of Community Organizations for Reform Now Web site, http://www.acorn.org/ (accessed September 7, 2004).

28. Ibid.

29. Ibid.

30. ACORN leader 4, personal communication, January 14, 2005.

31. ACORN leader 4, personal communication, September 10, 2004.

32. Association of Community Organizations for Reform Now Web site (accessed September 7, 2004).

33. ACORN leader 1, personal communication, August 25, 2004.

34. Association of Community Organizations for Reform Now Web site (accessed September 7, 2004).

35. Service Employees International Union Local 100 Web site, http://www.seiu100.org/ (accessed September 10, 2004).

36. Levin-Waldman, *The Political Economy of the Living Wage.*

37. COMM-ORG: The On-Line Conference on Community Organizing and Development, "ACORN News: August 6, 2003," http://comm-org.utoledo.edu/ (accessed May 31, 2005).

38. Ibid.

39. This story comes from the New Orleans Association of Community Organizations for Reform Now Web site (accessed May 31, 2005).

40. ACORN leader 1, personal communication, January 12, 2005.

41. Leslie Williams, "ACORN, Bankers Praised for Help in Home Buying," *Times-Picayune,* July 26, 1996, B4.

42. Isaac Martin, "Dawn of the Living Wage: The Diffusion of a Redistributive Municipal Policy," *Urban Affairs Review* 36 (2001): 470–496; Louis Uchitelle, "Economic View: Raising Minimum Wages, City by City," *New York Times,* September 28, 2003, 4.

43. ACT leader 1, personal communication, September 9, 2004.

44. ACT leader 2, personal communication, March 8, 2006.

45. ACT leader 1, personal communication, September 9, 2004; ACT leader 2, personal communication, January 17, 2005.

46. Sandra Barbier, "Community Organizers Join to Share Ideas," *Times-Picayune,* November 4, 1999, 1F.

47. Jeremiah leader 1, personal communication, February 24, 2006.

48. Ibid.

49. Barbier, "Community Organizers Join to Share Ideas."

50. Jeremiah leader 2, personal communication, September 10, 2004.

51. ACT leader 1, personal communication, September 9, 2004.

52. Editorial, "ACT Report Card," *Times-Picayune,* June 21, 1993, B4.

53. Rhonda Nabonne and Susan Finch, "School Board Gets List of Demands," *Times-Picayune,* May 14, 1998, A1; Dennis Persica, "N.O. Leaders Beware: Church Group Is on the Case," *Times-Picayune,* January 10, 1994, B1.

54. Coleman Warner, "Acts of Faith," *Times-Picayune,* October 23, 1994, A1.

55. Russell, "Public Housing in Some Areas of New Orleans Is Almost Unrecognizable Today."

56. Ibid.

57. Bruce Nolan, "Second Church-Based Group Ready to Help Change City," *Times-Picayune,* October 23, 1994, A7.

58. ACT leader 2, personal communication, January 17, 2005.

59. Valerie Faciane, "ACT Preparing for Gala Fund-raiser," *Times-Picayune,* October 10, 2002, 1.

60. Susan Finch, "License of Treme Tavern Revoked: Joe's Cozy Corner Scene of 2 Shootings," *Times-Picayune,* April 27, 2004, 1.

61. ACT leader 1, personal communication, September 9, 2004.

62. Jeremiah leader 1, personal communication, August 31, 2004.

63. Ibid.

64. Jeremiah leader 2, personal communication, September 10, 2004.

65. Bridge Collaborative, "Mission and Organizational Strategy," n.d. (given to author); Jeffrey S. Lowe, "Community Foundations: What Do They Offer Community Development?" *Journal of Urban Affairs* 26 (2004): 221–240.

66. Bridge Collaborative, "Mission and Organizational Strategy."

67. Ibid.

68. ACT leader 1, personal communication, September 9, 2004.

69. ACORN leader 1, personal communication, January 12, 2005.

70. For more on living wage campaigns, see Levin-Waldman, *The Political Economy of the Living Wage;* Martin, "Dawn of the Living Wage."

71. Stephanie Grace, "Way Cleared for Vote on N.O. Wages: Change Would Force Firms to Pay at Least $6.15 Hourly," *Times-Picayune,* June 30, 2000, A1.

72. ACT leader 2, personal communication, January 17, 2005.

73. ACT leader 2, personal communication, January 17, 2005.

74. Danny Barrett Jr., "Activist Group Holds Interfaith Service: Members Celebrate Top Accomplishments," *Times-Picayune,* May 5, 2005, 1.

75. Jeremiah leader 2, personal communication, September 10, 2004.

76. For more on community organizations as a resource that facilitates governance, see Peter Burns, *Electoral Politics Is Not Enough: Racial and Ethnic Minorities and Urban Politics* (Albany: State University of New York Press, 2006).

77. For more on the effect of broad-based coalitions on substantive representation of community groups, see ibid.

78. ACORN, "Katrina Survivors Association," n.d., http://www.acorn.org/fileadmin/KatrinaRelief/AKSA_Platform_PDF.pdf (accessed March 6, 2006).

79. Ibid.

80. Ibid.

81. Ibid.

82. ACORN, "ACORN Rallies for Return and Rebuilding," n.d., www.acorn.org (accessed February 21, 2006).

83. ACORN, "The ACORN Katrina Survivors Association Message to Members of Congress," n.d., www.acorn.org (accessed February 21, 2006).

84. ACORN, "ACORN Takes Action to Rebuild New Orleans," n.d. www.acorn.org (accessed February 21, 2006).

85. The author participated in this case, *Wallace v. Blanco,* No. 05-5519 (E.D. La.). The plaintiffs hired him to provide expert testimony on the likely effects of Louisiana election law on turnout of displaced voters.

86. In order to vote via absentee ballot, voters must first request an absentee ballot.

87. "Eastern N.O. Rebuilding Is Meeting Topic," *Times-Picayune,* November 4, 2005, 1.

88. Joseph Gyan, "Lower 9th Takes Step toward Recovery," [Baton Rouge] *Advocate,* March 2, 2006, 1.

89. Bring New Orleans Back Commission's Urban Planning Committee, "Action Plan for New Orleans: The New American City," January 11, 2006, http://www.bringbackneworleans.com; Martha Carr, "Rebuilding Should Begin on High Ground, Group Says," *Times-Picayune,* November 19, 2005, 1.

90. Bring New Orleans Back Commission's Urban Planning Committee, "Action Plan for New Orleans," 37.

91. ACT leader 2, personal communication, March 8, 2006; All Congregations Together, "Press

Advisory: Communities across New Orleans Declare Their Viability in Response to the Recommendations of the 'Bring New Orleans Back' Plan," n.d. (given to author).

92. ACT leader 2, personal communication, March 8, 2006.

93. PICO LIFT, "Louisiana Governor and Clergy Sign Rebuilding Covenant," http://www
.piconetwork.org/katrina/blancosignscovenant.pdf (accessed March 13, 2006).

94. ACT leader 2, personal communication, March 8, 2006.

95. Brian Friedman, "Group Says Plan to Rebuild Is Biased: Activists Decry the Shrinking of
N.O.," *Times-Picayune*, December 15, 2005, 99.

96. Ibid.

97. Ibid.

98. "Coalition to Push for Housing," *Times-Picayune*, December 9, 2005, http://www.nola
.com/newslogs/.

99. Michael Cowan, "Everyman for Himself or Crescent City Resurrection?" January 20, 2006
(given to author).

100. Ibid.

4. Division and Fragmentation

The El Paso Experience in Global-Local Perspective

Kathleen Staudt and Clarence N. Stone

El Paso is located directly on the U.S.-Mexico border, joined at the hip with Mexico's fifth-largest city, Ciudad Juárez and its 1.5 million people. Together, the metropolitan region is home to more than 2 million residents, most of whom share a Mexican heritage and the Spanish language. This is an "interdependent border":[1] people have friends and relatives on both sides of the border; they also shop and work on both sides of the border; political interests span the international border, albeit divided by two different sets of political institutions. The global joins the local, but local politics are quite peculiar in a terrain that contains the local governments of two sovereign nations.

This chapter examines local politics in the El Paso–Ciudad Juárez border region, an area that was part of northern Mexico until the Treaty of Guadalupe Hidalgo in 1848. Subsequently, El Paso became part of the U.S. western frontier, and Ciudad Juárez, part of Mexico's *frontera norte*/northern frontier. The area has long been a gateway for immigration that U.S. locals call the "Ellis Island of the Southwest." Most of El Paso's population, or 78 percent in the 2000 census, shares a Mexican heritage, whether first-, second-, or third-generation or even earlier. Until the civil rights era of the 1960s, the confluence of poverty, English-language domination, and discrimination produced domination by a small economic elite of white males.

We aim to analyze the post–civil rights era in El Paso, from 1980 to the present. Three questions occupy center stage: (1) Who are the changing occupants of political space in El Paso? (2) Why has the largest and oldest community-based organization avoided one of the most compelling border issues of the last decade: femicide in Ciudad Juárez? (3) Why did the end of dominance by an elite group not bring about democratic and inclusive governance?

In the 1970s and beyond, new players occupied El Paso's political space, and power relations altered somewhat with diverse political voices, new policy agendas, and a search for different political alignments. However, these new voices are selective, and the policy agendas make some issues visible and mute others. In the region, the global economy is a visible and obvious context, not only next door to

El Paso in Ciudad Juárez, but also on the U.S. side, where global forces have rendered garment production an anachronism. Cross-border activists seek to widen the local terrain to include transnational issues, such as violence against women, but they face enormous challenges in the border region's peculiar local politics.

We examine a wide variety of community organizations, from the emergence in the early 1980s of the El Paso Inter-religious Sponsoring Organization (EPISO), an affiliate of the Industrial Areas Foundation (IAF), and La Mujer Obrera (the Woman Worker), to the early 1990s for a look at the brief but significant life of Unite El Paso and the political representatives and agendas it spawned, on to the still thriving university-affiliated Collaborative for Academic Excellence, and then recently to city-sponsored neighborhood associations and a chapter of the Association of Community Organizations for Reform Now (ACORN), all of which organize around both issues and place. Our primary focus is on EPISO and IAF's emergent "metropolitan" strategy that involves a second IAF group, Border Interfaith. Despite El Paso's border location, for IAF, metropolitan is conceptualized as one side of the border, an obvious strategy given its affiliation with the Texas IAF and homegrown (to the United States) strategies that do not translate well across border and territorial lines. To illustrate the strengths and weaknesses of IAF strategy, especially the different issues, players, and structural and cultural styles (including the visibility of women and gender issues), we compare EPISO with the cross-border Coalition against Violence toward Women and Families at the U.S.-Mexico border (hereinafter called the Coalition). Both the IAF and the Coalition opened up political space, taking advantage of new political opportunity structure,[2] but the outcomes have been mixed, generating external resources for El Paso and international visibility for El Paso–Ciudad Juárez but not filling a vacuum left by an absence of effective leadership.

ORGANIZATIONAL MATTERS

Domhoff and other elite theorists have asked "Who rules?", answering the question with evidence about "corporate-conservative" coalitions networked through interlocking board memberships and social ties, some of them personal, face-to-face relationships.[3] While this superstructure could once be found in many cities and states, an emphasis on the top mutes the underbelly of networks in the middle and at the bottom. These less visible networks are too often overlooked. In El Paso, El Paso–Ciudad Juárez, and other cities, a combination of factors helped to facilitate challenges to the ruling elite, among them the civil rights and feminist movements, structural changes in representation rules and the consequent rise of identity-based leaders, and reformist organizations like El Paso's IAF affiliate. In cities with limited civic capacity, however, these new changes rest on a persistent base of patron-client relationships and other relics of limited democracy.

The importance of "networks" provides yet another conceptual tool. We consider two types. Horizontal networks bring strengthened power to coalitions, including formal and informal coalitions, to people, and to their issues, although coalitions involve potentially complex control problems. Vertical networks also have power-strengthening potential, involving external resources and ideas, but similar control problems. Mark Granovetter's conception of "the strength of weak ties" suggests that horizontal and vertical networks are useful organizing tools.[4] The lesson of his work is that personal (strong) relationships, supplemented with impersonal (weak) relationships, can augment the strength of those who challenge power. In the late twentieth century, cyberactivism surely qualifies as weak and impersonal. For activists, it is a challenge to assess the appropriate form of control and freedom, in the interests of getting their issues addressed in timely ways.

Let us apply these ideas to El Paso–Ciudad Juárez. If the border business sector once provided the uncontested "rulers," then El Paso's IAF and the Coalition represent the activists who came to challenge this older order. All of them, rulers and challenging activists alike, are, however, shaped by state, national, binational, and global institutions that facilitate or hinder their agendas. Over the last two decades, opportune spaces have opened in El Paso's deconcentrated political arena, groups have split (including in the business community), and targets of opportunity have become available as sources of change.

In the following, we examine the IAF affiliate and the Coalition movement through the lens of choices each has made about its targets, opportune political spaces, and membership bases. The IAF and antiviolence coalition have very different control strategies, affecting recruitment, socialization, and funding patterns. Ultimately, these factors affect their response to local issues and opportunities that they seize, including networking and coalition building (or their decision to avoid new opportunities for the threats posed to control).

The Texas IAF is an organization under state and regional (southwestern U.S.) direction. It carefully recruits and trains paid organizers who are placed in locales where a base of support has been developed, largely through faith-based congregations. IAF is built on an organizational rather than individual base. Training involves basic principles that are learned and applied: power analysis, the "iron" rule of self-sufficiency, power before program, self-interest, and the focus on "winnable" goals, among others. Leaders from congregations undergo IAF training, locally, regionally, and nationally. IAF periodically rotates organizers to maintain commitment to the central organization rather than deepened loyalties to the locale. To support IAF infrastructure, funds are raised from foundations, faith-based denominations, and membership fees from congregational operating budgets. Each affiliate is a legal nonprofit, tax-exempt organization. Start-up is a lengthy process, consuming years and considerable funds, including funds for technical assistance from IAF itself.

IAF affiliates undergo a lengthy process of relationship building, involving personal, face-to-face interactions within and across congregations. From this base, people share their stories at "house" meetings, from which issue agendas emerge. The issues tend to be broad-based, around which people can agree rather than become polarized. The issues must be palatable to people of different religious denominations, given the congregational base. Leaders interact at state and local training meetings and statewide conferences, including days on which hundreds of leaders around the state converge on the state capitol to push their carefully moderated issues in consistent ways across legislative districts.

IAF and its affiliates might be viewed as coalitions across horizontal congregational lines locally, and horizontal communities from a statewide perspective. All are vertically linked to a single, centralized organization, the IAF, rather than diverse statewide coalitions, for caution is exercised about coalescing with other organizations and agendas that do not practice IAF organizing principles or support their focused issues. IAF carefully researches issues, including the appropriate target and level of decision making. Overall, IAF organizations, built through careful socialization and control, work with congregations, many of which also share traditions of hierarchical control and embody a cautious approach to their work.

The Coalition is a loose, informal movement network of volunteers. It emerged quickly, in response to local issues. For the Coalition, "local" is the binational metropolitan area of El Paso and Ciudad Juárez. The Coalition is not a tax-exempt organization, but rather one that draws on individuals and organizations with an ideological or issue-based interest in reducing and ending violence against women. There are no paid organizers; time, labor, and money are provided at people's own expense, but without any dependencies or control. The Coalition has no organizing principles that it infuses into recruitment and training, but most participants share a feminist identity and a willingness to polarize meetings and events over issues involving male privilege or abuse. Such principles may not resonate with mainstream congregational bases. Ideological issues like these are long-term, involving difficult-to-identify winnable goals.

Femicide in Ciudad Juárez is a multipronged problem for which there are multiple targets and decision makers in two sovereign countries and their multiple layers of federalism. With more than 300 foreign (mostly U.S.) export-processing factories employing a fifth of a million workers earning a fraction of the wages of U.S. workers, the atmosphere of cheap disposable labor permeates the city. While Mexico is in transition to democracy, activists have great difficulty playing by pluralist reformist rules such as transparency and accountability from government. Human rights activists in comparable circumstances wonder: How to fight the *pulpo* (octopus)? The response is often to seize any and all opportunities to make problems visible and to use compelling symbols to do so.[5]

Local activists, from both sides of the border, bring personal, face-to-face relationships to problems, but they lack resources for widening the visibility and pressure. Faith-based organizations on both sides of the border have been slow to respond to violence against women in either country, much less the binational region. While Mexico's populist traditions make public protest common and compatible with its political culture, few expect activism for social justice from the institutionalized church and clergy. Moreover, male clergy do not resonate well with feminist language and practice. Coalition activists have been willing to network and coalesce with many regional, national, and international activists. In so doing, they helped expand visibility in exponential ways, but not necessarily ways that involved long-term commitments to sustaining themselves as a coalition.

We now consider the context and analysis of El Paso's move from concentrated power to fragmentation, along with the ways that its IAF affiliate and the Coalition responded to the open, opportune spaces for action.

THE HISTORICAL CONTEXT

The Rio Grande, or Río Bravo as it is called in Mexico, now divides the El Paso–Ciudad Juárez region. The Treaty of Guadalupe Hidalgo established the international borderline in 1848, but slight adjustments were made as late as the early 1960s with the Chamizal Agreement.

People of Mexican heritage have long populated the region in majority numbers, but on the El Paso side, the English-speaking settlers governed the region and dominated the economy. Historically, U.S. poll taxes and English-language muted Mexican-heritage voices. A patron-client political culture is deeply embedded in the region, characterized by the personal cultivation of favor among diverse people in a hierarchical system. Historically, machine-style, mostly conservative Democratic Party politics made political control by the few and quiescence by the majority the norm in El Paso.[6]

Only in the mid-1950s did El Paso elect its first Spanish-surnamed mayor, Raymond Telles, initially disturbing to the Anglo elite. Telles helped to dismantle partisan elections in the name of professionalism.[7] As in other cities in the United States, nonpartisan voting weakened the political party as a mediating, organized connection between citizens and their government. However flawed political parties have been as democratic organizations, their absence contributes to political fragmentation. County elections remain partisan, but outside the criminal justice area, county government in Texas is relatively impotent.

During the 1960s, El Pasoans became roused like counterparts elsewhere in the state of Texas over civil rights and Spanish-language discrimination. La Raza Unida became a third-party force in south Texas and elsewhere in the U.S. Southwest, challenging the Democratic Party to become more accountable to Mexican American people.[8] Federal response to the civil rights movement, as well as constitutional principles to desegregate schools, challenged discriminatory practices. El Paso's main school desegregation case, *Alvarado et al. versus El Paso Independent School District*, was settled in 1976, with assistance from the Mexican American Legal Defense and Education Fund (MALDEF), bringing attention to the overrepresentation of Spanish-speaking students in special-education classes and the underrepresentation of Mexican American faculty and administrators. However, the U.S. Commission on Civil Rights' six-volume series helped to document that high dropout rates and minimal expectations existed in many low-income, heavily minority schools across the state. Without federal tools, El Paso's majority could not crack local politics and the historic practices that perpetuated inequality and segregation.[9]

Free-trade dogma needed pilot testing, and the U.S.-Mexico border was a major site. Seeking to deconcentrate jobs in the capital city and to encourage foreign investment, Mexico established the Border Industrialization Program in the 1960s and the export-processing factories known as *maquiladoras*. Just as the Bracero Program that had authorized Mexican farm labor in the United States ended, Mexico's new industrial strategy took shape. Conjoined with Mexico's new strategy, the United States altered customs codes so that tariffs would be paid only on "value added" in export-processing production. U.S. jobs migrated across the border into Ciudad Juárez and Mexico's northern frontier, with Ciudad Juárez home to the largest number of Mexican jobs created in plants that assembled foreign exports. By the year 2000, Ciudad Juárez employed 250,000 *maquiladora* workers, a female-majority workforce, at jobs that mostly paid low wages (the equivalent of about five to ten U.S. dollars per day).

POLITICAL OPENINGS: A NEW OPPORTUNITY STRUCTURE?

Nationwide challenges to at-large elections affected El Paso when its at-large electoral system was replaced with district-based city council seats in the 1981 city charter. The three large school districts in the county eventually established district-based elections as well. The district system increased the likelihood of Mexican American representation in predominantly Mexican American areas. A new cast of characters ran for office and won, among them Mexican American, Spanish-surnamed people.

This era was associated with historic firsts. Paul Moreno was the first Mexican American to represent a part of El Paso in the state legislature. The first Mexican American to serve on the Ysleta Independent School District board, Alicia Chacón, won in 1970, only to have her victory contested. But she prevailed and, in 1990, went on to become elected as the state's first Hispanic county judge (the chief executive officer of the county). The second Hispanic in El Paso's history to be elected mayor served in the late 1970s.

El Paso has never been a wealthy community, but during the latter half of the twentieth century, its per capita income diminished markedly compared with the national per capita income. From comparability (102 percent to 100 percent) in 1950, El Paso's per capita income declined to 59 percent of national per capita income. While many factors contributed to this decline, a major factor was loss of heavy industry, unionized jobs (limited as they were) to nonunionized jobs in garment manufacturing. Such work became a magnet for job seekers, within and across the border, just as the *maquila* system drew migrants to Ciudad Juárez from Mexico's interior. The Chamizal Agreement (noted earlier), along with "urban renewal," resulted in the loss of scores of thousands of low-rent homes in south El Paso, near the downtown. Residents moved to cheap land, sold by developers (some of them cotton farmers eager to sell land in a nonviable agricultural economy) outside the city limits, in unplanned settlements known as *colonias*. Most *colonias* lacked paved roads and water and sewer systems. County government had no planning authority until the mid-1990s. Up to that point the state of Texas had absolved itself of responsibility to *colonia* residents' need for basic public utilities.[10]

In the early 1980s, garment factory workers, most of them women, faced job instability in the increasingly competitive contracting and subcontracting arrangements. El Paso once had its large garment manufacturers, Farah and Levi Strauss among them, but also medium-sized and small plants, including sweatshops. Some unscrupulous employers delayed wage payments to workers, then went out of business (and occasionally restarted their businesses under new names) without retribution save workers' protests. In this context, an organization called La Mujer Obrera (the Woman Worker) emerged to organize garment factory workers. It pursued conflict and polarization strategies in its early years that eventually yielded state laws with stronger penalties for employer fraud. In the 1990s, La Mujer Obrera spawned another arm, a community development corporation, El Puente CDC, a grant-getting player and social enterprise operation of its own.[11]

Historically, progressive Mexican American political representatives, as individuals, could do little to stem the systemic factors that undermined El Pasoans' ability to enjoy prosperity: low-wage garment industry jobs, in an era wherein production gradually went global; immigration policy and enforcement, decisions made in Washington, D.C., and implemented in the Border Patrol district offices like El Paso. The individual rights gained during the 1960s helped bring about changes in who held top political offices but did not add up to major power shifts. Organized power was necessary to nudge at power relations that favored the status quo.

IAF, EL PASO: EPISO

In 1981, the Texas Industrial Areas Foundation facilitated the creation of its second organization in the state, after Communities Organized for Public Service (COPS) in San Antonio.[12] IAF relies on trained organizers to build a faith-based power foundation: congregations affiliate with the organization, and their members, often lacking political experience, undergo training to speak publicly, engage with government, and challenge politicians to be accountable for their issues, in public accountability sessions that attract extensive media attention. In El Paso, the IAF affiliate was named the El Paso Inter-religious Sponsoring Organization (EPISO).

The El Paso Anglo establishment reacted with a vengeance. Media articles referred to "outside agitators." Businesspeople took out full-page newspaper ads about "the threat" posed by EPISO.[13] Churches divided over whether or not to affiliate with EPISO. The era was associated with conflict and polarization in a community that had practiced and prized quiescence and patron-client-style diplomacy with its passive-aggressive conflict styles. Accountability sessions were a source of potential embarrassment and bad publicity for political candidates.

Ultimately, EPISO organized primarily around a Catholic parish base, in south El Paso and the southeast area known as the "lower valley" of the Rio Grande, including *colonias*. In the 1980s, EPISO focused on public utilities and services, especially in *colonias*, as did Valley Interfaith in south Texas, with a similar population base as El Paso. IAF cultivated relationships with Texas politicians to call attention to the so-called third world conditions in the United States, along the border, where residents lacked water and sewer services. Initially, media visibility was an embarrassment to El Paso's established official and business community. Subsequently, EPISO's local leaders engaged with county, city, and public utility board leaders to foster the development of new water districts. Eventually, the state of Texas established policies and programs that supported more water and sewer lines and ultimately more control over developers who broke up land to sell for *colonia* settlements outside city planning limits. County and city officials joined the bandwagon for external funding.

Also in the mid-1980s, Texans began to focus on inadequate schools, especially for low-income and minority-group students. The legislature enacted new laws that altered teacher preparation programs, tested teachers, forbade athletes from play without passing grades ("no pass, no play"), and established accountability testing. Before serious accountability testing, low expectations, prejudice, and tracking systems within schools created a two-tiered education process, one that channeled many low-income and minority students into low-wage jobs, rather than higher education and employment. By the early 1990s, an accountability system put teachers and administrators in the spotlight. Thenceforth all students were expected to perform at (minimal) standards. Early results from accountability tests were dismal, and state-mandated public reporting for disaggregated data showed huge gaps by ethnicity/race and economic disadvantage.

In this context, the Alliance Schools strategy was born. The Texas IAF lobbied for capital investment funds, to be allocated by the Texas Education Agency, for which schools could apply to mobilize parents for greater educational achievement. Such outside funding was of mutual interest to schools and parents (within IAF organizations). Schools constantly search for outside resources, and IAF organizations were able to use the process as an organizing strategy. In El Paso, low-income parents, many of them Spanish-speaking with *primaria*-level (sixth-grade) education from Mexico, often felt intimidated by the "experts," teachers and administrators. As a result, the schools exercised carte blanche over education, without much parental oversight. Alliance schools built relationships between parents and teachers to raise expectations (often operationalized as increased proportions of students who passed the state-mandated tests) and to put students on pathways to college.

At its high point, El Paso was home to twenty-two Alliance Schools in the two largest districts. This represented approximately 10 percent of schools in the county. Parents, many of them trained by the IAF as leaders, were organized to engage with the educational bureaucracy. They participated in parent academies, where they acquired language and skills to negotiate for a voice at campus policymaking tables. Ysleta Elementary School became famous nationally for how parents—primarily mothers—exercised civic skills and achieved "wins," such as obtaining funding from the school board to remodel their campus, computers for students, and traffic lights for dangerous streets nearby.[14]

El Paso's unemployment figures are traditionally twice those of state and national figures. With the North American Free Trade Agreement (NAFTA) in place by 1994, the end of El Paso's garment industry was nigh, resulting in many "displaced workers." By 1997, El Paso's dubious distinction was to become the city with the largest number of NAFTA-displaced workers, scores of thousands of them middle-aged, Spanish-speaking women. NAFTA's side agreements and workforce development opportunities abounded, but few of them yielded strong job placement prospects. Hispanic women earn just 37 percent of white men's incomes.[15] La Mujer Obrera and its El Puente offshoot established several social enterprises, such as a restaurant and child care center, although employment generation was limited. Both groups acquired impressive grant-getting abilities to initiate projects, though their sustainability is uncertain.

EPISO's response to the unemployment and low-wage economy of El Paso was to facilitate the replication of the San Antonio workforce-training project that involved job placement. By 1998, Project Arriba was born. Arriba, recruiting a largely Hispanic female pool, is a workforce training program that involves two years of training and job placements into jobs that pay more than twice the minimum wage. Through early 2006, Project Arriba graduated more than 300 participants, with more in the pipeline. Prominent businessmen serve on Arriba's board, and substantial subsidies have been obtained from public sources, such as the Empowerment Zone and, more recently, community development block grant funds, with support cultivated from city hall. Critics allege that Project Arriba's recruitment strategies result in "creaming" English-speaking high school graduates eligible for community college enrollment, rather than displaced workers. Yet Arriba is the only viable living wage job strategy in the city.

Gender inequality is an omnipresent reality in politics. El Paso has had only one woman mayor in its history, and two or three women at any given time on its eight-person city council. Not only are gender wage inequalities profound in El Paso, but El Paso and Ciudad Juárez have serious domestic violence and femicide problems: El Paso police report 28,000 domestic violence complaints annually, and approximately thirty women die annually from domestic violence and serial killing homicides in Ciudad Juárez.[16] Since EPISO, like IAF generally, avoids polarizing issues at the community level, gender, women, and antiviolence are not part of its discourse and agenda.

MORE NEW ORGANIZED STAKEHOLDERS AND PLAYERS

EPISO is a very visible part of the political and civic landscape in El Paso, but it cannot claim full responsibility for changing dynamics. On school reform, for example, there is a wide range of players. In El Paso, as in Texas more generally, school district lines do not coincide with city boundaries. The city of El Paso is served by three school districts, two of which spread well beyond the city limits. Ysleta ISD, the second-largest school district, had strong, albeit controversial superintendent leadership under Anthony Trujillo, who directed special attention to lower-income, south-of-the-Interstate "border" schools in his mixed-income district.

In 1988, when Dr. Diana Natalicio was inaugurated as president of the University of Texas at El Paso (UTEP), she began to look for ways to involve the university more extensively in the community. Her inauguration came at a particularly significant time. Under the guidance of Sister Maribeth Larkin as lead organizer, EPISO proposed to the El Paso Chamber of Commerce a collaborative approach to public school reform, based largely on the model of the Boston compact. But the chamber proved reluctant to take on such an ambitious role. After President Natalicio became part of an ongoing and expanding dialogue, she brought into the discussion Dr. Susana Navarro, a native of El Paso, and someone who had an extraordinary body of experiences for addressing school issues, including work with the U.S. Civil Rights Commission.

With support from Sister Maribeth Larkin and an enlarged circle of groups in the El Paso community, in 1992, President Natalicio appointed Navarro as executive director of a newly created El Paso Collaborative for Academic Excellence, and Natalicio served (and continues to serve) as chair of the board for the collaborative. On the board, she is joined by the mayor, the county judge, the three urban school superintendents, the president of the community college, the head of the Texas regional education office, the head of the El Paso Chamber of Commerce, the head of the Hispanic Chamber of Commerce, and the lead organizer for EPISO. The aim is clearly one of bringing all the major institutional voices into the collaborative; appointments come from the position held and thus are not personal. It is particularly significant that EPISO is represented on the board because IAF organizations are quite cautious about alliances with other organizations and their agendas. However, EPISO's inclusion in the collaborative is not without tensions.

In its first decade, with an initial strategic embrace from the superintendent of the Ysleta School District, the collaborative became a strong presence on the public school front. It has garnered funding support from the National Science Foundation and philanthropic foundations for math and science teacher-training funds and other initiatives. By the late 1990s, comparisons with other major urban districts in Texas documented that El Paso surpassed Austin, Dallas, Houston, and San Antonio in accountability test improvement and narrowed gaps between ethnic/racial groups. It should also be noted that the collaborative runs a parent engagement network. Although the number of participants on each campus each year is small, the aim is twofold—to have each participant spread know-how to others, and to build a cumulative network by connecting each new class with its predecessors.

In another development, lawsuits filed against Texas over a property tax–based funding system toward more equitable school funding eventually produced more funds for El Paso and other property-poor regions. Like earlier school desegregation, MALDEF again provided legal assistance to the lead plaintiff school district in San Antonio and other plaintiffs, including two small districts in El Paso County, Socorro and San Elizario.[17]

More or less parallel in time, other significant developments also occurred. From 1992 to 1994, an extraordinary group of mostly strategically placed leaders came together to form Unite El Paso, a short-lived wider and inclusive network with a name and an agenda that changed the terms of policy debate. Soon-to-be state senator Eliot Shapleigh was key to instigating this mostly middle-class, multi-ethnic group of business, educational, and civic leaders in an intentional effort to bring together Anglo and Mexican American leaders and voices.[18] Approximately 150 Anglo and Mexican American business, education, and government leaders came together in the network. Many met at the downtown civic center, at a community summit on September 17 through 19, 1993, forming committees to address El Paso's assets and needs. The network emphasized the importance of collaboration and funding equity, particularly vis-à-vis state government.

Soon after, the idea of "fair-share funding" was born. El Paso lawyers and political representatives focused particularly on transportation formula funding that awarded more road construction and maintenance money to smaller cities (like Austin, mid-1990s) than to El Paso. A high-visibility court of inquiry was established, under the leadership of Judge Márquez, as a follow-up to the summit. Ray Caballero (later mayor) began to play a more visible role in leadership to document El Paso's funding. EPISO played no visible part in the event.

As part of a changing political scene, El Paso also had voter registration drives in the 1980s, including those fostered by the Southwest Voter Registration Project. By then, the Mexican American majority finally became a majority of the registered. However, voter turnout has been problematic, especially in state and local elections. In the 1990s, a nonpartisan voter drive emerged, known as Count Me In, under the leadership of Ray Caballero, who became El Paso's mayor in 2001. Although he was defeated after a single two-year term, Caballero was, nonetheless, a key figure in how the city's politics evolved.

By the late 1990s, an informal division opened between one group with ties to Unite El Paso, herein distinguished as the "populists," and another group known as the "developers." The developers are building contractor, concrete, and real estate business people who actively seek the expansion of city boundaries, settlements, and roads to facilitate the building of low-density housing across a wide terrain. They represent an extension of the past establishment, primarily Anglo and male. Developers and their political allies seek to augment the property tax base through growth and sprawl, but also construct low-cost housing. Alternative-development populists, or "populists" for short, seek investment for El Paso's small businesses and older neighborhoods, squeezed for capital, according to El Paso's Business

Summit of 1998. The populists became a driving force for the Border Health Complex initiative in south-central El Paso, near the border and the downtown, an area of housing decay and poverty.

While the developer and populist groups differed in their ideas about economic development, it was perhaps the difference in political style that set them apart even more. The populists were willing to use sharp criticism and lawsuits to achieve their demands, and they are viewed as abrasive and polarizing, while the developers worked behind the scenes through contacts and campaign contributions to create a "friendly business climate." Both groups recognize the need for more better-paying jobs in El Paso. In his mayoral term, Caballero gave special attention to the near-downtown south and south-central areas around new economic issues, such as a border health complex.

The business community in El Paso is fragmented organizationally. The El Paso Greater Chamber of Commerce is the largest organization, with on-and-off subsidies from the city government. El Paso has many chambers: the Greater Chamber of Commerce and the Hispanic, Black, and Korean chambers. In the late 1990s, the Leadership Research Council (LRC) emerged as a chief executive officer group to provide more dynamic leadership to El Paso business. LRC members probably leaned more toward the developer ideas, but they acquired an interest in education. In 2004, given lingering concerns about organized business leadership, yet other groups, known as the Paso del Norte Group and REDCO, emerged, focusing on regional economic development.

Frequent turnover in the mayor's office has added to the fragmentation of leadership. As a populist, Caballero was defeated after one term by Joe Wardy, who was backed by developers and courted closely by EPISO. Wardy, however, also proved to be a one-term mayor, despite developer backing and a huge edge in campaign funds. Low voter turnout (15 percent in the 2005 local elections) is a cloud over the legitimacy of all local officials.

El Paso's leaders are not of like mind about externally controlled decision making over the region's economy and future. The boom economy of Ciudad Juárez, which plays by far different economic, environmental, wage, and regulatory rules, makes El Paso's weakness abundantly clear to people. El Paso was once a community with locally controlled banks, but the last two decades saw major national banks acquiring several key banks. Populist leaders sought to make what they viewed as El Paso's colony-like status more visible. For example, Senator Shapleigh helped to found a youth policy analysis program known as Community Scholars. In its early years, the scholars documented that externally controlled banks extracted more resources from El Paso than are reinvested. Even as bankers took issue with the Community Scholars' methodology, front-page headlines gave play to the controversy. EPISO took no position on this issue, but it has courted managers of externally controlled banks to serve on the board of such efforts as Arriba. This does not endear populists to EPISO.

CONTEMPORARY TERRAINS: IAF GOES METRO, BUT NOT ACROSS THE BORDER

Several large Texas cities are home to two IAF organizations, including Houston and San Antonio. Any and all organizations develop perceptions that hinder or help their ability to expand. In San Antonio, for example, the original IAF affiliate, COPS, was perceived as a Mexican American organization, with a Catholic congregational base, and a separate organization was formed to appeal to Protestant churches, particularly in the African American community.

In El Paso, EPISO has its proponents and detractors, each with historic baggage. For those with negative perceptions, early EPISO organizing is remembered as confrontational, dividing congregations over whether to join. Some teachers and principals remember vivid examples of EPISO, which they perceived as trying to control or divide their schools, and some EPISO organizers are remembered as abrasive. Those with positive perceptions remember the attention that long-muted issues received: *colonia* water and sewer services; academic achievement and parental voice in low-income neighborhoods; workforce training for living wage jobs. Once people actually meet face-to-face with EPISO organizers and leaders, they often appreciate the reasonable and informed quality of efforts. EPISO's organizing base is a set of Catholic parishes in the low-income, lower valley region of southeast El Paso, near the border. However, in south El Paso parishes and schools, the high-poverty area close to downtown and the border, priests and school district personnel no longer welcome EPISO organizing. A new superintendent was hostile to organizing and replaced a key Alliance School principal without consulting parent leaders.

IAF organizations undergo constant change, just as contexts in which they work constantly change. As one of its principles goes, no permanent allies, no permanent enemies. EPISO has entered a second, less conflictual stage of organizing, augmenting and strengthening positive perceptions. It has been able to recruit leading businesspeople to boards like Project Arriba, including people from non–locally controlled banks about whom some populists are wary. In line with their strict training, EPISO's organizers and leaders choose battles carefully and avoid alliances with those perceived as polarizing or as articulating no-win issues, such as immigration.[19] Accountability sessions continue, and EPISO prizes those candidates who agree to support their agenda—currently, Project Arriba. For instance, during Caballero's campaign for reelection, the mayor refused to support subsidies for Project Arriba, and that fact was publicized heavily in the media and through word of mouth. His successful opponent, Joe Wardy, delivered on a promise to provide support for Project Arriba. He and other business leaders traveled to a Texas IAF training on workforce issues in San Antonio in June 2004. In July, the mayor altered the formula for the city's CDBG funds to accommodate Arriba but subtracted about that amount from the categories for homelessness, health, and child/youth. Critics view the redistribution of community development funds as "robbing Peter to pay Paul," and Wardy's subsequent defeat in his reelection bid was anything but a vindication of his choice.

Despite the border terrain, issues such as those involving immigration, cross-border wage disparities, and femicide in Ciudad Juárez are not part of EPISO's agenda. Because EPISO, as an IAF affiliate, is highly disciplined to focus on its main agenda, the organization forgoes opportunities to network and make broad cause around populist issues. Meanwhile, in political space that EPISO might have filled, scores of city-instigated neighborhood associations have emerged, as has an ACORN chapter. By 2004, ACORN claimed eighty local dues-paying members. Neighborhood associations have put a damper on developers' agendas, for some are organizing against sprawl and for the preservation of desert *arroyos*. It is ironic that the developers' candidate, Mayor Wardy, put into motion a Neighborhoods First initiative that has enabled civic organizations to challenge developers' agendas.

In spite of efforts by various organizations, including EPISO, voter turnout in El Paso continues to be low. In the Ysleta school board election of May 2004, EPISO's base territory, only 1 percent of registered people turned out to vote. Caballero's defeat in his bid for reelection notwithstanding, EPISO is in a weak position to claim that it is a major force in El Paso's fragmented politics. The populists assumed a more confrontational role but lacked the organizational base of EPISO.

Yet in the late 1990s, the lead organizer began conversations with congregations on the middle-class west side, including a synagogue and several Catholic and Protestant denominations. After several years of interdenominational meetings that involved field trips and speaker series, the Westside Interfaith Alliance (WIA) Steering Committee, a 501(c)(3) organization, was established in 2003, and fund-raising began. WIA was renamed Border Interfaith in 2004, for its prospective broader base than Westside. Steering Committee members involve clergy and lay leaders. The base congregations began "house meetings," and larger sessions attracted more congregations, especially its Public Life Institutes of 2005–2006, drawing approximately 150 potential leaders to each session. For Texas IAF, two organizations in a city offer the combined strength of a broad and diverse base among congregations, after a slow connection of the dots. Money is being raised, most of it from denominational but increasingly congregational sources, to support contracts with IAF and eventually to hire a full-time trained organizer. With IAF faithful to the "power before program" principle, years will go by before issues are articulated in goal-oriented ways. While Border Interfaith makes good use of technology for communication, including e-mail, EPISO and the state IAF generally are wedded to person-to-person meetings and phone calls.

The following section will illustrate differences between EPISO and the Coalition against Violence. Some obvious contrasts include those relating to organizational structure, style, and culture. Terrain also sets the groups apart, with EPISO focused on El Paso, and the Coalition on the even more fragmented binational borderlands of El Paso and Ciudad Juárez. Ultimately, though, EPISO and Border Interfaith have the potential for a position in the governing coalition (of El Paso), while the Coalition has little potential for such a role as evidenced in its narrow agenda, all-volunteer operation, and heavy dependence on the media. It could align itself with a broader coalition, if one were in place and were receptive, or with EPISO/IAF if these organizations were open to a wider agenda. But the supporters of the Coalition do not offer much likelihood of devoting energy and resources to a broad, multi-issue agenda. Both EPISO and the Coalition have external networks, but the link of EPISO and Border Interfaith to IAF is at the heart of reluctance to form local alliances with groups such as the Coalition. The Coalition's external allies pose no parallel constraint on local alliances.

COALITION AGAINST VIOLENCE

Violence against women transcends the border, but Ciudad Juárez has achieved infamy in the world for the murders of at least 370 girls and women from 1993 to 2003, a third of whom have been raped and mutilated before death.[20] Mexican police, at both the municipal and the state level, respond with indifference, impunity, and incompetence. Most residents do not trust the police generally, and more specifically view them as complicit and/or paid to offer protection for the perpetrators, alleged to be sons of the wealthy and/or drug traffickers (two categories in which there is overlap). The majority of Juarenses live below the poverty line, earning little more than the rock-bottom wage totaling twenty-five to fifty U.S. dollars weekly, in a city with hundreds of foreign export–processing factories, most of them U.S.-owned.

Extensive organizing and networking have occurred around the murders, and the Coalition is one of many groups involved in mobilizing awareness and pressuring governments to respond. It has a special place in organizing efforts because it is based in the border region, with deeper knowledge of the issues, people, and setting than the distant, weakly linked cyberactivists. The networking links and Coalition activists' use of local cross-border space produced extraordinary attention that exploded in exponential ways over a two-year period, as outlined later.

Community organizing is challenge enough in a single city, with shifting power relations and vacuums. The greater challenge faces nongovernment organizations

(NGOs) from two sovereign countries for a metropolitan strategy that combines El Paso and Ciudad Juárez through cross-border organizing. Many obstacles exist to cross-border organizing: language differences; cultural differences, even among people of Mexican heritage; differences in activists' access to discretionary resources, telephones, and Internet access; immigration documents; and a high level of fear. Yet borders are not total barriers, as organizations exist and success occurs under certain circumstances, such as transnational institutions that authorize and connect stakeholders with "foreign" treaties, policies, and budgetary resources; government staff and subsidies that support binational business as a regional economic development strategy; or sheer personal dedication.[21]

The Coalition against Violence toward Women and Families at the U.S.-Mexico border is an example of human rights networking at global to local levels. It is cochaired by an academic (female) and a former labor union organizer (male), with an organizational and individual base made up of antiviolence center staff, feminists, union activists, and university students. Coalition volunteers network in nonhierarchical fashion. The Coalition draws on activists from young to old with an ideological and/or personal interest in the problem, rather than on a congregational base. It collects no dues and raises no money. Although clergy are sometimes present to open and close rallies with prayer, the institutionalized church has dedicated little effort to the cause, despite the movement's use of religious icons and imagery, as discussed later.

While EPISO views the "community" as the city and county of El Paso, and its regional allies as other Texas IAF organizations who target state decision makers in Austin, the Coalition's "community" is El Paso–Ciudad Juárez combined. Official binational institutions are few and far between, but informal cooperation is constant, especially among elites, businesses, and activists. Business chambers in both cities cooperate formally, and special local and state government officials on both sides of the border draw on the public purse to facilitate commerce and trade. The local police departments have regularly cooperated with each other over auto theft.

Above and below cross-border networks is a seeping "cartel-ization" of Ciudad Juárez, which, like Tijuana, is home to drug transit operations that grew once the U.S. war on drugs shifted the Colombia connection from Miami to the 2,000-mile-long U.S.-Mexico border. The enormous drug-money profits generate corruption and collusion with officials.

The Coalition was born at a labor solidarity meeting in Ciudad Juárez with antiviolence activists in November 2001. It rarely misses the opportunity to critique the tenfold minimum-wage salary difference between El Paso and Ciudad Juárez, and U.S.-owned factories in complicity. Such a public posture does not endear Coalition activists to business partners. The Coalition consciously avoided tax-exempt 501(c)(3) status and the concomitant fund-raising, reporting, and bylaws structure. The number of its participants, all of them volunteers rather than paid organizers, expand and contract, depending on opportunities for actions. Actions emerge around crises—bodies found in the desert—and culturally significant seasons. Documentaries, like Lourdes Portillo's *Señorita Extraviada,* provide compelling visuals that rouse people to action.

Coalition stakeholders conceptualize violence against women as a binational problem, with binational solutions. Of the hundreds of victims, most of them Mexicans, victim lists count four El Pasoans, one Dutch, one Honduran, and one Guatemalan. Activists in and outside the Coalition create events to heighten awareness of the problem and pressure authorities into action. They use dramatic symbols, some of them quasi-religious, and occasions: public Día de los Muertos/Day of the Dead altars in October and November, to mourn and remember the victims; Women's History Month and International Women's Day (March 8), and V-Day (February) events to march against violence. The colors and icons are pink and black, contrasting a crucifix and its background. At the downtown international border-crossing bridge, a large wooden crucifix sits on which nails are hammered and victims' names are written.

Drawing on existent informal binational cooperation, in 2002, Coalition members called attention to police cooperation over stolen vehicles. When a stolen car is reported in El Paso, police authorities immediately coordinate with their counterparts in Ciudad Juárez. Coalition members wondered publicly, over and over: If police can cooperate over stolen cars, why can't they cooperate over murdered girls and women? In 2003, after a series of marches, then mayor Caballero, police chief Leon, and their counterparts in Ciudad Juárez held a press conference to announce cooperation over training and an international toll-free tip line into the El Paso Police Department, with assistance from the FBI. Changes like these are delicate matters, treading on national sovereignty issues. Moreover, with alleged police complicity in Ciudad Juárez and Chihuahua City, home of the state judicial police that investigates serious crimes like murder, activists are understandably ambivalent about police involvement.

Coalition activities are planned through face-to-face meetings and speedy listserv dissemination. Participants identify targets of opportunity to educate politicians and sustain media visibility. Under two mayoral administrations in El Paso, those of Caballero and Wardy, council members voted unanimously for largely symbolic resolutions against the violence and in favor of calls for binational cooperation, resolutions difficult to oppose. The Coalition also worked with state senator Shapleigh and state representative Norma Chávez, who introduced and negotiated passage for a resolution in the Texas legislature, complete with April 2003 hearings in Austin, at which Coalition testimony was given.

During the summer of 2003, the Mexico Solidarity Committee networked with the Coalition and the Washington Office on Latin America to facilitate a U.S. congressional delegation to visit Juarez, to meet with victims' families, including the mother of a disappeared U.S. national (from El Paso), officials, and NGO activists. Congresswoman Hilda Solís (from Los Angeles) led a delegation to Ciudad Juárez with representatives from Chicago, San Antonio, Tucson, and of course El Paso. They visited sites inside the city and at the desert periphery where multiple bodies had been found, and pink wooden crosses were erected to mourn the victims. Amnesty International released a seventy-page monograph detailing human rights abuses and police corruption. In November 2003, another congressional delegation, focused on NAFTA, also was briefed on the murders. The media on both sides of the border and from afar devoted frenzied attention to the murders. Elites and officials in Ciudad Juárez periodically express outrage at their city's image internationally, although they no longer publicly blame the murder victims, as was common during the 1990s.

Coalition activists prize networking at the local, binational metropolitan, national, and international levels, while maintaining personal contact with activists who work with antiviolence counseling centers and victims' mothers in Ciudad Juárez (for the binational digital divide is even greater across border and class lines between Mexico and the United States than within the United States). Networking through cyberactivism has an anarchic quality that allows speedy response among weakly tied activists, resulting in enormous political events, but relationships, as indicated later, are often tenuous.

In both 2002 and 2003, Coalition activists organized marches that brought activists together at the international border, with hundreds crossing into Ciudad Juárez. Journalists, including those working for papers based in Mexico City, New York, Los Angeles, Washington, D.C., and European cities, covered the murders and events. Border activists had invested considerable labor in speaking to visiting journalists and researchers. Playwright Eve Ensler, famous for writing *The Vagina Monologues* and authorizing its performance for fund-raising against violence through the Web site, named Esther Chávez Cano, who heads Casa Amiga, an antiviolence counseling center in Ciudad Juárez, one of 21 International Leaders for the 21st Century, shifting networking to a whole new level.[22]

Ensler visited Juarez for V-Day celebrations in 2003, for a protest at the Ciudad Juárez office of the state attorney general. Several universities held conferences on the issue, including UCLA's "Maquiladora Murders" conference from October 31 through the Day of the Dead. The conference attracted 1,000 participants, including a New York–based cyberactivist who broadcast the conference on the Internet. Resolutions have been introduced in both the U.S. House and Senate with bipartisan support. In Mexico, after lengthy delays, President Fox finally appointed a special prosecutor and an investigator at the federal level to address what had heretofore been defined as a state and local problem. Special Investigator Guadalupe Morfín issued a report in 2004 linking the murders to the climate of poverty and inadequate municipal infrastructure.

V-Day 2004 produced a crescendo of international visibility, with Eve Ensler and entertainers from Mexico City and Hollywood performing Ensler's *Vagina Monologues*, with a new monologue on the Ciudad Juárez murders, to huge audiences on both sides of the border and more than a thousand cities around the world. A cross-border solidarity march was organized, the largest ever in the region, drawing 5,000 to 8,000 crossers from local to distant locales. Ensler was present at a ceremony at the University of Texas at El Paso with a 1,200-person audience that honored four Coalition women, one of them a university student, as "vagina warriors." Language like this does not always resonate well with some of the NGOs in Ciudad Juárez, especially those that represent the murder victims' mothers.

Loose networking has not surprisingly produced misunderstandings, defensiveness, and competition over accountability: Who is and should be authorized to speak about the murders and domestic violence generally? Who is and should be authorized to strategize over solutions? One NGO in Ciudad Juárez, diminished to a handful of activists, seized whatever opportunity possible to criticize Ensler, Mexico City, and Hollywood celebrities for disrespect and broadening the agenda to violence against women generally rather than the murders alone. New York–based activists criticized localism or aligned themselves with some NGOs against others, without deep knowledge of the local terrain. Electronic communication, if cryptic and culturally insensitive, sparks a bitterness all its own. In these difficult circumstances, the Coalition operated carefully, trying to maintain bridges with all groups, in a contested terrain that achieves local solidarity across international borders.

The successes of the antiviolence movement are quite remarkable, but they may stem in part from the dramatic character of its focus—the murder of women. The Coalition's method of operation is not readily transferred to other issues, with less affective content—issues such as cross-border wage disparities. Thus the Coalition is not an illustration of how fragmentation can be overcome to build an effective multi-issue form of governance. Instead, it is an example of a strictly voluntary movement emerging to fill a vacuum left by more structured and conventional groups in a situation of high fragmentation.

CONCLUSION

As with many American cities, El Paso went through an era in which, without holding elected office, a small business elite de facto governed the city. The activism of the civil rights period and the changing character of the economy, especially in banking, brought an end to that time. The civic and political terrain of most cities became more complex, and in places such as San Antonio, community organizing has produced a more inclusive form of governance. El Paso shows why such an outcome is not predestined. The U.S.-Mexico border is one barrier to problem solving but, as the Coalition shows, not an insuperable one. Divisions within El Paso's business sector are perhaps another barrier to a broad-based effort at community problem *solving*. But perhaps the greatest barrier is a history of civic and political marginality experienced by those who occupy the lower ranks of society's system of stratification.

EPISO's position shows how difficult it is to build a wide and sustainable base of popular support. As an IAF affiliate, EPISO works through existing organizations, especially those with a faith base, to reach those outside the civic mainstream. It teaches important skills through its leadership development efforts. However, at the same time, in the IAF mold, EPISO is very much a creature of its lead organizer and is also heavily oriented toward its IAF connection. Hence EPISO has not sought to become part of a larger progressive movement, but IAF has spawned another affiliate with its promise for a broader metropolitan strategy after the careful start-up work of relationship building proceeds. EPISO's electoral influence is limited, and its ability to maintain an Alliance School base, much less expand that base, proved to be temporary. It has seen new organizing forces gain a foothold, and it did not take on one of the area's most dramatic issues, unsolved murders of hundreds of women on the Mexican side of the border. That vacuum was filled by a volunteer movement, the Coalition against Violence toward Women and Families, along with distant national and international networks, which apply pressure on the diffuse "octopus," rather than pursue short-term winnable goals around which clear self-interest is evident. The IAF precept against permanent alliances allows EPISO to make ad hoc alliances with selected local officials and a segment of the business sector. EPISO has thus protected its main agenda of workforce development but is nevertheless very dependent on these allies for needed resources. As a consequence, EPISO is not in a position to promote a broad progressive agenda or even be a major player in a governing coalition. A sister organization, Border Interfaith, has emerged in El Paso, but at this stage, it is not clear what that move will yield. At present, important issues go unaddressed, and the issues that get attention receive narrow treatment consistent with a highly fragmented civic and political arena.

In El Paso, although there are now many players, governing is highly fragmented. Piecemeal and selective problem solving is the order of the day. The absence of tight control by a small elite does not translate into a vital form of popular control, even when the civic landscape is populated with a variety of issue-focused organizations. The border is itself a limiting factor, one that so far has been overcome to a degree only in a confined but highly symbolic and emotional issue centered on the murders of women. The handling of economic and immigrant issues rests not with actors in the region but with national players on an international stage.

Still there are substantial issues that could be addressed locally. But it is clear that local government can act effectively only if it has a strong political base, giving it a sustained direction, including a capacity to garner allies at the state level. At present, the most effective voice is that of the developer faction, focused on near-term profits that can be gained from largely unchecked sprawl. This is a policy direction that fits comfortably with the particularistic benefits of a patron-client tradition. Initiatives like the border health complex require a longer time horizon and a more complicated mobilization effort—something well beyond the simple deals that come through patron-client networks. The Border Health Complex could serve the multiple aims of central-city revitalization, jobs and services for lower-income people, and a significant link into the postindustrial economy. It could therefore have a broad, diverse, and durable constituency base, but the political mechanism for building it is not in place. Populist politicians can win office, but they lack sustaining power. And such a move is beyond the scope of single-issue organizations such as the Coalition.

For those who look to community organizing as the means to bring about a forward-looking capacity to govern, the experience in El Paso is discouraging. EPISO illustrates the limitations of the community organizing model of political change. Some might point to IAF's tradition of confrontation politics as the stumbling block. However, we see a much bigger problem. It starts with premises about the nature of governing. The IAF model assumes that a governing capacity is in place and that the political task is to put pressure on that established capacity. Accountability sessions are built on that assumption. Confrontation is one tactic for exerting such pressure. Concentrating effort on a few salient issues is another. EPISO has gone from *colonias* to Alliance Schools to Arriba as signature issues, and has had success at the issue level with each. But what is the cumulative effect? In order to be free to take up new issues and keep a fresh supply of activity going, IAF also embraces the notion of no permanent alliances. In the large picture, the tactics are like guerilla tactics—hit and run, embarrass the established order, and seek to destabilize it through exacting a succession of concessions. IAF's approach provides visibility and even attracts resources. It does not, however, yield a share in a permanent capacity to govern. Its narrow and ad hoc approach to issues adds to and therefore does not overcome fragmentation.

There is another deep-running limitation in the community organizing model. Political instruments, whether they be community organizations, political parties, or tight-knit elite circles, all have built-in limitations. None is a neutral instrument that can be applied without consequences. The instrument itself has an impact because political instruments have maintenance needs and their characteristics enter the picture.

Consider closely El Paso's experience with EPISO. Local affiliates of IAF are just that, affiliates of a national organization. These affiliates are creatures of the central organization, and many of the operating rules serve to protect the center. Moving lead organizers around so that their lifeline is the national (or regional) organization is one example. It is not surprising, then, that many of the issues come out of the central organization and its lines of communication. Beyond that, at the local level, decisions seem to stem from the maintenance needs of the organization. For example, as a signature program for EPISO, Arriba became the policy tail that wagged the organization dog. Pragmatic issue-by-issue alliances can stand in the way of a larger vision of what is at stake, as in EPISO's tilt from the populist faction to the developer faction.

Steering clear of broad agendas and aiming for much narrower and therefore more clearly winnable issues means that, even when successful (Arriba is still a viable initiative), the organization has little leverage over the scope of opportunity and quality of life available to local residents. With limited resources, a focus on narrow and winnable issues makes sense—once the organization limits itself by steering clear of long-term alliances. Going it alone inevitably means that the resource base is confined and therefore the vision of what is feasible is also limited.

IAF's rationale is initially to go after small winnable victories in order to build confidence among members and acquire a reputation for political effectiveness. Then bigger issues can be tackled. The logic behind IAF's strategy is sound, but the practical experience in El Paso comes up lacking. For example, as a signature program, Arriba consumes much energy to sustain, and EPISO has yet to put forward a broad conception of what should constitute the governing agenda for El Paso. Pragmatism is no overriding virtue when it serves to limit the vision of what might be. Sustaining the organization is, of course, a reasonable concern, but when the mode of operation does not reach a scale capable of reorienting that often overlooked intermediate level of civic relationships and networks, it is time for rethinking. Creating a sister organization provides a wider base of financial support for the regional and central office. But if both organizations operate with highly limited agendas and leave largely untouched the intermediate level of civic relationships and networks, then they are not in a position to have much leverage over El Paso's future. There is a catch-22 that needs to be overcome. If a big-picture agenda looks unattainable, it lacks appeal. But if a narrow agenda comes across as inconsequential, then it does not matter if it is attainable. Over the long haul, its backers will lack appeal. To matter, winnable issues have to add up to something consequential.

A civic ecology of high fragmentation allows some narrowly defined and limited-vision aims to be pursued effectively, but in El Paso it has not served well the development of a democratically based capacity to define and take on major community problems. The end of rule by a small economic elite was a significant step. However, bringing to a close one order of governing is only a partial step in determining what will come next. Building a new and more inclusive order is the bigger challenge. Like most cities, El Paso has so far failed to pass that test. As presently practiced, community organizing seems unlikely to provide a sufficient capacity to meet that large challenge.

NOTES

1. Oscar Martínez, *Border People: Life and Society in the U.S.-Mexico Borderlands* (Tucson: University of Arizona Press, 1994).
2. Sidney Tarrow, *Power in Movement: Social Movements and Contentious Politics,* 2nd ed. (New York: Cambridge University Press, 1998).
3. G. William Domhoff, *Who Really Rules: New Haven and Community Power Reexamined* (New Brunswick, NJ: Transaction, 1978).
4. Mark Granovetter, "The Strength of Weak Ties," *American Journal of Sociology* 78 (1974): 1360–1380.
5. See Kathleen Staudt, *Violence and Activism at the Border: Gender, Fear and Everyday Life in Cd. Juárez* (Austin: University of Texas Press, forthcoming), chaps. 4–5.
6. Kathleen Staudt and Irasema Coronado, *Fronteras No Más: Toward Social Justice at the U.S.-Mexico Border* (New York: Palgrave USA, 2002), chaps. 2–3.
7. William D'Antonio and William Form, *Influentials in Two Border Cities: A Study in Community Decision Making* (Notre Dame, IN: University of Notre Dame Press, 1965); Mario T. García, *The Making of a Mexican American Mayor: Raymond Telles of El Paso* (El Paso: Texas Western Press, 1998).
8. José Angel Gutiérrez, *The Making of a Chicano Militant: Lessons from Cristal* (Madison: University of Wisconsin Press, 1998).
9. U.S. Commission on Civil Rights, *Mexican American Education Study,* 6 vols. (Washington, DC: U.S. Commission on Civil Rights, 1970–1974); Susan Rippberger and Kathleen Staudt, *Pledging Allegiance: Learning Nationalism in El Paso–Juárez* (New York: Routledge/Falmer, 2003).
10. Kathleen Staudt, *Free Trade? Informal Economies at the U.S.-Mexico Border* (Philadelphia: Temple University Press, 1998), especially chap. 3.
11. Staudt and Coronado, *Fronteras No Más.*
12. Dennis Shirley, *Community Organizing for Urban School Reform* (Austin: University of Texas Press, 1997).
13. Mary Beth Rogers, *Cold Anger: A Story of Faith and Power Politics* (Denton: University of North Texas Press, 1990).
14. Shirley, *Community Organizing for Urban School Reform.*
15. Manuela Romero and Tracey Yellen, *El Paso Portraits: Women's Lives, Potential and Opportunities, A Report on the State of Women in El Paso, Texas* (El Paso: YWCA, 2004), 16.
16. Ibid., 27, on El Paso domestic violence calls; Staudt, *Violence and Activism at the Border,* where her research with a representative sample of women aged fifteen through thirty-nine shows

a 27 percent rate of domestic violence of women with partners (similar to U.S. figures of 1 in 4), but a 70 percent response indicating a distrust of the police (common all over Mexico).

17. Gregory Rocha and Robert Webking, *Politics and Public Education: Edgewood v. Kirby and the Reform of Public School Financing in Texas,* 2nd ed. (Minneapolis, MN: West, 1993); John Sharp, *Bordering the Future: Challenge and Opportunity in the Texas Border Region* (Austin, TX: Comptroller of Public Accounts, 1998).

18. Victor Ortiz-González, *El Paso: Local Frontiers at a Global Crossroads* (Minneapolis: University of Minnesota Press, 2004), especially chap. 4.

19. Kathleen Staudt and Randy Capps, "Con la Ayuda de Dios? El Pasoans Manage the 1996 Welfare and Immigration Law Reforms," in *Immigrants, Welfare Reform, and the Poverty of Policy,* ed. Philip Kretsedemas and Ana Aparicio (Westport, CT: Praeger, 2004), 251–276.

20. Diana Washington Valdez, *Cosecha de Mujeres: Safari en el desierto Mexicano* (Mexico City: Oceana, 2005); Diana Washington Valdez, "Death Stalks the Border" (special two-part insert), *El Paso Times,* June 2002, www.elpasotimes.com; Lourdes Portillo, *Señorita Extraviada,* 2001, www.lourdesportillo.com; Amnesty International, *Intolerable Killing: Ten Years of Abduction and Murders of Women in Ciudad Juárez and Chihuahua City* (Washington, DC: Amnesty International, 2003), www.amnesty.org; Kathleen Staudt and Irasema Coronado, "Binational Civic Action for Accountability: The Murders of Women in Juárez," in *Reforming the Administration of Justice in Mexico,* ed. David Shirk (Notre Dame, IN: Notre Dame University Press, 2006); Staudt, *Violence and Activism at the Cd. Juárez–El Paso Border.*

21. Staudt and Coronado, *Fronteras No Mas.*

22. See www.vday.org.

5. Community Organizing and No Child Left Behind

Dennis Shirley and Michael Evans

One of the core tenets of urban regime theory is that public officials in leadership positions in cities do not have the civic capacity to govern on their own. Rather, as articulated by Clarence Stone, the "theory assumes that the effectiveness of local government depends greatly on the cooperation of nongovernmental actors and on the combination of state capacity with nongovernmental resources." Presiding over a fragmented system of public administration that requires constant negotiation with trade unions, federal and state authorities, and skeptical citizens, individuals such as mayors and school superintendents are compelled to collaborate with a broad range of business, nonprofit, and community stakeholders to stabilize tenuous social systems and achieve even the most modest of positive civic outcomes. Although there are a variety of different regime types—Stone identified three of the most common as corporate, progressive, and caretaker—in all of the types public officials can govern effectively only by carefully building and painstakingly maintaining "civic capacity" among disparate and oftentimes antagonistic groups and institutions.[1]

Urban regime theory is an especially helpful conceptual framework for understanding the multiple dilemmas of urban education in the United States today. From this vantage point, city schools are vulnerable to the whims of a wide variety of influences: single-issue local interest groups that are unschooled in the arts of negotiation, compromise, and mutual accountability; unfunded state and federal mandates that drain precious resources even as they nominally promise valuable goals such as civic participation and school accountability as gauged by pupil learning gains; and incursions of philanthropies and businesses into school systems that are intended to be helpful but betray little understanding of the complexities of urban education and often come with strings attached. Situated in complex, multiracial metropolitan and regional economies, urban schools constitute a network of "high-reverberation" social systems that are inherently tenuous, perpetually underfunded, and subject to a merry-go-round cycle of reforms that enter and exit the schools with little impact on pupils and their communities.[2]

Although urban regime theory does not endorse any special partisan agenda, it does entail several ramifications for the ecology of civic engagement as it pertains to schools, as follows. First, community activists should avoid Marxist or neo-Marxist interpretations about the "hegemony" of urban school systems, because these are not so much "systems" as "loosely coupled" institutions in which local actors, along the model of Lipsky's "street-level bureaucrats," exercise a modicum of discretion over their workplaces. As one kind of "street-level bureaucrats," urban teachers cannot control factors such as building maintenance and technical infra-structure, and so forth, but they can control the pacing of instruction, the degree to which they emphasize or neglect aspects of a given curriculum, and how much and what kind of interaction they will have with parents.[3]

Second, because of this lack of "hegemony" in the Gramscian sense of the term, it makes little sense for community-based organizations to develop an adversarial, protest-oriented approach to urban schools. Few American mayors stake their rep-utations on improving urban schools, and those few that do rarely have been able to point to much progress in pupil achievement. Given the reality of chronically underfunded urban school systems that are desperate for external resources, the issue is not so much to storm the barricades of urban school systems with hosts of new demands—or to place blame on overworked teachers and principals—but rather to build broad-based coalitions of stakeholders that will make education a citywide priority. Protest politics that demonize schools, from this perspective, only exacerbate the welter of conditions that lead to high rates of teacher turnover, failed school bond referenda, and low academic achievement for pupils in the systems.[4]

Stone's original research on Atlanta that articulated urban regime theory pre-ceded the rapid rise of neoliberal strategies that have led to the devolution of tradi-tional state services to nonprofit agencies and businesses in the last fifteen years. This devolution has impacted services from health care to environmental management to education and has led to the emergence of the "caretaker" paradigm as the dom-inant form of urban regime. As Orr's introduction to this volume indicates, a new, more complicated ecology of civic engagement marked by the diffusion and shar-ing of political power has followed the collapse of older ward politics with strong mayoral leadership. This new ecology has been characterized by the emergence of new nomadic business elites that feel little loyalty to a given urban community (given the feasibility, perhaps even the fiscal imperative, of outsourcing jobs); community-based organizations that break with traditional emphases on social protest and polit-ical empowerment and enter directly into service provision (as in the case of the Nehemiah homes run by the East Brooklyn Congregations); and uneven economic growth, with new jobs located primarily in the service sector rather than in manu-facturing (most often with no health care benefits and little job security).

In education, state devolution has taken a myriad of forms—through the exit option of home-schooling, charter schools that hire teachers outside of traditional union arrangements, support for faith-based after-school programs, and the ascendancy of private educational management organizations (EMOs) that take over and run what had been traditional public neighborhood schools in major urban centers such as Baltimore, Philadelphia, and Chicago. Roughly one-quarter of American schoolchildren are now receiving their education through another venue than that of attending their local neighborhood school.[5] Along with the increasing popularity of nontraditional superintendents and school governance models borrowed from the corporate sector, urban public school systems in the 1990s and in the first decade of the twenty-first century in many ways represented a specifically educational variant of neoliberalism in action.

THE NO CHILD LEFT BEHIND ACT

The No Child Left Behind Act (NCLB; P.L. 107-110) of 2002 extended this neoliberal spirit of innovation and reform in many ways. Under NCLB, the parents of children in low-performing schools have the option to remove them from those schools and send them to high-performing schools, including charters (the Republicans tried to include the option of sending the children to private schools, but there was too much opposition from the Democrats to advance this part of the act). Considerable funding was allocated to the providers of "supplementary educational services"—including private, for-profit EMOs—to assist children in failing schools. Combined with some of the legislation of the new Office of Faith-Based and Community Services, NCLB appeared to support the devolution of urban school systems and auxiliary educational services to the private sector and hybrid entities like charter schools that are exempted from teacher union contracts and in many ways freed of the constraints imposed upon traditional public schools.

At the same time that NCLB supported this devolution of urban schooling along the lines of neoliberalism, it also represented an unprecedented seizure of power in the educational arena by the federal government. Unique among Western nations, the United States has no clause in the federal Constitution regarding education, and this role historically has been allocated to states and local school districts. Now, for the first time, the federal government required three bold new reforms that would apply to all states and localities (except for those few outliers that might be willing to forgo needed federal revenues). First, states would be required to conduct regular tests of all public school pupils to track their progress. Second, the federal government put in place sanctions that could lead local public schools to be closed and their pupils dispersed. Third, the federal government encouraged the growth of EMOs and for-profit "supplementary educational services" at the same time that it expanded its surveillance of virtually all public school systems across the country.

It was an audacious undertaking and one that expressed the deep sense of frustration among legislators at the slow pace of educational change at the local and state levels. Especially for Republican Party leaders, stalled reforms indicated that their earlier efforts to improve American schools inaugurated under the Reagan administration had not garnered the desired results. In his first term in office, President Reagan had convened the National Commission on Excellence in Education, chaired by David Gardner, president of the University of Utah, to conduct a thorough study of American education. Entitled *A Nation at Risk: The Imperative for Educational Reform* and published in 1983, the report used dramatic language to alert the public to the problems in our educational system:

> Our Nation is at risk. Our once unchallenged preeminence in commerce, industry, science, and technological innovation is being overtaken by competitors throughout the world. This report is concerned with only one of the many causes and dimensions of the problem, but it is the one that undergirds American prosperity, security, and civility. We report to the American people that while we can take justifiable pride in what our schools and colleges have historically accomplished and contributed to the United States and the well-being of its people, the educational foundations of our society are presently being eroded by a rising tide of mediocrity that threatens our very future as a Nation and a people. What was unimaginable a generation ago has begun to occur—others are matching and surpassing our educational attainments.
>
> If an unfriendly foreign power had attempted to impose on America the mediocre educational performance that exists today, we might well have viewed it as an act of war. As it stands, we have allowed this to happen to ourselves. . . . We have, in effect, been committing an act of unthinking, unilateral disarmament.[6]

Critics faulted the report for overstating the nature and scope of the problem, and the military metaphors were seen by many as an inappropriate reference to Reagan's efforts to garner congressional support for his "strategic defense initiative" to provide a shield to protect the United States in the event of a nuclear attack by the Soviet Union. Lacking scholarly citations and carefully formulated to grab headlines, the report was subsequently subjected to a devastating critique by educational researchers David Berliner and Bruce Biddle. Emphasizing that the greater social stratification in the United States than in other industrialized nations explained the variation in academic achievement, they recommended a more ambitious effort to fortify the welfare state and strengthen local communities as promising strategies to improve pupil learning.[7]

Yet even the severest critics of *A Nation at Risk* tended to agree with the authors that Americans needed to acknowledge the emergence of a new, post-Fordist international knowledge economy that would create new markets and destroy old ones in the years to come. As the report observed,

Knowledge, learning, information, and skilled intelligence are the new raw materials of international commerce and are today spreading throughout the world as vigorously as miracle drugs, synthetic fertilizers, and blue jeans did earlier. If only to keep and improve on the slim competitive edge we still retain in world markets, we must dedicate ourselves to the reform of our educational system for the benefit of all—old and young alike, affluent and poor, majority and minority. Learning is the indispensable investment required for success in the "information age" we are entering.[8]

The authors of the report could hardly have imagined the manner in which fax machines, cell phones, the Internet, and lowered transportation costs would "flatten" the world and dramatically increase the speed and scope of communication, global financial transactions, and population mobility in the next two decades. Nonetheless, they accurately apprehended that momentous changes were under way—and that those without the human capital to compete in newly emerging global markets would suffer severely in the coming economic dislocations.[9]

In retrospect, it is now clear that A Nation at Risk was the beginning of what would be a complete transformation in the politics of the Republican Party in regard to education. Republican party platforms traditionally had advocated the abolition of the U.S. Department of Education, but now a growing segment of Republican leaders came over time to embrace the message of A Nation at Risk that the nation's economic prosperity and national security were inextricably connected with an effective system of education. Following the issuance of the report, a new bipartisan coalition of reform-minded legislators and educational policy advocates began developing political power and experimenting with marketplace models of reform and statewide standardized tests to raise pupil achievement. Combined with the openness of centrist and conservative Democrats to public-private ventures and the exasperation of liberal Democrats stymied by the persistently low academic performance of the poor and children of color, educational reformers in the Republican Party who wanted to pursue bolder strategies than simply additional funding for traditional schools saw—and were to capitalize upon—a policy that blended strong federal leadership with local devolution and experimentation. Pleased by the growing recognition of the importance of a federal role in the educational sector by Republicans, Democrats joined forces with them to support new legislation when the Elementary and Secondary Education Act was up for renewal after the election of President George W. Bush in 2000.

Supporters of NCLB—and it is important to remember that NCLB was initially supported by a broad bipartisan coalition—argued that the act presented a hitherto unprecedented historic possibility to marshal resources to reduce the academic achievement gap between white children on the one hand and black and Hispanic children on the other. They also argued that the nation needed to launch a direct attack on the tenacious problem of so many uncertified teachers instructing children of color in urban districts, and they viewed NCLB as real progress because it re-quired local districts to inform parents about the credentials of their children's teach-ers. NCLB advocates contended that the traditional urban public school systems had failed egregiously—and virtually no one argued that the standardized test data were not discouraging—and that in a fast-paced information age much was to be gained by making the education of all pupils a federal priority. Supporters claimed that the achievement gap between the test score results of white students and those of stu-dents of color had to be confronted by the nation and used to create a new civil rights movement focused on academic achievement. Advocates noted that, follow-ing the model used in Texas previously, NCLB requires subgroup assessments of English-language learners, students with disabilities, economically disadvantaged youth, and breakouts by race and ethnicity; it is not possible to conceal achievement gaps within aggregate totals of a school or district. Small wonder that for some champions of equity NCLB represented a historic turning point and the most prom-ising legislation in a generation for improving urban education.

With passage of NCLB into law, Congress and then President Bush changed the political opportunity structure in the nation's educational system. Since the local school districts and the states had not pushed through devolution, now the federal government would do it. Since many local school districts and the states had not put in place rigorous accountability provisions with real sanctions for low-performing schools, now the federal government would do it. Power shifted, one could say, in two directions simultaneously—toward market-based alternatives at the local level, and toward the surveillance capabilities of the U.S. Department of Education at the national level.

Who lost power in this reorganization of American education? Traditional urban public school systems, under attack for low pupil test scores and besieged with endemic infrastructural problems, appeared to be the primary losers. To address the new political opportunity structure, and to maintain as many of their traditional prerogatives as possible, they began devolving the authority to run their most troubled schools to new EMOs and providers of supplementary educational services. State departments of education also lost power; they would now either have to cut some services to allocate additional staff to design, administer, and report test data to the federal government, or seek new tax revenues to expand their staff to address the new mandates. Schools of education in colleges and universities, traditionally the supplier of the majority of the nation's teachers, also lost power, as NCLB provided clauses that supported "alternative routes"—often district-based or run by start-up nonprofits—into teaching. One could argue that local citizens and teachers also lost power, as local control, already shifting to the states over many decades, appeared further diminished with the rise of the new federally mandated accountability systems.

The new shift of power in the direction of the federal government, on the one hand, and nontraditional private or public-private ventures, on the other, represented a political structure with multiple new opportunities for educators—if they could find ways to capitalize on them. Power in the form of increased legitimacy in the eyes of policymakers and the public would be garnered by those schools and school systems that raised pupil achievement as measured on standardized tests. Entrepreneurial educators affiliated with EMOs had unprecedented opportunities to develop pilot schools and to demonstrate that they could outperform traditional public schools. Providers of supplementary educational services had new revenues with which to fund after-school and weekend programs to improve pupil achievement. The hope of policymakers was that this injection of a competitive, marketplace spirit into the educational field would catalyze change in moribund school systems and that low-income pupils of color would be the principal beneficiaries.

It took local and state legislators and school personnel considerable time to recognize the full import of this new political opportunity structure. The initial passage of NCLB, after all, resulted from a broad bipartisan effort. But two years after the passage of the act, a small group of dissidents had evolved into a full-fledged revolt. By March 2004, twenty-one states had proposed or passed measures to seek changes in NCLB or to exempt themselves from the act in its entirety. By April 2004, twenty-seven states had produced resolutions or bills calling for studies of the costs of NCLB, for full funding of its provisions by Congress and the president, or for opting out of its stipulations altogether. Maine and Utah passed bills prohibiting the use of state funds to comply with NCLB; the Virginia legislature voted ninety-eight to one for a resolution objecting to many parts of NCLB; and the Oklahoma House of Representatives voted unanimously for a resolution calling for the repeal of NCLB. At the time of this writing (March 2006), only three states have not sought waivers for provisions of NCLB or in other ways pushed back against the many mandates (most unfunded) that the act imposes on their schools.[10]

If a groundswell of opposition to NCLB could be documented, so could widespread confusion or indifference. One survey of twenty-six community organizers revealed that "with few exceptions" organizers "did not see NCLB as driving their local education organizing agenda or constraining the local political context for their work."[11] In this they appear to be similar to the American public at large, for whom NCLB has not been a priority; in one Gallup poll, 68 percent of respondents said they "knew little or nothing of NCLB."[12] The same kind of uncertainty, accompanied by some skepticism, was evident at a symposium for more than sixty educational organizers the authors convened along with Chris Brown, Eva Gold, Elaine Simon, and Mark Warren at the Harvard Graduate School of Education in February 2004. Community organizers are working on a number of complicated educational initiatives at the local level, following classical organizing approaches such as "one-on-ones," house meetings, research actions, neighborhood walks, cam-paigns, and accountability sessions. Many organizers are aware of NCLB, but in general they are withholding judgment until its ramifications for local organizing become clearer.

Part of the challenge of understanding NCLB concerns its many different sec-tions and ambiguities in key terms. The act itself is more than a thousand pages long, and even an abbreviated "Desktop Reference" version raises as many new questions as it answers.[13] "Teacher quality," for example, is a core concern of NCLB, but states are free to define teacher quality in different ways, so that comparisons between states are difficult, if not impossible. NCLB requires all schools to be able to demonstrate "adequate yearly progress" by reducing the number of students below proficient in each ethnic group by 10 percent from the previous year—but federal guidelines defining proficiency differ markedly from those of most states, with the result that in 2004 some 317 schools in California "showed tremendous academic growth on the state's performance index, yet the federal law labeled them as low-performing."[14] This is especially significant for educators because the over-all goal of NCLB is to have all of American public school students proficient as measured on reading and math tests by the year 2014, twelve years after the enact-ment of the law—yet "proficiency" inevitably comes down to a best guess on where a "cut score" on tests should be set.[15] For educators working in gateway communi-ties with high numbers of immigrant children—and there are thousands of these scattered through the cities of the United States—one may well wonder how one should go about raising the test scores of second-language learners year after year when so many children arrive in their schools lacking the most rudimentary knowl-edge of English.

Of separate concern are Sections 1111, 1114, and 1118 of NCLB, which initially appeared to support parent involvement in education. On close scrutiny, however, one learns that beyond an unfunded mandate that districts must create parent advi-sory councils to promote parent involvement, the involvement primarily consists in giving parents in underperforming schools options to select supplementary edu-cational services from outside of the public school system and in choosing char-ters or private schools as options for their children. For community organizers who are interested in improving conditions for *all* residents of a vicinity, NCLB appears to offer exit options for only a few parents rather than a strategy for uplifting *all* schools.

Yet NCLB presents daunting challenges for the public at large not only because of ambiguities in its language. At its core, it represents a fundamentally new theory of educational improvement—one that was first explored at the state level through "accountability systems" implemented as part of the "southern strategy" of both Republican and Democratic governors such as Mark White of Texas, Lamar Alexander of Tennessee, Bill Riley of South Carolina, and Bill Clinton of Arkansas in the 1980s and 1990s. Advocates of this approach contend that regular testing of pupils can provide valuable data about student academic achievement and teacher quality, and that in an era in which the human capital of states is increasingly important, citizens have the right to know just how well pupils are doing academically. Conservative advocates of testing have won allies on the liberal side of the political spectrum through two strategies. First, they have promised additional financial resources, especially for Title I (low-income) pupils in public school systems; second, by placing a spotlight on disparities between pupils of color and white students, they have insisted that the "achievement gap" between subgroups must be addressed as a matter of social justice.[16]

To understand just how broad and deep NCLB is as a school improvement act, one must grasp that it appropriated and then expanded and transformed the "southern strategy" in two ways. First, it "federalized" the accountability systems, requiring all states to develop processes for measuring pupil achievement and for reporting student data to the U.S. Department of Education. Second, NCLB brought market-based strategies much more radically into the educational arena than most state policies had done hitherto, with explicit references to exiting the public educational system in the case of underperforming schools. The language of management and markets is present throughout NCLB and its accompanying Department of Education materials. "The point of state assessments is to measure student learning," states the U.S. Department of Education in *No Child Left Behind: A Parent's Guide*. "A key principle of quality management is the importance of measuring what is valued (e.g., production rates; costs of materials, etc.)."[17]

The unclear facets of NCLB, combined with a new federally mandated, market-driven accountability system, have prompted some angry criticisms of the entire legislative package, especially by liberal advocates who felt betrayed when Title I funding was cut dramatically at a time of economic recession but the many sanctions of the accountability system remained in place.[18] Further, the public at large disagrees with many key elements of NCLB. For example, more than two-thirds of adults surveyed by the Gallup poll contended that "the performance of a school's students on a single test is not sufficient for judging whether the school is in need of improvement"; a majority of Americans would rather see more funding for struggling schools than see tax resources dedicated to outside agencies such as the "supplemental educational services"; and 81 percent worry that "basing decisions about schools on students' performance in English and math only will mean less emphasis on art, music, history, and other subjects."[19]

Yet advocates of NCLB have not been deterred from pressing their case and ensuring that the many statutes of the legislation are enforced. Supporters of NCLB view the criticisms and hesitations of citizens, such as those expressed here, as indicative of the typical problems to be expected with introducing any major new social policy and have rallied African American and Hispanic school leaders to stay the course.[20] Clearly, a more detailed investigation of this complicated and highly contested topic is necessary.

To examine the impact of NCLB more closely at the grassroots level, we now turn to three community-based organizations (CBOs), which can provide some insight into the manner in which NCLB is slowly but decisively shaping educational policies in the United States today. Those descriptions are followed by an analysis of the complex ecological interface between NCLB and organizing, considering in particular the overall political framing and import of NCLB. We will contend that the act is a complicated piece of legislation that appears to contradict teachers' sense of best practices and endorses measures with which the public at large disagrees. Ill-advised legislation is nothing new for community organizations, however, and there are some political opportunities for community organizations in NCLB, if they are able to capitalize upon them.

ACORN AND NCLB

The Association of Communities Organized for Reform Now (ACORN) has developed a differentiated response to NCLB. Before the passage of NCLB, parents in Chicago working with ACORN had observed high attrition rates of beginning teachers in the city. ACORN conducted research that revealed that 22.9 percent of Chicago teachers left the classroom after just one year, surpassing the 15.1 percent for public schools nationwide by a wide margin (although not for urban public schools, estimated at 20 percent).[21] In addition, Chicago ACORN studied educational research that indicates that teacher qualification variables are the strong predictors of student achievement after controlling for socioeconomic status.[22] Given this body of information—supplemented by the large numbers of educators teaching in fields in which they lack proper academic credentials—ACORN launched a campaign to try to stabilize the teaching force in Chicago and to recruit teachers into the schools who would stay in the profession and teach in areas for which they are certified. ACORN organizers thus welcomed NCLB's emphasis on teacher quality, which they viewed as a "handle" for improving instruction in the city's schools. "We had already read the research correlating teacher quality with full certification," ACORN organizer Madeline Talbott said, "and we were raising hell about the number of teachers in Chicago who didn't meet that definition. And the district was already responding to that, but then when NCLB came along, they knew that they *really* had to respond it."[23]

In this case, Section 1119 of NCLB, which pertains to teacher quality, served as a top-down mechanism of support for the grassroots organizing conducted by ACORN. It is important to note in this regard that ACORN did not appropriate uncritically NCLB's definition of teacher quality—which provides considerable flexibility to the states but is largely based on "full certification, a bachelor's degree and demonstrated competence in subject knowledge and teaching."[24] "We're expanding the definition of highly qualified teachers to include community perspectives," Talbott explained. "We want people who come from our communities, who see the potential in the kids, and who aren't afraid to hold them to high standards. And we want people who will stay! It doesn't matter if they're certified or not—if they don't stay, they're not highly qualified for us."

Chicago ACORN found that local organizing could coordinate with federal policy to support teacher quality. At a national level, however, ACORN was sharply critical of the administration of the new law, issuing a report less than a year after the bill's passage entitled *Parents Left Behind: A Study of State, Federal, and School District Implementation of No Child Left Behind*. "The implementation of NCLB gets a grade of D," the report stated, and continued, "The work so far is at an F level in general, but states and districts are still promising to turn in their homework."[25]

What was wrong with NCLB, according to ACORN? The CBO charged that "state and federal governments are not providing adequate assistance, guidance, and oversight to local school districts in implementing the provisions of No Child Left Behind. Children, primarily low income and minority children, are therefore suffering by not getting the kind of education they deserve." From this vantage point, many parts of the original legislation of NCLB represented genuine progress. "There are a number of promises in NCLB that are what we want—and anytime these promises are made by the government, we have new opportunities to re-ignite our communities," ACORN campaign director Amy Schur explained. "NCLB has sections in it about teacher mentoring, student assessment, and teacher quality that we like and that provide information about schools that our parents have never been able to get before." The problem was not the original language or intention of these sections of NCLB, but the manner in which billions of dollars of promised Title I funding were cut and other provisions of NCLB were implemented in a slipshod fashion. For example, Section 1116, which provides for-profit businesses with tax revenues to provide "supplemental educational services," has not been monitored, according to Schur, with the result that public schools are subject to close surveillance and potential closure due to lack of student achievement, but private businesses receive no such oversight.

According to ACORN organizers, the punitive portions of NCLB, which threaten to close underperforming schools and implicitly encourage experimentation in the private sector, have been well understood by urban school systems. In the

summer of 2004, the Chicago public schools, following the example of Philadelphia in the 1990s, announced plans to close 100 low-achieving schools and to turn
two-thirds of them over to EMOs. According to Talbott, ACORN views the privatization as a consequence of the school choice provisions of NCLB. Since ACORN
is committed to supporting a strong public school sector, it is now at odds with the
district on choice, even as it supports other progress on teacher quality.

ACORN is a community organization that is engaged in a process of selective
and constructive engagement with NCLB, using segments of the law to advance the
interests of ACORN constituents while at the same time working to make sure that
the act is focused on poor and working-class communities rather than mandates
that may have little relevance to urban and poor youth. ACORN has mounted a
campaign called "Invest in Schools, Invest in Kids," which not only demands full
funding of the sections of NCLB but also seeks to "refocus its attention on our kids,
our schools, and our communities." The campaign has sponsored events in more
than thirty cities and protested the May 2004 congressional vote to support a
budget resolution that would limit funding available in future years to a broad
range of domestic programs, including education. In addition, ACORN has linked
up with the NAACP Voter Fund, MoveOn.org, the National Education Association,
and the U.S. Hispanic Institute to mobilize for the restoration of $27 billion of
NCLB funding, as part of a Web-based campaign linked with house meetings and
regional actions.

PACT AND NCLB

For Aaron Dorfman, lead organizer and executive director of People Acting for
Community Together (PACT) in Miami, much of the debate about NCLB has had
little impact on schools in terms of their daily interactions with the community.
"Federal policy hasn't been a major factor in how we organize our work at the local
level," he observed, "but NCLB seems good to us because of the continued support
for standards. Our belief is that standards have been good for low-income kids
because it used to be that you could ignore your lowest achievers, and it's not set
up that way anymore."

Unlike other organizing networks, PACT explored the route of specific pedagogical and curricular interventions in Dade County schools. In 1994 PACT organized hundreds of "one-on-one" visits with parishioners from its member
congregations and found that its members were especially worried that their children in the public schools were not learning to read. Conducting follow-up
research, PACT found that direct instruction (DI), a heavily phonics-based
approach to reading, appeared to have an excellent track record in causing large

gains in student achievement. PACT subsequently organized a campaign to acquire funding and consent from the Miami–Dade County School Board to support DI in five pilot schools; that funding was authorized in 1996, and the number of schools using DI expanded to a cluster of twenty-six by the summer of 2004.

DI is controversial in educational research circles because many experts in literacy view it as an anti-intellectual strategy that requires teachers and students to follow a precise script, ignores differences among individual children, and is necessarily stilted in the dynamic setting of the classroom.[26] Nonetheless, other research does support DI, as long as it is not applied dogmatically and teachers use their professional judgment to make modifications and adapt strategies from a broad repertoire of approaches to teaching reading.[27] Recognizing the intensity of the debate about DI as an instructional method, PACT stipulated that a minimum of 80 percent of the teachers in any given school had to vote to adopt DI for the school to receive the special funding for curricular support and professional development it entailed.

In addition to its advocacy for the use of DI in schools, PACT established a program called PALS, for PACT Academically Linking with Schools, that linked a PACT leader from a member congregation with each of the twenty-six schools for purposes of coordinating site visits and rectifying problems in communication. "We were in those schools with our parents and congregation members a lot," Dorfman commented, "and we were continually hearing from teachers who said that 'All of my kids are reading, and I've never had that before.' "

Florida schools are graded by the state department of education, and Dorfman was pleased to observe that as an aggregate, the twenty-six schools were moving in the right direction, with some of the schools with the strongest collaborations with PACT registering the greatest gains. "We're not sure what led to the gains," he conceded, "but I expect it was a mixture of talented principals and teachers, DI, and the presence of PACT in the schools." In any event, he saw no problems with NCLB or with the larger accountability movement. "We're finding some handles with it," he said. "We think the overall approach has been good for the kids."

The generally positive evolution of the PALS schools with DI experienced an abrupt shift with the arrival of former New York City superintendent Rudy Crew as the new superintendent of Miami–Dade County on July 1, 2004. Crew was especially concerned about the lowest-achieving schools in the district, which he organized into a "School Improvement Zone" of schools that he targeted for improved curricula and enhanced professional development. Noting the high level of student mobility, Crew decided that all the schools in the zone needed to share a common literacy curriculum, arguing that this was particularly important because of the high-stakes literacy test required of all third graders for academic promotion in Florida. A committee of district staff, representatives from United Teachers of Dade, and literacy experts then selected a reading and writing program designed by Houghton Mifflin, one of four reading series approved by the Florida Department of Education. Crew then mandated the reading series for all elementary schools in Miami–Dade County. In taking this action, Crew received strong support from the school board as well as teachers' unions. They appreciated his leadership in raising teacher salaries early in his tenure and the professional development support that he provided teachers along with the new Houghton Mifflin literacy series.

PACT has not viewed this change of curriculum as fatal for its partnerships with schools, although its leaders do consider it a disservice to the children. Understanding the need for perpetual reorganizing in situations of dynamic turbulence like those of urban school systems, PACT has since changed its focus to support high-quality induction programs in the schools in a manner that shares some similarities with Chicago's ACORN. In addition to the twenty-six schools in Miami–Dade County with which it continues to partner, PACT engages in legislative campaigns related to education in Florida along with nine other organizations in the Direct Action and Training Network (DART). Together, the ten organizations make up the Federation of DART Organizations in Florida (FDOF), which advocates funding for universal pre-kindergarten offerings in Florida. Although there is some funding for prekindergarten in NCLB—primarily through the Early Reading First and William F. Goodling Even Start Family Literacy programs—it is not a major emphasis, and the campaign is not linked in any overt way with NCLB. Hence, as with DI, PACT pursues what it considers to be sound educational policies with little reference to NCLB, although the overall emphasis on academic achievement is viewed favorably.

THE TEXAS IAF

The Texas Industrial Areas Foundation (IAF) has developed a critical stance toward the kind of testing and assessment systems promoted by NCLB. In the 1990s, when one of us (Shirley) lived in Houston and conducted research on the Texas IAF's Alliance Schools, it was relatively common for the Texas IAF to convene parent academies that informed parents about the nature of the tests and why they were important in gauging their children's academic progress. At Zavala Elementary School—in many ways, the poster child of the Alliance Schools in the 1990s—the drive to improve the school began when an angry father noticed the discrepancy between his child's excellent grades and her poor results on the Texas Assessment of Academic Skills (TAAS).[28] Texas IAF organizers never endorsed the test as such, but they considered it to be a legitimate assessment tool, even if their own goals for higher level critical thinking went far beyond the minimum skills gauged by the TAAS.

Much has changed in the intervening years, however, in terms of how Texas IAF organizers now view the accountability systems. "The turning point for many of us came in February 2003 at our annual Alliance School conference," Sister Mignonne Konecny, lead organizer for Austin Interfaith, recalled. "That was when so many of our teachers and principals said that they were now getting lesson plans from their districts dictating what they should teach, that they were getting flooded with practice tests and benchmark tests to be given every Friday, and we were really getting the message that the tests had become punitive rather than diagnostic." Organizers and leaders now find that the tests drive so many educational practices in Texas that any kind of reflection, analysis, or skill acquisition not measured on the tests is marginalized in the curriculum. "For all intents and purposes, the tests now are the curriculum in Texas," Joe Higgs, an organizer in the Houston area, commented. "Districts are saying more and more that the test is going to be all that we teach, no matter what the cost."

According to Texas IAF organizers, a host of unethical practices are implemented in schools in which teachers and principals are pressed to raise test scores or face a range of punitive actions such as losing their principals or potential state takeovers. Rene Wizig-Barrios, an organizer with The Metropolitan Organization (TMO) in Houston, described a series of incidents that depict how extreme the new accountability measures have become:

> One of our principals was told by her district to make sure that homeless kids in a shelter shouldn't show up on testing day because they would depress the scores. Other principals have abolished free time for kids in first, second, and third grade. Principals tell us that they want to meet with us and work with us but that they're so much under the gun to raise test scores that they just can't make the time. And now we have this new law in Texas which says that if kids don't pass the TAKS [Texas Assessment of Knowledge and Skills] reading test in third grade they can be held back. That kind of pressure seems to us to be way too great to put on kids who are that little, and it's a major source of fear and stress for the teachers.

Wizig-Barrios concedes that she does not know how much of these kinds of actions were caused directly by NCLB. "It's hard to tell what comes from the principal, the district, the state, or NCLB," she said. It is striking to note that the more extreme Texas interventions—such as not allowing third graders to go on to fourth grade unless they pass the TAKS—go far beyond anything specified by NCLB. "Part of the pressure comes from NCLB, part of it comes from the state of Texas trying to meet the standards, part of it is the district, and part of it is from the schools, where people are scared out of their minds," Konecny commented.

In the climate of fear described by Texas IAF organizers, teachers stop collaborative work and adopt an "every man for himself" approach to raising their test scores. In this Kafkaesque world, seventh-grade teachers find that their pupils have not studied writing since the fourth grade, because that is the last grade at which writing was assessed by the TAKS. Fifth-grade teachers discover that their pupils have never had science or social studies because these subjects were never assessed before the fifth grade—all the emphasis was put on reading, writing, and mathematics, to get the annual TAKS scores up. "So all of a sudden the fifth graders are getting social studies and science crammed down their throats, since that is what is tested that year," Konecny observed.

Ironically, the intense pressure put on principals to raise test scores appears to contribute to a rapid turnover of school leaders, either because principals leave troubled schools as soon as they can or because districts are continually in search of new principals who they think can raise scores. Principals in many cities in Texas are now hired on one-year contracts; if their school's test scores are low, they are fired, and if the scores are high, they receive generous bonuses. As a result, principals have very real financial incentives to press their teachers to produce high test score results on the TAKS, even when such one-sided emphasis on cognition might undermine the social, physical, and ethical development of children.

In this kind of context, it is difficult to sustain community organizing to improve both a school and its immediate environment. "People are so anxious about testing that they try to do everything at once," Kevin Courtney, lead organizer with the El Paso Interreligious Sponsoring Organization (EPISO), said. "We have testing going on this week in one of our schools that had forty-eight kids in a classroom for the first seven weeks of the school year; there was barely enough space for the kids to even sit on the floor. They finally got them in another class, and now they're testing them for two straight days. It's a disaster, and it isn't just in our Alliance Schools; the paper is filled with letters to the editor from angry teachers every week."

Unlike ACORN and PACT, the Texas IAF evinces no enthusiasm for NCLB. While there is a sense that there is some value in disaggregating pupil test scores by race, ethnicity, and Title I pupils, Texas IAF organizers expressed no interest in the kind of national campaign for full funding of NCLB endorsed by ACORN. "There are some big businesses that are racking up on this thing, and making billions of dollars," Konecny said. "If they took all of that money that was put into the testing regime to free up teachers to create their own assessment models, we'd be a whole lot better off."

DISCUSSION

This brief review of three community organizations' relationships with NCLB indicates a range of responses of intermediary institutions' interpretations of this landmark piece of federal legislation. ACORN found parts of NCLB regarding teacher quality helpful for its campaign to improve teaching in Chicago and is organizing for full funding, especially of Title I. PACT is supportive of high standards for all children and believes that its endorsement of DI is creating a constituency of teachers and parents who are advancing pupil learning in measurable ways. The Texas IAF contends that NCLB is supporting a draconian culture of reprisals against struggling and underfunded schools, as well as promoting bad pedagogy for children. The Texas IAF decries the overall accountability juggernaut and pedagogical practices such as ending free time for early childhood pupils and retaining third graders who cannot pass the TAKS test, viewing such change strategies as driven more by conservative ideology than by educational research or teachers' convictions about best educational practices.

Given such heterogeneity of positions, any attempt to neatly summarize the relationship between education organizing and NCLB is out of the question. Although they employ many similar organizing strategies, these community organizations have developed independent interpretations based on their street-level conversations with their local leaders that have led them to create distinctive agendas. These agendas appear in part to be not only mutually incompatible but also in conflict with one another.

The tensions between the groups appear most clearly in the case of the IAF and PACT. For the IAF, the emphasis on accountability in schools has gotten out of control, and schools have been transformed from community sites with potentially democratic practices into extensions of a vast bureaucratic apparatus that values rising test scores above all else. The stance is not antitesting, but it is critical of the idea that departments of education—whether in state capitals or in Washington, D.C., really have sufficient information about the quality of learning in a school to render authoritative judgments based on pupil test scores. In this interpretation, teachers especially need to win back some professional autonomy so that they can have critical conversations with parents, with their colleagues, and with their pupils about instructional strategies, curricular choices, and exhibitions of pupil learning. The key vision of the teacher here is that of the teacher as a democratic public intellectual, with considerable discretion over materials, informed by mindful deliberation with parents and other community stakeholders. Accountability matters, from this point of view, but accountability indicators should be shaped by the teachers, pupils, and community members who stand to gain or lose the most in the process of educational change.

PACT cares about intellectual freedom, too—but PACT organizers report that this is simply not the primary concern among their teachers or other educational leaders. Rather, from the lens of PACT, teachers want good tools that will lead to solid educational results for their pupils. In this scenario, professional autonomy for teachers is secondary to a carefully scripted instructional approach that provides teachers with step-by-step procedures to use in teaching reading at the elementary level. Teachers in PACT-affiliated schools wanted Direct Instruction, PACT organizers argue, and PACT worked with legislators and educators to make sure that they got it until a new superintendent mandated a new instructional approach. With test scores moving in the right direction, PACT members were persuaded that the organization's school collaborations were working. Nonetheless, PACT has had to learn the painful lesson of many urban educators, for even when test scores appear to be positive, a shift in leadership at the level of a superintendent can lead to curricular changes mandated from above. PACT's inability to defend the continuity of DI in its PALS schools reflects the apparent weakness of CBOs once they move beyond the mobilization of civic capacity and become directly involved in the implementation of specific educational strategies.

ACORN is the only community organization that has incorporated into its repertoire of responses a national campaign to "invest in kids, invest in schools" that called for full funding of NCLB and for a refocusing of NCLB on the very messy and complicated on-the-ground realities of public schools. This national campaign is important because CBOs really cannot impact federal legislation at a purely local or even a statewide level. In addition, ACORN's strategic choice to link its sixty city organizations into a coalition with MoveOn.org, the NAACP Voter Fund, the National Education Association, and the U.S. Hispanic Institute in the fall of 2004 for nationwide house meetings to restore $27 billion of NCLB funding represented an innovative appropriation of the house meeting structure deployed by the Howard Dean campaign and extended by MoveOn.org during the 2004 presidential campaign. ACORN's coalition with the other national organizations represents a new strategic capacity to take its campaigns to the national level—the most appropriate level for engaging and redirecting federal legislation such as NCLB.

These different interpretations of educational change advanced by ACORN, PACT, and the Texas IAF matter tremendously for the internal life of schools and pupil learning. From the vantage point of ACORN and PACT, top-down federal policies can indeed support local learning in schools and communities, although CBOs must show considerable flexibility and a significant local power base to meet with their constituents to hammer out new policies and initiatives that capitalize on the opportunities in NCLB. For the Texas IAF, however, the entire emphasis on accountability has gone too far and is having detrimental effects on school climate and pupil learning. By demanding "adequate yearly progress" as defined primarily by tests scores, from this point of view, the federal government has undermined the democratic potential of local public schools and is promoting reform based on compliance with mandates that often go against educators' best judgments.

Insofar as the IAF protests test-driven reforms that are imposed upon teachers regardless of teachers' sense of best practices, the IAF may be helping to create activity settings in schools in which teachers can engage in meaningful dialogue with one another about best practices, develop collaborative activities that respond to the needs of their pupils and their pupils' communities, and, in a very different way, develop the educational capacities of schools as learning organizations. As Fisher and Shragge have noted elsewhere in this volume, part of the repertoire of community organizations should include direct action and social protest. If there is no space for teachers to protest practices which they consider to be inimical to pupil learning, teachers will perform rituals of "contrived collegiality" in which they give lip service to different reform models while continuing quietly with their own understanding of best educational practices.[29] Simply increasing the "classroom press" on teachers rarely is successful, because test-driven strategies tend to focus teachers on short-term rather than long-term goals, isolate them from other adults, limit their opportunities for reflecting on their practice, and deplete their energy.[30] If reformers do not invest the necessary time and effort to develop conjoint activities with educators who do the real face-to-face instruction with pupils, they will tend to find that the best teachers will either exit the system or engage in quiet efforts to undermine the reforms through passive resistance and general noncompliance.[31]

These considerations are particularly important because a large percentage of teachers disagree with many of the provisions of NCLB, particularly concerning the measurement of "adequate yearly progress." In one recent major survey of teachers, four out of ten teachers indicated that their school could raise test scores without improving pupil learning; nine of ten teachers disagreed that test scores were an accurate reflection of what their pupils who learned English as a second language knew; and a substantial majority of teachers reported that their state's accountability system led them to teach in ways that went against their personal convictions regarding best instructional practices.[32] If Richard Ingersoll's findings are accurate that on the aggregate "the good school is characterized by high levels of teacher control," the Texas IAF's struggle to create educational activity settings in which teachers can follow their consciences and do the best teaching they can appears to be of critical importance for improving education in the state.[33]

Like PACT and the Texas IAF, ACORN has developed a repertoire of strategies that mobilize its community base and create a climate of creative dialogue with public school officials. Although ACORN still uses a variety of direct action tactics and readily deploys confrontational strategies against public officials and businesses when warranted, these more adversarial politics do not seem to characterize most of their work in school reform. Chicago ACORN has collaborated with the public schools to raise awareness of teacher quality problems and to develop "grow your own" teacher preparation programs that train indigenous community residents to become teachers. New York ACORN has started "small schools" that emphasize leadership training and civic engagement. National ACORN is waging a campaign for full funding of NCLB, emphasizing the importance of compliance with the act rather than a protest against it. Through all these cases, ACORN documents the chronic underfunding of urban schools, develops "relational capital" with district, state, and national policymakers, and fights to gain whatever leverage—be it in the form of certified teachers, Title I funding, or effective strategies to retain highly qualified teachers—that can be used to improve city schools.

ACORN, PACT, and the Texas IAF offer three different models of community organizing for school reform in the era of NCLB. The three CBOs demonstrate just how heterogeneous intermediary institutions can be and just how complicated the ecology of civic engagement is in the educational arena in the era of NCLB. There is little evidence of collaboration between the groups, even when they operate in the same cities and represent the same constituencies (especially since ACORN recruits individual members, and both the Texas IAF and DART, the national group with which PACT is affiliated, are congregationally based). Nonetheless, both the Texas IAF and ACORN serve on the Partnerships for Change Planning Commit-tee of the Center for Community Change (CCC). It may be that independent groups such as the CCC that provide technical assistance to CBOs—but are not CBOs themselves—can help to broker broader networks or at least strategic part-nerships that will develop civic capacity in the educational arena.

Such collaborative ventures are critical to help local, grassroots groups over-come competitive relationships (which is difficult, since they often rely on the same philanthropies for supplements to their institutional or individual membership dues) and to develop the kinds of political power that could have an impact at the national level. It would be appropriate—indeed, highly desirable—for the CBOs to interrogate the very concept of "leaving no child behind" in our current social and economic context. The rhetoric appears to suggest that education is a panacea that, if applied, will assure children of integration into the American mainstream, with plentiful opportunities and jobs that pay a living wage. In this connotation, Americans continue a long tradition of social theorizing that places a dispropor-tionate burden on schools for rectifying social inequalities. This strategy has not worked well in the past, and there is no evidence that it will succeed in the current context.

To be "left behind" in the United States today means not only lacking an edu-cation but also being mired in poverty. If one seeks to "leave no child behind" in terms of an antipoverty strategy, one would have to come up with a very different set of social policies—and not just educational policies—than have been imple-mented in the United States since the 1960s. One-third of the poor in the United

States are children;[34] childhood poverty in our country has increased by more than 50 percent in the last quarter century;[35] and when compared with the twenty-four other nations measured in the Luxembourg Income Study, "the United States leads all nations in having the highest rates of child poverty at 22.3 percent, with the overall average standing at 9.9 percent."[36] This social policy failure, one can submit, will not be addressed adequately by putting in place the new accountability systems and getting all children to a level of "proficiency" on the tests by the target year of 2014. Rather, one would need to understand and address the nature of uneven development in a rapidly globalizing economic context—and putting this burden on schools shifts moral responsibility away from those more complicated, politically contentious, and ethically burdened domains of struggle.[37]

None of this is to gainsay the value of the work of community organizations engaged at the grassroots level to improve schools and neighborhoods. Yet if one seeks a measure of educational justice for children, putting the burden of equity on the schools is egregiously unjust in an era in which the income gap between the richest and poorest Americans has grown to a hitherto unprecedented magnitude. As many Americans with high school diplomas have discovered in the recent recession, even those with relatively high levels of technical skill are subject to downsizing and have been compelled to resort to jobs that pay poorly and offer no benefits; indeed, there are now as many Americans who are on-call, temporary, or contract workers as there are members of labor unions.[38]

Having noted the gravity of the increasing class stratification in the United States and the failure of antipoverty economic and social policy, however, does not mean that education should not be a central strand of federal educational policy. Title I funding has been a lifeline for many schools serving large numbers of poor and working-class students, and CBOs such as ACORN that wage national campaigns based on restoring full funding for Title I are right on target. The disaggregation of pupil test score data by race, class, ethnicity, and learning disability can be a critical tool of progressive social policy; insofar as NCLB accountability measures have brought to light the differential achievement of youth of color in predominantly white schools, they have appropriately indicated that schools must indeed educate all pupils, rather than burying the poor academic achievement of some pupils in more flattering aggregate numbers. By acknowledging the importance of teacher quality for student achievement, NCLB has provided local groups like ACORN chapters with "handles" for organizing and for collaborating with school districts to develop innovative community-based programs for recruitment and retention of teaching staff. NCLB is an extraordinarily complicated piece of legislation, and educational activists who are willing to do the hard work and find elements in it to benefit their schools and community should be able to do so in a way that improves pupil achievement and creates civic capacity.

In considering the opportunities contained within NCLB, it is important to note that local activists can redirect federal policy in their states and districts to advance agendas that have emerged through community organizing. However, the professional skills needed to apply for federal grants essentially exclude poor and working-class people from the grant application process—except as tagalongs on others' grants. In this regard the expertise of organizers or educational leaders is a sine qua non of successful grant writing; NCLB does not promote the kind of "empowered participatory governance" that Archon Fung has demonstrated can serve to bring poor and working-class people into leadership positions in public schools and other social service settings.[39] NCLB *could* have promoted participatory governance, but rather than enabling a democratic ideal of civic engagement, it encouraged a market-driven ideology promoting exits from struggling public schools—in spite of the uneven record of such school choice ventures.[40]

Of course, many CBOs have found ways to cross political lines in the past, and it would appear that a skillful incorporation of federal priorities (such as teacher quality) with local goals (such as parent engagement) could nonetheless be achieved. Insofar as ACORN has found ways to couple federal legislation with the local drive for teacher quality, it is "making democracy work" and creating power, as one would expect from urban regime theory.[41] Community organizing is hard work, and NCLB does nothing to make it easier. The challenge in this context, as always, is to develop strategies to create "mileux of innovation"[42] that will capitalize upon openings such as those that can be found in NCLB—or in any other local, state, or federal legislation—to advance the interests of poor and working-class communities.

NCLB remains problematic, however, from the vantage point of the larger failure of American society to tackle and reduce our poverty rates; there simply is no reason why European nations should have greater success in this regard, other than a failure of political will in the United States. Poverty is much more than just not having money in the United States; it truly does mean being "left behind" in terms of the safety of one's neighborhood, the quality of one's housing, and the overall provision of public services in everything from libraries to hospitals.[43] In addition, NCLB is also problematic if one does not acknowledge the kinds of curricular distortions that Texas IAF organizers described in the schools with which they are working and ignores teachers' concerns about ways in which the current "accountability" drive undermines and distorts pupil learning.

On the other hand, NCLB does represent progress in attempting to address the "achievement gap" between white pupils and pupils of color; further, the effort to raise teacher quality, even when done in the rather heavy-handed manner of a federal bureaucracy, is critical insofar as poorly prepared teachers simply have not been able to teach students adequately in their academic subject matter. There are now more than 200 CBOs in the United States that are engaged in education organizing; the Institute for Education and Social Policy at Brown University estimates that the number of community organizations working with schools has more than quadrupled since 1996.[44] Those community organizations may find ways to take advantage of the opportunities in NCLB while still maintaining a bold, outspoken, and critical stance toward its problematic aspects. Although it is a daunting challenge, community organizations may be able to recapture the rhetoric of the act—which, after all, was originally derived from the Children's Defense Fund—and use it to advance a broader antipoverty civic engagement strategy for improving education and increasing economic justice.

NOTES

1. Clarence N. Stone, "Urban Regimes and the Capacity to Govern: A Political Economy Approach," *Journal of Urban Affairs* 15 (1993): 6.

2. Clarence N. Stone, Jeffrey R. Henig, Bryan D. Jones, and Carol Pierannuzi, *Building Civic Capacity: The Politics of Reforming Urban Schools* (Lawrence: University Press of Kansas, 2001), 47.

3. Karl E. Weick, "Educational Organizations as Loosely Coupled Systems," *Administrative Science Quarterly* 21 (1976): 1–19; Michael Lipsky, *Street-Level Bureaucracy: Dilemmas of the Individual in Public Services* (New York: Russell Sage Foundation, 1980).

4. Larry Cuban and Michael Usdan, *Powerful Reforms with Shallow Roots: Improving America's Urban Schools* (New York: Teachers College Press, 2003).

5. Bruce Fuller, "The Public Square, Big or Small? Charter Schools in Political Context," in *Inside Charter Schools: The Paradox of Radical Decentralization*, ed. Bruce Fuller (Cambridge, MA: Harvard University Press, 2000), 12–65.

6. National Commission on Excellence in Education, *A Nation at Risk: The Imperative for Educational Reform* (Washington, DC: U.S. Government Printing Office, 1983), 5.

7. David C. Berliner and Bruce J. Biddle, *The Manufactured Crisis: Myths, Fraud, and the Attack on America's Schools* (New York: Perseus, 1995).

8. National Commission on Excellence in Education, *A Nation at Risk*, 7.

9. Thomas L. Friedman and Oliver Wyman, *The World Is Flat: A Brief History of the Twenty-first Century* (New York: Farrar, Straus and Giroux).

10. Monty Neill, Lisa Guisbond, and Bob Schaeffer, *Failing Our Children: How "No Child Left Behind" Undermines Quality and Equity in Education* (Cambridge, MA: Fairtest, 2004), 132; National Education Association, "Growing Chorus of Voices Calling for Changes in NCLB," http://www.nea.org/esea/chorus1.html (accessed November 22, 2004).

11. Leigh Dingerson, Chris Brown, and John M. Beam, *26 Conversations about Organizing, School Reform, and No Child Left Behind* (Washington, DC: privately printed, 2004).

12. Lowell C. Rose and Alec M. Gallup, "The 36th Annual Phi Delta Kappa/Gallup Poll of the Public's Attitudes toward the Public Schools," www.pdkintl.org/kappan/k0490pol.htm (accessed May 30, 2006).

13. U.S. Department of Education, *No Child Left Behind: A Desktop Reference* (Washington, DC: U.S. Department of Education, 2002).

14. Sam Dillon, "Bad School, or Not? Conflicting Ratings Baffle the Parents," *New York Times*, September 5, 2004, A1.

15. Bella Rosenberg, *What's Proficient? The No Child Left Behind Act and the Many Meanings of Proficiency* (Washington, DC: American Federation of Teachers, 2004).

16. Education Trust, *ESEA: Myths versus Realities: Answers to Common Questions about the New No Child Left Behind Act* (Washington, DC: Education Trust, 2003); Linda Skrla, James Joseph Scheurich, Joseph F. Johnson Jr., and James W. Koschoreck, "Accountability for Equity: Can State Policy Leverage Social Justice?" in *Educational Equity and Accountability: Paradigms, Policies, and Politics*, ed. Linda Skrla and James J. Scheurich (New York: RoutledgeFalmer, 2004).

17. U.S. Department of Education, *No Child Left Behind: A Parent's Guide* (Washington, DC: U.S. Department of Education, 2003), 13.

18. Deborah Meier and George Wood, *Many Children Left Behind: How the No Child Left Behind Act Is Damaging Our Children and Our Schools* (Boston: Beacon Press, 2004).

19. Rose and Gallup, *The 36th Annual Phi Delta Kappa/Gallup Poll*, 3.

20. Education Trust, *ESEA*.

21. Association of Community Organizations for Reform Now, *Parents Left Behind: A Study of State, Federal and School District Implementation of No Child Left Behind* (Washington, DC: ACORN, 2002).

22. Linda Darling-Hammond, "Teacher Quality and Student Achievement: A Review of State Policy Evidence," *Education Policy Analysis Archives* 8, no. 1 (2000), http://epaa.asu.edu/epaa/v8n1 (accessed August 15, 2006); Andrew J. Wayne and Peter Youngs, "Teacher Characteristics and Student Achievement Gains: A Review," *Review of Educational Research* 73 (2003): 89–122.

23. This quotation from Talbott and all subsequent quotations from community organizers were acquired either from telephone interviews conducted by Shirley in September and October 2004 or during a two-day symposium on education organizing convened on September 30 and October 1, 2004, by the Institute for Education and Social Policy at New York University in New York City.

24. U.S. Department of Education, *No Child Left Behind: A Parent's Guide*, 20.

25. Association of Community Organizations for Reform Now, *Parents Left Behind*, 6.

26. Ernest R. House, Gene V. Glass, Leslie D. McLean, and Decker F. Walker, "No Simple Answer: Critique of the Follow Through Evaluation," *Harvard Educational Review* 48 (1978): 128–160; Kathleen K. Manzo, "Study Challenges Direct Reading Method," *Education Week* 23 (2004): 3; Curt Dudley-Marling and Patricia C. Paugh, "The Rich Get Richer; the Poor Get Direct Instruction," in *Reading for Profit: How the Bottom Line Leaves Kids Behind*, ed. Bess Altwerger (Portsmouth, NH: Heinemann, 2005), 156–171.

27. See Gary L. Adams and Siegfried Engelmann, *Research on Direct Instruction: 25 Years beyond DISTAR* (Seattle, WA: Educational Achievement Systems, 1996); Marcy Stein, Douglas W. Carnine, and Robert C. Dixon, "Direct Instruction: Integrating Curriculum Design and Effective Teaching Practice," *Intervention in School and Clinic* 33 (1998): 227–234.

28. Dennis Shirley, *Community Organizing for Urban School Reform* (Austin: University of Texas Press, 1997).

29. Andy Hargreaves, *Changing Teachers, Changing Times: Teachers' Work and Culture in the Postmodern Age* (New York: Teachers College Press, 1994).

30. Michael Huberman, "Recipes for Busy Kitchens," *Knowledge: Creation, Diffusion, Utilization* 4 (1983): 478–510.

31. Andy Hargreaves, *Teaching in the Knowledge Society: Education in the Age of Insecurity* (New York: Teachers College Press, 2003); Richard M. Ingersoll, *Who Controls Teachers' Work? Power and Accountability in America's Schools* (Cambridge, MA: Harvard University Press, 2003); and

Linda M. McNeil, *Contradictions of School Reform: Educational Costs of Standardized Testing* (New York: Routledge, 2000).

32. Joseph J. Pedulla, Lisa Abrams, George Madaus, Michael Russel, Miguel Ramos, and Jing Miao, *Perceived Effects of State-Mandated Testing Programs on Teaching and Learning: Findings from a National Survey of Teachers* (Chestnut Hill, MA: National Board on Educational Testing and Public Policy, 2003).

33. Ingersoll, *Who Controls Teachers' Work?* 223.

34. Mark R. Rank, *One Nation, Underprivileged: Why American Poverty Affects Us All* (New York: Oxford University Press, 2004), 32.

35. Lee Rainwater and Timothy M. Smeeding, *Poor Kids in a Rich Country: America's Children in Comparative Perspective* (New York: Russell Sage, 2003), 29.

36. Rank, *One Nation, Underprivileged,* 33.

37. Jean Anyon, *Radical Possibilities: Public Policy, Urban Education, and a New Social Movement* (New York: Routledge, 2005).

38. Griff Witte, "As Income Gap Widens, Uncertainty Spreads: More US Families Struggle to Stay on Track," *Washington Post,* September 20, 2003, A1.

39. Archon Fung, *Empowered Participation: Reinventing Urban Democracy* (Princeton, NJ: Princeton University Press, 2004).

40. Jeffery R. Henig, *Rethinking School Choice: Limits of the Market Metaphor* (Princeton, NJ: Princeton University Press, 1994).

41. Clarence Stone, *Regime Politics: Governing Atlanta, 1946–1988* (Lawrence: University Press of Kansas, 1989).

42. Manuel Castells, *The Information Age: Economy, Society, and Culture,* vol. 1, *The Rise of the Network Society* (Malden, MA: Blackwell, 2000), 35.

43. Rainwater and Smeeding, *Poor Kids in a Rich Country;* Rank, *One Nation, Underprivileged.*

44. Kavitha Mediratta, with the Community Organizing Research Team, *Constituents of Change: Community Organizations and Public Education Reform* (New York: Institute for Education and Social Policy, New York University, 2004).

6. Political Opportunity, Venue Shopping, and Strategic Innovation: ACORN's National Organizing

Heidi Swarts

ACORN, the Association of Community Organizations for Reform Now, plays a unique role among efforts to advocate for poor and working-class Americans. Founded in 1970, ACORN represents "low to moderate-income" people, or poor and working-class people. From the beginning, it has seen itself as both a poor people's interest group and part of a broad populist movement for social change. ACORN has been struggling against shrinking government resources for social needs for thirty-five years. Its national staff has continuously innovated, developing new methods to mobilize resources and recruit members.

ACORN differs from faith-based or congregation-based community organizing (CBCO), the other dominant form of nationally coordinated community organizing, in several ways. These include its structure as one centralized national organization, its consistently national ambitions, and its degree of experimentation. I argue that these features help explain why ACORN has significantly greater experience with successful national organizing campaigns than most other national organizations that conduct community organizing.[1] One analysis that ACORN commissioned credits the organization with $12 billion of redistributive programs.[2] While any such analysis requires verification, this figure is plausible. The appendix to this chapter lists a sample of ACORN national policy outcomes.

In the introduction to this volume, Marion Orr argues that changes in American and global political economy have caused community organizing to respond with altered strategies. This is true for ACORN, although the organization always had ambitions to become a national movement.[3] However, both how it went about doing this and its ability to do so changed. Like all grassroots organizations, ACORN learned that increasingly, the locus of power and resources has moved beyond cities and states. The national campaign tactics analyzed in this chapter represent pragmatic responses to a political context of shrinking public investment in community needs and services. These responses include strategies that target the private sector for resources; government regulatory instead of redistributive strategies; and finding ways to leverage its limited power and resources so it can better target higher-level venues in both public and private sectors. The latter include far more participation than previously in broad national coalitions and marshaling many different sources of pressure at once. These are creative responses to ACORN's limitations.

This chapter examines why ACORN was an "early adopter" of national-level organizing. Changes in the ecology of community organizing that reduced political openings as well as internal organizational factors help explain why ACORN has increasingly turned to national campaigns. First I compare the organization to the CBCOs and outline the barriers to national-level campaigns that all community organizations face. Then I argue that ACORN has developed national campaign strategies in response to the diminished public sector and loss of urban political power. These take two forms: the incremental, decentralized groundswell, and the simultaneous multilevel campaign. Finally, I will assess the campaigns and their implications for community organizing as a whole.

ACORN AND COMMUNITY ORGANIZING

Scholars have documented how progressive organizations have increasingly come to be run by paid staff far removed from an active grassroots membership base.[4] Some national organizations contract door-to-door fund-raising to separate national canvassing operations rather than integrating fund-raising with building locally based organizational strength. In contrast, ACORN, like the CBCOs, is a national organization of active city organizations with roots in local neighborhoods. It raises a significant percentage of its funds from family membership dues of $120 per year; more is raised internally from other local fund-raising.[5]

Some advocates of congregation- or institution-based organizing have criticized ACORN for lacking a strong emphasis on leadership development and local organizational infrastructure. However, although ACORN's culture and practices are different, it does train indigenous leaders both locally and nationally. My research indicates that effective leadership among ACORN locals varies significantly, based on multiple local factors. For example, like other organizations, some ACORN chapters particularly benefit from talented organizers, strong neighborhood networks, and a relatively stable and employed population. Also, as part of the ecology of the community organizing sector, ACORN reaches many that congregation-based organizations do not. CBCOs as a group are racially diverse: according to a 2001 survey, member institutions are 36 percent predominantly white, 35 percent predominantly black, and 21 percent predominantly Hispanic.[6] Many are cross-class. While CBCOs and ACORN have overlapping constituencies, ACORN's membership is more uniformly low-income and is overwhelmingly African American and Latino. Many members live in inner-city neighborhoods with extremely high poverty and few community institutions. In inner-city African American neighborhoods, it is not uncommon for church members to commute in from the suburbs to their childhood churches, while the lower-income local residents remain uninvolved.[7] Door-to-door outreach allows ACORN to recruit neighborhood residents into meaningful advocacy and civic engagement.

Many CBCOs in particular emphasize leadership development, democratic process, and the importance of highly developed local infrastructure. For example, one CBCO senior staff member taught a group of new activists that "too much citywide action with locals not doing anything leads to problems, because the self-interest of people is at the local level" and that the local church organizing team was more important than the citywide organization. While grassroots vitality is usually necessary for major translocal campaigns, these views can become a kind of localism that valorizes grassroots strength more than policy change. Presumably, developing civil society organizations of the disempowered is not just an end in itself but a means for exercising power and winning meaningful gains. The power of ongoing organized constituencies is essential for winning changes that benefit excluded groups. However, no community organization, no matter how well trained the leaders or extensive the networks, has won any outcome to compare with such achievements as women's suffrage or the Voting Rights Act—victories won by national social movements that have waxed and waned with larger social movement cycles.[8] No single organization can achieve such outcomes. Increasingly ACORN and the national congregation-based networks are launching strategic collaborations with each other, as well as beyond the community organizing sector.

Barriers to National Organizing

It may seem odd for "community" organizing to undertake "national" campaigns; its domain would seem to be the local community. However, community organizing must be seen through another lens: not "community" as opposed to "national," but "community" as opposed to "workplace" organizing. Like labor organizing, community organizing is populist, concerned with bettering conditions for nonelite, ordinary working Americans. Scholars such as Theda Skocpol have demonstrated that large cross-class federated voluntary associations have engaged in influential national policy advocacy since the nineteenth century.[9] However, there are many disincentives for contemporary community organizations to undertake national campaigns.[10] First, the citizens' organizations best suited to influence federal policy tend to be public interest groups with specialist staffs and large, checkbook memberships that provide the resources they need.[11] The traditional source of clout for poor and working-class grassroots groups, in contrast, is their members. Members are less fungible than money; engaging them in national politics requires funds for a mobilization infrastructure, and resources are particularly scarce for working-class organizations. Experience in grassroots organizing does not translate easily into policy expertise or savvy on Capitol Hill. Specialists in local political arenas usually lack the knowledge, resources, and expertise that effective national advocacy requires. Community organizations' numbers, though significant, are far smaller than those of the civic and fraternal organizations in their heyday. ACORN's poor and working-class members are especially challenging to mobilize, as the poor have low rates of civic engagement and typically also lack both a sense of efficacy and hope for change.[12]

As a poor people's organization, ACORN has a major challenge in mobilizing resources. It has few "conscience constituents," and its contentiousness makes it eligible only for the tiny part of the philanthropic sector that funds confrontational community organizing. Yet among groups that conduct robust local community organizing, ACORN is a clear leader in conducting national organizing campaigns. Since 1970, as table 6.1 shows, ACORN has grown from an active organization in one city (Little Rock, Arkansas) to ninety-two cities.

EXTERNAL FACTORS IN ACORN'S ACCELERATION OF
NATIONAL ORGANIZING

Global and national political and economic change has altered the ecology of community organization. The political process theory of social movement dynamics emphasizes the influence of such broad changes on specific political contexts.

**Table 6.1. Growth of ACORN
Chapters, 1970–2005**

Year	No. of States	No. of Cities
1970	1	1
1975	3	8
1980	24	35
1985	27	39
1990	27	40
1995	28	41
2000	29	46
2005	40	92

Scholars have argued that these shifts in opportunity predict better than some other factors when social movements will emerge and decline.[13] Openings in opportunity occur based on several factors. These include widened political access such as African Americans gained when they moved from the Jim Crow South to northern cities and gained the franchise in key electoral states.[14] In urban politics, city council elections by district rather than at-large (citywide) widen political access to grassroots groups because they are more able to elect and influence politicians if officials are accountable just to one district. Relations with elite actors can provide opportunity. Influential allies can assist community organizations, while divisions among elites can motivate some elites to seek the allegiance of constituencies with otherwise little influence. In addition to political opportunity, political process–oriented social movement scholars usually consider two other factors when explaining social movement emergence, growth, and decline: the availability of social networks and organizations as movement vehicles, and cultural processes, including collective identity formation and advantageous framing of issues.

Additional external political factors that influence actors and outcomes are state capacity and new threats. While concentrated state power can supply challengers with few openings, dispersed and fragmented state authority may also deny political opportunity to activists.[15] Government may lack the political capacity or authority to resolve dilemmas of public policy. For example, some citizens' organizations have sought regional planning solutions to problems stemming from urban sprawl. Not only are there powerful lobbies opposing restrictions on growth, but in areas with many separate municipalities, local political authority is fragmented and offers little leverage for groups seeking regional policymaking.[16]

Scholars have noted that political opportunity must be perceived in order to be seized.[17] ACORN's development and shifting strategies were not an automatic response to transparently shifting opportunities; rather, its choices result from the interaction between leaders' goals and ideology and their perceptions of external opportunities. No doubt possible opportunities were missed, while some efforts were made in the face of little opportunity. However, over time ACORN experienced organizational learning. Its national leadership exhibited an increasing openness to potential opportunities in new venues as well as recognition of constraints.

Declining Opportunity, Multiplying Threats

The environmental changes that affected ACORN's strategic choices include accelerated threats—since the Reagan administration, the conservative assault on redistributive policies and aid to cities—and the long-term decline of cities' intertwined economic and political power. The interstate highway system, the Federal Housing Act, and Veterans Administration home loan policies subsidized the growth of suburbs at the expense of cities. As corporations became increasingly vulnerable to global competition, they simply abolished jobs or moved them overseas. Cities experienced capital flight, the loss of middle-class residents and their tax revenues, the decline of federal and state aid, falling working-class wages (in real dollars), and the ravaging of inner-city neighborhoods. Cities are therefore more vulnerable to businesses' demands for subsidies as they compete with other cities for corporate facilities and their tax revenues. The gradual decline of cities' economic and, partly as a consequence, political power relative to suburbs has reduced their resources and their ability to respond to redistributive demands. The gradual replacement of cities by suburbs as the electoral center of gravity; the southern shift from Democratic to Republican; and the skillful mobilization of antitax, antigovernment discourse and voters by new conservative think tanks and Religious Right organizations reduced the opportunities for community organizations to force redistribution of resources to their neighborhoods. However, these forces may also pose a unifying threat to poor and working-class neighborhoods and their advocates.

Community organizing did not adapt quickly to these changes; scarce resources, limited organizational capacity, traditions of localism, and a history of "turf wars" and competition with other organizations worked against the broad coalitions and shift in organizing scale that national-level organizing usually requires. However, organizations gained experience working together nationally to pass the Community Reinvestment Act in 1977, and since then to defend it from numerous threats from the banking industry and its allies. After the abolition of Aid to Families with Dependent Children in 1996, many organizations came together through the Center for Community Change's Campaign for Jobs and Income Support, which helped stave off some later cuts to the federal welfare budget. The election of George W. Bush in 2000 and his administration's hostility to social welfare programs and labor rights stimulated unprecedented levels of electoral organizing in 2004 by community organizations, labor unions, other liberal and left constituencies, and ACORN. Both real and threatened political-economic assaults forced activist groups like ACORN to identify and create new pockets of opportunity.

Political Opportunity and Venue Shopping

Political scientist Sarah Pralle notes that "most advocacy groups will search for alternative decision venues and/or policy arenas when external political opportunities significantly change."[18] ACORN has begun to focus more on national targets (corporations, the 2004 presidential election, congressional legislation) that increasingly wield authority over the conditions of life in cities. However, when there is little opportunity in a more far-reaching and potentially advantageous venue, ACORN will move to a more local and less demanding venue. For example, when there appeared to be little opportunity for a major national increase in the mini-mum wage, ACORN experimented with city- and state-level wage increase cam-paigns. In 1996, Missouri ACORN ran a statewide ballot initiative that would have raised the state's minimum wage to $6.25. Heavily outspent by business in conser-vative Missouri, the initiative failed, but it passed overwhelmingly in St. Louis. Mis-souri ACORN then reverted to a less far-reaching living wage campaign for St. Louis, targeting only companies with city contracts. ACORN has historically not shied away from overly ambitious campaigns, like the Missouri ballot initiative[19]— but organizations that must mobilize their own resources cannot lose campaigns indefinitely. Therefore, ACORN has been motivated to change venues.

As ACORN has increasingly conducted national-level campaigns, it has sought alliances with increasingly diverse groups. In order to place education on the 2004 national campaign agenda, ACORN joined the National Mobilization for Great Public Schools, along with the National Education Association, MoveOn.org, the Campaign for America's Future, the NAACP Voter Fund, and the U.S. Hispanic Leadership Institute.[20]

Under the constraints of an extremely hostile national political environment, ACORN has developed two types of national campaign. When no national venue is promising, ACORN organizes a series of local campaigns that wins incremental victories while it helps build a movement. When there is a promising national venue, ACORN runs a national campaign active simultaneously at multiple levels: its city locals, often its statewide organizations, and its national organization. Table 6.2 summarizes these two types of campaign.[21] Both types of campaign include coordinated local grassroots action in ACORN cities across the country. The dif-ference is degree of openness of a national decision venue.

Incremental Groundswell: Series of Local Campaigns

The series of local campaigns works as an incremental groundswell and relies on fast replication to alter the public discourse and ideally the political climate for more ambitious campaigns. It is useful when there is little political opportunity for national policy change. The classic example is the living wage movement, called that because of its classically movementlike qualities: it began locally, succeeded, was replicated, and spread quickly across the country. It is a national strategy because it is nationally coordinated and staffed, and because it is implemented nationwide. There may even include some work in Congress or with federal bureaucrats; for example, although a national minimum-wage increase was unlikely, ACORN worked with Senator Ted Kennedy's office on national minimum-wage increase legislation. ACORN also collaborated with 2004 vice presidential candidate John Edwards to promote state wage hike campaigns in Ohio, Michigan, and Arizona.

Table 6.2. Characteristics of ACORN Organizing

	Incremental Groundswell: Series of Local Campaigns	Simultaneous Local-State-National Campaign
Decision venue	Series of local or state venues, coordinated by ACORN national headquarters	Can be market-based or political • if corporate campaign, one national venue • if political campaign, can be venues at multiple levels
When used	When national venue (e.g., Congress) offers little or no opportunity	When national venue offers most far-reaching result, or when resolution of a local grievance requires a national corporation or branch of national government
Example	Living wage "movement": series of ordinances passed by individual municipalities	Household Finance, the United States' largest lender of subprime loans
Strategy	Series of local victories creates momentum; goal is to change expectations and level of discourse. Helps *create opportunity* by (1) winning incremental victories and (2) creating broad coalitions to support more far-reaching local or national reforms, such as: • Extensions of LW ordinances to more employers; • Labor peace provisions (agreeing to not interfere with organizing campaigns) • State minimum-wage increases	Local chapter tactics • identified loan victims • documented predatory business practices • protested local Household Finance offices • local media campaigns • sought local legislation to curb loan practices State-level tactics: • **Legal:** Pushed state attorneys general to sue Household • **Legislative:** sought local legislation to curb loan practices • **Regulatory:** Pushed banking regulators to act National-level tactics: • **Legal:** Two class-action lawsuits • **Shareholder resolution** introduced at Household shareholders meeting • **Media campaign** about loan practices targeting Wall Street analysts

The real wages of low-wage workers have declined since the 1970s, and the political climate for a national minimum-wage increase has been hostile since the last such increase in 1996, from $4.25 to $5.15. The living wage movement represents an incremental strategy that, in itself, affects only a small fraction of the working poor—those who work for private firms that hold contracts with, or receive subsidies from, local governments. A common argument opponents make is that such a policy gives a city a competitive disadvantage. However, city contractors often supply services that are less mobile than other forms of business, and other cities are likely to have a living wage policy as well. Living wage ordinances only affect about 1 percent of a city's workers. The strategy, therefore, is not primarily an economic but a political strategy to build coalitions and broader public support for higher wage standards.[22] ACORN provides technical assistance and leads some campaigns, but most campaigns feature broad religion-, labor-, and community-based coalitions. The movement has helped reframe the public discourse about wages, bringing into focus the fact that the legal minimum wage is well below the poverty level. It has built a national movement in which 140 city and county living wage policies have been enacted, with many more city, county, and university campaigns under way.[23]

This consciously incremental strategy resulted from hostility by the presidency and Congress to raising the minimum wage. But this is also a strategy that has helped *expand* opportunity by (1) framing the issue of wages as an issue of economic justice, and (2) building a broad organizational infrastructure that can exert pressure from below for state minimum-wage increases.[24]

Simultaneous Local-State-National Campaign

The local-state-national, or simultaneous multilevel campaign operates in many venues at once, using multiple tactics with the ultimate goal of building pressure at the highest level of decision venue: a national corporation, one or more branches of national government, or both. While the incremental groundswell campaign can be thought of as horizontal, the simultaneous multilevel campaign features a kind of vertical integration in which tactics aimed at all levels of the target are employed simultaneously.

One campaign typically produces multiple outcomes. First, it pressures a major national corporation to reform a policy such as refusing to offer mortgages to residents of inner-city neighborhoods, or engaging in deception and requiring usurious interest rates for subprime loans. For example, ACORN won a commitment of $360 million from Ameriquest for below-market mortgages for first-time home buyers. Second, it negotiates the terms of the new policy, which include funding for ACORN to broker the new service (such as locating first-time home buyers and counseling them, which reduces the risk to the lender).²⁵ This not only delivers valuable services but also mobilizes resources for ACORN. It creates programs, pays staff, and channels a portion of the funds back into organizing. In addition, it identifies potential new ACORN members, who supply dues and build organizational capacity.

The first major example of the multilevel campaign used the Community Reinvestment Act (CRA) as a wedge to pry open major banks to demands for investment in inner-city communities. ACORN filed its first CRA challenge in St. Louis in 1985. The 1990s saw a massive wave of bank mergers and acquisitions. Frequently these mergers made capital for urban communities even more inaccessible, but the CRA made federal bank regulators' approval of the mergers conditional on some degree of investment in local communities. By filing challenges to banks that applied for merger and acquisition approval, ACORN could bring banks to the bargaining table. These financial institutions preferred a settlement with ACORN to full-scale review by federal banking regulators.²⁶

The process is well illustrated by a 1991 campaign, prompted by North Carolina National Bank's plan to merge with C&S/Sovran to create NationsBank. According to an ACORN report to the Annie E. Casey Foundation, the merger would have created the fourth-largest financial institution in the country.²⁷ However, North Carolina National Bank had a record of taking local deposits but not making local loans, instead sending profits back to Charlotte, North Carolina. One risk of bank mergers is that small local banks that have relatively good local lending records get swallowed up by larger entities that do not. ACORN saw this risk and also saw the potential of gaining access to what would become the largest bank in many southern cities, where ACORN had a strong presence. In a typical tactic, ACORN conducted research and discovered that North Carolina National denied black and Latino loan applications from two to four times as often as white loan applications, even controlling for income: "Middle income Black applicants were seven times as likely to have their loans denied as middle income white applicants."²⁸ ACORN enlisted community allies and elected officials, including House Banking Committee chair Henry Gonzalez and Senate Banking Committee chair Donald Riegle, to call for public hearings by the Federal Reserve Board. At this point in a campaign, ACORN typically engages in a spate of tactics to gain publicity and create pressure, in this case for the bank to submit a plan for community investment to the Federal Reserve as part of its merger agreement.²⁹ The Fed approved the merger but included an agreement between NationsBank and ACORN in which the bank agreed to fund ACORN Housing Corporation to recruit, screen, and counsel low-income and minority applicants for new low-cost mortgages. This mortgage product featured interest at 1 percent below market rate, which ACORN claims "alone was worth hundreds of millions of dollars to AHC borrowers."³⁰

ACORN has made more than forty-five such agreements with banks, as well as many agreements with companies providing ancillary products, such as home insurance and the secondary mortgage market. In 1992 the Federal National Mortgage Association (Fannie Mae) agreed to a $55 million pilot program to purchase mortgages from banks that had agreements with ACORN. The program adopted the kinds of terms that make mortgages possible for ACORN borrowers. These included down payments as low as $1,000 or 3 percent of the sales price, and the use of nontraditional proofs of creditworthiness, such as rent or utility payment records.

Bank campaigns and other multilevel national campaigns employ a wide variety of tactics at all levels to meet their goal. A good example is ACORN's campaign against predatory lending by Household Finance. Predatory lenders offer subprime mortgages and other loans, often with hidden costs and astronomical interest rates, to low-income borrowers, one-third to one-half of whom are actually eligible for "A" loans, the best quality home loans.[31] ACORN used a dizzying array of simultaneous local, state, and national tactics to put more pressure on Household Finance (see table 6.2). By May 2002, the banking newsletter *Retail Banker International* reported:

> Household Finance, one of the leading US specialists in consumer credit, appears to be losing the battle to clear its name. Already under attack on several fronts for alleged predatory lending practices, it now faces a new and alarming adversary. Carl McCall, the man in charge of the finances of New York State, has called on Household to take drastic action to reform its business practices. McCall controls the state's retirement fund, which holds shares in Household worth over $100 million. His remarks, which include a clear threat to sell the shares if things do not improve, are likely to make ethical funds and other socially aware investors take notice. And if they start selling it will put further pressure on Household's share price.[32]

Ultimately Household Finance settled the suit by the fifty state attorneys general for $484 million to victims of predatory lending policies; it also funded a $72 million Foreclosure Avoidance Program for at-risk borrowers, administered by ACORN.[33] In the absence of a progressive national administration leading reform efforts, organizing individual corporate campaigns helps build a broader constituency for regulatory reform at the state and national levels.

In 2003, ACORN assumed management of Project Vote, a leading voter mobilizing nonprofit organization since 1982. From 1982 until the 2004 registration campaign, Project Vote claims to have registered and mobilized more than 3 million new low-income and minority voters.[34] In preparation for November 2004, using ACORN's network of neighborhood chapters, Project Vote mounted a massive voter mobilization campaign in fifty-one cities in fifteen of the seventeen presidential "battleground" states. More than 10,000 workers and volunteers registered more than 1.12 million new voters in low-income African American and Latino neighborhoods. They contacted a similar number of registered but new or infrequent voters during November, and a total of 2.2 million voters on election day.[35]

One result, far overshadowed by the larger defeat of the Kerry campaign, was a precedent-setting achievement: the first time a minimum-wage increase was passed in a southern state. Florida ACORN collected close to a million signatures to place a minimum-wage increase measure on the November 2 ballot, partly as a strategy to boost low-income voter turnout. The measure passed by 72 to 28 percent and raised the minimum wage to $6.15 in May 2005, indexed annually to inflation. About 850,000 workers gained $2,000 each of additional annual full-time income.

ACORN's Earned Income Tax Credit (EITC) outreach campaign delivers a service while fighting poverty in the aggregate, mobilizing resources for ACORN, and reaching out to potential new members. In 2003, the Marguerite Casey Foundation awarded ACORN a two-year, $1.5 million grant for grassroots organizing and outreach, primarily on the EITC, in three pilot cities. ACORN became one of hundreds of community-based organizations that collaborate with the IRS's Community Partners Program. The outreach seeks the 10 to 20 percent of eligible families unaware of what is now the largest remaining federal entitlement. According to the Center on Budget and Policy Priorities, the federal credit now lifts more children out of poverty than any other government program: 4.9 million people, including 2.7 million children, in 2002. The politically popular entitlement rewards parents who work.[36]

In conducting outreach and free tax preparation for EITC-eligible families, ACORN delivered a service for which it was well qualified by its on-the-ground network of organizers and ACORN members. In its first year, the ACORN sites in New Orleans and Miami were ranked first (of sixty-five and thirty-nine sites, respectively) in number of tax returns prepared.[37] This program occupies what is surely the narrow ground of shared self-interest between ACORN and the Internal Revenue Service. The IRS supervisor of this program found ACORN so effective that he worked with the organization to expand from three cities in 2003, to forty-five in 2004, and eighty in 2005.[38] Table 6.3 provides a list of recent ACORN campaigns in each of these two categories.

These two kinds of national strategy are successful adaptations to formidably difficult conditions for a redistributive politics. Very limited opportunities combined with accelerating threats to working people's interests have challenged ACORN to search for venues where limited but significant gains were possible.

However, this does not explain why ACORN, relative to many other community organizations, including the CBCOs, began national organizing much earlier and has developed a growing repertoire of tactics. Organizational features specific to ACORN help explain why.

Table 6.3. Examples of ACORN National Campaigns

Incremental Groundswell: Series of Local Campaigns	Simultaneous Local-State-National Campaign
• Adequate charity or reduced-price care in hospitals: seeks individual agreements with hospitals as well as ordinances	Bank campaigns using the Community Reinvestment Act: ACORN has won agreements with more than 45 banks
• Inclusionary zoning: campaigns for zoning that includes affordable housing provisions in new developments	Predatory lending: • Ameriquest • Citigroup, two campaigns • H&R Block • Jackson-Hewitt • Wells Fargo
	2004 and 2006 Voter mobilization campaigns
	2004 Education campaign

ACORN'S EARLY ADOPTION OF NATIONAL ORGANIZING: SOME ORGANIZATIONAL FACTORS

Its structure as one national organization, its need to find creative solutions to the problem of resources, and its consistently national vision and goal to create a broad-based social movement all predisposed ACORN to respond early to the changing ecology of organizing. ACORN's internal structure was designed for national coordination. However, the new tactics it has developed in response to the changing environment have allowed it to win significant gains.

ACORN's Structure: One National Organization

ACORN's organizational structure as one national organization with local and state chapters, not a CBCO "network" with legally autonomous affiliates, made it far easier to mobilize the entire organization in national campaigns. The national networks that conduct CBCO are organizationally and legally decentralized: that is, they are networks of independent 501(c)(3) nonprofit organizations, each of which has its own board of directors. Such organizations have the authority to choose their own campaigns and hire and fire their own staff organizers. (In practice, authority is shared among local leadership, local staff, and national network staff, and the balance of power among them varies by network.) Local CBCOs can be highly democratic but slower to coordinate. CBCOs have more institutional layers than ACORN: whereas ACORN members are individuals and families, each legally independent CBCO is a federation of *other* 501(c)(3) organizations—its member religious congregations. Each of these has a local organizing committee that may agree or disagree with a given course of action. A CBCO's citywide board of directors may also resist attempted coordination from the network it consults with. As an independent organization, its independent identity may be stronger than its identification with the IAF, PICO, the Gamaliel Foundation, or DART; indeed, it may have switched from one network to another over its history. However, ACORN's relatively centralized control allows it to make fast decisions and move quickly to launch nationally coordinated campaigns. It retains legitimacy because it pursues issues with broad local support.

Although the boards of directors of ACORN locals set local policy, crucially, the head organizer (since 1970, Wade Rathke), not the elected local ACORN boards, has the ultimate authority to hire and fire all staff, including local organizers.[39] Organizers primarily report to the ACORN national office and only secondarily to the local board. In contrast, most local CBCOs, even if affiliated with a national network, can hire and fire their own staff. In ACORN, national decisions (except staffing) formally rest with the national board of directors, and local boards choose local campaigns and approve participation in national campaigns, but their identity is as part of one national organization.[40]

Finding Resources for a Poor People's Organization

As organizations of organizations, CBCOs require dues from their member congregations. They also tap into national denominational funders. In contrast, ACORN's members are poor and working-class individuals and families. One motivation for ACORN's national corporate campaigns is its ability to extract concessions from banks, mortgage lenders, and other companies and then negotiate funds to support new programs, which ACORN administers. ACORN multilevel campaigns have won funding for loan counseling, access to low-cost mortgages and improved subprime loan products, campaigns to recruit applicants for the EITC (an important national redistributive policy) and the child care tax credit, and free tax preparation. A portion of these funds finds its way back into organizing. The process of service delivery itself helps ACORN boost visibility and reach new potential members.

A Consistently National Vision

While community organizing sometimes builds deep, democratically led local capacity to the exclusion of other goals, ACORN is unabashedly national. Like a union local, ACORN fights local battles, but like the AFL-CIO, ACORN has a national vision that includes influencing electoral politics.

Since 2000, both PICO and the Gamaliel Foundation did launch national organizing campaigns. However, since the 1970s, ACORN organized locally but also launched national campaigns. Like the CBCOs, ACORN defines its strength as its base in local communities. However, for thirty years it has also tried to batter its way into state and national electoral and legislative politics, experimenting with one method after another. Perhaps it was a combination of hubris and naïveté that led ACORN to target the 1980 presidential election when it was only six years old. In 1976 founder Wade Rathke proposed a plan to expand ACORN from three to twenty states by 1980, run delegates in caucus states, and influence the national Democratic platform.[41] The 20/80 Campaign sought to break down ACORN localism, build ideological coherence, and ultimately build a national social movement. By not endorsing a candidate, it lost potential allies such as labor, which ran into the arms of the Democratic Party after Reagan's 1980 victory and the decline of opportunity for progressive groups.[42] Ultimately ACORN failed in its attempts to influence the Democrats, but it succeeded in expanding to twenty states. Perhaps this very grandiosity, combined with dogged determination and a willingness to experiment and learn from its mistakes, has been ACORN's greatest asset.

Because ACORN is not a 501(c)(3) tax-exempt organization, it can endorse and run candidates for office and participate in political party activity. This gives it more tactical options for state and national campaigns, including running and endorsing candidates for office. ACORN has backed various third-party efforts such as the New Party, and in New York State ACORN helped found the Working Families Party. ACORN developed local political action committees (PACs) to interview and endorse candidates for office.

Consistent with its national vision and unlike most groups that specialize in local organizing, ACORN has long had a national staff of issue specialists dispersed in nine offices throughout the country, who advise nationally coordinated campaigns. The CBCO networks consult with policy experts to varying degrees—for example, the Gamaliel Foundation has "strategic partners" with which it works closely in developing policy analyses and campaign ideas. However, ACORN has had its own internal policy experts for well over a decade. Its national staff members function somewhat like a think tank of specialists in different organizing areas: research, national legislative campaigns (in Washington, D.C.), communications, financial industry campaigns, agreements with banks for new low-cost loan products, low-cost housing development, living wage campaigns, and overall political strategy (voter mobilization, ballot initiative campaigns, and other campaigns targeting city and state elected officials). In part, this staff specialization emerged from successful strategies that become institutionalized in ongoing programs. For example, when it became clear that citywide campaigns to legislate a "living wage" were a successful incremental strategy for raising wages, one ACORN organizer became the national living wage campaign specialist. ACORN considered it advantageous to position itself as the expert in living wage ordinances, and to build a national living wage movement by aiding non-ACORN campaigns. Since 1998, it has staffed a Living Wage Resource Center that assists both ACORN and non-ACORN campaigns. The resource center tracks campaigns, disseminates research, provides materials and technical assistance, conducts organizing trainings and conferences, and links fledgling campaigns to lawyers and resources.

This section has examined internal structural, historical, and ideological factors that predisposed ACORN to attempt national campaigns. ACORN's structure as one centralized organization, its goal of building a national poor people's movement, and the infrastructure of national staff specialists that it put in place are reasons ACORN was one of the first to respond to the mix of opportunities and threats ushered in by a globalizing economy and a conservative resurgence.

ANALYSIS AND IMPLICATIONS OF ACORN'S NATIONAL CAMPAIGNS FOR COMMUNITY ORGANIZING

A brief look at how ACORN has responded to specific dimensions of political opportunity illustrates how social movement entrepreneurs not only respond to, but actively seek to create and expand opportunity.

ACORN seeks windows of opportunity at the local, state, and national levels. With incremental groundswell campaigns, ACORN has determined that there is little opportunity for federal or (usually) state action and has focused locally in the hopes of creating more opportunity at higher political levels. Multilevel local-state-national campaigns act at multiple levels, and multiple venues at each level. They also have a synergistic quality in which tactics combine to produce results in multiple locations. For example, voting is undertaken at all political levels, so a national voter registration campaign motivated by a tight presidential election has beneficial results locally in cities such as Columbus, where 50,000 newly registered low-income voters got local politicians' attention.

ACORN's 2004 voter mobilization campaign, in which it claims to have mobilized 2.2 million newly registered and infrequent low-income voters to the polls, was a response to the highly competitive 2002 presidential election, which widened electoral access to the poor. With exceptions, such as the 2000 election in

Florida, this access was not legally denied, but voters were demobilized and inert. However, the results were the same as if 1.125 million Americans gained and used a new legal right to the vote. The difference is that political entrepreneurs produced this result.

Influential allies have been important to ACORN campaigns. In the 1990s, President Clinton's greater interest in urban problems opened HUD to ACORN, which made some gains in tenant organizing protections in HUD properties. ACORN has long-term relationships with politicians such as Senator Ted Kennedy. However, after 2000, when opportunity for national victories was so small, perhaps the allies that made the most difference have been state regulators and attorneys general with a shared interest in curbing predatory lending, or corporations that make settlements with ACORN and then share an interest in creating a level playing field for their industry.

The Florida minimum-wage increase and the fact that the four states ACORN targeted for a 2006 minimum-wage hike are "red states" suggest that the opportunities for class-based economic populist campaigns in such states are greater than popular wisdom might assume. One reason for this is that "red states" in the Sunbelt are experiencing rapid, largely Latino immigration. Not only ACORN but the CBCO networks all have identified immigration issues as a major national priority, and CBCO's Catholic base is a natural way into these communities. Immigrants' rights is an issue that should lend itself to, and will need to draw on, the broadest possible coalitions among community organizations and their allies.

All groups that represent low- and moderate-income Americans have experienced shrinking opportunities and heightened threats to their interests from the increasingly hostile political environment since 1980. However, I argue that internal organizational factors predisposed ACORN to respond early by launching national campaigns. These include structural factors, such as ACORN's form as one national organization with a national board of directors and staff, able to quickly identify national goals and mobilize its locals. Also, ACORN's need for resources has motivated it to identify new funding sources, such as the private corporations it targets for reform. Beginning with its use of the Community Reinvestment Act to pressure banks to invest in poor neighborhoods and provide new low-cost loan products, ACORN developed a corporate campaign strategy that was inevitably national, as it mirrored the structure of the national corporation. The organization then applied this model to a number of banks and adapted it to other financial issues such as home insurance and predatory lending practices.

Aspects of ACORN's culture and history were also favorable to national-level organizing. Much congregation-based organizing beginning with the Industrial Areas Foundation has contrasted "community organizations" with "movements," which it portrays as excessively ideological, decentralized, sporadic, and often focused on symbolic moral victories or embarrassing politicians rather than on real change.[43] ACORN, however, has sought to create a national populist movement for low- to moderate-income Americans. It has long allied itself with labor, which has a national political mission, and whose resources help make possible campaigns that transcend the local. ACORN also has a willingness to experiment with new tactics at multiple venues.

ACORN has undergone organizational learning. Historically it identified building national power narrowly as building the ACORN organization. This widespread tendency among community organizing has caused many groups, including the major congregation-based networks, to long avoid coalition work. However, particularly as decision venues have moved from local to national levels, organizations are even less able to win battles on their own. ACORN has become especially open to collaboration with a wide variety of groups.

The organization's history has implications for the debate launched by Piven and Cloward on the role of disruption versus organization building in winning outcomes for poor people.[44] Organization need not mean the decline of militance, and the threat posed by disruptive direct action is historically contingent. As Meyer and Tarrow have pointed out, since the 1960s, conventional protest has become institutionalized.[45] National ACORN director Steve Kest noted that "whenever ACORN opens a new office, they recapitulate the phases of exerting power: first 20 to 50 people show up and protest. It will have an impact, the mayor will run out there, but [authorities] become inured to this." With regard to the kind of direct action that threatens significant disruption, Kest commented that "the opportunities for disruption and disorder have changed. There are fewer opportunities than back then. Then the assumption was that it would lead to progressive change. Today it could just as well lead to repression. It's true that ACORN still has a bias toward direct action because we think the experience of going through that is key to our leaders developing a political consciousness through throwing themselves on the line. It builds commitment, awareness, a sense of people's own power. But it's never enough."[46] In unfavorable contexts, often with strategic and personnel deficits, ACORN uses strategic and organizational innovation to leverage limited resources into significant achievements. This requires creativity in pioneering new tactics and targets. ACORN's most innovative campaigns actually *create* political opportunity for itself and other actors, as well as economic opportunity for constituents, their neighborhoods, and, ironically, the business corporations that ACORN initially protested in order to force negotiation, reform, and investment in low-income neighborhoods.

APPENDIX

Major Acorn Policy Outcomes

Living Wage Movement

Initiator or lead coalition member in twelve successful living wage campaigns. Participant in four other successful campaigns.[47]

Maintains Living Wage Resource Center with a full-time staff person, who provides technical assistance to non-ACORN campaigns nationwide as well as to ACORN campaigns. Resource center web site disseminates information on all campaigns (140 successful campaigns), model ordinances, etc.

Sponsored three National Living Wage Training Conferences for campaign organizers, both within and outside ACORN.

*Coalition Leader or Member, Successful Statewide
Minimum-Wage Increase Campaigns*

1999   Massachusetts:[48] Raised minimum to $6.75; increased state earned income credit.

2003   Illinois: $5.50 in 2004, $6.50 in 2005. First midwestern state to increase minimum wage.

2004   Florida: Raised to $6.15/hour in May 2005, annual increases indexed to inflation. First southern state to increase minimum wage; 850,000 workers affected, $2,000 additional annual full-time income.

2004   New York:[49] $7.15/hour phased in over two years, beginning with a raise to $6.00 on January 1, 2005; 1.2 million workers affected.[50]

2006   Missouri, Arizona, Colorado, and Ohio raised their minimum wage when ballot initiative campaigns that ACORN helped lead won.

Earned Income Tax Credit and Child Tax Credit Tax Refunds

2004   ACORN-run pilot project: free tax preparation centers in three cities achieved average gain of $1,789 for eligible families.

2005   ACORN-run free tax preparation centers in forty-five cities help 10,000 low-income families file tax returns; 52 percent qualify for Earned Income Tax Credit ($7.6 million) and $2.9 million in Child Tax Credit refunds.[51]

2006   ACORN free tax preparation centers expanded to seventy-five cities, aiding 27,000 families and yielding $36 million in tax refunds.

Community Reinvestment

Housing Loan and Insurance Programs for Low- and
Moderate-Income Borrowers

1994	Allstate and Nationsbank: Signed $10 million agreement for below-market mortgages.
1996	Prudential Insurance:[52] Dropped requirement of a minimum $50,000 market value for home insurance policies. Other requirements waived, 20 percent discount for applicants trained in home safety by ACORN Housing Corp.
2000	Ameriquest: ACORN negotiated agreement to provide $360 million, three-year pilot loan program for low-income home buyers. Targeted 10,000 people in ten cities, administered by ACORN Housing Corp. Precedent-setting subprime lending program.[53]
2004	Citigroup: ACORN negotiated partnership to deliver new mortgage and bank account products for immigrants.

ACORN Housing Corporation

Loan counseling provided to 160,000 borrowers, 1986–2005.
Recruited and assisted 60,000 families to become first-time homeowners.
Estimated value of mortgages, 1995–2005: $5.75 billion.[54]
Rehabilitated more than 850 vacant and abandoned housing units.[55]

Predatory Lending Reform

National Legislation

Helped stop legislation that would have preempted all state and local laws regulating predatory lending (Rep. Bob Ney, R-Ohio).

Settlements with ACORN

2001	Citigroup: ACORN successfully pressured Citigroup, the nation's largest bank, and Household Finance to stop predatory high-interest single-premium credit insurance to homeowners. These were the only two major lenders that offered the product.
2004	Ancillary to ACORN campaign: $484 million settlement of suit by fifty state attorneys general whose lawsuit was triggered by ACORN-organized formal complaints by Household Finance victims
2004	Citigroup: Reformed subprime loan products.[56]

2004   H&R Block: National agreement to eliminate administration fee for
            Refund Anticipation Loans (RALs) and provide fuller disclosure.[57]
2004   Household Finance: $72 million Foreclosure Avoidance Program for
            at-risk borrowers.[58]

Voter Registration

1996   Illinois: ACORN sued the state of Illinois in 1996 for not complying
            with the National Voter Registration Act ("motor voter law"). Illinois
            was one of five states that did not comply with this law, which directs
            states to offer voter registration to citizens where they apply for dri-
            ver's licenses, library cards, and welfare and other public services.
2003–2004   Registered 1.1 million new voters in low-income black and Latino
            neighborhoods since July 2003. Registered voters in fourteen of sev-
            enteen presidential election battleground states.

Selected Local Acorn Policy Outcomes

Elections

1998   New York: With labor, ACORN spearheaded formation of the Work-
            ing Families Party, the first community-labor party with official bal-
            lot status in New York State in more than fifty years.
1999   Chicago: Former Chicago ACORN president, endorsed by ACORN
            PAC, elected alderman of Chicago's Fifteenth Ward.
1999   New York: ACORN and labor partners helped upset twenty-five-year
            GOP hold on Hempstead, Long Island City Council, electing two
            Democrats also running on the Working Families Party line.
2003   New York: Letitia James won first victory by a third-party candidate
            for New York City Council in two years.
2005   New York: ACORN member Wayne Hall elected mayor of Village of
            Hempstead, Long Island, New York, listed on both the Democratic
            Party and the Working Families Party ballot.

Education

1995   Seattle: Library created for low-income high school. Librarian hired;
            $20,000 allocated for books.
1996   St. Paul: ACORN elementary charter school opened in St. Paul, teach-
            ing students in English, Spanish, and Hmong.
1997   New York: City schools chancellor responded to ACORN charges of
            racism with plans to broaden access to gifted programs.

1997	New York: Two ACORN high schools opened in New York City.
1998	Chicago: ACORN High School, dual-language charter school, opened in Mexican American neighborhood.
2000	Oakland: Oakland ACORN won three-year battle to reopen the abandoned Woodland Elementary School as an ACORN community school.
2001	Chicago: Chicago ACORN won agreement to hire 3,000 new teachers, almost double the number hired in previous years.[59]
2001	New York: ACORN and teachers' union pressured New York City not to privatize five public schools with for-profit Edison Schools.
2004	New York: New York Department of Education provided $1.6 billion for new lead teacher program in South Bronx schools.[60]

Welfare/Workfare

1997	Los Angeles: ACORN wins grievance procedure for workfare workers, the first in the country.
1997	New York: ACORN-organized Workers Organizing Committee of WEP (Work Experience Program, workfare) wins improved conditions for workfare workers. Judge rules Giuliani administration must provide WEP workers at sanitation and transportation departments with protective clothing, equipment, and other services. In unofficial election, 99 percent of 17,000 city workfare workers voted for representation by ACORN.
1997	Philadelphia: ACORN won free transit passes for people moving from welfare to work within city of Philadelphia.
2000	New York: ACORN WEP Workers Organizing Committee wins grievance procedure for workfare workers.
2001	Los Angeles: ACORN-organized home child care providers win grievance procedure for minimum-wage violations. (Day care is essential for many workfare recipients who have jobs.)

Housing

1998	Dallas: ACORN convinced city to increase funding to pay for home repairs for more than 500 senior citizens.
1998	St. Louis: In test case of new regulations, ACORN got Mercantile Bank's Community Reinvestment Act rating downgraded from outstanding to satisfactory based on racially discriminatory home loans.
2000	Baltimore: ACORN helped pressure HUD to renegotiate thousands of FHA loans.

2001	California: Coalition including ACORN helped pass California Assembly Bill AB 489, the first California statewide restrictions on predatory lending.[61]
2001	St. Louis: Coalition including ACORN passes Proposition H, a tax to raise $5 million a year for a housing trust fund and health care for the poor. Taxed out-of-state purchases of more than $2,000.
2002	California: Senate passes ACORN-proposed Bill 1403, tenant-protection law giving renters sixty instead of thirty days to vacate when month-to-month rental agreements are terminated without cause.
2002	Los Angeles: Coalition including ACORN won creation of a $100 million housing trust fund.
2002	New York: City council adopted ACORN's anti–predatory lending ordinance.

Restricting Predatory Lending

2001	Oakland: Won anti–predatory lending legislation.
2003	Arizona: Led campaign that prevented passage of industry-backed bill protecting predatory lending.
2003	Arkansas: Helped strengthen provisions of new anti–predatory lending legislation.
2003	Connecticut: Coalition including ACORN won state legislation to reduce abuses of Refund Anticipation Loans.
2003	New Jersey: Coalition including ACORN passed new anti–predatory lending legislation.
2003	New Mexico: Coalition including ACORN passed new anti–predatory lending legislation.
2004	Massachusetts: Coalition including ACORN won legislation prohibiting loan prepayment penalties, required loan counseling, and limited loan fees.
2004	Minnesota: Collaborated with state attorney general to win state legislation to prevent scams targeting families at risk of foreclosure.
2005	Seattle: City council passed anti-RAL legislation that requires full disclosure or legal redress by RAL lenders.[62]

Utilities

| 2001 | Chicago: Coalition including ACORN won concessions from Peoples Gas, including additional $1 million for residents in arrears on high heating bills; city of Chicago increases aid by $2 million. |

NOTES

1. The only national organization of which I am aware that has similar or greater national experience and accomplishments is the Center for Community Change (CCC) in Washington, D.C. The CCC began as a technical assistance consulting organization for all kinds of community organizations, but it evolved into an umbrella organization that organizes coalitions and national initiatives and brokers relationships between community organizations and funders. Interview, Laura Barrett, Gamaliel Foundation, October 12, 2004.

2. Lisa Ranghelli, "The Monetary Impact of ACORN Campaigns: A Ten Year Retrospective," February 16, 2005 draft, author's possession.

3. For example, see the ACORN-produced book *This Mighty Dream: Social Protest Movements in the United States*, by John Beam, Madeleine Adamson, and Seth Borgos (New York: Routledge and Kegan Paul, 1984).

4. Harry Boyte, *Everyday Politics* (Philadelphia: University of Pennsylvania Press, 2005); Theda Skocpol, "Advocates without Members: The Recent Transformation of American Civic Life," in *Civic Engagement in American Democracy*, ed. T. Skocpol and M. P. Fiorina (Washington, DC, and New York, Brookings Institution and Russell Sage Foundation, 1999), 461–510; Theda Skocpol and Morris P. Fiorina, "How Americans Became Civic," in Skocpol and Fiorina, *Civic Engagement in American Democracy*, 27–80; Theda Skocpol, *Diminished Democracy: From Membership to Management in American Civic Life* (Norman: University of Oklahoma Press, 2003); Dana R. Fisher and Paul-Brian McInerney, *Civic Engagement and the Canvass* (Circle Working Paper 26, January 2005), http://www.columbia.edu/~drf2004/ (accessed March 27, 2006).

5. ACORN formerly ran its own national canvass operation but ceased when its effectiveness waned during the 1980s. Its locals conduct numerous other grassroots fund-raisers (a few still conduct a canvass), the locals and the national organization seek foundation funds, and the organization has won millions from private corporations to support both community redevelopment and organizing. For data, see Heidi Swarts, *Organizing Urban America: Secular- and Faith-Based Progressive Movements* (Minneapolis: University of Minnesota Press, 2007).

6. This is based on survey data from the 100 CBCOs that responded from a total of 133 surveyed. Mark R. Warren and Richard L. Wood, *Faith-Based Community Organizing: The State of the Field* (Jericho, NY: Interfaith Funders, 2001), presented on COMM-ORG: The On-Line Conference on Community Organizing and Development, http://comm-org.wisc.edu/papers.htm (accessed April 12, 2006).

7. Data are from my own fieldwork in St. Louis (see Swarts, *Organizing Urban America*) and from R. Drew Smith, *Beyond the Boundaries: Faith-Based Organizations and Neighborhood Coalition Building* (prepared for the Annie E. Casey Foundation by the Faith Communities and Urban Families Project, the Leadership Center, Morehouse College, November 2003), http://www.aecf.org/publications/data/3_btbreport.pdf (accessed November 9, 2005).

8. On social movement cycles, see Sidney Tarrow, *Power in Movement* (New York: Cambridge University Press, 1998).

9. Skocpol and Fiorina, *Civic Engagement in American Politics*, 211–248.

10. ACORN and the various CBO networks are all slightly different on this dimension. Saul Alinsky and the Industrial Areas Foundation have both had a national vision at various times; however, the IAF today is organized as six suborganizations working regionally as well as locally. PICO and the Gamaliel Foundation have begun nationally coordinated campaigns only very recently, in the year or two before the 2004 election, although both have worked at the state and

regional level. DART, the smallest network (with about twenty-two affiliates), has the slightest infrastructure for national campaigns.

11. Jeffrey M. Berry, *The New Liberalism: The Rising Power of Citizen Groups* (Washington, DC: Brookings Institution Press, 1999).

12. They have as little free time as the more affluent, less money and education, and fewer civic skills. See Sidney Verba, Kay Lehman Schlozman, and Henry E. Brady, *Voice and Equality: Civic Voluntarism in American Politics* (Cambridge, MA: Harvard University Press, 1995).

13. Scholars such as William Gamson, Charles Tilly, and Peter Eisinger wrote influential early works that highlighted features of the political context as causal factors in social movement emergence and success. See W. Gamson, *The Strategy of Social Protest* (Homewood, IL: Dorsey Press, 1975); C. Tilly, *From Mobilization to Revolution* (Reading, MA: Addison-Wesley, 1978); Peter K. Eisinger, "The Conditions of Protest Behavior in American Cities," *American Political Science Review* 67 (1973): 11–28. In his 1982 study of the civil rights movement, Doug McAdam proposed a "political process" model as an alternative to earlier models, especially the dominant model, which stressed organizational factors and the availability of external resources; see Doug McAdam, *Political Process and the Development of Black Insurgency, 1930–1970* (Chicago, University of Chicago Press, 1982). A collective restatement of the approach was made in D. McAdam, J. D. McCarthy, and M. Zald, eds., *Comparative Perspectives on Social Movements* (Cambridge: Cambridge University Press, 1996). Tarrow used the approach in his synthetic summary of social movement theory: Sidney Tarrow, *Power in Movement: Social Movements, Collective Action, and Politics* (Cambridge: Cambridge University Press, 1998).

14. See McAdam, *Political Process and the Development of Black Insurgency;* and Frances Fox Piven and Richard A. Cloward, *Poor People's Movements: Why They Succeed, How They Fail* (New York: Vintage, 1979).

15. H. Swarts, "Setting the State's Agenda: Church-Based Community Organizations in American City Politics," in *States, Parties, and Social Movements: Protest and the Dynamics of Institutional Change,* ed. J. Goldstone (Cambridge: Cambridge University Press, 2001), 78–106.

16. Ibid.

17. Doug McAdam, Charles Tilly, and Sidney Tarrow, *The Dynamics of Contention* (Cambridge, Cambridge University Press, 2001); also the debate from *Sociological Forum* reprinted as part 1 of *Rethinking Social Movements,* ed. Jeff Goodwin and James M. Jasper (Lanham, MD: Rowman and Littlefield, 2004).

18. Sarah Pralle, "Shopping Around: Environmental Organizations and the Search for Policy Venues" (paper presented at the annual meeting of the Western Political Science Association, Oakland, California, March 17–19, 2005), 13.

19. The source of this puzzling trait is unclear, and there is inadequate space here to analyze it. As one longtime national staffer said, "We're accountable to members, and members are ambitious, and say things like 'let's take over city council.' ... When people get fired up that's when they join. Back in 1995 they thought it was ridiculous that the minimum wage was $4.25." I can hypothesize that the reason for this characteristic may have to do with qualities of its founders and leaders; the fact that compared with conventional nonprofit sector organizations, ACORN has few resources and thus less to risk by failure; or the fact that ACORN's underpaid organizers are willing to contribute long hours of labor, and those who stay form a cadre with a strong collective identity and allegiance to ACORN. One labor organizer has referred to ACORN as a "cult"; anonymous interview with author.

20. The coalition claimed that "nearly 4,000 house parties were held—the single largest mobilization for public schools ever—where parents, teachers and community members came together to discuss local and national issues and made plans to take action and make sure that education is

a priority on every level of government." Allison Conyers, "4,000 House Parties Call for Quality Education," ACORN press release, September 24, 2004.

21. Maude Hurd and Lisa Donner, with Camellia Phillips, "Community Organizing and Advocacy: Fighting Predatory Lending and Making a Difference," ACORN report, n.d., author's possession.

22. Carol Zabin and Isaac Martin, *Living Wage Campaigns in the Economic Policy Arena: Four Case Studies from California* (Center for Labor Research and Education, Institute of Industrial Relations, University of California, June 1999), http://www.iir.berkeley.edu/livingwage/pdf/livwage.pdf (accessed on January 30, 2005).

23. This is as of November 2006; more have been passed since. The source is the ACORN Living Wage Resource Center Web site, which is probably the most up-to-date source of information on these ordinances; it is cited by the Economic Policy Institute and other research on living wage campaigns. Although ACORN's claims about its own work should be taken with proper skepticism, ACORN only claims leadership or direct participation in a minority of all living wage campaigns.

24. Traci Hukill, "Chasing Amy," *Metroactive,* October 15–21, 1998, http://www.metroactive .com/papers/metro/10.15.98/index.html (accessed April 10, 2006).

25. ACORN has also served this outreach and service-provision function as part of the IRS's national free tax preparation service for low-income individuals, conducting outreach in poor neighborhoods to recruit applicants for the Earned Income Tax Credit.

26. These include four federal agencies: the Federal Reserve, the Office of the Comptroller of the Currency (OCC), the FDIC, and the Office of Thrift Supervision.

27. "Capital & Communities: A Report to the Annie E. Casey Foundation on ACORN's Work to Revitalize Low and Moderate Income Communities," n.d., http://www.ACORN.org/index.php?id=686 (accessed June 24, 2005).

28. Ibid.

29. ACORN wanted the bank to "1) work with community groups to create loan counseling programs; 2) reform underwriting and pricing policies to more flexibly accommodate low- and moderate-income borrowers; 3) establish lifeline bank accounts and government check cashing; 4) maintain and expand branching in low- and moderate- income neighborhoods; 5) decentralize corporate power sufficiently to allow for local credit needs; and 6) fund financial intermediaries to provide technical assistance for multifamily housing development by non-profits." Ibid.

30. Specifically, the agreement provided $125,000 for ACORN Housing Corporation (AHC) to help low-income and minority applicants in Dallas, Houston, and Washington, D.C.; the mortgages were fixed rate with no ballooned payments, down payments as low as $500, a 95 percent loan-to-value ratio, and 1 percent below-market interest.

31. Maude Hurd, letter to federal banking regulators, October 17, 2001, fanniemae.com/news/pressreleases/0710/html (accessed June 17, 2005).

32. "Household Losing the Public Relations Battle," *Retail Banker International,* May 13, 2002.

33. The Foreclosure Avoidance Program provides interest rate reductions, waivers of unpaid late charges, deferrals of accrued unpaid interest, and loan principal reductions to borrowers at risk of home foreclosures.

34. Project Vote, "Our Mission," http://projectvote.org/index.php?id=119. It was independent until 2003, when it approached the Industrial Areas Foundation and ACORN to pursue affiliation. ACORN accepted the offer.

35. "ACORN's 2004 Voter Participation Campaign," report, author's possession.

36. A family of four with two children and one full-time worker earning $7 per hour would

net $13,600 per year, several thousand dollars below the poverty line. This worker in 2004 qualified for an Earned Income Tax Credit of $4,300 and a Child Tax Credit of $395. Joseph Llobrera and Bob Zahradnik, "A Hand Up: How State Earned Income Tax Credits Help Working Families Escape Poverty in 2004. Summary," Center on Budget and Policy Priorities, http://www.cbpp.org/5-14-04sfp.pdf (accessed June 20, 2005).

37. ACORN cannot require EITC recipients it contacts to join. At best no more than 50 percent of those invited during the EITC outreach join, but ACORN is still gaining new members and recognition.

38. Ron Smith, IRS chief of corporate partnerships, telephone interview, June 24, 2005.

39. ACORN bylaws, author's collection.

40. Local control of local campaigns not only is consistent with community organizing's ideology of democratic participation but also is pragmatically effective in motivating local activists to participate, especially in new chapters. For example, in April 2005, New Orleans ACORN pursued neighborhood infrastructure repairs for water main leaks, while in Watts, Los Angeles, ACORN members marched for safer streets and won three new stop signs.

41. At the 1980 Democratic National Convention, ACORN won a commitment to establish a poor people's commission, but in 1982 the Democratic National Committee essentially killed it. However, the campaign expanded ACORN's organization, won it national visibility, and changed its self-image. ACORN history taken from Gary Delgado, *Organizing the Movement* (Philadelphia: Temple University Press, 1986).

42. Ibid.

43. For this view, see Edward T. Chambers and Michael A. Cowan, *Roots for Radicals: Organizing for Power, Action, and Justice* (New York: Continuum International, 2003).

44. See *Poor People's Movements: Why They Succeed, How They Fail* (New York: Vintage, 1979).

45. David S. Meyer and Sidney Tarrow, eds., *The Social Movement Society: Contentious Politics for a New Century* (Lanham, MD: Rowman and Littlefield, 1998).

46. Steve Kest, interview, August 4, 2004, Brooklyn, New York.

47. Municipalities in which ACORN led successful campaigns include St. Louis; St. Paul; Minneapolis; Boston; Oakland; Denver; Chicago; Cook County, Illinois; New Orleans; San Francisco; Sacramento; and New York City. In addition, ACORN participated in successful campaigns in San Jose; San Diego; Broward County, Florida; and Detroit.

48. The Massachusetts Needs a Raise Coalition (the Massachusetts AFL-CIO, Neighbor to Neighbor, the Tax Equity Alliance of Massachusetts, and the Coalition against Poverty). Greater Boston Legal Services Web site, http://www.gbls.org/employment/organizations.htm (accessed April 21, 2005).

49. The New York coalition was the $5.15 Is Not Enough Coalition, mobilized by New York's Working Families Party, of which ACORN is a founding member. In both the coalition and the party, ACORN and labor unions were primary driving forces.

50. Minimum wage for restaurant employees who receive tips was also raised from $3.30 to $4.60 in two years.

51. This is an average of 10 percent more than other IRS Volunteer Income Tax Assistance (VITA) program sites.

52. The exclusion of homes with flat roofs (the majority of Philadelphia's urban housing) was waived, there was no requirement for credit reports and no mandatory ratio of market value to replacement cost, uniform statewide inspection requirements were imposed, and insurers were willing to insure homes with vacant and abandoned buildings on the block.

53. The program capped fees at 3 percent, included no prepayment penalties, held interest

rates at half a percentage point below average, and featured no requirement for credit life insurance. ACORN provided financial education and loan counseling.

54. Estimated by multiplying the mean mortgage value of ACORN Housing's largest lender, Bank of America, by the number of mortgages made through ACORN Housing Corp., 1986–2005. Memorandum, Bruce Dorpalen, ACORN Housing Corp., 2005, author's possession.

55. ACORN Housing Corporation was founded in 1986 and as of August 2004 had offices in thirty-seven cities.

56. Citigroup agreed to reduce prepayment penalties and cap points and fees at 3 percent of loan amount.

57. RALs are short-term loans that provide people with their tax refunds earlier; interest rates are exorbitant, however, and borrowers are often not informed of them.

58. Provides interest rate reductions, waivers of unpaid late charges, deferrals of accrued unpaid interest, and loan principal reductions to borrowers at risk of home foreclosures.

59. Chicago ACORN based demands on its research on schools in four low-income neighborhood schools. It characterized 28 percent to 40 percent of teachers in schools studied as underqualified.

60. This program is a project of the Community Collaborative to Improve District 9 Schools (CC9), which includes six community-based organizations, including ACORN. Other participating organizations deliver services, while ACORN primarily contributes community organizing.

61. The law limits interest to no more than 8 percentage points above the current yield on Treasury bonds; fees on loans cannot exceed 6 percent of the total loan.

62. ACORN claims that RALS tax preparers sold RALs to more than 17,000 low-income Seattle area families in 2002.

7. Higher Power

Strategic Capacity for State and National Organizing

Richard L. Wood

This chapter studies an organizing effort of the PICO National Network, which organizes in poor, working-class, and middle-class neighborhoods in the United States, mostly in urban areas.[1] PICO engages in "faith-based community organizing" to generate democratic pressure to advance the interests of its nonelite, highly multiracial participants.[2] The research reported here goes beyond other studies of grassroots organizing through its focus on efforts to influence policymaking on health care, public safety, education, immigrant rights, and housing at the *state and national levels*.

Efforts to build democratic movements in urban America have recently gained renewed scholarly attention.[3] These analyses have generally promoted a cautiously optimistic reading of the prospects for urban democratic reform. But they focus on local movements and thus beg the question, When so much of the decision making that determines the quality of life for poor, working-class, and middle-class Americans occurs "over the heads" of local political leaders, how influential can locally rooted social movements be? Are they relegated to fiddling on the margins of social policy—perhaps extracting minor concessions, but powerless to impact the decisions of economic elites who control global financial and informational flows, national political elites whose policies determine the availability of resources to meet urban needs, or the state-level elites who distribute those resources? Together, these state- and national-level decisions severely constrain local options; can community organizing effectively reshape those constraints?

Furthermore, as noted in the introductory chapter of this volume, changes in the national culture and political economy have reshaped the ecology of civic engagement in ways that present new challenges. Deindustrialization of the American economy and the delocalization of many of the corporations that remain in cities virtually require community organizing to project power into higher-level political arenas if participants wish to have real impact. Meanwhile, the political and cultural bases from which to build such civic power have themselves been eroded: on one hand by a new hyperpartisanship in Congress and national politics, and on the other hand by the decline of a *culture* of civic engagement in American life.[4] Can community organizing efforts hope to simultaneously address the economic challenges facing low-income communities, political stagnation in the national capital, *and* the cultural challenges of sustaining long-term civic engagement?

This chapter begins to answer these questions by examining two prominent sites of higher-level power projection by faith-based community organizing (FBCO) groups. Examining first the ten-year track record of the PICO California Project, I will argue that the evidence shows that such efforts can attain significant influence at the state level—even in the largest, arguably most politically complex state of the nation (California, with a population of 40 million and a vast and sophisticated media market). This retrospective analysis provides strong evidence of political impact and strategic capacity at the state level, but it can tell us little about the actual dynamics underlying this strategic capacity, or how well that capacity might translate up to the national level. For the latter, I examine the organizing process of PICO's currently emergent New Voices national campaign to reshape domestic policy in Congress, gradually launched during 2002–2005.

This analysis thus assesses the factors shaping the internal strategic structure and strategic capacity within two supralocal organizing efforts: at the state level via documentary evidence, interviews with key participants, and ethnographic data, seeking insight into the factors that have allowed the PICO California Project to generate significant influence; and at the national level via a more contemporaneous analysis drawing on a year and a half of participant-observation, interview, and archival data to assess the potential strategic strength of PICO New Voices.[5] The conclusion argues that, beyond the potential political gains of such work, its *culture-shaping* dimensions offer crucial tools for democratic leaders engaged in all kinds of "public work."[6] The conclusion also suggests the constraints imposed on such efforts by the current hyperpartisanship of national politics.

CONTEXT

When launched (PICO California Project in 1996, New Voices in 2002), each of the organizing efforts analyzed here faced significant hurdles: First, though some of PICO's local community organizations had impressive track records, strong political roots, and significant local power, others were not nearly so strong. Second, these organizations had little prior experience in supralocal political arenas and little expertise on that level. Third, these organizations operate on budgets far short of what their opponents can mobilize—the typical local organization having an annual budget of only $150,000 (in 2000 dollars).[7] Fourth, the relatively friendly terrain— that is, friendly for claims making in favor of government programs and policies supporting urban residents of moderate means—of the political discourse descended from Roosevelt's New Deal had clearly lost its hegemony, supplanted by a discourse in which such claims must struggle uphill to gain legitimacy.

Thus, at face value the decision to launch these supralocal campaigns from within the PICO network seems quixotic. Influencing these higher-level political arenas presented significant hurdles of funding, expertise, political sophistication, and scale that PICO had never faced before. Likewise, as a determinedly nonpartisan organization, PICO had little chance of tapping into the deep pockets of party-linked financiers that might otherwise be natural candidates for funding such efforts. Perhaps most significantly for the New Voices effort, the more obvious route toward national influence would be via a coalition linking similar efforts by other faith-based community organizing networks. Together, these networks (PICO, IAF, Gamaliel, DART, IVP, RCNO, and OLTC, plus a few independent efforts) represent more than 160 local organizations, including essentially all the major metropolitan areas and many other primary cities of the country.[8] As of 1999, for which systematic national data exist, those organizations incorporated 4,000 member institutions (87 percent religious congregations, the rest mostly unions, public schools, and neighborhood associations) in thirty-eight states, which together included approximately 2 million institutional members.[9] Since then, the field has grown significantly, perhaps by 20 percent, and now has a presence in all but a handful of states.[10] The same studies, along with the chapters by Swarts and Burns in this volume, show how effective FBCO work can be at the local level. These organizations are capable of projecting significant local political influence; table 7.1 shows one assessment of that capacity, the ability to mobilize large numbers of people into the public arena.[11] In most cities, an organization capable of mobilizing 500 or 1,000 people focused on specific policy proposals can wield significant influence in local politics—especially when that constituency is as racially and ethnically diverse as these are.[12]

Table 7.1. Projecting Power: Highest Attendance at Political Actions Sponsored by Local Organizations

Maximum Reported Attendance at a Local Political Action	Number of FBCO Organizations ($n = 100$)
1,000 or more (max = 10,000; mean = 1,807)	27 organizations
400–900	36 organizations
120–350	28 organizations
Less than 100	9 organizations

If coordinated around a coherent issue initiative, a cross-network national cam-paign built on this power basis would appear to hold real potential for significant national influence. But such potential is simply off the table at present: although PICO and some of the other networks continue to engage in local collaborative efforts with one another or with groups such as labor unions or the neighborhood organizing group Association of Community Organizations for Reform Now (ACORN), past attempts at larger-scale, cross-network collaboration have gener-ated significant frustration and disillusionment. Only internally does there appear to exist the political trust necessary to undergird such an effort.

PICO's decision to launch supralocal work resulted from a simple political cal-culation: although its federations often can wield real influence over local decisions, PICO found such influence increasingly inadequate to meeting the challenges fac-ing its constituents in "working families." In the context of municipal dependence on monetary flows controlled at the state and federal levels under the new federal-ism (and many unfunded federal mandates), local decision making kicks in only *after* more substantial decisions are made; the decisions that these organizations previously could influence occurred only *within* vast constraints imposed by those higher-level decisions. Thus, attempting to influence state and federal decision mak-ing became increasingly necessary if PICO leaders were to respond adequately to the challenges they faced.

These factors explain the decision to move up to higher-level political arenas. But how effective could PICO be there?

POLITICAL IMPACT OF THE PICO CALIFORNIA PROJECT

In 1993, California faced tight fiscal constraints, and both the governor's office and the state assembly were controlled by the GOP—which, at least at first blush, rep-resented an unlikely ally for work addressing urban social concerns (though, as we shall see, PICO has worked collaboratively with politicians of a wide variety of stripes, including many Republicans). Yet for the reasons cited earlier, gaining a voice in statewide policy seemed imperative. As I will argue, that PICO was ulti-mately able to do so successfully offers the best initial insight into the organiza-tion's strategic capacity. Furthermore, the organizational and strategic lessons learned in California have significantly shaped the national effort.

For my brief purposes here, two kinds of evidence will document the effort's success: specific victories gained at the state level, and comments from key inform-ants in state government and political society regarding PICO's influence.

Public education, health care, and to a lesser degree housing policy have been the focus of PICO's statewide efforts. Initially, the organization used its preexisting ties to Governor Pete Wilson (established by PICO's San Diego Organizing Project when Wilson was mayor there) and its ability to mobilize people from throughout California to influence educational policy: first at a 1995 assembly in San Jose, where some 1,500 people met the U.S. secretary of education and state superintendent of schools and demonstrated PICO's political credentials, gradually building up to a successful 1998 campaign to convince Wilson and the state legislature to provide $50 million for after-school programs in poor districts around the state. The organization also played an important role in placing on the ballot the 1998 Proposition 1A to provide $9.2 billion for school repair and construction—which passed despite California's powerful antirevenue lobbies, with PICO mobilizing crucial support for its eventual passage. In 1999, building on a successful program forged by PICO's local Sacramento affiliate, the statewide effort worked with legislators and the state education secretary to develop legislation for $15 million for a parent-teacher home visitation project, extending it to 450 public schools statewide. This legislation has been renewed annually ever since, with PICO successfully fighting to protect it during budget-cutting years—particularly in 2002, when in the face of the worst budget crisis in California history PICO mobilized almost 4,000 residents to a statewide political action to preserve funding for vital programs in health care, education, and housing. The home visitation program has now received $150 million and is widely hailed for fostering educational success by linking families more actively to schools and teachers. Finally, in 2004 Governor Arnold Schwarzenegger signed PICO-sponsored legislation for $30 million in incentive money for local school districts to establish smaller high schools, again building on the work of local affiliates.[13]

In 2000, the California Project turned its focus to health care policy.[14] Bringing 3,000 middle- and low-income residents from around the state—the most multiracial political gathering of this size in the state capital in years, which itself turned the heads of government staffers and politicians—the organization won passage of the Cedillo-Alarcon Clinic Investment Act of 2000, dedicating $42 million to improving the infrastructure of health clinics in the state, which serve large numbers of the poor and working poor (in 2001, PICO helped gain $10 million in annual funding increases for these primary care clinics). The 2000 action also generated attention to health policy within the administration of Governor Gray Davis, whose political platform had included virtually no agenda for health care. Initial success was limited but important: the state dropped intrusive quarterly reporting requirements for MediCal (the state's version of Medicaid, the federal program for low-income health care), allowing some half million families to maintain their health coverage more consistently. Most substantially, after initial setbacks the California Project worked with the heads of both houses of the state legislature to obtain the state's commitment to expand health coverage to some 300,000 working-poor parents. Under sustained political pressure from PICO and its organizational allies (including the AARP, the California Medical Association, and the California Primary Care Association), the federal government agreed to waivers making more than $400 million available for this program, and the state agreed to use its share of tobacco lawsuit settlements (more than $400 million per year) to support health care, committing $200 million to match the federal funding. Though the latter funding was held up by the state's 2002 budget crisis, as this chapter goes to press (2006), the program remains alive, and PICO is leading a ballot initiative to dramatically increase funding for the Healthy Families Program and related efforts.[15]

On housing policy, PICO has seen much more limited success. Nearly 3,000 statewide residents attended a 2001 meeting in San Francisco, at which state treasurer Phil Angelides agreed to support affordable housing funding, and this effort led to a $20 million increase in California's tax credit for low-income housing. However, in the state's extraordinarily expensive housing market, this funding can hardly be considered a large win, and a 2004 bond initiative to which PICO's San Francisco affiliate dedicated significant organizational resources was defeated (narrowly missing the 60 percent vote needed for passage in California's "tax reform" environment).

This brief review of PICO's successes in the California public arena represents one way of showing that this faith-based community organizing model has the strategic capacity to generate high-level influence. But equally important for long-term influence is how the organization is perceived by political insiders in the state. To assess this, Paul Speer and his colleagues interviewed key informants in California state government and elite political society regarding their perceptions of the PICO California Project.[16] Overall, the interviewees expressed a great deal of respect for the organization's professionalism and rootedness in "real communities and real people"; as one informant noted, the organization "has gained recognition in state politics because many representatives, lobbyists, and experts have begun to recognize the strong relationship the PICO California Project has with the home communities of its affiliates." Other statements that capture the tenor of these interviews include the following: "More than any other organization, the PICO California Project's leadership is comprised of representatives of a diverse cross section of the population of California. Perhaps most importantly, its leadership encompasses a unique population of the disenfranchised"; and "Grassroots groups are often unfocused and undisciplined in their work, often have trouble staying on message. . . . The PICO California Project, however, does not share any of these weaknesses."

Key strengths of the effort seen by these interviewees included the perception that PICO is "disciplined, focused, and competent"; has organizational infrastructure at both local and state levels; represents a diverse constituency; and frames socioeconomic issues from the moral high ground.[17] Thus, in interpreting these interviews, Speer argued:

> The Project is seen as effective because they . . . act on issues both locally and statewide. . . . Another strength is the great legitimacy the organization has with local elected representatives. . . . [Elite interviewees noted that members] were a diverse group, representing a number of ethnicities and age groups . . . and that PICO California Project does not have a financial interest in the resolution of any issues of concern to the organization. Rather, the group has a "pure self interest in true social justice that is absolutely unique."[18]

PICO's unique position in California politics was emphasized repeatedly by interviewees: "The organization's faith-based orientation made it quite unique in the power arena of the state capital . . . and lent a 'moral credibility' to PICO's issue work."[19] Another informant noted that she had "never seen that kind of sophistication" in a grassroots organization.[20] Still others called PICO "a bomb exploding the business-as-usual style of politics";[21] argued that its work has "resulted in progress [on health care] that would have never been made without the organization";[22] and said "of all the grassroots organizing groups in California politics, none are as effective as the PICO California Project."[23]

The primary weakness cited by these elite political informants concerned the inherent limitations of PICO's political culture of broad internal consultation on all significant decisions. As one noted: "The organization is based on and directed by its leadership [i.e., not staff-driven]. . . . When strategic decisions must be made, leadership is brought together to discuss plans and decide as a community which direction they will take. [Staff] cannot make those decisions. . . . This decision-making structure makes it difficult for the organization to be flexible and respond to rapid changes in political debate and strategy."[24] Notwithstanding this weakness—to which I shall return—the overall picture that emerges in Speer's analysis is as follows: "The organization also enjoys real and powerful connections with legislators and representatives at the State Capitol. The organization is able to call upon these connections to put strong pressure on local representatives to address the concerns of the organization's leadership. This kind of political connection has not been developed by any other grassroots organization working in the State [and the organization is seen as] very savvy about the political process . . . [the organization] understood the nuances of negotiation, which was highly effective during her work with the Governor."[25] Thus, PICO appears to have made a significant impact on the policy process in California, bringing previously marginalized voices into that process to an extent unmatched in these political insiders' experience; as one summarized the organization's political access: "[PICO] has a great deal of power and entree, certainly to a greater extent than most organizations. . . . Even in critical times when there is a huge crush of demands . . . PICO can still get in the door and still get respected. That's rare for someone who doesn't have $100,000 to donate."[26]

Finally, note that—despite fears of some participants at the start of the effort—projecting state-level power does not appear to have undermined PICO's local organizing: in the context of building statewide influence, PICO in California expanded from ten local affiliate organizations in 1993 to twenty such affiliates in 2005, representing more than 350 congregations (which PICO claims gives it a presence in more than half of the state's legislative districts and representation of some 400,000 families affiliated with sponsoring congregations). Indeed, it arguably *strengthened* local organizing by creating resource flows into which affiliates could tap by influencing city and county decision making (particularly as local governments drew on tobacco settlement money to fund health care for working-class residents, and on state affordable housing money generated through the PICO-supported bond measure to fund local housing initiatives).

PICO California Project executive director Jim Keddy, working with organizers and leaders from throughout the state, was the architect of the work throughout the period. His assessment of what PICO California Project has accomplished is somewhat more sober. In the 1998–2001 period, he notes, "We were able to shift pretty significant resources toward our priorities, during a time when the state had money. . . . After the stock market crash [of 2001], we got into a situation of playing defense, trying to protect programs that serve working-class families." Keddy went on to note that PICO underwent a great deal of strategic learning in the latter period, regarding the nature of the taxation system, how the state spends money, and how to run statewide initiatives (which are crucial in California)—and that in many ways PICO was successful, in the sense that California has not had the huge cuts in social spending faced by working people in many states. But he noted, "we want to get out of playing defense, and really play offense again." By 2006, that was happening: PICO was working on a major statewide ballot initiative to expand and fund health coverage for children in California.[27]

The trajectory of the PICO California Project thus highlights the challenges presented by projecting power into supralocal political arenas, but it also demonstrates PICO's ability to do so. Perhaps, then, even projecting national power might be more promising than it appears. Might PICO's thirty years of experience organizing in local communities and ten years organizing at the statewide level in California (and more recently in Louisiana, New Jersey, and Colorado) provide a basis for projecting power nationally? New Voices is PICO's effort to answer that question. Though it is too early to know whether that national effort will succeed or fail, we can examine the factors that might plausibly contribute to a successful national organizing strategy. Before empirically considering the emergent New Voices campaign, I offer some analytic categories to help us do so.

UNDERSTANDING SUCCESS AND FAILURE: STRATEGY,
ORGANIZATION, AND SOCIAL NETWORKS

Political strategy is notoriously recalcitrant to generalizable analysis, in that it is always highly emergent and context dependent. But recent studies of social movements have begun to offer real insight into the internal factors that drive some efforts toward success and others toward failure. Not satisfied with either purely structuralist or purely rationalist accounts of movement success—which emphasized resource mobilization and selective incentives, respectively—this recent work pays greater attention to internal cultural, political, and strategic dynamics within such movements.[28] Gamson's pioneering work launched the "strategy" facet of this effort, generating an academic firestorm of controversy over the best way of measuring movement strategy and success.[29] Ultimately, the best evidence and interpretation suggest that Gamson largely got it right.[30] Three facets of this reanalysis of movement strategy will be especially important here. First, movements whose goal is the *displacement* of elites systematically fail; to have reasonable hope of success within the American polity, movement strategists must frame their goals in ways that do not require elite displacement in order to succeed. Reform (perhaps radical reform, but reform nonetheless), negotiation, and compromise are the watchwords of success in institutional politics. Second, factionalism also leads to failure; to succeed, movement leaders must avoid the kinds of organizational problems that lead to such factionalism. Third, for reform movements that do avoid factionalist disputes, the greatest predictor of success is a movement's existence during a time of broad crisis: that is, concessions to movement demands tend to occur during times of system crisis (presumably as an elite strategy to preserve their legitimacy during crises), so movements that simply last long enough to be around during a time of crisis are more likely to succeed. Movement longevity thus increases the chances of success.

But what leads to movement longevity? Frey and colleagues suggest close attention to internal movement dynamics: "Internal politics remain critical to the success of excluded groups."[31] Previous work examining the internal political culture of community organizing argues that the crucial dynamics of internal politics are processes of cultural interpretation and meaning construction—and suggest that PICO has mastered those dynamics rather successfully, at least in its stronger local projects.[32] Thus, the FBCO movement examined here clearly has mastered these initial challenges: PICO (and FBCO organizations generally) pursue reformist goals, generally avoid internal factionalism, and have built organizations enduring for years or decades. This chapter therefore only briefly alludes to these minimal conditions of success and instead focuses on the strategic and cultural factors that undergird success.

Thus, the strength of looking at a contemporary movement just emerging into the national political arena: there we can see at work the dynamics of movement politics, cultural interpretation, organizational strategy, and meaning construction—the very stuff of "internal politics" understood broadly, including but not limited to goal framing and the fight against factionalism. Two recent analyses of movement structure and strategy will help us understand the key factors that contribute to movement success. We can think of these as the internal strategic structure and the strategic capacity of a movement.

Internal Strategic Structure

Michael Chwe's agent-based modeling of the influence of network structures and participants' strategic situations suggests that we must think simultaneously about structure and strategy in analyzing movements for collective action.[33] First, it matters whether the members of a network being mobilized generally carry a low or high threshold for collective action. For our purposes, "collective action" means active participation in PICO's national New Voices effort, including its associated political action. "Threshold" here means whether a particular individual will participate if she perceives a relatively small number of fellow activists prepared to participate (low threshold); or will do so *only* if she perceives a large number of others prepared to participate (high threshold). Chwe's model shows that the "strategic situation"—the mix of high versus low thresholds in the network being mobilized—matters greatly for what kind of organization is necessary to effectively sustain the effort. *If* participation thresholds are high, the organizing effort must construct broad networks with significant numbers of "weak ties" linking subgroups. Only in that way will individuals be connected to enough others in the organizing effort so that they can "see" large numbers of other likely participants, and thus meet their high thresholds. *If* participation thresholds are generally low, the organizing effort need not focus on constructing such broad networks linking large numbers of individuals: tight-knit local groups built on mostly "strong ties" to one another are sufficient to undergird widespread mobilization into action. Thus whether strong ties or weak ties are more crucial at a given moment in an organizing effort depends vitally on whether participants hold high or low thresholds for action at that particular time.

Chwe shows that scholars must take this into account to explain movement success. But note, too, that this insight captures part of the art of community organizing: professional organizers and primary leaders within the movement must at least intuitively know people's thresholds and craft their emerging network organizations accordingly. This need not be a product of abstract thinking and strategizing; indeed, it is much more likely to be a product of intuitive "feel" and expert knowledge gained through the practice of organizing.[34] Since such thresholds may well not be static but rather emergent (shifting with participants' political anger, motivation, and other factors), organizers and primary leaders must be assessing the internal strategic situation constantly (note that this represents a very different dimension of "strategy" than that discussed by Ganz, below).

As we will see, during the early stages of PICO's initial mobilization around the national strategy, participants expressed significant concern that it might be impossible to succeed, that it was too difficult to project sufficient political power to affect national decision making. We can think of this as a high-threshold situation: potential participants recognized the need to mobilize national political leverage in order to improve life in their communities, but they would invest themselves in doing so only if they were convinced that enough others would do so—and "enough" here meant a lot of people. In this high-threshold context, the organizing effort had to construct many ties across various local organizing projects, states, and regions of the country—that is, had to invest organizational time in generating weak ties to complement the strong ties that its participants already carried from congregation-based organizing locally.

Equally important, Chwe shows that in almost all strategic situations, a *mix of weak and strong ties* within the movement is optimal. So, again, building an effective national mobilizing structure involves balancing strong and weak ties: strong ties to reinforce solidarity within, commitment to, and the meaningfulness of participation; weak ties to overcome high thresholds to action by increasing members' perception of sufficient probable participation by others.

A final set of insights provided by this agent-based modeling approach bears directly on this analysis: collective action is much more "robust"—that is, much less subject to collapse and demobilization—when communication within the organizing effort is partially *reciprocal*. That is, the organizing effort is much more likely to collapse if communication flows only in one direction, so that participants cannot be confident that they know each other's actual inclinations to participate. In contrast, reciprocal communication allows participants to monitor their strategic situations and thus gain the confidence to act. Chwe suggests that such reciprocity occurs partly through the ongoing sharing of political feelings such as anger—this allows participants to gauge one another's actual inclination to take action.[35] But the *optimal* internal communicative situation in a movement involves a mixture of reciprocal communication (for the reasons mentioned earlier) and one-way communication (which facilitates flow of information from low-threshold to high-threshold members, thus increasing the likelihood of aggregating up and taking action). Thus, a successful supralocal organizing movement must foster extensive reciprocity of communication while also preserving situations in which communication is more structured from above. As we will see, these strategic conditions for success (the right balance of weak and strong ties and of one-way and reciprocal communication) imply specific aspects of organizational culture and organizational authority.

Strategic Capacity

Also crucial to movement success is strategy in a quite different sense: the timing, tactics, and targets of the movement.[36] As Ganz argues, the usual ways of assessing movement strategy (through such concepts as political opportunity structure, leaders' charisma, and even "strategy" itself) help little in analyzing the creativity involved in developing effective strategy.[37] He focuses instead on "strategic capacity"—the ability of leaders to learn from political experience, gain access to crucial information from the political environment, and strongly maintain their own motivation. He argues that we can study the impact of strategic capacity on movement success far more effectively than we can study the impact of strategy itself. This is true a fortiori in studying the early stages of PICO's national effort: its strategy might be evaluated retrospectively, ten years from now, but strategic capacity provides better entrée into assessing its current potential, promise, and challenges.

Ganz argues that strategic capacity is the product of two sets of factors, grouped under "leadership" and "organization":

Leadership: Strategic capacity is likely to be greater if the movement has leaders that mix strong and weak ties within and outside the movement (similar to Chwe's analysis, but here focused not on the internal ties among participants but on the external ties of key strategists); leaders whose past biographies make some political insiders and others political outsiders;[38] and leaders whose past political experiences give the movement ready access to diverse tactical repertoires, thus creating alternative political possibilities.

Organization: Strategic capacity is likely to be greater if the movement organization includes structures for deliberation that are regular, open, and authoritative; draws on resources (both money and people's talents) that come from multiple constituencies (including from the groups it is trying to mobilize); fosters "focal points for creative decision-making";[39] and provides structures of accountability that keep leaders tied to the interests of salient constituencies and involve what Ganz terms democratic or entrepreneurial accountability rather than bureaucratic accountability (i.e., people gain authority and status via either political entrepreneurship or democratic election, rather than being chosen from above in the organization).

Ganz's overall explanatory framework, the "strategic process model" of movements, argues that qualities of leadership and organization drive the movement's strategic capacity, which shapes the creative linking of movement timing, tactics, and targets, which in turn shapes movement success.

Ganz's excellent empirical analysis of farmworker organizing in the 1960s shows that the United Farm Workers' organizational characteristics led to its "strategy unfolding in a community, statewide, and long-term arena," which offered significant strategic advantages in comparison to the parallel AFL-CIO organizing effort among farmworkers.[40] This parallels the important historical pattern whereby the most successful civic associations have adopted a "federated" structure that parallels the local-state-federal structure of government in the United States.[41]

Overall, the prior work reviewed here suggests that the strategic efficacy of collective movements depends on the interaction of four sets of specific factors: the organizational, leadership, network, and cultural factors summarized in table 7.2. To recapitulate, the newness of PICO's national organizing effort does not allow a retrospective assessment of movement strategy, but we are able to examine an equally important question: How do internal movement dynamics *generate* the strategic characteristics listed in table 7.2? Rather than assuming that movements gain strategically advantageous qualities as some kind of "found objects," I ask how such qualities emerge *through the organizing process*. Retrospective assessments are

Table 7.2. Strategic Capacity: Organizational, Leadership, Network, and Cultural Factors Contributing to Success

Organizational Factors

Deliberative structure	Regular, open, authoritative; "focal points for creativity"
Resource flows	Money and people from multiple constituencies, including base
Accountability	Entrepreneurial or democratic >> bureaucratic accountability
Organizational structure	Federated (local-state-federal) organizational structure

Leadership Factors

Leaders' biographies	Mix of insiders/outsiders
Repertoires	Key leaders bring mix of political repertoires

Network Factors

External networks	Mix of strong and weak ties to diverse external institutions
Internal networks	Mix of strong and weak ties among organizing participants; generally, weak ties >> strong ties if action thresholds high

Cultural Factors

Goal framing	Against displacement goals
Internal politics	Promoting unity; effective undermining of factionalism
Internal communication	Reciprocal communication extensive, including communication regarding participant "feeling"; some one-way communication
Monitoring	Regular assessment of participants' action thresholds
Meaning construction	Cultural interpretation and construction of shared meaning of national organizing

of little use in answering this question; we need instead to analyze the actual process of political organizing in situ, as it unfolds in real time. I turn now to a brief ethnographic assessment of PICO's strategic capacity as it is being built through national-level organizing.

STRATEGIC CAPACITY IN PICO NEW VOICES: ORGANIZATION, LEADERSHIP, NETWORKS, AND CULTURE

To launch the New Voices national campaign, PICO leaders and organizers had to deal with significant doubts within their own federations; to be successful, they will have to overcome significant strategic barriers. As PICO associate director Scott Reed, a key architect of the New Voices effort, suggested in an interview, "Our leaders increasingly understand the need for the federal-level action, but are constrained by their own realities and by political realities in Washington, D.C., in bringing it about." How are participants confronting those barriers, and what do the emerging factors of organizational structure, leadership, network ties, and culture suggest about the resulting strategic capacity?

Note first that one of the most insightful scholars of grassroots political organizing in the United States is quite skeptical of the strategic capacity of the faith-based community organizing field in general.[42] This is a sobering assessment, not to be dismissed. The breakthrough by some FBCO efforts to new levels of political influence *of itself* offers little assurance that such efforts have developed the kinds of strategic creativity, internal democratic accountability, or learning capacity that Ganz argues underlie successful strategy in the long term. But note, too, that Ganz's interpretation emerges from his exposure to models of organizing in particular networks and regions of the country. Ganz thus offers a healthy skepticism, but one that must itself be subjected to critical inquiry: does it apply to *all* faith-based community organizing efforts? Conversely, have particular efforts developed organizing cultures with strategic capacities that transcend the debilitating limitations that Ganz sees? PICO's New Voices initiative offers an ideal setting for beginning to answer these questions: an emergent organization facing new strategic opportunities that challenge its existing strategic repertoire.[43]

Before PICO would move toward national-level work, key players in the network had to embrace two things: a *need* to influence national policy, and the *possibility* of doing so successfully. In a different setting, these moves might have been made by authoritative leaders or a dominant clique, and simply imposed from above; alternatively, they might have bubbled up from below in some long-term process of shared experience and political discernment. In PICO, neither of these scenarios played out. Rather, a handful of key strategists—not a formally designated role but rather those inclined to think about broad societal trends and PICO's overall strategic position—began thinking about the obstacles facing local federations as their leverage over social policy narrowed. This group coalesced around and is led by Reed.

Before those discussions proceeded beyond initial stages, however, the culture of PICO—in which local federations have long-established autonomy and decision-making authority—dictated a broadly consultative process.[44] Within this organizational culture, any move to impose a national strategy from above would have delegitimized the whole effort. This was further reinforced by the experience of the PICO California Project: as executive director Jim Keddy recalled, "Our statewide work would never have worked if we'd [just] relied on the organizers. It took off when the [volunteer] leaders really took control of it." There *was* a top-down component to the initiative in the sense that Reed and network director John Baumann made the decision (in the absence of outside funding for starting a national drive ex nihilo) to place the idea on the agenda of the annual meeting of PICO organizers and to provide initial funding for the effort. But they then went out to the roots of the organization for discussion and discernment: to the core lay leaders, clergy, and staff of local federations.

The first such convening took place in November 2002 in New Orleans. At that meeting, Reed and others presented their analysis of the reasons in favor of a national effort, as well as the opportunities and difficulties confronting such an effort. This generated a wide-ranging discussion of the obstacles to success, the limitations of local federations, and yet the urgent need to change the dynamics of federal policymaking. The upshot of that meeting was support for initial work toward building a national campaign, but a strong sense that it would have to be organically linked to existing local efforts—complementary to them and *buttressing their local power,* not simply feeding off of them. This would become typical of how the national effort would proceed: rather than making a final and unconditional decision to move nationally, at each step of the way the architects of New Voices asked participants to discuss the effort and endorse moving forward with specific steps, testing the political waters both internally and externally.[45] Such decision making—fully *deliberative* but without the clear *authoritative structure* for which Ganz argues—has occurred at each subsequent stage of the campaign: at least every six months, groups of participants from PICO's almost fifty local federations come together to discuss their experience and formulate strategy.

In a sense, a particular kind of internal political culture within PICO plays the role that Ganz posits ought to be played by the structure of an organization. This alternative places a significant strategic burden upon the political artisans who craft PICO's organizational culture—can the resulting political process meet the strategic challenges PICO faces? I turn now to analyze the cultural dynamics within the

New Voices effort, with our eyes on political implications but also on the subtle cultural dynamics of this public work.

Cultural Dynamics, Structure, and Strategic Capacity

The national strategy session in April 2004 demonstrates the key cultural and organizational dynamics of the effort. Some 150 lay leaders, clergy, and organizers came together in Washington, D.C., for three days of joint strategizing and meetings with congressional representatives and policy think tanks. I here offer brief glimpses of the key dynamics that occurred there, related to the cultural, network-building, organizational, and leadership factors that shape strategic capacity.

On the first evening of the April 2004 national meeting, San Diego layperson Gloria Cooper, for many years a high-profile voice in the PICO California Project, led the group in self-introductions. The most common theme expressed: a sense of intimidation by the power represented by the nation's capital, and fear of confronting it. The focus of the evening was a "faith reflection" by Rev. Heyward Wiggins, the pastor of Faith Tabernacle, an African American Pentecostal church in Camden, New Jersey: "My Lord, we come together truly with no strength of our own, but only in your spirit. . . . magnify yourself. . . . allow your children to have their minds and hearts challenged and changed, to be empowered, to be hopeful, to understand the mission that lies ahead of us. . . . My brothers and sisters . . . it is no longer enough to have lofty metaphorical phrases, you must *walk, act, and stand firm* to confirm your faith in God." Note how a superficial "political" reading of Wiggins's presentation might see this as only an effort to "motivate" his listeners. This is of course correct as far as it goes, but note too the deeper effort to *construct shared meaning* among participants by interpreting their current position in light of shared mission and scriptural commitments. This process continued as Wiggins drew on the scriptural account of the ancient Hebrew people hesitating in fear before crossing the Jordan River into the promised land to invite participants to reflect on where they stood at this moment: their fears paralleled the ancient Israelites' fears, and their intention to influence national politics placed them imaginatively "on the banks of the River Jordan"—desiring a promised land of national influence but intimidated by the prospect.

Note the dynamic here: all want collective action, but all are fearful of failing—a classic situation of strategic *monitoring:* Who will step forward "into the water" first? In the powerful prophetic tradition of African American Christianity, Wiggins here invoked both Dr. Martin Luther King's regular citation of God's promise to "never, ever leave us alone" and the original account of crossing the Jordan River: "So the priests are called to carry the ark across: it represents [God's] power, honor, and glory. As the priests held it up, God called them to step in first, so the people will cross over." He got a standing ovation at this point; my own notes from the event say simply, "Folks are eating this up; he's a terrific preacher." Wiggins went on to argue this did *not* mean clergy being the primary leaders of the effort, but *did* mean that they not hold back fearfully; only in that way would lay leaders find the courage to be the primary leaders.

For our purposes, note the way that this reflection interprets these days devoted to national organizing as linked to the liberation of the ancient Jewish people, to the civil rights struggle in America, and as a time of legitimate choice: people are fearful but can choose to overcome this fear. Again, this *constructs shared meaning* among participants, anchored in the power of the preached word in this Pentecostal strand of Christianity. But, crucially, note how this choice was framed: Rev. Wiggins interpreted the intimidation and fear that participants were experiencing as akin to the people's fear at crossing the Jordan, and he challenged them to overcome their fear and choose to move forward. This was a moment of *one-way communication* that created energy and enthusiasm for the New Voices project, thus helping push the group past their thresholds for collective action.

A second core element was introduced by Gloria Cooper as she identified the four goals of the meetings: "to discern together whether our local federations are ready to launch this national effort"; "to create relationships with each other, around the country"; "to develop relationships with our own federal officials"; and "to create the opportunity for us as PICO to change federal policy on those issues we all have in common." These goals—at this stage, simply goals, not achievements—emphasized *reciprocal communication, deliberation,* and developing the kinds of *internal and external networks* characterized above as *"weak ties"*: links across geographic locations within PICO and to external government officials. Cooper then asked for brief reports on the issues and accomplishments of each local group, and in dialogue with participants from around the country drew out lessons that might inform New Voices demands for policy reform nationally. These interchanges represent *reciprocal communication* across different federations and levels of the PICO organization.

In the final core element of the evening, Scott Reed highlighted where the project had been and where it stood as these meetings began:

> Eighteen months ago, when we gathered in New Orleans, fifty groups asked this question: "Can we begin to work together, work with our federal representatives, to generate a voice that needs to be heard in this country?" Now look at this map, with ribbons over the whole country [indicating links between fifty participating federations in fourteen states]. We begin to inch a little further into the river, right pastor? . . . We're seeking changes that are not going to be offered by the Democratic *or* Republican party. They will seek to *manage* the change . . . to bend it to their own interests . . . so how we engage

Washington is important—we'll try to learn from one another how to nurture those relationships [with Congress] in a way that translates into political capital on issues.

He went on to outline a proposal that had emerged from discussions prior to this gathering:[46]

> We are *proposing* a strategy—we don't impose our will on any project. We are suggesting that we find clarity on this proposal in the next two days. We want to create awareness in our federal officials of what's happening in our neighborhoods, by having every project conduct a town hall meeting or public action in the fall. Imagine for a minute: what if we have fifty PICO projects in coordinated meetings with our ninety congressional representatives? And remember 45 percent of those officials are Republican, a little more than half are Democrats—imagine them sitting in the same room, on the same day, all across the country. We'll create an awareness of how [federal policy affects our communities]. We'll create an opportunity not just to bring resources back home, but to say to Washington what needs to change.

Finally, Reed noted that over the next two days, "we'll learn from each other about ways we can accomplish this, and how we can strengthen relationships with our [congressional] representatives in ways that help us move forward." Reed's approach here is best understood as cultivating the *internal politics* of the organizing effort: he fosters an internal conversation that preserves space for differing political viewpoints and levels of commitment to national action. Throughout this presentation, Reed engaged in a great deal of interchange with participants, asking how they were feeling about the effort or whether their colleagues "back home" were ready to link their work to national efforts; other moderators similarly "checked in" with participants regularly. These "check-ins" are best understood as a form of *monitoring of participants' action thresholds;* they help key leaders assess whether or not others are moving toward action. More ambiguous is the *deliberative structure* at work here: throughout the meetings, deliberation occurs regularly and openly—and authoritatively in the limited sense that broad opposition to the national effort would presumably have prevented PICO from moving forward. But—perhaps because such opposition was a real possibility at these early stages of the effort—a yes-or-no vote was never held to decide definitely whether to proceed. The openness of PICO's process meant real deliberation occurred regularly, and as we shall see, real creativity entered into that process in unexpected ways, but *authoritative deliberation* in Ganz's sense occurred only in less formal ways. In the conclusion to this chapter, I consider the implications of these complexities.

A similar tenor permeated the next day's meetings, framed by initial prayer and song and punctuated by occasional group humor, but underlain by a striking seriousness of intent regarding the reform of national policymaking. Participants broke up into small discussion groups, each with a particular focus such as "preparing to meet elected officials," "developing talking points," "developing and nurturing political relationships with elected officials," and "moving issues at the local level and connecting this to federal level." In the latter group, organizer Gina Martinez noted that "ideally, we want to integrate the national, state, and federated work all fully into our local work. . . . I don't think we're there yet, but that's our goal." Another organizer noted that "long-term, this national work absolutely helps our local work, but short-term that's not always so clear . . . we need to be asking that all the time." Drew added, "It also makes really clear the need to grow the organization—to find new congregations, get new leaders involved, raise the capacity of the organization to do higher level work." A Lutheran pastor talked about how the San Diego Organizing Project worked: "We identify an issue locally, start looking for what the higher-level connections might be, like federal policy or federal money that affects education." He went on to note that the experience of the PICO California Project had given them "a model for doing this that people know." A leader from the California Project noted the importance of new habits like "*always* asking what the higher-level connections might be, what opportunities might exist at the state or federal level." A Florida participant emphasized the power that congressional relationships can bring to an organization by noting that "when we moved our issue work from being completely unsuccessful to when we finally won, the *only thing that changed* that was that we had developed relationships with our federal officials." In this small group, participants also simply chatted about how excited they were—and, as one said, "nervous, but not scared any more"—to be moving toward impacting national policy.

The small-group discussions and report-backs that followed them served to generate *focal points for creativity* within the organization, within which all participants could propose new ideas and strategies and offer lessons from local political work for broader consideration. Among the insights generated: how much more polarized and partisan federal-level politicians were, and how this forced the local PICO group to adapt its approach; the value of photo opportunities for building ties to collaborative politicians; the almost desperate need among Washington-based politicians for local allies back in their districts, and how to use that need strategically; and the need to educate politicians about how faith-based organizing differs from "politics as usual." None of this appeared to be scripted, but rather emerged from local activists analyzing their own experience. It thus represents at least the beginning of a broadly participative *deliberative structure* within the organization. The small-group interaction also extended *weak ties* across federations and (more substantially) simply offered informal venues for extensive *reciprocal communication* about both strategy and emotion. Note, too, that one participant commented: "After our last time here, our congressperson told us that she knew that we had folks contacting other congresspeople around the country. That's reorganizing power, when they know our connections." This highlighted the advantages of PICO's emerging national structure, what might be described as *proto-federated*, with strong local political capacity, a few statewide projects of varying capacities, and the beginnings of political capacity at the federal level. Note, however, that this is not a full federated structure in Skocpol and Ganz's sense discussed earlier, with local chapters nested consistently within state structures and the latter linked to a centralized national office. Whether PICO moves in that direction—and whether this is the "right" structure in the current context—remains to be seen.

Organizer Gordon Whitman summed up the conversation to this point: "We do good local and state organizing. . . . We know what it means to put the mayor in front of ourselves and push, cut an issue [locally] . . . and sometimes at state level. At federal level, we're not so clear on how to do it . . . we need to learn this. But [given the impact of federal policy on local communities], it's as hard *not* to do it as it is to do it—we've been fighting with one arm behind our back, and are learning to untie it and bring it out into the fight."

The rest of the morning was spent reporting from research and local policy work regarding specific policy initiatives that might provide vehicles for New Voices to impact legislation in the five focus areas that had emerged out of PICO's local work: affordable housing, immigrant rights, health care access, public schools, and public safety (framed as "hometown security"). Participants then prepared for afternoon meetings with their congressional representatives.

New Jersey organizer Joe Fleming, another key architect of the national campaign, sent the group off by extending the earlier biblical metaphor:

> Well, the first effect of putting your foot into the Jordan River is that you stir it up, muddy the waters a little. But it'll gradually get clearer. . . . Decisions made here [in Washington, D.C.] either help or hurt our own communities. We want to look at what we've learned, look at next research steps as you meet with your federal officials. . . . It's the sum of our relationships at the federal level that is going to determine how well we can have an impact at the federal level. It may not all be clear yet, but that's okay . . . it'll come clearer. . . . Please come back here at 7:00 P.M., when we'll figure out our next steps and larger strategy.

The evening's discussion involved reports from the day's meetings with congressional representatives and aides, and thinking about how PICO would choose the policy areas on which to focus. Leaders suggested the right policy initiative ought to entail a "good opportunity," defined as either "a bill already in Congress or enough relationship with a congressperson that we can introduce a bill"; something with a "moral dimension, something that resonates with our values," a "sense of urgency" and "appeal in both parties"; an issue that "allows us to reach new partners"; something related to issues that local PICO groups had already worked on; and "something we can win." These were discussed and recorded as criteria for selecting issues. Reed then elaborated:

> Eventually, I think we will want to choose to move on something that gives expression to who we are, something that is bold and evocative . . . what we're calling our prophetic initiative, our prophetic voice. . . . It's important that we be clear: We have a lot of work to do still, don't want you to leave with the impression that we're ready to select a national issue—we're not there yet. We're going to be able to filter some possibilities through these lenses you've been talking about, move *toward* making a choice.

Throughout the day's work, note the interplay of instrumental politics, the articulation of an ethical vision to drive the political work, and the construction of a shared culture of public work—and the refusal to let the language of "morality" be overly narrowed to exclude the socioeconomic issues facing struggling communities. This kind of "cultural work" moves well beyond the recently fashionable focus on "framing" political issues in moral language, which in practice too often amounts to further instrumentalizing people's ethical commitments.[47] Here, ethical commitment, politics, and cultural dynamics interpenetrate relatively seamlessly in concrete organizing for a better society.

Participants would gather the next day to prepare to take their experiences back to local organizations, through dynamics similar to those already reported here: more promotion of unity through ritual, prayer, and song; construction of shared meaning by using scriptural and democratic references to interpret their experience in dealing with federal power; one-on-one conversations about how participants were feeling about returning home; reporting on new ties (external and internal) established on this trip; and planning how to forge new ties to congressional representatives in the months ahead. Thus, three days in Washington, D.C., involved effort at several levels: *promoting unity* in the face of skepticism or misunderstanding "back home" regarding national-level work; cultivation of *internal and external networks* involving both *strong and weak ties;* reinforcing PICO's emerging *proto-federated structure* by better integrating PICO's work at the local, state, and federal levels; and fostering a *deliberative structure* in which authority functions in neither bureaucratic nor democratic mode. The cultural dynamics lent themselves to *construction of shared meaning,* regular mutual assessment of *action thresholds,* and a combination of *reciprocal and one-way communication.*

Only the closing sequence must be mentioned here: Reed invited everyone to exchange phone numbers and call each other periodically, saying, "We want to build some accountability not just in your local organization, but also across the whole country." More important, another key architect of the national initiative, Joe

Givens of New Orleans, invited all to participate in a ritual of solidarity: a joint reading of a statement entitled "The Prophetic Voice" that had been drafted by clergy members active in PICO, as a kind of vision statement for the New Voices campaign. I will consider the backgrounds of the key clergy shortly; here, the crucial point is the diversity of their perspectives: Black Pentecostal, Roman Catholic, white Protestant, and African American Baptist traditions were all represented, as were sharply divergent political viewpoints: from a progressive intellectual viewpoint drawing on the writings of social critic Cornel West to the views of a self-declared "Republican businessman from southern California"—and a variety of other perspectives.[48]

The PICO National Network and this particular national gathering would continue to wrestle with this tension, as it reflects differences that coexist legitimately within the network and are regularly negotiated via participants' shared commitment to "a fundamental commitment to the well-being of low- and middle-income people."[49]

Leadership Factors

Two additional influences on strategic capacity remain to be examined briefly, the first of which is leadership factors. Recall Ganz's argument that a pair of leadership factors are crucial to shaping a movement's strategic capacity: the *biographies* of key leaders and the *repertoires of action* that they bring to the movement. Table 7.3 lists the key personnel (organizers, clergy, and lay leaders) who have been most central to the New Voices effort so far.[50]

Though interpreting this information is necessarily an approximate exercise, the following conclusions are plausible. First, there is impressive diversity of racial, geographic, and religious background within the strategic core of the New Voices initiative, as well as significant gender diversity. This represents an important achievement and may represent an important pool for strategic creativity: there is no evidence of a single demographic profile of core participants that threatens to narrowly constrain strategic capacity and perception, parallel to the factors that Ganz shows can undermine strategic creativity. But note, too, that this promises strategic creativity only in a rather vague sense, in that the links from religious, geographic, racial, and gender background to political strategy are not obvious.

More sobering is the relatively narrow base of professional and organizational background represented within the New Voices strategic core: it is heavily weighted in favor of those whose primary organizational experience lies narrowly within church structures and the specific field of faith-based community organizing. As a result, PICO might in the future suffer from an overly narrow political repertoire

Table 7.3. Biographical Backgrounds of Key Strategists within PICO New Voices

Person	State	Race/Ethnic Group	Religion	Professional Experience/Other
Organizers				
Scott Reed	CA	White	Lutheran	All FBCO organizing
Joe Givens	LA	African American	Catholic	Democratic Party and FBCO
Joe Fleming	NJ	White	Catholic	Community organization and FBCO
Denise Collazo	FL/CA	Hispanic	Southern Baptist	Harvard and FBCO
Gordon Whitman	MI/PA	White	Jewish	Legal aid attorney, political organizing, and FBCO
Clergy				
Heyward Wiggins	NJ	African American	Evangelical	Pastor, working-class employee
Roy Dixon	CA	African American	Pentecostal	Businessman, Republican, pastor
George Cummings	CA	African American	American Baptist	Professor, pastor, social critic
Kendall Baker	CA	White	United Church of Christ	Pastor and writer
Amelia Adams	LA	African American	Pentecostal	Pastor, working-class employee
Norm Rhotert	MO	White	Catholic	Pastor, 40 years FBCO
Harold Mayberry	LA/CA	African American	African Meth. Episcopal	Pastor
Tip Tipton	FL	White	Presbyterian	Pastor
Lay Leaders				
Janelle Highfill	CO	White	Presbyterian	FBCO, professional
Bea Bernstein	CA	Hispanic, second-generation immigrant	Catholic	Clerical work and longtime FBCO
Susan Molina	CO	Hispanic	Catholic	Public schools and FBCO
Gloria Cooper	CA	African American	Pentecostal	Activist and longtime FBCO
Paula Arceneaux	LA	African American	Catholic	City employee
Bob Rosterfort	MO	White	Catholic	Manager

or lack of access to national political insiders. Although this is not surprising, and neither outcome is inevitable, Ganz's analysis suggests that, left unaddressed, these factors might place important limitations on the efforts' strategic capacity.

Both of these strategic leadership challenges might be overcome, but doing so will require incorporating new members into the strategic core, cultivating new strategic allies among elite political players, building strong alliances with other organizations, or dramatic strategic creativity.

Resource Flows

The final influence on strategic capacity is resource flows. Ganz argues that this organizational factor is critical in shaping strategic capacity. In particular, strategic creativity is less constrained when resources flow from multiple constituencies (i.e., are decentralized) than when an organization is dependent on centralized and hierarchical resource flows.

Resource flows within the PICO effort can be addressed briefly here. Two kinds of resources are crucial and look quite different in New Voices. The flow of *people* into the effort is quite decentralized: organizers, clergy, and leaders are involved to varying levels essentially from throughout PICO's geographic base. Note, however, that the vast majority come from local faith communities, a narrow base in a non-geographic sense. The flow of *money* is highly centralized. Up to 2004, the effort was funded almost entirely from the internal resources of the national PICO office—approximately a half million dollars. More recently, some $300,000 has been provided by national foundations, including the Carnegie Corporation, the Nathan Cummins Foundation, and the Hazen Foundation, plus related major funding from the Marguerite Casey Foundation.[51] All this represents funding from relatively elite institutions rather than the kind of constituency-generated money that Ganz argues reinforces internal accountability and strategic capacity.

If five years into the future PICO has successfully raised major funding to sustain the effort, this early history will be correctly seen as well-invested seed money that launched faith-based community organizing into its first serious national-level effort. If, on the other hand, at that point the New Voices effort has folded (whether for lack of funding or other factors), substantial blame may lie in the effort's narrow resource base and the lack of diverse accountability associated with it (to outside organizations, to churches, to other constituents, and most crucially to the base). Or perhaps what Ganz called "resourcefulness"—the strategic creativity of motivated leadership—may outmaneuver resources on the complex terrain of national politics. But the New Voices effort could also starve for lack of resources before its resourcefulness bears fruit. Thus, financing New Voices—whether from internal or external issues—remains a critical strategic challenge.

CONCLUSION

PICO's efforts to project nonpartisan political power into the state and national arenas are analyzed here to assess the strategic situation of efforts to project power from local organizing into higher-level political arenas. At the level of state politics, the PICO California Project shows that significant political influence is possible. But we should be clear: PICO's work has impacted but not revolutionized California politics, which will continue to respond to national, global, and local financial factors well beyond the reach of community organizing pressures. PICO has successfully advanced particular interests of working families and helped many find a public voice. This is an impressive track record of public work, but the need for deeper democratic transformation remains and is constrained by powerful economic and political forces.

At the national level, PICO's New Voices campaign appears to incorporate significant resources for generating strategic capacity, as well as significant liabilities. In the analytic terms utilized here, New Voices has successfully created deliberative structures that occur in regular and open formats and include organizationally created "focal points for creative decision-making" to foster strategic creativity. The rich diversity of racial backgrounds (and to a lesser extent religious background and gender) within the strategic core suggests little risk that the resulting deliberation will fall into the racial exclusivism, anti-institutionalism, or similar obstacles to political creativity that litter the landscape of democratic politics in America.[52] A potential counterweight to national strategic capacity, however, lies in the rather narrow leader biographies, resource flows, and perhaps political repertoires within the New Voices campaign. This will have to be overcome with new alliances and new resource flows.

Similarly, relational ties at all levels within the internal structure of the network—often very strong ties within sponsoring congregations, somewhat weaker but still relatively strong ties across congregations within a local federation, and weak but intentionally cultivated ties across federations—represent a central font of strategic capacity. PICO's careful cultivation of this kind of social capital through its relational organizing model has borne fruit in generating one of its greatest strategic assets. By forging an internal culture of democratic practices and public work, this effort challenges one of the key long-term disabilities that undermines democracy in America.

The quality of PICO's external ties is more mixed. The effort carries strong links within the religious arena; strong bipartisan links to local political leaders; mostly new and emerging bipartisan links to national political representatives; some nascent linkages to nationally prominent public policy centers; weak ties to labor unions and other potential allies; and relatively slim links to key centers of power within the national political parties. In addition, PICO's presence in only sixteen states may limit its ability to project national power. At this stage, the effort is too young to adequately assess these external networks.

The flow of authority and accountability within New Voices is complex. Though, as noted earlier, the deliberative structure is both regular and relatively open, how *authoritative* it is has been left intentionally ambiguous. PICO represents neither the kind of representative democracy that Ganz prefers nor the kind of bureaucratic structure that Ganz criticizes, in which power flows from above. Rather, New Voices incorporates a third category, *entrepreneurial authority*, in which enterprising leaders who bring insight and creativity to bear on the tasks of organizing find it quite possible to rise within the PICO structure. Ganz cites entrepreneurial authority approvingly—indeed, it appears to be the key dynamic in the early, successful days of the United Farm Workers and its antecedents[53]—but does not comment on it extensively. PICO's version of entrepreneurial authority allows authority to flow relatively freely within the organizing structure rather than being defined from above—though ultimately many strategic decisions are made by the strategic core. At present, this does not appear to this observer to be problematic. In the long term, however, it may not be possible to institutionalize entrepreneurial authority in a stable way, so that the organization may have to push toward more firmly structured democracy or suffer the costs of bureaucratic stasis.

Finally, the foregoing account suggests that the cultural factors underlying strategic capacity are an area of particular strength within New Voices. The framing of reformist goals, the promotion of unity, the combination of reciprocal and one-way communication, the monitoring of participants' thresholds for action, and cultural interpretation and the construction of shared meaning are all tasks at which PICO has become expert—drawing widely on the talents of organizers, clergy, and lay leaders. Along with the organization's internal relational fiber, expert cultural work may represent PICO's greatest resource for creative political strategy.

Together, these factors suggest that this emerging national effort holds real promise for strategic efficacy. As this chapter was being written, New Voices sponsored sixteen assemblies attended by some 8,000 constituents, at which congressional representatives, senators, and other politicians were asked to pledge their commitment to a new way of doing federal business in PICO's key issue areas.[54] In a clear adaptation of the PICO California Project's 2003 strategy, these assemblies occurred "back home" in representatives' congressional districts, where PICO's local organizations can best generate popular pressure—a tactic for exerting national leverage that showcases PICO's strategic capacity. Shortly after the November 2004 national elections, the network sponsored a clergy press conference at the U.S. Capitol that garnered extensive media coverage and highlighted PICO's rather different understanding of "moral values" than the one widespread in that election.[55]

Subsequently, New Voices engaged heavily in the work of channeling national political attention to rebuilding in the wake of Hurricane Katrina.

But powerful constraints rooted in the current political and economic context apply a fortiori to the New Voices national effort: massive federal deficits, deep antigovernment and antitax currents in national culture, and the hyperpolarization of congressional and presidential political dynamics argue against any irenic reading of PICO's national opportunities. To succeed, New Voices leaders will have to overcome these constraints. They strive to do so *not* simply as partisans on one side of current battles—though on any given issue their preferences may line up with one side more than the other—but through two fundamental strategies: by constructing a culture of sustained public engagement that directly challenges the antipolitical tone of a national popular culture of escape from politics, and by striving to forge a centrist coalition around particular issues (currently, health care for uninsured working families) that can draw support from both parties and make policy headway despite partisan polarization. In confronting partisan polarization directly, PICO's ambition risks failure. But the combination of creative cultural work and strong organizing capacity in local congressional districts may create sufficient strategic capacity to overcome those risks—if New Voices can broaden its strategic networks and resource base.

In closing, I would suggest three implications of this analysis. First, New Voices demonstrates that, with the right leadership and the careful cultivation of more deliberative and participative organizational structures, the established political capacity of faith-based community organizing can generate the kind of strategic capacity for which Ganz calls. Second, this analysis challenges faith-based organizing participants at all levels to reject any complacency the power they now exercise and to forge organizations with deeper strategic capacity: our present national political incapacity simply demands this. Third, this analysis calls current and potential strategic partners of faith-based community organizing—funders, religious leaders, political organizers, policy experts, and scholars—to reinforce the most promising strategic developments within the field and to forge broader alliances more capable of tying national political life to a workable vision of a good society.

NOTES

1. The name PICO National Network was officially adopted in 2004; previously, the organization was known as the Pacific Institute for Community Organization. PICO has been analyzed in several publications: Stephen Hart, *Cultural Dilemmas of Progressive Politics* (Chicago: University of Chicago Press, 2001); Paul W. Speer, *People Making Public Policy in California: The PICO California Project* (Nashville, TN: Vanderbilt University, 2002); Heidi Swarts, "Setting the State's Agenda: Church-Based Community Organizations in American Urban Politics," in *States, Parties,*

and Social Movements: Protest and the Dynamics of Institutional Change, ed. Jack Goldstone (New York: Cambridge University Press, 2001); and Richard L. Wood, *Faith in Action: Religion, Race, and Democratic Organizing in America* (Chicago: University of Chicago Press, 2002).

2. Michael Gecan, *Going Public* (Boston: Beacon Press, 2002); Richard L. Wood and Mark R. Warren, "A Different Face of Faith-Based Politics: Social Capital and Community Organizing in the Public Arena," *International Journal of Sociology and Social Policy* 22, nos. 9/10 (Fall 2002): 6–54.

3. Harry C. Boyte and Nancy N. Kari, *Building America: The Democratic Promise of Public Work* (Philadelphia: Temple University Press, 1996); Gary Delgado, *Organizing the Movement: The Roots and Growth of ACORN* (Philadelphia: Temple University Press, 1986); Gecan, *Going Public;* Hart, *Cultural Dilemmas of Progressive Politics;* Paul Osterman, *Gathering Power* (Boston: Beacon Press, 2003); Heidi Swarts, "Moving without a Movement: Organized Churches and Neighborhoods in American Politics" (Ph.D. diss., Cornell University, 2001); Mark Warren, *Dry Bones Rattling* (Princeton, NJ: Princeton University Press, 2001); Wood, *Faith in Action.*

4. Carmen Sirianni and Lewis Friedland, *Civic Innovation in America* (Berkeley: University of California Press, 2001).

5. In addition, the intellectual and empirical context of this study draws on the author's prior ethnographic research on faith-based community organizing as a broad national field much wider than PICO, and on PICO's own local- and state-level work in California and elsewhere. Mary Ann Flaherty and Richard L. Wood, *Faith and Public Life* (New York: Ford Foundation and Interfaith Funders, 2002); Wood's "Religion, Faith-Based Community Organizing, and the Struggle for Justice," in *Cambridge Handbook of Sociology,* ed. Michele Dillon (New York: Cambridge University Press, 2003); and Wood and Warren, "A Different Face of Faith-Based Politics."

6. Boyte and Kari, *Building America.*

7. Wood and Warren, "A Different Face of Faith-Based Politics."

8. These networks and regions of particular strength are the Industrial Areas Foundation (five regional groupings); the Gamaliel Foundation (Midwest); Direct Action, Research, and Training (Florida and Ohio); the InterValley Project (New England); the Regional Congress of Neighborhood Organizations (Southern California); and Organize! Leadership and Training Center (Massachusetts).

9. Wood and Warren, "A Different Face of Faith-Based Politics."

10. Though data comparable to the systematic 1999 data do not exist, a rough comparison can be made: the essentially exhaustive 1999 survey documented 133 local faith-based community organizing efforts nationwide. The field has clearly grown since then, to perhaps 160 or 180 organizations. The lower figure would represent a 20 percent increase—though note that we do not know if the newer organizations are as large as the more established organizations.

11. Data are from Table 8 in Wood and Warren, "A Different Face of Faith-Based Politics."

12. See Tables 4, 5, and 6 in ibid. For a broader assessment of the strategic position of the FBCO field, see Mark R. Warren and Richard L. Wood, *Faith-Based Community Organizing: The State of the Field* (Jericho, NY: Interfaith Funders), 2001.

13. The strategy behind this legislation: use state funding to leverage far larger amounts of money in local school funding, in part by shifting the state's matching formula from a fifty-fifty split with local districts building new schools, to 60 percent state funding if the high school will serve 500 or fewer students. The legislation also included $5 million to reconfigure large schools to produce smaller internal academies. In the effort, PICO relied on research showing that students—especially those from less privileged backgrounds—benefit academically and socially from smaller school settings.

14. Wood, *Faith in Action.*

15. PICO-California (the current name for the former PICO California Project) is a leading force within the group sponsoring the November 2006 ballot initiative. Other members of the Coalition for a Healthy California include the American Cancer Society, the American Heart Association, and several professional health care organizations.

16. See Speer, *People Making Public Policy in California.* Those interviewed included fourteen key informants from state-level government and political society, half primarily linked to educational policy and half to health care policy. They included a former attorney general, the secretary of education, the press secretary for a cabinet official, two state senators, the policy director for the Speaker of the assembly, and the CEO of a statewide community clinic association; staff persons to the state senate president pro tem, the Office of the Governor, and the state senate Office of Health; and officers or lobbyists from the California Medical Association, the AARP, and the Union of Health Care Workers.

17. Ibid., 25.

18. Ibid.

19. Ibid.

20. Ibid., 39.

21. Ibid., 43.

22. Ibid., 40.

23. Ibid., 35.

24. Ibid.,40.

25. Ibid., 26.

26. Ibid., 43.

27. All quotations in this paragraph are from author interview with Jim Keddy (January 2005); see also Peter Schrag, "The Cost of Good Works in a Bad System," *Sacramento Bee,* February 1, 2006, B7. As this book went to press (November 2006), the ballot initiative was narrowly defeated, with 52% voting against it following a $65 million anti-tax campaign by tobacco companies (*Sacramento Bee,* November 13, 2006). PICO California immediately launched an effort to work with Republican Governor Schwarzenegger to provide insurance to all California children (*Sacramento Bee,* December 1, 2006).

28. James M. Jasper, *The Art of Moral Protest* (Chicago: University of Chicago Press, 1996); Francesca Polletta and James M. Jasper, "Collective Identity and Social Movements," *Annual Review of Sociology* 27 (2001): 283–305.

29. William A. Gamson, *The Strategy of Social Protest* (Homewood, IL: Dorsey Press, 1975); William A. Gamson, "Understanding the Careers of Challenging Groups: A Commentary on Goldstone," *American Journal of Sociology* 85 (1980): 43–60; William A. Gamson, "Political Discourse and Collective Action," in *From Structure to Action: Comparing Social Movement Participation across Cultures,* ed. Hanspeter Kriesi, Bert Klandermans, and Sidney Tarrow (Greenwich, CT: JAI Press, 1988), 219–244.

30. R. Scott Frey, Thomas Dietz, and Linda Kalof, "Characteristics of Successful Protest Groups: Another Look at Gamson's Strategy of Social Protest," *American Journal of Sociology* 98 (1992): 368–387.

31. Ibid., 384.

32. Hart, *Cultural Dilemmas of Progressive Politics;* Swarts, "Setting the State's Agenda"; Richard Wood, "Religious Culture and Political Action," *Sociological Theory* 17 (1999): 307–332; Wood, *Faith in Action.*

33. Michael Chwe, "Structure and Strategy in Collective Action," *American Journal of Sociology* 105 (1999): 128–156.

34. See the work of Dreyfuss cited in Bent Flyvbjerg, *Making Social Science Matter: Why Social Inquiry Fails and How It Can Succeed Again* (New York: Cambridge University Press, 2001).

35. See Chwe, "Structure and Strategy in Collective Action," 151, where he uses the 1989 Tiananmen Square demonstrations in Beijing as an example.

36. Marshall Ganz, "Resources and Resourcefulness: Strategic Capacity in the Unionization of California Agriculture, 1959–1966," *American Journal of Sociology* 105 (2000): 1003–1063.

37. In developing this model, Ganz draws extensively on recent work on meaning, creativity, and cultural reception. Theresa M. Amabile, "Creativity and Innovation in Organizations," in *Research in Organizational Behavior*, vol. 10, ed. B. M. Staw and L. L. Cummings (Greenwich, CT: JAI Press, 1996), 123–167; Jerome Bruner, *Acts of Meaning* (Cambridge, MA: Harvard University Press, 1990); Wendy Griswold, "The Fabrication of Meaning: Literary Interpretation in the United States, Great Britain, and the West Indies," *American Journal of Sociology* 92 (1987): 1077–1117.

38. In this article, Ganz's evidence that the UFW leadership's mix of political insiders and outsiders gave it a strategic advantage in comparison to Agricultural Workers Organizing Committee's heavy reliance on political insiders provides crucial insight. But one also wonders whether the UFW's weak ties to high-level political insiders at the national level contributed at later stages of the movement to the union's difficulty in consolidating its pathbreaking gains. I will return to this matter later, in thinking about PICO's long-term prospects.

39. John Lofland, *Social Movement Organizations* (New York: de Gruyter, 1996), 1027.

40. Ganz, "Resources and Resourcefulness," 1024.

41. Theda Skocpol, Marshall Ganz, and Ziad Munson, "A Nation of Organizers: The Institutional Origins of Civic Voluntarism in the United States," *American Political Science Review* 94 (2000): 527–546.

42. Marshall Ganz, "Making Democracy Work? Review of *Dry Bones Rattling* by Mark Warren," *Contexts* 1 (2002): 62–63.

43. New Voices does not represent the only site in which faith-based community organizing may transcend the limits that Ganz sees. There appear to be initiatives in other networks and within PICO that are breaking out of the strategic limitations that Ganz analyzes. But that process is necessarily uneven, and Ganz's diagnosis rings true in a significant number of settings, including some that project impressive local power.

44. Much of Ganz's skepticism about the democratic promise of this form of organizing is premised on his understanding of the working of authority within these organizations. PICO's internal culture is quite different in this regard than the much more hierarchical model of authority that Ganz has seen in other settings.

45. It is important not to be naive in accepting that this kind of process of ongoing consultation necessarily represents democratic decision making: in my ethnographic experience in the broader field of community organizing, such decision making can be quite democratic—but it also can be quite hierarchical, with staff driving the decisions through the power their role carries.

46. Italics mark Reed's verbal emphases. The key participants in these prior discussions, and in New Voices strategy formulation generally, were organizers Scott Reed, Joe Givens, Denise Collazo, Gordon Whitman, and Joe Fleming; leaders Gloria Cooper, Bea Bernstein, and Janelle Highfill; joined subsequently by several clergy and other lay leaders whose biographies are discussed later in the chapter.

47. George Lakoff, *Moral Politics: How Liberals and Conservatives Think*, 2nd ed. (Chicago: University of Chicago Press, 2002).

48. Note that this gathering represents impressive diversity from *within* the broad terrain of American Christianity, including its immigrant expressions. Though congregations from Jewish,

Muslim, Buddhist, Unitarian, and other faith traditions sometimes participate in faith-based community organizing, Christian congregations predominate in this work generally and in New Voices. Regarding Cornel West: the speaker drew especially from his *Prophesy Deliverance! An Afro-American Revolutionary Christianity* (Philadelphia: Westminster Press, 1982). See also Mark David Wood, *Cornel West and the Politics of Prophetic Pragmatism* (Urbana: University of Illinois Press, 2000), and West's *The Cornel West Reader* (New York: Basic Books, 1999).

49. Though beyond my purposes here, see Kleidman's argument regarding the negative consequences of nonideological organizing. Robert Kleidman, "Volunteer Activism and Professionalism in Social Movement Organizations," *Social Problems* 41 (1994): 601–620.

50. Note that this cutoff is somewhat arbitrary, but these are the organizers, clergy, and laypeople most centrally involved in the key question here: strategic direction and organizational deliberation regarding New Voices. A broader listing of overall public leadership would reflect greater diversity among participants, particularly with regard to Latino leaders and clergy, and African American organizers.

51. Author interview with national fund-raising coordinator Denise Collazo, December 2004. She notes, "We've been building toward [serious national money], but it's hard to get start-up money. Funders want to fund particular issues, particular campaigns . . . more money will come once we get to the stage of having particular issue campaigns."

52. Todd Gitlin, *The Twilight of Common Dreams: Why America Is Wracked by Culture Wars* (New York: Metropolitan Books, 1995).

53. For example, Ganz notes that farm workers "selected themselves" into leadership roles within the UFW and its predecessors (Ganz, "Resources and Resourcefulness," 1029).

54. For examples, see coverage in the following newspapers: *San Diego Union-Tribune*, October 18, 2004; *Los Angeles Times*, October 18, 2004; and *Denver Post*, October 17, 2004.

55. See coverage in the following newspapers on November 19, 2005: *Oakland Tribune, San Francisco Chronicle, New Orleans Times-Picayune, Orange County Register, Atlanta Journal-Constitution,* and *North County (San Diego) Times.*

8. Contextualizing Community Organizing

Lessons from the Past, Tensions in the Present, Opportunities for the Future

Robert Fisher and Eric Shragge

Community organizing is "hot" now. While some may think of it as little more than an artifact from the 1960s, it is both older and more contemporary. It has roots dating back at least to the late nineteenth century and continues today with a vibrancy and variety of expressions uncommon for such conservative times. Efforts from community development corporations to national organizing networks proliferate and expand widely. Foundations reflect and fuel this growth. After funding individual-oriented efforts in the 1980s and then family-oriented ones in the 1990s, many foundations turned in the late 1990s to community as the locus and vehicle of critical social initiatives. Theorists were ahead of foundations regarding the salience of community work. New Social Movement theory instructs that community-based organizing both in cultural and geographic communities has become the dominant form of resistance and social change since the 1960s.[1] These theorists argue that organizing at the community level proliferates widely in a postindustrial world, as industrial forms of organizing around labor and class become less salient. Communitarian theorists underscore the growing clamor for community and connection as a result of our decontextualizing global order.[2] More recently, the critique of Skocpol argues against the professionally managed advocacy organizations, often based in Washington, D.C., that dominate contemporary civic life and have taken the place of more participatory, membership-based, federated forms of local engagement.[3] Whether theorists see the membership-based community efforts about which we write as proliferating, declining, or displaced, attention increasingly focuses on their importance. For scholars, however, the challenge is to get below general observations to a closer look at the complexity, competing ideologies, and variety within community organizing that are revealed in the longitudinal analyses and case studies offered in this volume.

This chapter underscores not only the proliferation and diversity but also the disconnects and limits of community organizing. It first discusses the varied types of community organizing that have persisted over time and asserts some selective lessons learned from them. In addition, this chapter focuses on several important tensions in the field of community-based social change. The first is the tension between different traditions and visions of community-based work. One, most often referred to as *community organizing* or *social action,* makes demands on both public-sector and private-sector targets. It seeks greater social intervention, improved conditions, and social, urban, and economic programs. It uses mobilization and the power of people to work toward change. It offers an extrapolitical or extraparliamentary approach, because it (1) lacks the necessary power to have its claims heard and power exercised through official channels and/or (2) seeks a fundamental change in the social, political, and economic structure. Its opposition can be a means and a vision, a strategy as well as an alternative worldview. To achieve broader ends it employs a variety of tactics, from direct action to negotiation and partnering with those in power. In contrast, other organizations work within a framework called community development, which focuses on improving communities through a variety of self-help or service programs. These programs may be financed from the outside, but their goal is to improve local conditions through local solutions. They too may have broader objectives, as with oppositional groups, but it is more common for them to follow a pluralist politics that seeks to win incremental victories and deliver services within a context of current power relationships or modestly shifting ones. We will discuss other ways of classifying organizations later, but it is important to point out the diversity and coexistence of a range of political stances within what can be described as community organizing.

A second tension emerges from an examination of the results of progressive community organizations. There are many of these throughout the United States, as illustrated later in this chapter, that work on a variety of social and economic issues. The larger of these organizations have the capacity to organize multicity campaigns, and some have a strong regional presence. Some of the organizations have long traditions; organizations affiliated with the Industrial Areas Foundation (IAF) date back to the late 1930s. However, despite local successes this work has not significantly impacted the wider national agenda or translated into the traditional political arena. Except for coordinated national networks with broad agendas such as ACORN, which has been in existence for more than thirty years but has grown remarkably with the recent interest in community-based initiatives, progressive work on the ground remains at the level of the local community, sometimes at the regional level, but rarely contributes to the national agenda in a significant way.

A third tension results from the fragmentation of the field of community organizing. Though the political context has been stacked against these organizations, in part their limited success results from the absence of connection between them. The many progressive initiatives have not been able to find ways to unite into a broader social movement or coalition for social justice. This might have a lot to do with differing origins, traditions, suspicions between leaderships, differences in their social bases, and competition for limited funds. However, until these divisions are addressed more effectively, the progressive tendencies within the community sector remain largely limited to the local arena.

Finally, there is an ongoing tension between local community organizing and social movements. These movements have played a key role in opening political opportunities for a variety of local organizing activities. The early work of Alinsky in Chicago would not have succeeded if it had not been for the militancy of the industrial labor movement. Similarly, in the 1960s, Alinsky's work built on the strength of the civil rights movement. On the other hand, once in place, local organizations have had difficulty connecting to wider social movements. For example, there has been little connection between the wave of youth activism linked to anticorporate globalization and progressive local organizations. This disconnect, like some of the other tensions noted earlier, poses challenges to the field of community organizing at the same time the field is experiencing a significant revival. We will explore these tensions later in this chapter.

TYPES OF COMMUNITY ORGANIZING

In the interest of sharpening the discourse, we have drawn upon the two dominant approaches usually cited in the literature: community development and social action. Of course, these dominant types overlap and interact within and between organizations. Nor is this a static situation. Organizations change dominant strategies over time, not uncommonly from social action to community development. The work of one affects the other, even if unintentionally. For example, the very existence of social action efforts can give community development initiatives more room to maneuver and often more funding for their work. Nevertheless, in general at any given moment organizing efforts tend to prefer community development or social action. In a nutshell, social action represents an engagement in the struggle for social change through organizing people to pressure government or private bodies. Central to this perspective is an oppositional politics and the use of conflict strategies and tactics.[4] This kind of organizing may challenge social inequalities and oppressive power by offering an alternative politics, a critique of current conditions and power relations. Or it may focus on specific winnable local demands. In contrast, community development assumes a shared interest in society. It seeks primarily to bring together diverse community interests in a common process that contributes to the well-being of the community as a whole.[5] It often results in a strengthened sense of community, referred to as community building, and/or delivers tangible community projects such as housing or social services.[6] The development approach is best illustrated by efforts to strengthen the local (usually neighborhood) economy through either neighborhood protection efforts or more contemporary community development corporations (CDCs) and groups like Habitat for Humanity, which build affordable housing for low-income tenants and homeowners.[7] Community building focuses less on service delivery and economic improvement and more on developing community identity and connection. While it is currently seen as more connected to the community development strategy, community building is viewed now as important by both perspectives.

Of course there is much more complexity in the world of community organizing than appears in any simple dualism. For example, aside from the differences between community development and social action approaches, community-based efforts range from small, poorly funded, informal, local organizations focused on a single issue and/or cultural identity to large, much better funded, more formalized, regional and national networks of community organizing efforts working on a number of broad issues that seek national impact. Boyte criticizes staff-dominated citizen action groups that primarily canvass "members" and remain without substantial roots in communities or impact on community institutions.[8] Despite the diversity and divisions in the field, this chapter is guided by a single critical assumption: for community organizing to have a true social change orientation, both directions are simultaneously required. Organizing is about both building community *and* engaging in a wider struggle for social and economic justice. We will conclude with an approach that recognizes the limits of the action/development duality and asks how each contributes to building social integration or opposition.

ESSENTIAL LESSONS FROM THE PAST

A few lessons must suffice, but they are essential to contextualizing contemporary discourse about the practice of organizing. First, community organizing has a long history. Community organizing has been an ongoing, integral, and significant part of civil life for more than a century. People continue to choose in astounding numbers to participate in voluntary-sector, civil society activity, including community organizing and development projects. This is a historical phenomenon. Americans turn most easily to community organizations at the grassroots level to build community, participate in public life, and meet individual and collective needs. With the devolution of the nation state and the shifting of public responsibility to nonprofits and community groups, this may be even truer today than it was a hundred years ago.[9]

Second, community organizing cuts across various political stances and strategies. Although almost all community organizing is a public activity that brings people together to discuss and determine their collective welfare, it is not inherently radical, liberal, conservative, or reactionary. Nor is it inherently democratic and inclusive or authoritarian and parochial. It is above all an extrapolitical activity, a strategy used by different segments of the population to serve certain interests, achieve specific goals, and advance clear or ill-defined ideologies and political perspectives. For example, right-wing groups have flourished in the past few decades as social action groups. The form an organizing project takes depends on a host of factors, especially the ideology and goals of its leadership, the goals and needs of the constituency being organized, the sources of funding, and the broader social ecology is which the effort is situated. We should never assume that just because an effort is a community organization that it inherently seeks progressive social change. Nor should we accept claims that community-based efforts are not political—that they are just about building relations and partnerships to better serve their communities. All community work is political, that is, about power, whether the community efforts are explicit or implicit, intentional or not, about their political nature. In order to understand the full range of community organizing efforts, we use a definition of power that reflects both pluralist and conflict theory. Lipsitz says that "power in the modern world is not just a matter of allocation of resources, it is also a matter of legitimation."[10] Winning victories and a place at the bargaining table is essential to community organizing efforts. They want to influence policies, programs, and governance. But for those with a more oppositional orientation (discussed later), building a larger power bloc and mobilizing constituents and allies requires challenging the basic legitimacy and practice of those in power, as well as providing alternatives to it.

Third, the relationship between local community organizing and national (or international) social movement activity is critical to understanding the origins, nature, and success of local efforts and the importance of social action community organizing. Often local efforts serve as the building blocks of broader movements, what sociologists call social movement organizations (SMOs). These SMOs can provide the democratic spaces, organizational opportunities, skill development, and political education critical to broader movement building. Like social movements they serve a significant political role by (1) pushing new issues onto the public stage, (2) legitimizing previously ignored claims, (3) having these claims cause divisions in the larger society and with more formalized political institutions and processes, and (4) forcing political parties and other institutions to address these heretofore ignored grievances. By opposition we mean both contestation for power with elites and activity that seeks to build an alternative to existing structures and relations. It extends beyond issues of governing and governance to influencing far broader social change.

Social movements provide opportunities, direction, and support for such local efforts. Even more than community organization, they have the power to force claims, politics, strategies, and tactics onto not only the local but also the state and national political stage, thereby legitimizing and catapulting them beyond traditional barriers. Consider the civil rights movement, which began based on generations of prior local work as well as local efforts after World War II. It grew to national proportions and spawned, directly and indirectly, organizing efforts at that time such as the New Left, the Student Nonviolent Coordinating Committee, and the Black Power movement, not to mention later efforts around the rights and power of women, other ethnic and racial minorities, gays and lesbians, and so forth.[11] The social ecology and strategies of the civil rights movement were not limited to official channels, at either the local or national level. As with all successful movements, however, its impact was much greater than the sum of its local parts. It is this heritage of and interaction with social movement opposition that recently has been dropped out of the discourse related to community organizing.

Fourth, community organizing efforts develop in a broad context that heavily influences the effort as well as the overall dominant form of community organizing in any era. Social movements are one critical part of that broad context. The social ecology in which an organizing effort is situated heavily influences its daily practice and long-term objectives. That context includes the local neighborhood or cultural community; the city, suburb, or rural environment; the metropolitan area; the state; the nation; and the globe, all contributing to a multilevel social ecology of community organizing. They all reflect varied levels, which both situate and influence community-based efforts. Clearly, local conditions directly nurture, spawn, and limit community organizing projects. The participants (organizers and members) and a myriad of conditions at the grassroots level combine to mold consistently unique organizing experiences. But while community organizing projects have a significant nature and existence at the local level, they are also products of a broader context that extends to national and even international political-economic developments. In large degree, the macro political-economic context heavily influences the goals and strategies, the general tenor, the type of organizing selected, and the likelihood of success of local efforts.

THE IMPORTANCE OF CONTEXT: A HISTORICAL OVERVIEW

Throughout the twentieth century, dominant forms of community organizing emerged in different eras. The liberal reform political economy of the Progressive Era, the period from approximately 1900 through 1917, responded positively to the impulse for reform at national, state, city, and community levels. Although other types of community organizing existed in this period, it was the integrated approach that blended community development and social action—exemplified in the best of the social settlement houses—which dominated the era.

In the Great Depression of the 1930s the community development approach had much less salience and support. As capitalism collapsed, as one reform solution after another failed to halt the economic depression, the social action type, most notably the urban populist work of Saul Alinsky in the Back of the Yards neighborhood in Chicago, came to dominate grassroots activity. The hotly debated and precarious political economy of the era legitimated citizen action and political ferment at the factory as well as the communities where workers lived. Alinsky's work drew on the militant organizing in the 1930s and 1940s derived from the union and radical movements. It proposed to "rub raw people's resentments" as a way to get them involved and fight the established powers.[12] Conflict was not the only strategy and tactic used by Alinsky and his staff. Community building, developing relationships in the community, and winning trust and support through "one-on-one" encounters were also important parts of the work. Opposition almost always includes a broad variety of tactics. Conflict is one of many means community members and organizers use to win power. But it was central to Alinsky's strategy.

In the post–World War II era the conservative cold war economy stifled social action and encouraged more accommodationist forms of community development, both at home and abroad. Of course, community development efforts, such as homeowners' and property associations, had a long history. But conservative eras, such as that created by the cold war politics of the postwar era, tied this necessity for neighborhood associations to a reactionary politics. Segregationist goals were intertwined with community betterment, interconnecting the protection of property values with a politics of neighborhood exclusion.[13]

The relationship between the national political economy and community organizing is not a one-way street where the dominant form of community organizing is determined by the national political economy of an era. The historical process is a much more complex dialectic. In the 1960s and the first part of the 1970s, when the social action type of community organizing came to dominate again, the national political economy both produced the change and was the product of it. The grassroots resistance of the southern civil rights movement, the student New Left, and the rebellion in black urban slums pushed the national political economy left, expanded the political discourse to legitimate grassroots resistance, and demanded the passage of social legislation to address the needs of the poor and people of color. The interconnection between the broader social movement and local-based community organizing was clear and critical. The shift in political economy at the national level, expanded with Lyndon Johnson's Great Society and War on Poverty programs, encouraged both social action and community development approaches, though social action infused almost every effort. On the heels of these developments Boyte heralded a "backyard revolution" in the making.[14]

It is this interpenetration between the national political economy and community organizing that comes across so vividly in the history of community organizing efforts. The legacy of Alinsky organizing, the civil rights movement, and the New Left are examples of oppositional social action strategy grounded in popular democracy and direct action. We will see that with the period of restructuring beginning in the late 1970s, new practices that were more embedded in processes of governance and service delivery began to dominate.

CONTEXTUALIZING CONTEMPORARY PRACTICE

The importance of the national, even global, political economy in shaping the nature of community organizing is evident in the past few decades, especially in (1) the proliferation of the community organizations with a variety of mandates and practices, (2) the increasing importance of the community development and community-building approach, and (3) the widespread adoption by most community-based efforts of more moderate strategies and the dramatic decline in salience of oppositional strategies and conflict tactics. Throughout the 1980s and 1990s the legacy of social action community organizing diminished.[15] These changes take on even greater significance in light of the broad proliferation of community efforts and even broader interest in the practice and potential of community organizing.

In the 1980s the United States made a clear turn to neoconservative politics at the national level. The twelve years of Reagan/Bush policy from 1981 to 1993 promoted a neoconservative agenda grounded in promoting corporate interests and right-wing programs, policies, and discourse. Responding to the heightened demands of an emerging global economy and the challenged status of U.S. corporations in it, neoconservatives sought to cut social costs. They went after labor unions, government programs, and claimant movements; they shifted even the limited political dialogue about human needs completely to corporate needs; they delegitimized the public sector and public life and pushed people into increasingly private spheres and private conceptions of the good life.[16]

In the neoconservative decades of the 1980s and 1990s, the impact of national context on local organizing was enormous. A wide variety of efforts continued to promote democratic resistance and left insurgency, but it was the neoconservative political economy that largely determined the direction of most community organizing during the decade, moderating them and pushing them away from oppositional strategies. In fact, the load shedding of public responsibility by the national government foisted new burdens as well as opportunities on local groups. The dramatic increase of nonprofit organizations in the past three decades, including but not limited to community-based efforts, is a manifestation of this national policy. Clearly the proliferation of community work since the late 1970s should be seen as an outgrowth of 1960s activism and a growing desire for democratic participation. But the proliferation of such community work must also be understood as well as a by-product of neoconservative politics and policies.

Rinku Sen argues that three contextual trends have had a major impact on progressive organizing since the 1970s. These are "the resurgence of conservative movements and the power gained by such movements in the United States since the early 1970s; the character and organization of the new economy, which is distinguished by the rising use of neo-liberal policies and contingent workers; and the continued and unyielding role of racism and sexism in the organization of society."[17]

This chapter will focus on the first contextual trend. The emergence of the neoconservative movement and neoliberalism (the more global variant of neoconservatism in the United States) as the ideology that defines social and economic policies has had a contradictory impact on the community sector. The increased importance of community organizations for economic and urban development is a reflection of the processes of globalization and the consequent rearrangement of power at both the national and the local level. Local restructuring is at stake because the nation-state has revised its traditional role and functions. Consequently, the regulation function of the state has been redefined, relying on market and related competition, as well as local nonprofit associations for provision of goods and services.

There are many different paths from what Jessop describes as the shift from the Keynesian Welfare National State (KWNS) to Schumpeterian Workfare Postnational Regimes (SWPR).[18] But regardless of the specific route, all subordinate social policy to economic policy with downward pressures on working conditions, and all seek to get people to become "enterprising subjects" and less dependent on state welfare programs. They diminish national governments, place greater emphasis on local, regional, and supranational levels of government, and accord new powers to social partnerships with related processes of negotiation.

The combination of extensive use of public-private and other partnerships and the involvement of diverse stakeholders in building agreements for how to adjust to the international competitive realities is coupled with expansion and support for the third sector and the social economy. The neoliberal ideology places markets at the center and implies that they should be open and, as far as possible, "liberated from all forms of state interference."[19] Both governments and foundations have policies that have promoted local entrepreneurial strategies both private and social, as well as accommodating investment through private-public partnerships. The process is contradictory insofar as these bodies have been active in promoting and supporting community organizations. And it is paradoxical that these organizations have moved into a vacuum created by the cutting of public services while also having to respond to the deteriorating social and economic conditions.[20]

In the United States, the Reagan-Bush-Clinton period recast the role of the state, and the agent of social change was redefined from the people and the government to the corporations.[21] The government launched unprecedented attacks on the power of trade unions and the poor in order to minimize social costs and support corporate allies in the competitive globalized market. In addition, the full force of the technological revolution transformed the industrial core of the United States into decaying centers of unemployment and despair. Community organizations, faced with mounting social problems such as poverty and unemployment, and without resources, were forced to be innovative; they created new forms of support and social solidarity. Food banks, shelters for the homeless, self-help organizations, and economic initiatives aimed at meeting basic needs and urban revitalization emerged. In some cases, such as community economic development, new formal partnerships were established, drawing community organizations and other actors into a consensus-building process, often with banks and other businesses formerly seen in the social action model as the cause of community problems. The community efforts of the 1980s and 1990s tended to lose their explicit political edge and found a new place alongside government and the private sector in reconstructing social and economic provision.

MODERATION OF COMMUNITY ORGANIZING

In the 1980s and 1990s, the dominant community organizing practice became community development.[22] In a social action model, power is the goal, a valuable commodity that enables people and their communities to get things done. Neo-Alinsky organizations, for example, try to "give people a thirst for power."[23] Recent models of community development define power in terms of technical skills or as untapped capacities resting within the community—internal power, which the community already possesses but needs to develop or access. Community work focuses on building relationships in the neighborhoods, developing partnerships with the powerful, using consensus strategies and tactics in order to actualize community capacity. This is important and valuable work that has tended in the past two decades, not always by choice, to adopt more conservative, businesslike strategies and tactics. As economic support for social services and solving social problems declined due to opposition at the federal level and shrinking tax bases at the local level, and as political discourse in the nation revolved around free-market solutions to all problems, many community organizing efforts moved more into the business of economic development.[24]

This trend was nowhere more evident than in the rapid growth and spread of community development corporations (CDCs), which dominated the field of community organizing from the early 1980s through the mid-1990s. CDCs began in the 1960s and experienced a "second wave" in the 1970s, when under the Carter administration they became central components of the limited, but significant, federally assisted neighborhood development movement. Beginning around 1980, however, CDCs found government support drastically cut. A new, third wave of CDCs developed in the privatization campaigns of the Reagan years and were forced into becoming much more businesslike than their predecessors. They had to exhibit "business talent and development skills once thought to be the exclusive province of the for-profit sector."[25]

The bottom line for most CDCs, as with seemingly everything else in these decades, was economic success. The primary goals were to "correct the market's failure to provide jobs and services to the community," as well as help build a nonwhite middle class by developing highly specific and measurable development projects in which neighborhood people could work for their own economic betterment.[26] Most avoided political controversy, were dominated by professionals with a technical orientation, had narrow memberships bases, and rejected social action activity. Although market demands forced most CDCs to become so oriented to economic success that they were not able to sustain their social action work, they did not always give up on these goals by choice. They were often forced into it, and then adapted to it. This was true of social action organizers as well. Neo-Alinsky organizer Shel Trapp saw a natural progression in his work. First, organizations defend the neighborhood; then they take an "offensive" stance. "That's when you start to link development with organizing."[27] Robert Rivera, an IAF organizer, put it similarly: "There are two types of organizing. One that is for, the other is against. Now you have to be for something. It's a different style of organizing."[28] But at play in the 1980s was more than a "life cycle" of organizing. Community economic development and building community partnerships with local economic and political elites became the dominant form of community organizing because of the demands and constraints of organizing in a neoconservative political economy. Of course many efforts held on to conflict strategies and tactics, even while combining them with economic development projects, especially older efforts with roots in the politics of the "sixties" such as ACORN, National People's Action, and the Center for Third World Organizing. But the pressures against social action turned most away. From the late 1970s to the mid-1990s, community economic development seemed to become virtually synonymous with community organizing.

Of course, while CDCs have become to a large extent private market developers and followed a path of consensus development and the conservative trend in local work, a fuller picture of the relationship between CDCs and community organizing is more complicated. As noted previously, CDCs have a complex history with multiple generations recognized in the literature, and these have shaped the vision that they carry into their practice of community development.[29] They often began, for example, as organizing efforts. DeFilippis describes those created in the late 1970s and early 1980s as emerging out of protest movements. "They [second-generation CDCs] emerged out of localized problems and conflicts, and it was not ideologically inconsistent to deal with local-scale problems as a developer rather than an adversarial activist."[30] With the transformation of the relationship between the state and community organizations, described earlier, there was greater pressure on CDCs to take on a state replacement role and become the key local service provider.[31]

In the past decade, while community economic development work has remained significant, a new community-building emphasis developed in response in large part to the discovery of worsening community conditions and relationships, especially in but certainly not limited to poor and minority communities. Communitarian authors such as Putnam and Etzioni argue for the rebuilding of "social capital" as a means of re-creating civil society.[32] The emphasis is on the local as a way of creating participation of citizens in socially oriented networks. Similarly, Kretzmann and McKnight construct an important perspective combining community building and community development that is based on the analysis that the prospect for outside help is bleak because of budgetary constraints and that significant community development can take place only when local people and local institutions discover and invest their own resources and efforts. The basic goal is to mobilize assets to build community involving "virtually the entire community in the complex process of regeneration."[33]

From a social action perspective, this version of community building emphasizes consensus and collaborative strategies, de-emphasizes community tensions, and ignores the causes of many community problems. It usually does not deal with underlying structural and contextual issues that caused community problems, such as banks that redline the community, corporations that abandon it, absentee landlords who run it down, or private and public policy that undermines it. The new community building posits itself as an alternative to both the social work model, which for McKnight[34] reduces citizens to clients, and to the Alinsky/social action model, which Kretzmann and McKnight[35] dismiss as grounded in community deficits and problems rather than community assets. As with Mike Eichler's "consensus organizing" strategy, there is a basic understanding that the context of the 1980s and 1990s required new models of organizing that could be "sold as a real conservative program."[36]

Returning to Sen's observation on the changing context, we can see two important elements. Changes in work have important consequences for asset-based practice. With the loss of regular work and the precarious employment that replaced it, the hours of work have become redefined, and they are predictable. Working in part-time low-wage sectors destabilizes family life because members often have to balance several jobs with irregular hours. As a consequence, there is neither the time nor the energy to participate in such new forms of community life. The availability of predictable time shapes the possibilities for voluntary commitments. With the restructuring of wage labor, this is not a realistic option for many members, particularly of low-income communities. From a social action perspective, the prescriptions of McKnight and the others create an idealized and decontextualized view of community. Similarly, when a feminist analysis is added, the idea of community as a voluntary means of caring becomes problematic. Feminists have argued that women who participate in the labor market have a double day, with both domestic and wage labor. Currently with the realignment of state services and the appropriation of them in the community, this further increases the demand on women, who traditionally have provided much of local direct and unwaged services.[37]

Social action groups have been affected as well by the moderating influence of the conservative context. Most neopopulist, political activist community organizing efforts during the 1980s and early 1990s adopted more moderate strategies and a more moderated version of oppositional politics. Battle lines shifted. "To a surprising extent the grass roots no longer 'fight the power.' They fight for a share of the power. Sometimes they win a sizable share. . . . [Sometimes they] team up with the established elite that they once derided and that once spurned them."[38] Even National People's Action (NPA), another organizing network based in Chicago, one criticized by some organizers as too confrontational, opposed in the early 1990s being "out in the streets making symbolic statements, when you can be in the boardroom negotiating specific agreements that win for neighborhoods."[39]

Consider the evolution of the Industrial Areas Foundation, the direct descendant of Alinsky organizing, which currently has about sixty-two organizing projects around the nation, but it is in Texas where the IAF network is the strongest. Throughout the state, in San Antonio, Houston, El Paso, Austin, Fort Worth, and the Rio Grande Valley, IAF organizers and active members struggle for utility reform, improved public education, government accountability, health care for the indigent, and basic public services, including water and sewers for the "colonias." Most visibly, they organize "get out the vote" efforts to promote bond packages to help IAF neighborhoods, hold "accountability sessions" to keep politicians publicly in line with IAF objectives, encourage voter registration, and work to improve "alliance schools" by halting the dropout rate, stopping drug use and violence, and getting parents more involved. More quietly, in the day-in and day-out practice of community organizing, they serve as "schools of public life," empowering neighborhood residents by giving them an opportunity to do something about public issues that have "frustrated [them] all their lives."[40]

IAF organizations do all this remarkably well, as many commentators have noted. Applebome proposed in 1988 that the IAF Network is "in ways large and small . . . changing politics in Texas."[41] Mary Beth Rogers, who served as chief of staff to former Texas governor Ann Richards, concluded that the IAF efforts in Texas "are virtually the only organizations in America that are enticing working poor people to participate in politics."[42] Mark Warren's more recent study of the Texas IAF, written within the social capital discourse, is equally flattering. Warren sees the Texas IAF as an impressive example of "community building to revitalize American democracy."[43] Without doubt its achievements and victories have been many.

But it is not a static organization. While still following much of the Alinsky style of organizing, the IAF adapted a new organizing strategy in the 1980s and 1990s to meet the needs of new constituents and the demands and openings of a new conservative context. Whereas most CDCs look for consensus, IAF groups focus on the importance of "standing for the whole."[44] Of course, many in power still see IAF as a radical protest group, and even during Alinsky's lifetime some IAF projects, such as The Woodlawn Organization, shifted from "conflict to coexistence." IAF remains a strong, progressive, and democratic voice; it is a powerful organization with dynamic leaders, a large mass base, a confrontational style, and substantial funding. But in a conservative context this success came with costs. The funding tended to be more for moderate projects such as building civic capacity in public schools. Moreover, the more moderate strategy encouraged IAF organizers to distance themselves from radicals and social movements. Whereas the early Alinsky took pride in being a radical, in the IAF radicals are seen as alienated outsiders. "IAF now almost makes a fetish of its commitment to moderates," noted veteran organizer and trainer Mike Miller.[45] The strategy of moderation, the commitment to moderates, the grounding of IAF efforts in mainstream religious institutions, and a definition of power that emphasizes building relationships may have led, however, to a politics that limits the parameters of IAF's work and its overall long-term effectiveness.

Of course, organizations cannot "do it all." In such a complex recipe, especially in a conservative context, other features of organizing pull energy and attention away from social action community organizing. In addition, pressures for development, traditional community building, and demands for accountability make it hard for organizations to find the flexibility to carry out an action agenda. Even in ACORN, which has done a better job of both continuing its progressive politics and using direct action tactics, one staff member, commenting on the Comprehensive Community Initiative in the South Bronx in which ACORN was funded by the Edna McConnell Clark Foundation to "do it all," noted, "It's a real struggle to not compromise our work culture to fit [this project]. We spend a lot of time making sure that our culture stays intact. . . . Direct action is our culture."[46]

REINSERTING OPPOSITION

It is no paradox neoconservatives call for neighborhood-based solutions and "empowerment" of citizens; they know well that these are less expensive strategies for problems that require costly national and global solutions and neighborhood-based initiatives. Without the existence of a social movement able to push the national political discourse left, win funding for social programs and redistributional policies, and struggle for state power, we can expect, at best, incremental change from the top and important but modest victories at the grass roots. Whatever the context ahead, community organizing, even with its limits, will remain essential: as schools of democracy and progressive citizenship; as seeds of larger resistance efforts; as demonstrations of the persistence of public life in an increasingly private world; as the vehicles of struggle in which we win victories, develop skills, forge identity, and legitimate opposition; and as potential grassroots components of the next major social justice movement. To play such roles, however, community organizing must both build on and go beyond the contemporary context. It must benefit from the new skills and strategies learned in the past generation and challenge the neoconservative political economy, which heavily shaped organizing in the past decades. While the history of community organizing makes clear that national context is fundamental, it also instructs that opposition—ideological and direct action challenges—is essential to push the context, policies, and programs toward meeting basic human needs and implementing more democratic processes.

Take, for example, the work of ACORN and its recent successes around both predatory lending and predatory tax preparation. Using a national network now located in some sixty-five cities, towns, and rural areas, as well as new efforts in Canada and Peru, ACORN continues to use a variety of strategies and tactics to move the issues that most affect its primarily low-income constituents, issues for which ACORN can get funding support and on which it can win, and issues around which ACORN can generally build the organization while keeping closely tethered to its overall identity as part of a larger social justice movement. In the predatory lending campaign, ACORN brought a number of major financial businesses, including Household Finance Corporation, one of the largest banking and lending agencies in the world, to the bargaining table through a variety of tactics such as broad participation by community members in direct actions at Household corporate sites, board meetings, and the homes of members of the board of directors;

public relations in local and national media, including newspapers, radio, and television; legislative initiatives at the local, state, and national levels; regulatory campaigns at multiple levels; and shareholder strategies. ACORN was able to win significant victories with Ameriquest, Citigroup, and Household Finance, all major financial institutions.[47]

ACORN also demonstrated a variety of strategies and tactics in a national campaign around the exploitation by commercial tax preparers of low-income residents eligible for the Earned Income Tax Credit (EITC), who are encouraged to take, at often exorbitant interest rates, a Refund Anticipation Loan (RAL) in order to get their tax refund quicker. Research by the Brookings Institution concluded that in 2001 of the $32.4 billion in refunds under the EITC program targeted at the working poor some $1.9 billion went to commercial tax preparers.[48] RALS are usurious short-term loans that charge an annual percentage rate of anywhere from 67 to 774 percent.[49] ACORN, which noticed this problem was affecting its members, determined that H&R Block and Jackson-Hewitt offices were actively operating in the same low-income communities that ACORN was organizing. ACORN met with policy analysts who had done work on this issue, secured funding from the Marguerite Casey Foundation for a direct action campaign targeting H&R Block and Jackson-Hewitt, and utilized similar tactics as in the predatory lending campaign. Especially effective was ACORN's ability as a national network of local community efforts to mobilize protests in the winter of 2004, during the early part of tax season, at some fifty offices of H&R Block on the same day and on more than one occasion. The turnout of members participating in the actions varied, but the chanting, aggressive demands, anger against the injustice of these predatory practices, bad publicity in national and local media, and the fact that those protesting were community people all got Block's attention. While the results of the campaign are still uncertain, the fact that H&R Block signed a negotiated agreement with ACORN within five months of the first protest points to the power of ACORN's social action organizing. It demonstrates the effectiveness of direct action strategies and tactics, when coupled with a national network and a relatively steadfast ideological commitment to fighting against class and race inequity and for a more democratic and egalitarian society.

BRIDGING THE DIVIDES

Another significant challenge for contemporary community organizing is to address the fragmentation that exists not only between community development and building approaches, on the one hand, and social action efforts, on the other, but also between grassroots community organizing efforts themselves, as well as between community organizing efforts and contemporary social movements. If community organizing is to have an impact greater than the sum of its parts, these divides must be addressed.

The first divide is the disconnection between community organizing efforts themselves, undermining their overall impact. Until very recently the national and regional networks—IAF, ACORN, Gamaliel, National People's Action, PICO National Network, and others—essentially acted as though they were ignoring each other. Most of them ignored comparable organizing in the workplace or efforts around culture and identity rather than geography. Increasingly, local efforts steeped in the development and service tradition do form coalitions with each other—for example, around homelessness, AIDS, or domestic violence—but this is less common with the social action efforts. More recently connections have improved. The national networks have been working with labor unions around living wage, immigrant, and get-out-the-vote campaigns. ACORN has close ties with the Service Employees International Union (SEIU) in Texas and Louisiana. Moreover, ACORN and Gamaliel have been working together in an inside-outside relationship in metropolitan areas where ACORN continues to organize in inner-city neighborhoods and Gamaliel focuses on inner-suburban communities with similar problems. But historically and still predominantly today these organizing efforts tend to work alone, ignoring the work of counterparts and, at their worst, putting down the efforts of the others. This tension has a long history and results from solid choices about where to put scarce resources and the obvious limits of coalition work. There are also ideological and practice divisions, not to mention competition for limited funding. But what seems to keep them apart as well are narrow issues of turf, organizational maintenance, personalities, and sometimes even a tradition of arrogance bred by a political culture hardened to outsiders. As the world and its challenges become larger and more integrated, community organizations are rethinking this isolation. The very fact that globalization foists its social problems onto communities that are unable to handle them underscores the need for larger, more powerful organizations to confront them.[50] This point is not lost on the national networks, especially ones like IAF and ACORN that have been around for more than a generation. ACORN, for example, has doubled its number of locals since 2003, an extraordinary rate of growth. Nevertheless, the divides that separate organizing efforts remain wide and daunting.

The second divide is with social movements. As the challenges to community organizations become greater, the need for connection with contemporary social movements becomes more obvious. Local organizing, with all its benefits, has its limits, especially in our globalizing context. Our world is increasingly characterized by centralization of power and decentralization of production.[51] Economic power concentrates as the task of cleaning up the mess of neoliberal policy and economic globalization fragments. Unless organizing can both build on and surpass a localist focus, the result could be internally directed local democracies and corporate control of everything else. New community developers recognize the local basis of democracy. They are correct in their encouragement of participation in the building of "civil society." There is a base of people with expertise who participate in a wide variety of community activities. But the local is only the beginning, and a single community organization or even a single national network, no matter how effective, is terribly overmatched by the size and power of corporations and governments. Democracy has to build outward and confront the wider agenda that has been universally accepted by corporate leaders and politicians of all stripes. Clearly, the opposition has to be constructed from the ground up, but it must also connect to global concerns and developments and especially to oppositional movements working for social change. Unlike some who think the nation-state has been surpassed by the new global economy,[52] and therefore is inappropriate as a target of organizing, we propose, along with others, that community efforts need to expand their work beyond the local to put the state back in to regulating corporate practice and ensuring the welfare of its citizens.[53] Problems lived locally are connected internationally and mediated by governments. In the United States those public bodies tend to be weak and underfunded, so groups like ACORN have had more recent success targeting private corporations. Nevertheless, the connections between public and private are there to be made. Appropriate alliances and demands have to be made to build effective politics at all levels. Public policy remains essential to any long-term social justice agenda. Community organizing with a social action politics has the greatest potential to articulate demands and promote alliances, which reach beyond the local community.

The best way to do so is to mend the huge disconnect and divide between community organizing efforts and contemporary social movements. Consider the youth/antiglobalization social movement, a strong force prior to September 11, 2001, and the war in Iraq. As impressive as they were, the Battle in Seattle and the A16 demonstration in Washington, D.C., needed to be grounded in actual organizing and daily practice. It is no wonder community organizers, especially those in the national networks, dismissed contemporary social movement activists because they were "not really organizers" and "don't have a base." Organizers were critical of antiglobalization road show politics in which confrontations at international meetings became played out without much ongoing programmatic activity. We propose that politicized community organizations can serve as bridges between mass events and between mass events and local alliance-building and popular education. Politicized community organizations such as ACORN can serve as day-to-day, on-the-ground organizing opportunities for those first engaged and mobilized by the larger social movement. At the same time, we need wider political organizations to promote demands and alternative visions that can sustain local struggles. Some like ACORN propose an alliance of community organizing with labor organizing and electoral politics, as seen in their work with the SEIU and the Working Families Party in New York. Effective community organizing needs a national, even an international, social movement, just as this broader movement depends on grassroots organizing. As noted earlier, this is a key lesson in the history of community organizing. The dialectical relationship between social movements and local organizing is essential to understanding both the potential and the limits of local work.

The third divide is between the community development and social action models of organizing. The action and development models and the related litera-ture examine practice elements and strategies. The politics tends to be limited to what can be described as "pragmatic reformism," that is, improving social condi-tions within the boundaries of what exists. How can community organizing move beyond this and contribute to greater social change and a politics of redistribution that underscores the United States as a shared, democratic, and inclusive commu-nity? The issue is complex; it is not easy to separate limited gains from long-term social change because engagement in the "real world" inevitably leads to pushing for specific victories. The difference between those practices that are limited to specific gains and those that see practice as part of a process of wider social change is due to factors such as intention, vision, process, and alliances. Both action and development can contribute to social change or can play a role in maintaining the status quo. Both can also have a lasting impact by changing the consciousness of the groups they serve, thus creating conditions for mobilization for social and polit-ical change.

The renewal of activism in the current period challenges the split between social action and development. The mobilizations on issues of international trade have brought together actors and organizations from a variety of social and political movements. The mobilizations that received extensive media coverage represent one aspect of their activities. There has been extensive local organizing at the core. Younger activists, interviewed by Shragge, did not split along the action-development divide but saw their work, whether it was developmental such as loan funds or collective gardens or organizing labor or fighting corporate power, as being in opposition to the relations of power in the society dominated by the interests of large international capital.[54] Similarly, the literature on this new wave of activism does not distinguish between action and development but examines the common-ality of opposition.[55] The link that facilitates these approaches to organizing has been the blending of social movements and local or community organizing. Ac-tivists become organizers at the local level and find local activities that allow for the expression of their oppositional politics. This is not new. The social movements of the 1960s and the 1970s produced similar results as first the student movement and

New Left and then the women's movement established local organizing and service projects that linked their radical politics and community organizing practice. Eventually some of these services became mainstream, such as homeless or domestic violence shelters. Based on these experiences and with our analysis of the moderation and contemporary role of community organizing, we present another conceptualization, both attempting to make the politics more explicit and acknowledging the underlying complexity of practice.

Table 8.1 addresses the tension between the development and action approaches and their relationship to the question of social change. It also provides a new model for understanding community practice. The terms *integration* and *opposition* are used to contrast the politics of practice. Integration strategies are used to increase people's participation in the system as it is or to enlarge resources or distribute some goods a little more fairly without challenging the basic assumptions of the system itself. This can happen either through pressure group tactics or through a variety of social programs. For example, local organizing to pressure the municipal government to improve traffic patterns or garbage pickup can better the quality of life in a neighborhood but does not challenge the domination of the car or the patterns of waste production. Similarly, programs such as job readiness attempt to place people in the labor market but do not necessarily raise questions about working conditions or about the pattern of linking jobs to participation in consumer culture. Integration practices support the maintenance of the fundamental power relations of our society and are designed to help people either meet their needs or make gains within existing structures and processes. It assumes that the system can expand to accommodate and bring people into either the jobs or the lifestyles defined by corporate capitalism. They do not question the limits and competitive nature of the system. Organizing within this approach does not go beyond the limitations of a singular focus on either local winnable demands or service and development.

Those working on the opposition side understand local organizing as part of a process of fundamental social change. This can include both organizing opposition to different aspects of society, such as specific policy or forms of oppression and inequality, and creating local alternatives such as cooperatives and services. These practices challenge the basic relations of power and create an alternative political and social culture based on democracy and direct control by citizens of these organizations. Further, the process of reaching these ends occurs through mobilizing citizens to play an active role. This is a key element, and the one aspect of practice that has been reduced since the 1980s. Power relations can be challenged and shifted only through the collective actions of citizens. Community organizing, to be a force for social change, has to be able to mobilize locally but must act in conjunction with wider alliances that share a politics of opposition.

Table 8.1. Redefining Community Practice Models

	Integration	Overlapping Practices	Opposition
Development	Service provision and development initiatives based on professional leadership and a consensus model **Tradition:** asset building (e.g., McKnight)	Service provision at the local level	Building alternatives that create new democratic or nonmarket economics, new practices that are "prefigurative" **Tradition:** feminist services or green urban development (collective community gardens)
Action	Pluralist pressure group organizing **Tradition:** pluralist pressure groups (e.g., Alinsky)	Organizing people in a neighborhood to pressure for local improvements	Social movement organizing and critical consciousness, challenging the legitimacy of existing power relations **Tradition:** Social movement organizing— locally (e.g., antiglobalization activism)

Source: Eric Shragge, *Social Activism and Social Change: Lessons for Community and Local Organizing* (Guelph, Ontario: Broadview Press, 2003), 198.

The differences are not always clear-cut, and it is hard to classify actual day-to-day practices. It is for that reason the middle column—overlapping practices—is added to the table. For example, community-building and community development processes also have the potential of moving people into action. In some respects, the actual activities are less important than the processes around them. This means, for example, that specific demands, campaigns, or services at the local level are integral to community organizing and fall within a process of building opposition. The process of organizing is what is important, not just the outcome. This includes raising critical consciousness in those participating in the organizing process about the necessity of social transformation as the means to achieve social justice and democracy. Fabricant and Fisher propose that "community building stripped of political intention tacitly demands that neighborhoods solve their problems within the confines of present economic and political arrangements. . . . Through the community building process and their own lived experience, residents come to understand that personal need and community problems are rooted beyond the neighborhood to the structural arrangements of the society as a whole."[56] In addition, local work must be connected to broader social movements and coalitions that are part of a struggle for social change. Gutierrez and Lewis, for instance, understand specific activities by feminist organizers at the local level as tied to the broader social movement.[57] Table 8.1 illustrates the dimensions of integration and opposition along with the action and development approaches and traditions in order to illustrate each approach. The quadrants have to be understood as types that show the general orientation of practice. The day-to-day reality is more complex. However, community organizing has to move beyond the traditional divides and become part of both a wider opposition movement and its local face.

CONCLUSION

This chapter makes a case for community organizing that is willing to build opposition, use confrontation as part of its diverse arsenal of strategies and tactics, and emphasize organizing that begins at the local level and builds outward. The argument for more than two decades has been that social action is passé. This critique came first from neoconservatives outside of the field of organizing. If you risk social action, your organization will pay the price of being marginalized and defunded. This is always a risk. Grassroots social change is never easy; it is inherently an audacious act. But we think several factors create the conditions that make opposition more acceptable and more effective. Economic competition and uncertainty have left many with little stake in the status quo. The contradictions of our contemporary world—the growing class inequalities, the revival of ethnocultural hatreds, heightened repression, the increased salience of right-wing regimes, and the continued wanton degradation of the Earth, to name but a few—continue to mount. The tyranny of the "marketplace" and pursuit of the corporate agenda have been arrogant and successful. People have fundamental needs that are unmet and which the new community development cannot meet. Support for the neoliberal order is fragile; chinks in the armor, let alone a major crisis, could engage many people. A combination of uncertainty and a lack of legitimization of the social order creates conditions for opposition and contestation. Challenges to the existing order, in the national campaigns of ACORN and in the earlier antiglobalization protests in Seattle and Washington, D.C., confront the corporate proponents of social moderation, which fear the expanded social costs of democratic dissent and economic democracy. Even with the events of September 11, 2001, and the turn to even more conservative regimes since 2000, including the Bush victory in 2004, it seems limited and shortsighted for organizers, activists, and community-based service providers not to seriously consider the potential of reinserting social action in their work as a way to build a broader opposition and alternative politics.

NOTES

Selected parts and earlier versions of this chapter first appeared in other works of ours, including Robert Fisher's *Let the People Decide: Neighborhood Organizing in America*, and Eric Shragge's *Activism and Social Change: Lessons for Community and Local Organizing.*

1. B. Epstein, "Rethinking Social Movement Theory," *Socialist Review* 90 (1990): 35–66; Robert Fisher and Joseph Kling, eds., *Mobilizing the Community: Local Politics in the Era of the Global City* (Newbury Park, CA: Sage, 1993).

2. Michael Sandel, "Democrats and Community," *New Republic*, February 22, 1988, 20–23.

3. Theda Skocpol, *Diminished Democracy: From Membership to Management in Civic Life* (Norman: University of Oklahoma Press, 2003); Theda Skocpol and Morris Fiorina, eds., *Civic Engagement in American Democracy* (Washington, DC: Brookings Institution/Russell Sage Foundation, 1999).

4. Saul D. Alinsky, *Reveille for Radicals* (New York: Vintage/Random House, 1946); S. Kahn, *How People Get Power* (Washington, DC: NASW Press, 1994); J. Rothman, "Three Models of Community Organization Practice," in *Strategies of Community Organization*, ed. F. Cox (Itasca, IL: Peacock, 1968); Robert Fisher, *Let the People Decide: Neighborhood Organizing in America*, updated edition (Boston: Twayne, 1994).

5. Rothman, "Three Models of Community Organization Practice."

6. The social action model is similar to that developed as the "social action" and "political activist" models, respectively, in Rothman, "Three Models of Community Organization Practice," and Fisher, *Let the People Decide*. The community development model combines the community-building and economic development components as expressed in what Rothman, in "Three Models of Community Organization Practice," calls "locality development" and Eric Shragge, in *Community Economic Development: In Search of Empowerment*, 2nd ed. (Montreal: Black Rose Books, 1997), refers to as community economic development.

7. Fisher, *Let the People Decide;* Michael Davis, *City of Quartz* (New York: Vintage, 1992).

8. Harry Boyte, *Backyard Revolution* (Philadelphia: Temple University Press, 1980); Harry Boyte, *Everyday Politics: Reconnecting Citizens and Public Life* (Philadelphia: University of Pennsylvania Press, 2004).

9. Michael Fabricant and Robert Fisher, *Social Settlements under Siege: The Struggle to Sustain Community Organizations in New York City* (New York: Columbia University Press, 2002).

10. G. Lipsitz, *A Life in the Struggle: Ivory Perry and the Culture of Opposition* (Philadelphia: Temple University Press, 1988), 241.

11. Aldon Morris, *Origins of the Civil Rights Movement* (New York: Free Press, 1984); Fisher, *Let the People Decide.*

12. Alinsky, *Reveille for Radicals.*

13. Fisher, *Let the People Decide.*

14. Boyte, *Backyard Revolution.*

15. J. Cocks, *The Oppositional Imagination* (London: Routledge, 1989).

16. Robert Fisher and H. Karger, *Social Work and Community in a Private World: Getting Out in Public* (New York: Longman, 1997).

17. Rinku Sen, *Stir It Up: Lessons in Community Organizing and Advocacy* (San Francisco: Jossey-Bass, 2003).

18. B. Jessop, "Liberalism, Neoliberalism, and Urban Governance: A State-Theoretical Perspective," in *Spaces of Neoliberalism: Urban Restructuring in North America and Western Europe*, ed. N. Brenner and N. Theodore (London: Blackwell, 2002), 105–125.

19. N. Brenner and N. Theodore, "Cities and Geographies of 'Actually Existing Neoliberalism'" in *Spaces of Neoliberalism: Urban Restructuring in North America and Western Europe*, ed. N. Brenner and N. Theodore (London: Blackwell, 2002), 2.

20. Fisher, *Let the People Decide*; Benjamin Marquez, "Mexican American Community Development Corporations and the Limits of Directed Capitalism," *Economic Development Quarterly* 7 (1993): 287–295; Shragge, *Community Economic Development*; Eric Shragge, *Activism and Social Change: Lessons for Community and Local Organizing* (Guelph, Ontario: Broadview Press, 2003); J. Panet-Raymond and R. Mayer, "The History of Community Development in Quebec," in *Community Organizing: Canadian Experiences*, ed. B. Wharf and M. Clague (Toronto: Oxford University Press, 1997), 29–61.

21. Fisher and Karger, *Social Work and Community in a Private World.*

22. Fisher, *Let the People Decide*; Marquez, "Mexican American Community Development Corporations"; Eric Shragge, "Looking Backwards to Go Forward: The Quebec Community Movement 30 Years Later," *Intervention*, no. 110 (October 1999): 53–60; Shragge, *Activism and Social Change*; Panet-Raymond and Mayer, "The History of Community Development in Quebec"; Neal Pierce and Carol F. Steinbach, *Enterprising Communities: Community-Based Development in America* (Washington, DC: Council for Community-Based Development, 1990).

23. Fisher, *Let the People Decide.*

24. N. Pierce and C. F. Steinbach, *Corrective Capitalism: The Rise of America's Community Development Corporations* (New York: Ford Foundation, 1987).

25. Ibid., 30.

26. Marquez, "Mexican American Community Development Corporations."

27. Shel Trapp quoted in J. Katz, "Neighborhood Politics: A Changing World," *Governing*, November 1990, 49.

28. R. Rivera, lecture, University of Houston, April 18, 1991; J. DeFilippis, *Unmaking Goliath: Community Control in the Face of Global Capital* (New York: Routledge, 2004).

29. Fisher, *Let the People Decide*; DeFilippis, *Unmaking Goliath.*

30. DeFilippis, *Unmaking Goliath*, 51.

31. Ibid., 53.

32. R. D. Putnam, "Bowling Alone: America's Declining Social Capital," *Journal of Democracy* 6 (January 1995): 65–78; A. Etzioni, *The Spirit of Community: Rights, Responsibilities, and the Communitarian Agenda* (New York: Crown, 1993); A. Etzioni, ed., *New Communitarian Thinking: Persons, Virtues, Institutions, Communities* (Charlottesvile: University Press of Virginia, 1995).

33. J. Kretzmann and J. McKnight, *Building Communities from the Inside Out: A Path toward Finding and Mobilizing a Community's Assets* (Chicago: Acta Publications, 1993), 345.

34. J. McKnight, *The Careless Society: Community and Its Counterfeit* (New York: Basic Books, 1995).

35. Kretzmann and McKnight, *Building Communities from the Inside Out.*

36. M. Eichler, "Consensus Organizing" (lecture, University of Houston, Graduate School of Social Work, November 15, 1990).

37. S. McGrath, K. Moffat, and U. George, "Community Capacity: The Emperor's New Clothes," *Canadian Review of Social Policy* 44 (1999): 9–23.

38. M. W. Newman and L. Williams, "People Power: Chicago's Real Clout," *Chicago Sun Times*, April 6, 1990, 12.

39. S. Trapp, "Dynamics of Organizing," *Disclosure*, March–April 1992, 2.

40. Cortes in H. Boyte, *Commonwealth: A Return to Citizen Politic* (New York: Free Press, 1989), 191.

41. "Changing Texas Politics at Its Roots," *New York Times,* May 31, 1988.

42. M. B. Rogers, *Cold Anger: The Story of Faith and Power Politics* (Denton: North Texas State University Press, 1990).

43. M. Warren, *Dry Bones Rattling* (Princeton, NJ: Princeton University Press, 2001), 1.

44. "Standing for the Whole," in *Texas IAF Network: Vision, Values, and Action,* ed. Pearl Caesar (Austin: Texas IAF Network, 1990), 13.

45. M. Miller, "Saul Alinsky and the Democratic Spirit," *Christianity and Crisis* 52 (May 25, 1992).

46. P. Brown, A. Branch, and J. Lee, *Neighborhood Partners Initiative: The Startup Chicago: A Chapin Hall Report* (University of Chicago, 1999), 35.

47. M. Hurd and S. Kest, "Fighting Predatory Lending from the Ground Up," in *Organizing Access to Capital: Advocacy and the Democratization of Financial Institutions,* ed. G. Squires (Philadelphia: Temple University Press, 2003), 119–134.

48. B. Katz and D. Jackson, *Purging the Parasitic Economy,* Web exclusive, September 7, 2004, www.brookings.edu/metro/20040907_metroview.htm (accessed September 8, 2004).

49. C. C. Wu, J. A. Fox, and E. Renaurt, *Tax Preparers Peddle High Priced Tax Refund* (Washington, DC: Consumer Federation of America and the National Consumer Law Center, 2002), 1–29.

50. M. Sandel, "Democrats and Community."

51. D. Montgomery, "What the World Needs Now," *Nation,* April 3, 1995, 461–463.

52. J. Brecher and T. Costello, *Global Village or Global Pillage: Economic Reconstruction from the Bottom Up* (Boston: South End Press, 1994).

53. J. Midgley, *Community Participation, Social Development, and the State* (London: Methuen, 1986); D. Lehmann, *Democracy and Development in Latin America: Economics, Politics, and Religion in the Postwar Period* (Philadelphia: Temple University Press, 1990).

54. Shragge, *Activism and Social Change.*

55. W. F. Fisher and T. Ponniah, eds., *Another World Is Possible: Popular Alternatives to Globalization at the World Social Forum* (New York: Zed Books, 2003); B. Shepard and R. Hayduk, eds., *From Act Up to the WTO: Urban Protest and Community Building in the Era of Globalization* (London: Verso, 2002); M. Prokosch and L. Raymond, eds., *The Global Activist's Manual: Local Ways to Change the World* (New York: Thunder Mouth's Press/Nation Books, 2002).

56. Fabricant and Fisher, *Social Settlements under Siege,* 259.

57. L. M. Gutierrez and E. A. Lewis, "Education, Participation, and Capacity Building in Community Organizing with Women of Color," in *Community Organizing and Community Building for Health,* ed. M. Minkler (New Brunswick, NJ: Rutgers University Press, 1999), 216–229.

9. Community Organizing for What?

Progressive Politics and Movement Building in America

Peter Dreier

Civic engagement and political participation (including voting) do not occur automatically. They require mobilization—that is, organizations with resources to reach out, identify, recruit, educate, and mobilize people to get involved. For example, Rosenstone and Hansen show that a "decline in mobilization" accounts for much of the drop-off in voting in recent decades.[1] As personal contact gives way to TV advertising and direct mail, and as political parties, labor unions, and other groups have lost much of their capacity to mobilize low-income and working-class citizens, civic engagement suffers. The wide class disparities in voting that we take for granted in the United States do not exist in other democratic societies.

The current progressive Left has no unifying vision, strategy, or mobilization vehicle. It has, instead, a huge mosaic of organizations that focus on separate issues and separate constituencies. There is a growing recognition by community organizers—as well as those in the labor, environmental, feminist, and other social movements—that this fragmentation of progressive forces undermines the effectiveness of each component of the broader movement. Moreover, all of them are playing on a constantly changing economic, demographic, and political field that requires constant rethinking of strategies. If community organizing is to make a difference, it has to address these challenges. Here I examine the strengths and weaknesses of community organizing, and the challenges it faces, at the start of the twenty-first century. This chapter reviews the world of community organizing as part of the broader movement for progressive social change.

THE PROGRESSIVE LANDSCAPE

To those progressives suffering from political hopelessness, Rick Perlstein's book, *Before the Storm*, about how conservatives recovered from the devastation of Barry

Goldwater's 1964 defeat, offers some solace and lessons. At the time, almost every pundit in the country wrote the conservative movement's obituary. Goldwater's right-wing supporters were viewed as fanatics, out of touch with mainstream America. But the GOP's right wing regrouped. With the help of conservative millionaires, corporations, and foundations, the right-wing leaders created new organizations, think tanks, and endowed professorships at universities to help shape the intellectual climate and policy agenda. They created a network of right-wing publications and talk radio stations. They recruited a new generation of college students, funded their campus organizations, and got them internships and jobs within conservative organizations and with conservative government officials and agencies. They identified potential political candidates and cultivated and trained them. They brought together the two major wings of the conservative movement—the business conservatives and the social/religious conservatives—in an uneasy but relatively stable coalition to elect conservative Republicans. Then they took over the atrophied apparatus of the Republican Party. They helped change the political agenda. In 1980, they elected Ronald Reagan. In 2000, they helped Bush steal the election. In 2004, they helped Bush win a second term, almost fair and square.[2]

Let us consider the landscape of the progressive movement. For the sake of argument, let us assume that the annual operating budget of the progressive movement added up to $25 billion. That includes the organizing, advocacy, and research staffs of the labor movement, the thousands of local community organizing groups and the major community organizing networks (some of which are covered in this volume), environmental groups like the Sierra Club and Greenpeace, national women's groups like NOW, civil rights and immigrants rights organizations, gay rights groups, the network of "public interest" groups like Common Cause, Public Campaign, the Center for Responsive Politics, the Public Interest Research Groups, and the Naderite networks (like Congress Watch), and civil liberties groups like People for the American Way, and the ACLU. Let us add the national policy groups and think tanks like the Economic Policy Institute, the Center for American Progress, the Center on Budget and Policy Priorities, and many others, and some local counterparts like the Center on Wisconsin Strategy and the Los Angeles Alliance for a New Economy. Throw into the mix the budgets of various progressive media outlets—*Mother Jones, The Nation, American Prospect, Sojourners, Ms., Dollars & Sense,* the Air America radio network (which includes the Al Franken Show), Web sites like AlterNet, TomPaine.com, and Common Dreams, and many others. Include the various progressive nonprofit public interest legal groups like the Mexican American Legal Defense and Education Fund (MALDEF), the National Association for the Advancement of Colored People (NAACP) Legal Defense Fund, Lamda Legal Defense Fund, the National Women's Law Center, and others. Add the various national and regional organizer training programs. This list does not even include the various political action committees (the union PACs, Emily's List, and others), the liberal churches and Jewish groups, the AARP, MoveOn.org, or various peace, human rights, and international "solidarity" groups.

Now let's reshuffle the deck. If progressives were starting from scratch and had, say, $25 billion a year to spend, how should they spend it? How many organizers? Researchers? Lawyers? Public relations and communications staff? What kind of organizations—single issue and multi-issue? How much would be allocated to unions, community organizing, environmental groups, women's rights groups, civil rights organizations, and gay rights groups? In what parts of the country—which cities, states, congressional districts—should they focus organizing work? How many staff would be based in Washington, D.C.? How many in "the field"? What issues should they focus on? What policy agenda?

Obviously, this is not how the real world works. Every organization emerges out of specific circumstances, develops its own constituency and issues, raises money from members and outside funders, and tries to expand to fill a niche. There is no progressive king or queen to assemble all these resources and make a rational allocation of money based on some agreed-upon criteria. But this mind game does help us think about the condition of progressive forces in the United States and how progressives might want to build an effective movement that was able to take political power.

THE FRAGMENTED MOSAIC OF COMMUNITY ORGANIZING

In the late 1960s, the United States witnessed the beginnings of what Harry Boyte called a "backyard revolution," a mushrooming of local community organizing groups and community development organizations, hoping to stem and perhaps reverse the decline of urban (primarily minority) neighborhoods.[3] With some funding from private foundations, thousands of community groups emerged that worked on a variety of issues, using a variety of organizing strategies, and with uneven effectiveness. Almost every U.S. city (and a few suburbs) now has at least one community group that does organizing. Some cities have dozens of such groups.

When people read about or see large-scale protest demonstrations in the media, they rarely think about the organizational resources required to make them happen. Mobilizing protests is only one aspect of effective organizing. Few people recognize how hard it is to build membership-based community organizations among the poor. It is extremely labor-intensive, requiring constant attention to identifying and developing leaders, building organizations, raising funds, engaging in traditional lobbying and occasional direct action, conducting research and policy analysis, and developing media savvy and other skills.[4]

Many (perhaps most) of the community organizing groups that emerged in the last four decades eventually fell apart or remained small and marginal, unable to sustain themselves financially, economically, and politically. A few hung in, grew, and gained in strength, in part by becoming part of broader networks at the city, regional, or national level.[5] No one really knows how many community organizations exist, the total size of their budgets, the number of staff people who work for them, how long they have been in business, how many are linked to larger networks, or how effective they are. This makes any serious evaluation of the strengths and weakness of community organizing, or these organizations' role in progressive politics, difficult.

What seems clear, however, is that among the thousands of community organizations around the country, most engage in relatively modest efforts. These include, for example, pressuring the police to close down a local crack house, getting city hall to fix potholes, or getting the parks department to clean up a local playground. Some groups are more ambitious. Their community organizing has included forming tenant unions, building community development corporations, combating banks' redlining, challenging police abuses, fighting against environmental and health problems, mobilizing against plant closings and layoffs, and reforming public education and even setting up charter schools. In some cities, housing activists have joined forces with unions and other groups to push for inclusionary zoning laws and municipal housing trust funds, such as the $100 million annual fund in Los Angeles enacted in 2002.[6]

Community organizations have won many neighborhood-level and municipal victories. Some organizing networks have built statewide coalitions to address state-level issues and change laws, regulations, and priorities. But the hard truth is that despite the tens of thousands of grassroots community organizations that have emerged in America's urban neighborhoods, the whole of the community organizing movement is smaller than the sum of its parts, as Paget described (and bemoaned) in 1996 and is still true today.[7] With some important exceptions, described later, community groups that do win important local victories are not always capable of building on their success and moving on to other issues and larger problems. For the most part, community-based organizing has been unable to affect the national agenda—or, in most cases, even state agendas. As a result, these organizations often improve only marginally the conditions of life in many urban neighborhoods.

Compared with groups like organized labor (with 13 million members) or even AARP (with 35 million members), community organizing groups are not very powerful at the national level. But that may not be the appropriate criteria. ACORN, for example, is just one of many organizations that do "community organizing," just as the Service Employees International Union (SEIU) is one of many organizations that do "labor organizing." Some of this fragmentation problem is due to "turf" competition between groups for funding, membership, and media attention. Some of it is due to the way funders, particularly foundations, evaluate organizing groups, requiring each group to identify its accomplishments, distinguishing them from the accomplishments of other groups within a broader movement. Some of it, as Burns describes in his chapter on New Orleans, is due to the reality that different groups, often in the same city or metropolitan area, sometimes work on similar issues but do not join forces. Likewise, Shirley and Evans's chapter on local school reform efforts shows how three organizing groups, ACORN, PACT, and Texas Industrial Areas Foundation (IAF), never collaborate, "even when they operated in the same cities and represent the same constituencies." With a few local exceptions, the various community organizing networks and groups do not work together, forge a common sense of purpose, or engage in common campaigns.

Observers of community organizing sometimes examine the differences between various "schools" of organizing. There are certainly differences between various organizing networks and training centers in terms of the class and racial/ethnic base of their constituencies, how or whether they deal with religious congregations, how they train leaders, how they raise money, and other matters. But those engaged in the organizing typically exaggerate the distinctions—what Freud called the "the narcissism of small differences." Wood's chapter on PICO, Staudt and Stone's chapter on EPISO (an IAF affiliate), and Swarts's chapter on ACORN, for example, reveal more similarities than differences.

As Fisher and Shragge observe in their chapter, community organizing today still feels like an "interest group," a cluster of organizations that use a common strategic approach but do not form a "movement." This is not inevitable. For example, there were many divisions within the civil rights movement (over strategies, tactics, and goals), but there was also some coordination and a sense of common history and purpose. There is no umbrella group for community organizing comparable to the labor movement. The labor movement is now split into two separate umbrella groups (the AFL-CIO and the Change to Win coalition), but even so, the reality is that the world of community organizing is much more fragmented, and thus less effective, than it could be.

While community organizing can be looked at as a separate political strategy and approach to social change, it is best examined as part of a broader progressive movement, with consideration given to whether it contributes to the Left's efforts at building political power for poor and working-class people. The purpose of progressive politics and movements is to reduce the level of poverty and the level of class, racial, and gender inequality in the nation, promote sustainable growth, and promote peace and human rights at home and overseas.

Despite our vast wealth, no other major industrial nation has allowed the level of sheer destitution that exists in the United States. In light of this reality, it is understandable that community organizing proponents often talk about their work in terms of "organizing the poor." One of the most important roles for progressives is to organize the poor to speak and advocate for themselves, so that they are at the political table and able to bargain and negotiate for their own concerns. But as a strategy for political and policy change—especially at the state and federal levels—this, on its own, is inadequate. Basic arithmetic tells us that the poor alone do not constitute a majority in any city, state, or congressional district, so that any effective organizing requires allies who are not poor.

For purposes of organizing, the demographic characteristics of the poor are important. We can figure out how many live in cities, suburbs, and rural areas and what the race and gender breakdowns are. We should know how many live in high-poverty neighborhoods and where those neighborhoods are. We should know which state legislative and congressional districts they live in and what proportion of eligible voters they represent in each district. We can identify how many are the "working poor" with steady jobs, how many are marginally employed, and how many are jobless. We can find out how many lack health insurance, how many live in housing that is too expensive, how many are hungry, how many face environmental dangers in the communities and workplaces, how many send their kids to underfunded schools.

But how does this information inform organizing? Without being part of a broader movement, there is no way for organizing groups to decide how to allocate progressive resources, to prioritize where and how to organize, to figure out which campaigns would be most effective in recruiting and mobilizing the people. Instead, different organizations—unions, community groups, environmental justice groups, and others—make decisions based on where they are located, what they are interested in doing, where they can get money, and other concerns. Currently, the Left is simply too fragmented to act in any coherent way. It operates on the principle of "let a thousand flowers bloom" and hopes that some of the flowers will grow into gardens.

THE REVIVAL OF COMMUNITY ORGANIZING

Community organizing emerged in the early 1900s, when the United States was becoming an urban and industrial society and when most urban workers were employed in factories and lived in nearby neighborhoods. It also emerged at a time when the U.S. working class, disproportionately composed of immigrants and their children, was part of a growing industrial labor movement.

In the early 1900s, New York City, like other industrial cities, was a cauldron of seething problems—poverty, slums, child labor, epidemics, sweatshops, and ethnic conflict. Out of that turmoil, activists created a progressive movement, forging a coalition of immigrants, unionists, muckraking journalists, settlement house workers, middle-class suffragists, tenement and public health reformers, upper-class philanthropists, and radical socialists. Although they spoke many languages, the movement found its voice through organizers, clergy, and sympathetic politicians. Their organizing involved both workplace battles and community struggles. Although these issues involved separate campaigns and constituencies, there was considerable overlap because many of the activists saw themselves as part of a broader movement. Their efforts produced laws that improved factory conditions, slum housing, and sanitation, among others. Many of the activists and leaders of that era—such as Francis Perkins, who became President Franklin Roosevelt's secretary of labor—helped lay the foundations of the New Deal decades later.

During the Great Depression of the 1930s, Saul Alinsky originally viewed community organizing as a partnership with labor unions. As Orr notes in chapter 1, the people who worked in Chicago's slaughterhouses worked in the same factories, lived in the Back of the Yards neighborhood, went to the same churches, participated in the same sports leagues, and were members of the same unions. The people who lived in that neighborhood were "citizens" and "community residents" as well as "workers." The problems they faced were interconnected. As a result, Alinsky viewed both labor organizing and community organizing as dual strategies for addressing the problems facing working-class people. Unions helped community groups win victories around municipal services and jobs; community groups helped unions win victories against the meatpacking companies and other employers.

Alinsky had a tremendous influence on the next generation of community organizers. He inspired many civil rights, student, and antiwar activists to move to urban ghettos and organize the poor. Many adopted his ideas about strategy, tactics, and building "people's" organizations. His theories influenced organizers in the early years of the environmental movement, feminism, and consumer activism. His ideas were particularly important in shaping the growing efforts of community organizing, even as organizers revised his theories to adapt to changing circumstances, constituencies, and issues.

But one of Alinsky's key strategic impulses was noticeably absent from the upsurge of community organizing in cities around the country during the 1960s, 1970s, and 1980s. This was the connection between community and labor organizing. One important exception was the work of Cesar Chavez and the United Farm Workers union. The southern civil rights movement provided much of the impetus for community organizing in northern cities in the 1960s. A number of New Left activists moved from campuses to urban neighborhoods to organize the poor.[8] Some community organizing efforts were funded by the mid-1960s federal antipoverty program, through grants to social service agencies, legal services offices, and Model Cities programs. Veterans of these efforts helped expand community organizing initiatives, which mushroomed in the 1970s and 1980s.

The issues around which urban residents organized varied greatly. Community groups formed to protest racial discrimination by employers, landlords, and real estate agents, as well as school segregation and inequities in school funding. Tenants organized in many cities to expand renters' rights.[9] Another major target of urban protest was the federal urban renewal program, which was implemented by local governments and sometimes labeled "Negro removal" because of its impact of bulldozing black areas in cities. Community activists protested plans for highway construction that sliced through low-income neighborhoods. Organizers also pushed for stronger police protection, and limits on police abuse, in minority neighborhoods. They opposed the razing of housing and small businesses to make way for megaprojects such as convention centers, sports complexes, and upscale housing developments. They mobilized to oppose expansion of hospitals, airports, and other institutions encroaching on their neighborhoods.

Some community organizing groups also engaged in service delivery and community development activities. They started community development corporations (CDCs) to help turn their protests against the urban renewal bulldozer or bank redlining into positive visions of stronger neighborhoods. With some exceptions, foundations preferred channeling funds for these service and development efforts, which were less controversial than protest and conflict. In 1970, 100 CDCs existed. By the 1990s, at least 2,000 CDCs operated around the country, with support from private foundations, local and state governments, businesses, and religious institutions. Many of the early CDCs struggled to undertake physical redevelopment projects. They lacked the financial, developmental, and management experience needed to construct and manage low-income rental housing competently. Although a few of these early groups managed to survive, grow, and prosper, many fell on hard times and ultimately went out of business. Some of their housing projects were mismanaged; some fell into foreclosure. In the 1980s, starting with the Reagan administration, the federal government instituted sharp cuts in assistance for low-income housing, exacerbating the abandonment of inner-city areas by private landlords and developers. This new wave of CDCs emerged to address the deepening decline of inner cities, against overwhelming odds, which included an unsympathetic federal administration, patchwork financing, high-risk development projects, and undercapitalization. For community groups, service and development efforts provided a steadier source of funding but sometimes led to tensions with their organizing work. Only a handful of CDCs got involved in community organizing and mobilization.[10]

Community organizing groups generally operated on shoestring budgets, funded by government grants, foundations, and some membership dues. They had few staff persons. Their organizers were generally inexperienced, and there were few people or resources available to provide training and mentoring. By the late 1960s, only a few organizations—such as Alinsky's IAF (Chicago) and the Highlander Center (Tennessee)—were available to provide training. The number of training centers expanded in the 1970s and 1980s—such as the Midwest Academy, the National Training and Information Center, and others—and helped expand the number of community organizing groups, link them together into networks, and strengthen their capacity.

Many of these local neighborhood and community organizations won some victories, but they often had difficulty sustaining their accomplishments. This limitation was due in part to a lack of sustained funding, as well as to organizations' inability to develop strategies for strengthening their base and moving on to new issues. In addition, the resources or authority needed to address a neighborhood's problems are often not available at the neighborhood level, and not even at the city level. This was particularly problematic as U.S. cities faced an increasingly serious fiscal crisis in the 1970s, making it difficult for local governments—even the most progressive local regimes—to address the problems facing low-income people and low-income neighborhoods. Some organizers recognized that battles at the local level can win improvements in people's lives but that real solutions to the nation's economic and social problems—including urban problems—required changes in federal policy.

THE CHANGING PLAYING FIELD FOR ORGANIZING

The success or failure of progressive movements must be examined in the context of broader trends. What obstacles and opportunities did they confront? Were they able to take advantage of opportunities? In hindsight, it may appear that progressive successes (as well as failures) were inevitable. In fact, they were the result of leaders' decisions about tactics and strategies, and their capacity to mobilize people, to recruit allies, and to identify openings and possibilities and take advantage of them, often against enormous odds.[11] Marion Orr discussed the changing political and economic ecology of central cities in chapter 1. In the following, I outline some broader trends, reminding the reader that to be effective, progressive organizing groups must adjust their strategies and coalition efforts to adapt to the broad changes in the economic, demographic, and political landscape.

The Urban Fiscal Crisis

Typically, community organizing groups want more funding for housing, police and fire protection, hospitals, schools, parks and playgrounds, and other munici-

pal functions. But since the 1970s, municipal governments and many state governments have confronted chronic fiscal crises. City governments are often perched
on the brink of fiscal distress. Even in cities with strong economies, local public
officials compete on a playing field tilted toward their suburbs, with few mecha-
nisms to promote city-suburb cooperation so that suburban wealth can be tapped
to help reduce poverty or promote private investment that generates good jobs.
Urban politicians worry that higher taxes on business and the middle class, higher
wages, and more regulations on employers and developers will exacerbate further
flight to the suburbs, to other states, and even to other countries. Most urban leaders are trapped in what they perceive to be a fiscal straitjacket.[12] To the extent that
progressive victories require additional funding resources as well as regulatory policies, it has become more difficult for progressive groups to win significant victories at the municipal level. Without additional federal funding, it is difficult for
cities to seriously address their housing, infrastructure, public safety, education,
and other problems. Progressive local regimes (such as those of former mayor
Harold Washington in Chicago, former mayor Ray Flynn in Boston, and current
mayor Antonio Villaraigosa in Los Angeles) have helped promote the agendas of
community organizations, but they are limited in resources and authority to solve
even local problems. In her chapter, Swarts observes that ACORN's shift to national
campaigns occurred in part because cities had less and less to offer. Burns writes
about the lack of resources available to public officials in New Orleans. Staudt and
Stone suggest that this is also true in El Paso.

The urban fiscal crisis, the decline of ward-level political machines, and the
retrenchment of government services have led some municipal governments to forge
"partnerships" with community-based organizations to provide a variety of social
services. In her chapter, Swarts describes ACORN's programs, such as housing loan
counseling and Earned Income Tax Credit (EITC) tax preparation. Staudt and Stone
describe EPISO's efforts to coordinate job training. As Fisher and Shragge note in
their chapter, this is a two-edged sword. When community organizing groups engage
in development and service delivery, this can shift part or even all of their focus and
energies. Some groups are able to walk this tightrope better than others.

Decline of Urban Power Structures

In the 1930s, the Back of the Yards Neighborhood Council took on the powerful meatpacking companies in Chicago. In the 1960s, the FIGHT organization in Rochester,
New York, another affiliate of Alinsky's IAF, challenged the Eastman Kodak Corporation, that city's dominant employer. In the period after World War II, urban politics were dominated by pro-growth coalitions that pushed for the physical
redevelopment of downtown areas. Typically, they were preceded by the formation

of organizations of corporate leaders such as the Coordinating Committee in Boston, the Committee of 25 in Los Angeles, the New Detroit Committee, and Central Atlanta Progress. These groups brought together the key business leaders to smooth over differences, forge a corporate consensus on public policy, marshal elite support for a pro-growth agenda, and promote local involvement in the federal urban renewal program. Most of these corporate-sponsored urban policy groups, weakened by changes in the corporate economy, are no longer the powerful bodies they were in the 1950s, 1960s, and 1970s. As Orr writes in his chapter, referring to FIGHT's battle with Rochester's dominant employer, most major local employers are now branches of large companies, run by branch managers. These managers have less of an economic, political, and personal stake in the city and region. Burns shows how New Orleans, once ruled by an exclusive social aristocracy and business elite, has become what he describes as a "nonregime city"—a city without a coherent corporate power structure or governing regime. Staudt and Stone show how the tight-knit Anglo business community that ruled El Paso for many years has gradually been transformed, allowing new groups, including a new Latino professional class, to exercise some influence.

This transformation has consequences for community organizing. For example, groups working against bank redlining no longer can confront the directors of the local bank on their own turf. These banks are now run from distant boards. Local unions, community groups, and environmental groups working to restrain Wal-Mart can find local organizing "handles," but they must find ways to work together across the country to influence decisions made in Bentonville, Arkansas, where Wal-Mart is headquartered. Without some kind of national network or movement, local groups are limited in their ability to bargain with large corporations and influence federal policy.

The "Business Climate" and Capital Mobility

Whenever community organizations, unions, environmental organizations, and other progressive groups propose policies to make business act more responsibly, business leaders react in horror that it will destroy the incentive to invest and will hurt the business climate. As a result, most officials accommodate themselves to the business community's priorities. Although many local officials want to improve conditions for the poor and near poor, they also want to make their cities attractive places to do business and retain middle-class residents. Living wage ordinances, "linkage" fees on new commercial buildings that target the funds for affordable housing, business taxes, clean-air laws, inclusionary zoning laws that require housing developers to incorporate units for low-income families, and rent control challenge business's priorities and are thus labeled as "anti-business."

Corporations may be bluffing when they threaten to leave if cities enact such laws, but it is hard for local officials, unions, and community groups to know for certain. Business warnings are not always empty threats. Even sympathetic politicians are not sure when businesses are bluffing, and politicians tend to err in favor of business.

Although some businesses are mobile, many are tied to the local economy. Progressive city officials and activists need a clear sense of when business threats are real and when they are not. This knowledge would spare cities costly bidding wars and prevent businesses from playing municipalities off each other to attract private investment. At the national level, federal laws actually promote competition between cities, regions, and states. The Taft-Hartley Act, for example, allows states to enact antiunion "right-to-work" laws. Our federal system allows cities to establish their own property tax rates and cut special deals for particular investment projects, exacerbating bidding wars for business. Progressives need to fight for federal and state legislation that puts restrictions on bidding wars between cities and states for private investment. Tax, environmental, labor, and other laws should be reformed to make it more difficult for companies to play Russian roulette with our cities. We need to enact a common national standard and establish a more level playing field.

Suburbanization

More than half of the U.S. population—and more than half of all voters—live in suburbs. The 1992 presidential election was the first in which suburbanites represented a majority of voters. In the 2004 elections, some analysts attributed Bush's reelection and other Republican victories in key swing states to voters in the newer (exurban) suburbs, especially among lower-middle-class churchgoers, many of them regular congregants of new "megachurches" that have grown along with suburban sprawl.[13]

Almost half of the nation's poor live in suburbs, too. There is a widening economic divide *within* suburbia, as a recent Brookings Institution report on economic segregation reveals.[14] Suburbanites are not a homogeneous constituency that lacks any shared interests with central cities. Perhaps a third of all suburbs are doing worse than central cities on such indicators as poverty rates and the incidence of crime. Congress and many state legislatures are dominated by suburban districts. But most community organizing groups have focused on low-income areas of inner cities that typically are represented by liberal Democrats who occupy reasonably "safe" seats in state legislatures and Congress. This is no longer adequate in terms of building political strength. In terms of influencing policy, strength in inner-city neighborhoods gives community groups an important role in influencing municipal politics.

But such influence is insufficient for winning victories in state and federal politics. The progressive Left needs a strategy for building a base in the swing state legislative and congressional districts that are primarily outside cities.[15] Without an organizing strategy and policy agenda that address the concerns of some significant sector of suburbanites—especially but not exclusively those in inner-ring suburbs—community organizing and labor unions will become victims of these trends.

The building blocks for an effective progressive movement today start in cities and move outward to working-class suburbs and some liberal middle-class suburbs. Some labor unions and community organizing networks recognize this and have begun to reach out to the suburbs, often in alliance with religious congregations, whose denominations include urban and suburban institutions. They must find common-ground issues that can help them develop a *regional agenda* to channel jobs and economic development into declining business districts, in contrast to cutthroat competition between cities in the same region trying to outbid each other for private investment or to limit suburban sprawl and traffic congestion.

Immigration and Racial/Ethnic Diversity

America's neighborhoods, cities, and metropolitan areas are highly segregated by race. But as many demographers have noted, the demographic trajectories of our major metropolitan areas are more complex and diverse than ever before. They are no longer dominated by the dynamic of whites fleeing to the suburbs as central cities become increasingly populated by blacks. The massive wave of immigration over the last four decades and the increased suburbanization of blacks, Latinos, and Asians have moved our metropolitan areas beyond the paradigm of "politics in black and white." Although most large central cities, such as New York and Los Angeles, are becoming less white, they are also becoming less black, as African Americans suburbanize and as immigrants and their children take the place of the native born. Most suburbs are also becoming more heterogeneous in racial and ethnic terms.

Unlike in the 1960s and 1970s, these transitions are not pitting whites against blacks but are creating more complex patterns. Although the full political implications of this shift have yet to play out, new forms of ethnic expression and, in some cases, cooperation are being overlaid on the black-white racial tensions that drove urban politics in the postwar period. The emerging politics of interethnic relations is not going to be easy, but at least it is less likely to be locked in racial polarization. More complex interracial coalitions will form.

With obvious exceptions, racism and racial discrimination are more subtle and less overt than they were in the past. Nevertheless, considerable documentation indicates that landlords, real estate agents, appraisers, lenders, police, doctors, and others today treat whites differently than they treat blacks and Latinos, even when income is factored in. Anyone stopped for "driving while black" can attest to this. It may be possible that *intentional* discrimination has been reduced over the past few decades, but that more covert, *institutional* forms of racial discrimination persist.

Public opinion polls consistently show that white Americans are more supportive of laws against racial discrimination and of racial integration in neighborhoods and schools than they were twenty-five or forty years ago. But it is difficult to mobilize public support around more subtle forms of racial discrimination or around institutional practices that result in racially disparate outcomes but which appear, on the surface, to be racially "neutral" in intent or procedure. The backlash against affirmative action is one symptom of this. Clearly the Bush administration's response to the Katrina disaster, particularly in New Orleans, resulted in part from the fact that New Orleans is a majority black (and mostly Democratic) city. But accusations that Bush was a "racist" met with considerable skepticism among opinion leaders.

These dynamics create dilemmas and opportunities for progressive organizers. Community organizing groups have a long history of dealing with racism and discrimination by schools, employers, banks, landlords, and police, but, as Santow describes, rarely have they been successful at addressing the problem of residential segregation. How do we deal with the reality of racism and segregation and still find a common ground for building majoritarian support?

Militarism and Globalization

A discussion of the challenges facing progressives would be incomplete without some focus on the military-industrial complex and the dilemmas of globalization. We will never solve our domestic problems as long as we continue to spend such a large part of our federal budget on national defense. Today, almost two decades after the end of the cold war and in spite of all the talk about a "peace dividend," the United States has not significantly reduced its reliance on military spending. Indeed, the "war on terrorism" has necessitated increased federal funding for war and "homeland security."

This reality has three serious consequences. First, there is not enough money in our federal budget to adequately fund domestic economic and social programs. Second, our private economy is still dominated by military research and production, which means we divert much of our scientific and technical expertise to defense and invest too little in civilian industries. Third, the United States uses its military, economic, and political influence to promote many regimes overseas that limit human rights and workers' rights. This provides a friendly business climate for corporate investment, but it promotes a "race to the bottom" in terms of working and living conditions, what some call the "Walmart-ization" of the economy. In general, the community organizing movement has few links to movements that focus on human rights, militarism, opposition to unregulated free trade, and solidarity with movements at home and overseas that promote fair trade. In part this is a function of the limits of "localism," and in part it is a result of the internal culture of community organizing groups that focus on domestic issues.

The Internet and New Technology

The introduction of the Internet, e-mail, cell phones, the blogosphere, and other new technologies has made communication easier and faster. It has accelerated corporate globalization by allowing firms to access information quickly and efficiently from different parts of the world. It has made it easier for government officials and agencies to communicate with citizens and vice versa. It has changed how candidates campaign for office and how interest groups participate in campaigns, including fund-raising, voter education, and voter turnout. The new technology has also made it easier for grassroots activists to communicate with each other, educate and alert people about pending issues, and mobilize people for letter-writing campaigns, rallies, elections, and other efforts. The emergence of groups like MoveOn.org and daily blogs about political issues has reshaped the political landscape.

ORGANIZING NETWORKS, FEDERATED ORGANIZATIONS,
AND SOCIAL MOVEMENTS

In *Diminished Democracy,* Theda Skocpol laments the decline since the early 1900s of mass-membership grassroots and mixed-income organizations and their replacement with advocacy and lobbying groups run by professional staff with little capacity to mobilize large numbers of people.[16] She discusses the importance of having "federated" organizations—national organizations with local chapters that are able to mobilize members at the local and national levels simultaneously. Among community organizing groups, ACORN best represents a "federated" structure. Its constituent base consists of its chapters in cities across the country, primarily in low-income areas. As Heidi Swarts discusses in her chapter, ACORN also has a national infrastructure and the capacity to wage campaigns simultaneously at the local, state, and national levels. More typically, organizing groups that have local chapters and also want to influence national policy forge networks, some looser than others, usually on one issue. In recent years, several issues have catalyzed local organizing groups into working together at a national level, sometimes as part of a federated structure, or as part of a network or coalition of organizations. To illustrate, I review five examples—community reinvestment, environmental justice, living wage, sweatshops, and immigrant rights. Each reveals why local community organizing is essential but insufficient to address America's changing economic, demographic, and political conditions.

Community Reinvestment

The community reinvestment movement is a place-based movement that has linked local groups to change federal policy and negotiate with national and local lenders. It emerged in the 1970s to address the reality of declining urban neighborhoods and persistent racial discrimination in housing and lending. At that time, a number of astute activists began to recognize that many long-term homeowners and small-business owners—even those who were obviously creditworthy—were finding it increasingly difficult to obtain loans from local banks and savings-and-loans institutions to repair their homes or expand their businesses. Local activists and organizers concluded that their neighborhoods were experiencing systematic disinvestment known as redlining. Banks accepted deposits from neighborhood residents but would lend money primarily to home buyers in suburbs. Activists tried to convince bankers to revise their perceptions and practices. Other efforts involved consumer boycotts—"greenlining" campaigns—against neighborhood banks that refused to reinvest local depositors' money in their own backyards.

Some neighborhood groups achieved small victories, including agreements between banks and community organizations to provide loans or maintain branches in their neighborhoods. Eventually, activists working on similar issues around the country discovered one another and recognized their common agendas. From such localized efforts grew a national "community reinvestment" movement to address the problem of bank redlining.

Community groups came together to focus attention on the role lenders played in exacerbating neighborhood decline and (to a lesser extent) racial segregation. Its first major victory, the Home Mortgage Disclosure Act (HMDA), was passed by Congress in 1975, followed by the Community Reinvestment Act (CRA) in 1977.[17]

The CRA had minimal impact at first but gained momentum in the 1980s, despite resistance from the Reagan and Bush administrations and their appointed federal bank regulators. But by the mid-1980s, local activists coalesced into a significant national presence. The networking of local groups organizing around the same issue made it possible for them to learn from one another through several national organizing networks and training centers, particularly National Peoples Action (NPA), ACORN, the Center for Community Change (CCC), and the National Community Reinvestment Coalition (NCRC), as well as the Woodstock Institute and Inner City Press. These networks provided groups with training and linked them with one another to make the federal government more responsive to neighborhood credit needs. Through these networks, grassroots groups pressured Congress to strengthen both the CRA and the HMDA several times in the late 1980s.

The most important aspect of the CRA was that it provided local groups with an "organizing handle" to use with banks and government regulators. By requiring banks to meet community needs as a prerequisite for obtaining various approvals from federal bank regulators, and by giving consumer and community groups the right to challenge these approvals, the CRA provided the groups with leverage to bring banks to the negotiating table. The community reinvestment movement's effectiveness resulted from its ability to identify organizing campaigns and policy remedies at the local, state, and national levels simultaneously. These remedies included local linked deposit laws, state linked deposit and antiredlining laws, and, of course, the enactment, and then the strengthening and improved enforcement of, the federal HMDA and CRA. Consequently, groups could organize, and achieve victories, on several fronts. Local groups joined forces on state- and federal-level campaigns. Under pressure from community groups and national advocacy networks—and from some elected officials, bank regulators, and the media—banks responded with increased investment in previously underserved communities.

Thanks to these laws, and to grassroots organizing, the community reinvestment climate has changed dramatically in the past few decades. Banks are now more proactive in working with community organizations to identify credit needs and create partnerships to meet them. Government regulators are more active in evaluating lenders' CRA performance, despite resistance from the banking industry. The community reinvestment movement pushed many banks to reluctantly increase their lending in minority and poor neighborhoods that had once been written off. The CRA has resulted in more than $1 trillion in private investment being channeled into urban neighborhoods. The homeownership rate of blacks and Latinos has increased significantly since 1977, and the homeownership gap between whites and racial minorities has narrowed.

Environmental Justice

In the mid-1980s and early 1990s, a new form of community-based organizing grew to national scale with the visible emergence of the environmental justice (EJ) movement, which criticized the mainstream environmental movement for its class and racial bias. The "mainstream" environmental movement, with its focus on conservation and the protection of wildlife and open space in remote areas, dates back to the early 1900s. At that time, a more radical wing of the movement, based in urban areas, focused on public health, tenement reform, workplace safety, and access to urban parks and recreation areas. The former wing of the movement was dominated by affluent Americans; the latter wing was led by a combination of working-class activists and middle-class reformers.[18]

A new wave of mainstream environmentalism emerged in the late 1960s and 1970s, its beginnings identified with Earth Day in 1970. Its efforts overlapped with the emerging consumer movement, typically identified with Ralph Nader. Its early victories included the passage of the Clean Air Act, the Clean Water Act, and the Occupational Health and Safety Act; creation of the Environmental Protection Agency (EPA) and the Occupational Safety and Health Administration; consumer-friendly informational and warning labels on medicines, cigarettes, and other products; and the shutdown of many existing nuclear power plants. Most of the major environmental organizations, such as the Sierra Club, the League of Conservation Voters, the Audubon Society, the National Wildlife Federation, the Wilderness Society, and Friends of the Earth, were overwhelmingly white and middle-class in terms of their staff and membership. To different degrees they were national public interest and advocacy groups that rarely mobilized members for action. Some of the more radical environmental groups, such as Earth First and Greenpeace, were more decentralized but shared with the mainstream groups their predominantly white and middle-class membership.

In the 1980s, the EJ movement challenged the mainstream environmental groups for their lack of diversity and for ignoring the concerns of low-income and minority communities. It helped redefine environmentalism, linking its issues with public health, workers' rights and occupational health, land use and transportation, and economic and housing development. It focused on issues such as the siting of toxic waste facilities, public health, access to parks and open space, and land and water rights. It represented a convergence of community organizing, civil rights, environmentalism, and, in some cases, labor unionism.

For example, in the 1970s, the United Farm Workers union linked immigrant worker rights to health and the use of pesticides. In 1982, in Warren County, North Carolina, residents protested against a proposed PCB landfill. The protest was unsuccessful, but it helped spawn a new movement and a new environmental awareness. Subsequently, the U.S. General Accounting Office conducted a study of hazardous waste landfills in the Southeast and found that blacks were a majority of the population in three of the four off-site landfills (not associated with an industrial facility) in the region. In the mid-1980s, Mexican American women in Los Angeles organized Mothers of East Los Angeles (MELA) to stop the construction of a state prison in their neighborhood. In 1987, members of MELA fought successfully against the siting of a hazardous waste incinerator near their community. A few miles away, women in South Central Los Angeles organized the Concerned Citizens of South Central to successfully fight a proposed solid waste incinerator, the LANCER project, targeted for a neighborhood that was more than 52 percent black and 44 percent Latino.

Research began to confirm the patterns of environmental racism and injustice identified by these groups. In the late 1970s, sociologist Robert Bullard examined the siting of garbage dumps in black neighborhoods in Houston and identified systematic patterns of injustice. He wrote several reports and papers based on this research, culminating in *Dumping in Dixie* in 1990.[19] In 1987, a report by the United Church of Christ's Commission for Racial Justice, *Toxic Wastes and Race in the United States,* found common themes among these different efforts. It popularized the concepts of environmental racism and environmental justice, concepts that focused attention on racial disparities in the siting of toxic facilities and public health indicators such as cancer and asthma rates; the failure of mainstream environmental organizations to address these concerns; and the failure of government environmental agencies and laws to deal with such disparate racial outcomes.[20]

As local groups became aware of each other, often at environmental conferences or through the media, they recognized their common outlook and concerns. A turning point came in 1991 when groups came together at the National People of Color Environmental Leadership Summit in Washington, D.C., attended by more than a thousand activists from all fifty states, as well as other nations. The summit participants forged alliances and networks. According to Chang and Hwang, "the new language made it possible for local grassroots organizers to begin to understand their work differently. Soon regional environmental justice networks began springing up across the country."[21] In the South, black organizations joined to fight hazardous waste proposals and to clean up communities. In the Southwest, Latino and indigenous organizers formed the Southwest Network for Environmental and Economic Justice (SNEEJ). In the Northeast, West Harlem Environmental Action (WEACT) led the fight over the North River sewage treatment plant, drawing in activists across twelve northeastern states, which resulted in the formation of a multistate regional network, the Northeast Environmental Justice Network (NEJN). The Farmworkers Network for Environmental and Economic Justice began in 1993 when several labor leaders held a historic meeting of independent farmworker groups. They also advocated international approaches to farmworker issues and invited the Confederación Nacional Campesina (CONFENACA) from the Dominican Republic. By the late 1990s, the network included farmworker groups from nine states. Given their emphasis on economic justice, it is not surprising that these groups made connections with organized labor, seeing a common bond between workers exposed to toxic chemicals on the job and communities exposed to poisoned groundwater.

The EJ movement has had an impact on several fronts. It has influenced federal policy to become more sensitive to racial disparities in terms of both environmental hazards and environmental laws. For example, in February 1994 the Clinton administration issued Executive Order 12898, charging each cabinet department to "make achieving environmental justice part of its mission," with the EPA as the lead agency. Clinton's EPA administrator, Carol Browner, created an "office of environmental justice" and appointed a national environmental justice advisory council dominated by environmental advocates. The EJ movement has also influenced the mainstream environmental movement to become more aware of racial and income concerns, as well as the diversity of staff and leadership. The Sierra Club, for example, now has an ongoing campaign around toxic dumping in poor and minority areas through which it has forged ties with local environmental justice groups. The EJ movement has also pushed the mainstream groups to forge closer ties to organized labor, to find common cause around fighting for safer workplaces and healthier communities, pushing for "clean energy" solutions that create jobs, holding corporations accountable, resisting the framing of issues as "jobs versus the environment," and working together around fair-trade agreements that include environmental and workers' rights.

Living Wage

A dramatic example of organizing success is the growing number of cities that have adopted living wage laws, a tribute to the alliances between unions, community organizations, and faith-based groups that have emerged in the past decade. Baltimore passed the first living wage law in 1994, following a grassroots campaign organized by Baltimoreans United in Leadership Development (BUILD), an IAF affiliate, and the American Federation of State, County and Municipal Employees (whose members work for local governments). By 2004, community, labor, and religious coalitions had won living wage ordinances in 117 cities.

The movement received a major impetus from efforts by city governments to contract public services to private firms paying lower wages and benefits than prevail in the public sector. Proponents have also been motivated by the proliferation of low-wage jobs in urban areas. The movement was also spurred by Congress's failure to raise the national minimum wage, which has not been adjusted since 1997, when it was increased to $5.15 an hour.

Yet these underlying factors alone do not account for the movement's success in getting so many cities to adopt local living wage laws in so short a period. As Martin and others (including Swarts's chapter in this volume) have shown, the movement's effectiveness is due in large measure to the existence of two national networks and federated structures—the labor movement and ACORN—that have both spearheaded local living wage campaigns and spread their strategic and tactical experience to new cities.[22]

The national unions and ACORN's national office have provided training, research, fund-raising, strategizing, and coordination. ACORN's "federated" structure made it possible to juggle a number of local living wage campaigns at the same time. This is also why the IAF was unable to build on its initial innovative success in Baltimore. The IAF is a much looser national network. Each local or regional group is essentially on its own in terms of designing campaigns, hiring staff, and raising money. Moreover, ACORN's close ties to the labor movement provide resources for national and local living wage efforts that would not be available to a locally based organization on its own.

Living wage laws cover only a small proportion of a city's workforce (about 12,500 out of 1.7 million workers in the city of Los Angeles), typically employees of firms that do business with city government. In recent years, voters in San Francisco, Santa Fe, and New Orleans endorsed ballot initiatives to create citywide minimum wage laws that set minimum wages significantly higher than the federal level. As Burns discussed in his chapter, the New Orleans law was overturned in state court.

The living wage movement has built on these local successes to widen its horizons of political and economic reform. It has helped change the public's view of the poor and the social contract. Two decades ago, the concept of a "living wage" was a radical idea. Today, it is part of the mainstream public debate. President Clinton's rhetoric that government policy should "make work pay" helped shift public attitudes. Today, there is widespread popular support for the Earned Income Tax Credit, which provides income assistance to the working poor. The popularity of Barbara Ehrenreich's best seller about the working poor, *Nickel and Dimed,* and growing protests against Wal-Mart's low pay indicate that concerns about inequality and poverty are moving from the margin to the mainstream of American politics.

ACORN's strategy, in conjunction with unions, church groups, and others, to inject the living wage issue into state ballot measures is another important step. In early 2004, ACORN initiated a statewide ballot measure in Florida to raise the state minimum wage, registered thousands of residents, mostly in low-income, minority neighborhoods in cities, to increase turnout on election day, and won a decisive victory the following November. After its victory in Florida, ACORN and its labor allies planned and successfully organized grassroots minimum-wage initiatives in six other states in 2006, particularly where Democrats had a chance to expand, or hold on to, key offices. The strategy increased voter turnout and provided candidates with their margin of victory in Missouri, Montana, Ohio, and elsewhere. Activists also hoped that this state-by-state strategy would lay the groundwork for raising the federal minimum wage. These victories helped Democrats win a majority in the Senate in 2006. In November 2006 after the Democrats won majorities in Congress, they pledged to raise the federal minimum wage to $7.25 an hour.[23]

Global Sweatshops

In the early 1900s, the battle against sweatshops was fought on local turf. Unions sought to organize immigrant garment workers (typically women and young girls) and, along with their allies among middle-class reformers, pushed for local and state legislation regulating wages, hours, and safety conditions in the teeming sewing factories of New York, Chicago, and elsewhere. The movement made steady progress. Its achievements were so significant that in 1953, International Ladies' Garment Workers' Union (ILGWU) president David Dubinsky claimed that "we have wiped out the sweatshop."[24] By the mid-1960s, "more than one half of the workers in the U.S. apparel industry were organized and their real wages had been rising for decades."[25]

Today's antisweatshop movement fights on a global battlefield. Like its earlier counterpart, it is a coalition of consumers and workers. It was jump-started by the labor movement in the mid-1990s, was fostered by college students, and has been aided by environmentalists, feminists, consumer groups, religious groups, and human rights advocates. It draws on some of the strategies and tactics of community organizing, waging campaigns for corporate responsibility and government regulation of business, and using innovative strategies to address the challenges posed by organizing on a global political playing field.

The apparel industry is the most globalized, footloose, and exploitative industry in the world. It is dominated by giant retailers and manufacturers (brand names) that control global networks of independently owned factories. Low wages reflect not low productivity but low bargaining power. An analysis in *Business Week* found that although Mexican apparel workers are 70 percent as productive as U.S. workers, they earn only 11 percent as much as their U.S. counterparts. In industries whose production can easily be shifted almost anywhere on the planet, worker organizing is extremely difficult. The antisweatshop movement emerged in the 1990s to organize consumers as workers' allies.

The explosion of imports has proved devastating to once well-paid, unionized U.S. garment workers. The number of American garment workers has declined dramatically, although in a few cities, notably Los Angeles, garment employment has expanded, largely among immigrant and undocumented workers. Recent U.S. Department of Labor surveys found that more than nine out of ten such firms violate legal health and safety standards, with more than half troubled by serious violations that could lead to severe injuries or death. Working conditions in New York City, the other major domestic garment center, are similar. Retailers squeeze manufacturers, who in turn squeeze the contractors who actually make their products.[26]

Two exposés of sweatshop conditions captured public attention. In August 1995, state and federal officials raided a garment factory in El Monte, California—a Los Angeles suburb—where seventy-one Thai immigrants had been held for several years in virtual slavery in an apartment complex ringed with barbed wire and spiked fences. They worked an average of eighty-four hours a week for $1.60 an hour, living eight to ten persons in a room. The garments they sewed ended up in major retail chains, including Macy's and Robinsons-May, and being sold with brand-name labels such as B.U.M., Tomato, and High Sierra. Major newspapers and TV networks picked up on the story, leading to a flood of outraged editorials and columns calling for a clampdown on domestic sweatshops. Then, in April 1996, TV celebrity Kathie Lee Gifford tearfully acknowledged on national television that the Wal-Mart line of clothing that bore her name was made by children in Honduran sweatshops, even though tags on the garments promised that part of the profits would go to help children. Embarrassed by the publicity, triggered by a National Labor Committee report, Gifford soon became a crusader against sweatshop abuses.

In August 1996, the Clinton administration brought together representatives from the garment industry, labor unions, and consumer and human rights groups to grapple with sweatshops. After intense negotiations and much controversy, in April 1997 the Department of Labor issued an interim report, and in November 1998 the White House released the final forty-page report, which included a proposed workplace code of conduct and a set of monitoring guidelines. Several labor and human rights groups quit the Clinton task force to protest the feeble recommendations, which had been crafted primarily by the garment industry delegates and which called, essentially, for the industry to police itself. This maneuvering would not have generated much attention except that a new factor—college activism—had been added to the equation.

The campus movement was started by a handful of college students who had worked as summer interns at Union of Needletrades, Industrial, and Textile Employees (UNITE), the garment workers' union, and sought to find a way to link college students (in their roles as consumers) and labor issues. It began in the fall of 1997 at Duke University when a group called Students Against Sweatshops persuaded the university to require manufacturers of items with the Duke label to sign a pledge that they would not use sweatshop labor. Following months of negotiations, in March 1998 Duke's president and the student activists jointly announced a detailed "code of conduct" that barred Duke licensees from using child labor and required them to maintain safe workplaces, pay the minimum wage, recognize the right of workers to unionize, disclose the locations of all factories making products with Duke's name, and allow visits by independent monitors to inspect the factories.

The Duke victory quickly inspired students at other schools, and the level of activity on campuses accelerated. In the summer of 1998, disparate campus groups formed United Students Against Sweatshops (USAS), which had weekly conference calls to discuss its negotiations with Nike, the Department of Labor, and others. It sponsored training sessions for student leaders and conferences at several campuses where the sweatshop issue is only part of an agenda that also includes helping to build the labor movement, the North American Free Trade Agreement (NAFTA), the World Trade Organization, women's rights, and other issues. Antisweatshop activists employed the USAS listserv to exchange ideas on negotiating tactics, discuss media strategies, swap songs to sing during rallies, and debate the technicalities of defining a "living wage" to incorporate in their campus codes of conduct. Within a few years, some 200 colleges and universities adopted antisweatshop codes of conduct in response to student protest.

The antisweatshop movement has been able to mobilize wide support because it has struck several nerves among today's college students, including women's rights (most sweatshop workers are women, and some factories have required women to use birth control pills as a condition of employment), immigrant rights, environmental concerns, and human rights. At the core of the movement, however, is a strong bond with organized labor. Unions and several liberal foundations have provided modest funding for student antisweatshop groups. Since 1996, the AFL-CIO's Union Summer placed thousands of college students in internships with local unions around the country. The campus movement is also linked to a number of small human rights watchdog organizations—Global Exchange, Sweatshop Watch, and the National Labor Committee—that operate on shoestring budgets and provide technical advice to student activists. These groups have brought sweatshop workers on speaking tours of American campuses and have organized delegations of students to investigate firsthand sweatshop conditions in Central America, Asia, and elsewhere.

Global apparel firms make clothing for the $3 billion college market in thousands of factories around the world. Neither the universities nor the student activist groups had the resources to monitor all these workplaces and hold them accountable to the antisweatshop standards. Their solution, announced in 2005, was the Designated Suppliers Program (DSP), which commits universities to purchase much of the clothing bearing campus logos only from factories that have been approved by an independent board that evaluates employers' respect for workers' rights. With the help of the Worker Rights Consortium (WRC), USAS identified a number of factories around the world—particularly in Asia, Mexico, Central America, and the United States—that could qualify under these more stringent worker-friendly standards. By mid-2006, nineteen major universities and colleges and universities had agreed to support the DSP. Student activists believe that if enough universities adopt these standards, the number of sweat-free factories will steadily increase. This will demonstrate that even in the highly competitive global clothing industry, companies can do the right thing by their employees and make a profit.

Immigrant Rights

In early 2006, a grassroots immigrant rights movement emerged on the national scene. It was catalyzed by widespread opposition to a congressional bill, sponsored by Representative James Sensenbrenner, that would have turned all illegal immigrants into felons and criminalized aid to them by employees in welfare agencies and religious organizations. Opponents mobilized millions of immigrants and their supporters across the country in protest rallies and other activities. These protests generated enormous media attention and forced both political parties to rethink their positions on immigration reform.

Although the news media generally characterized the movement as coming "out of nowhere," the reality was more complex. Labor unions, community organizations, and immigrant rights groups had been mobilizing around similar issues since the late 1990s. When President Bush was elected in 2000, it appeared he would try to forge a compromise legislative plan around guest workers and gradual legalization. In 2001, unions and immigrant rights groups collaborated with the Mexican government to persuade Bush and the Congress to grant legal status to many illegal immigrants, but 9/11 derailed any momentum around immigrant rights in Washington.

Despite this, grassroots groups around the country, including unions, continued to push the issue in various ways. The Los Angeles labor movement's success in unionizing and mobilizing immigrant workers had helped persuade the national AFL-CIO to change its long-standing opposition to legalizing undocumented immigrants. In June 2000, more than 20,000 people attended a rally at the Los Angeles Sports Arena, sponsored by the Los Angeles County Federation of Labor, that called for amnesty for undocumented workers. The participants were mobilized primarily by labor unions (especially SEIU, the Hotel Employees and Restaurant Employees [HERE] union, and UNITE) but also by religious organizations and community organizations, including immigrant resource centers.[27] Similar labor-sponsored public forums were held in other major cities around the country to highlight this new stance and build support for federal legislation.[28]

In 2003, HERE initiated a two-week campaign, the Immigrant Workers Freedom Ride, involving more than 900 immigrants and supporters, in eighteen buses, who traveled from Los Angeles, Seattle, and eight other cities to Washington and New York to raise awareness about immigrants' rights. The brainchild of Los Angeles HERE leader Maria Elena Durazo, it drew support from the same network of unions, religious groups, immigrant rights resource centers and advocacy groups, and civil rights organizations. As their buses crossed the country, they held rallies in more than 100 cities. The organizers self-consciously sought to build bridges across racial lines. In each city, they invited immigrant workers from Haiti, China, Mexico, Africa, and elsewhere to speak. The New York rally drew 100,000 people. According to the *New York Times,* "The demonstrators called for granting legal status to illegal immigrants, for creating more family reunification visas and for increased workplace protections for immigrants because they are often exploited on the job. In addition, the demonstrators called for an end to civil liberty violations against immigrants, complaining that many law-abiding immigrants have faced harassment and detentions since the September 11 terrorist attacks."[29]

In January 2004, President Bush reignited the debate by declaring, "The system is not working." This helped fuel right-wing anti-immigrant groups and right-wing radio talk jocks, who interpreted Bush's statement as favoring amnesty or legalization. This, in turn, triggered growing hostility toward immigrants by local, state, and national Republican politicians and grassroots anti-immigrant groups. In early 2005, the Minutemen, an anti-immigrant volunteer group, began patrolling the Mexican border to "catch" undocumented immigrants trying to get into the United States. Some politicians called for Congress to allocate money to build a fifteen-foot-high wall on the U.S.-Mexican border.[30] This growing grassroots nativism increased the sense of urgency among immigrant rights groups. But it was the House of Representatives' passage of the Sensenbrenner bill that catalyzed the mass mobilizations.

A turning point was a February 2006 statement by Cardinal Roger Mahony of the Archdiocese of Los Angeles. Mahony declared that if the Sensenbrenner bill became law, he would tell priests to defy the requirement that they check for residency documents before providing assistance. "Giving a sandwich to a hungry man could theoretically be a criminal act," he said.[31] With this statement, the head of the nation's largest Catholic archdiocese (with its huge immigrant population) essentially endorsed civil disobedience as a tactic to oppose the Sensenbrenner bill. It was an important stimulus for the mobilizations that would follow the next month.

Los Angeles was ground zero for the immigrant rights movement, so it was no surprise that the first mass protest, which mobilized more than 500,000 people, occurred in that city on March 25, 2006. According to the *Washington Post,* this protest "put the immigrant movement on the map."[32] The County Federation of Labor, the Coalition for Humane Immigrant Rights, the Central American Resource Center, and the Catholic church spearheaded the local effort while simultaneously reaching out to national groups and other local groups.

The success of the Los Angeles protest, including major attention from newspapers and broadcast media in English, Spanish, and other languages, inspired organizers around the country. SEIU and UNITE/HERE's national staffs, along with other organizations and networks (the National Capital Immigrant Coalition, the National Council of La Raza, and the Catholic church, as well as the Center for Community Change) joined forces, creating the We Are America Alliance (forty-one immigrant resource groups, unions, churches, day laborers, and Spanish-language disc jockeys) to oppose the Sensenbrenner legislation and called for a national "Day without Immigrants" protest. They used e-mail and conference calls, and occasionally meetings, to brainstorm and plan the May 1, 2006, mobilization. Protests and boycotts took place in more than seventy cities. Millions of people participated—at least 400,000 in Chicago alone. Many immigrants took the day off from work to underscore the importance of immigrants to the national economy. In many cities, stores, restaurants, and factories were forced to close for lack of employees. Farmworkers in California, Arizona, and elsewhere refused to pick lettuce, tomatoes, grapes, and other crops. Truck drivers, who move 70 percent of the goods in the ports of Los Angeles and Long Beach, did not go to work. Although the vast majority of immigrants were Latino, organizers made sure to involve organizations representing immigrants from non-Spanish-speaking countries.[33]

The immigrant rights movement has already demonstrated its capacity to mobilize large numbers of people in cities across the country. Whether it can sustain and institutionalize its activities is still unclear. The different groups within the movement—a network of networks—do not agree on short-term and long-term goals. They do not yet have a coherent lobbying strategy around agreed-upon legislation. They still have not shown whether the movement can "transform the marchers into voters for lasting gains."[34] Leaders of the various groups within the movement have been meeting—hosted by the Center for Community Change, among other organizations—to iron out differences, strategize, coordinate, and figure out how to raise money. The labor unions, and some foundations, are the primary sources of funds for the movement. As a result, the unions have disproportionate influence within the network.

The emergence of separate immigrant rights organizations underscores the importance of ethnic, racial, immigrant, and community identities as catalysts for organizing. Alinsky would certainly understand this. But he viewed the labor movement as the linchpin of progressive politics and as the key mobilizing force for working people in their workplaces and communities. His initial Depression-era effort in Chicago organized Polish, German, and Irish immigrants through unions, churches, sports leagues, and community organizations. With the current immigrant rights movement, we appear to have come full circle in terms of the mosaic of organizations involved, although they are now organizing on a larger playing field.

WHAT NEXT? OPPORTUNITIES AND OBSTACLES FOR
PROGRESSIVE ORGANIZING

From the 1930s through the early 1970s, the American "social contract" was based
on the premises of the New Deal—a coalition led by the labor movement, its
strength focused in cities, its core constituency immigrants and their children,
African Americans, and, to a lesser extent, white southern small farmers, with allies
among middle-class reformers (i.e., planners, intellectuals, journalists, social workers) and some liberals within the business community. During this postwar era, the
United States experienced a dramatic increase in per capita income and a simultaneous decline in the gap between the rich and the poor. The incomes of the bottom half of the class structure rose faster than those at the top. Urban community
organizing as we know it—based on the Alinsky model and its offshoots—was not
a major component of the New Deal coalition.

In the 1960s, many progressives hoped to build on this foundation. Representing the left wing of the Democratic Party, United Automobile Workers (UAW) president Walter Reuther had been making proposals since World War II to renew and
expand the New Deal and engage in national economic planning. He advised Presidents Kennedy and Johnson to champion a bold federal program for full employment that would include government-funded public works and the conversion of
the nation's defense industry to production for civilian needs. This, he argued, would
dramatically address the nation's poverty population, create job opportunities for
African Americans, and rebuild the nation's troubled cities without being as politically divisive as a federal program identified primarily as serving poor blacks.

Both presidents rejected Reuther's advice. (They were worried about alienat-
ing southern Democrats and/or sectors of business that opposed Keynesian-style
economic planning.) Johnson's announcement of an "unconditional war on
poverty" in his 1964 State of the Union address pleased Reuther, but the details of
the plan revealed its limitations. The War on Poverty was a patchwork of small initiatives that did not address the nation's basic inequalities. Testifying before Congress in 1964, Reuther said that "while [the proposals] are good, [they] are not
adequate, nor will they be successful in achieving their purposes, except as we begin
to look at the broader problems [of the American economy]." He added that
"poverty is a reflection of our failure to achieve a more rational, more responsible,
more equitable distribution of the abundance that is within our grasp."

Although Reuther threw the UAW's political weight behind Johnson's programs, his critique was correct. Since the 1960s, federal efforts to address poverty
have consistently suffered from a failure to address the fundamental underlying
issues. Most progressives understood that the civil rights victories, such as the Voting Rights Act, Civil Rights Act, and Fair Housing Act, were a necessary but not

sufficient condition for reducing poverty and inequality. It was at this point that community organizing played a significant part in local and national politics—demanding, and in some cases implementing, antipoverty and community development programs, fueled in part by the requirement that local residents get to participate in these programs. Even so, the most influential supporters of the War on Poverty were liberal labor groups, civil rights organizations, and, with much ambivalence, many big-city mayors. In the 1960s and 1970s, cities were still very important in terms of the size of the population, the number of voters, the location of jobs and of union members, the composition of congressional districts, and the power of their congressional representatives (such as New York Congressman Adam Clayton Powell).

In the 1970s, the New Deal and Great Society gains were supplemented by other victories that emerged out of civil rights, women's rights, and environmental and consumer activism, fueled by the emergence of the Naderite network, feminism, environmental groups, and an upsurge in community organizing. These included affirmative action, the Clean Air Act and other environmental laws, strong regulations on business regarding consumer products and workplace safety (such as OSHA), and significant improvements in the legal and social rights of women, including reproductive freedoms. The major victories that emerged from community organizing (linked to civil rights) were HMDA (1975) and the CRA (1977), which resulted from the ability of groups to link local and national campaigns around bank redlining.

Many community organizations were born in the 1970s in the aftermath of the civil rights and antiwar movements, when activists were rethinking how to build (or rebuild) a progressive movement for social change. These groups emerged at a time when the post–World War II prosperity—fueled by the rise of the United States as a global superpower, steady economic growth, a narrowing gap between rich and poor—was coming to an end.

Starting in the mid-1970s, major U.S. corporations began an assault on the labor movement and the living standards of the poor and working class. This view was best expressed by *Business Week* in its issue of October 12, 1974: "It will be a hard pill for many Americans to swallow—the idea of doing with less so that big business can have more. . . . Nothing that this nation, or any other nation, has done in modern economic history compares with the selling job that must be done to make people accept this reality."

Since the late 1970s, liberals, progressives, and Democrats have been on the defensive, seeking to protect the key components of the New Deal, Great Society, and subsequent victories from being dismantled by the increasingly powerful right-wing forces—led by the uneasy alliance between big business and the religious Right, and the mainstream of the Republican Party.

Surveys find that Americans are generally in favor of activist government. For example, a majority of workers support unions, most Americans are pro-choice and want stronger environmental and gun control laws, and most Americans believe that the minimum wage should be raised and that the nation should do more to combat poverty. But liberals and progressives have not been successful in countering conservative forces in terms of the political infrastructure or an ideological "frame" or message. Progressives have not yet found a twenty-first-century agenda to replace the New Deal and the Great Society, to counter the right wing's "antigovernment" message, and to find a way to protect and expand social democracy at home in the midst of globalization.

The challenge and opportunity posed by Wal-Mart (and the Wal-Martization of the economy) illustrate the dilemma confronting the progressive movement. There is growing interest among different constituencies—women, immigrant rights, labor, environmentalists, faith groups, fair trade activists, and small business—in challenging Wal-Mart. Unions in Los Angeles and elsewhere have worked closely with churches and community groups to stop Wal-Mart from opening supercenters in their areas. But a "stop Wal-Mart" campaign cannot be sustained. Campaigns to "unionize Wal-Mart" and "hold Wal-Mart accountable" (for better wages, health care benefits, and so on) make more sense. Over the next decade, major unions—SEIU, Teamsters, UFCW—will be waging major campaigns to unionize Wal-Mart and make the company a more responsible corporate citizen. Community organizing can play key roles in these campaigns if they view themselves as part of a broader movement and forge alliances with unions and other organizing groups.

Progressives understand that we really cannot solve our nation's economic and social problems—including the problems facing the urban poor—without changes in federal policy. What is needed is a policy agenda around which progressives can agree, a new way of framing this agenda to mobilize public opinion, and a political strategy to mobilize voters to win a majority in Congress. For example:

1. To level the playing field for union organizing campaigns, we need to reform the nation's unfair labor laws.
2. To improve conditions for the growing army of the working poor, we need to raise the federal minimum wage and expand participation in the Earned Income Tax Credit.
3. To address the nation's health care crisis, we need some form of universal national health insurance.
4. To provide adequate resources for housing poor and working-class families, we need a national housing trust fund or other legislation to expand federal subsidies.
5. To improve our public schools, especially those that serve the nation's poorest children, we need to increase federal funding for smaller classrooms, adequate teacher training, and sufficient books and equipment. We cannot rely primarily on local or even state funding for public education.

6. To provide families with adequate child care, we need a universal child care allowance that reaches families regardless of income. This can be accomplished only with federal funding and some state matching formula that accounts for variations in states' (and parents') ability to pay.

7. To redirect private investment in cities and older suburbs, we need to provide sufficient funds to clean up toxic urban brownfields.

8. To address the problems of growing traffic congestion, we need federal funds to improve public transit of all kinds, as well as federal laws to limit tax breaks and other incentives that promote suburban sprawl and "leapfrog" development on the fringes of metropolitan areas.

Political victories are about more than technology and election day turnout. They are about message and movement. Successes on election day are a by-product of, not a substitute for, effective grassroots organizing in between elections. Over the past century, the turning points for improving American society involved large-scale mobilizations around a broad egalitarian and morally uplifting vision of America, a progressive patriotism animated by "liberty and justice for all." These movements drew on traditions of justice and morality. They redefined the rights and responsibilities of citizens, government, and business. In the Gilded Age, it was agrarian populism and urban Progressivism. During the Depression, it was the upsurge of industrial unionism linked to Roosevelt's New Deal. In the 1960s and 1970s, it was the civil rights, women's rights, and environmental movements, promoting a vision of how the nation's prosperity should be shared by all but not squandered for future generations.

The United States today is holding its breath, trying to decide what kind of society it wants to be. Progressive forces are gaining momentum but still lack the organizational infrastructure needed to effectively challenge conservatives' message and movement. They have begun to invest in building that infrastructure—think tanks, grassroots coalitions, technology, staff recruitment, identification and training of candidates. Community organizing has an important role to play as part of a broader progressive movement.

NOTES

1. Steven Rosenstone and John Mark Hansen, *Mobilization, Participation, and American Democracy* (New York: Macmillan, 1993).

2. In his book *Politically Incorrect: The Emerging Faith Factor in American Politics* (Dallas: Word, 1994), Ralph Reed, former director of the Christian Coalition, recounts how his movement built itself up from scratch, utilizing the network of conservative pastors and churches and providing sermons, voter guides, get-out-the-vote training, and other resources to create a powerful organizational infrastructure.

3. Harry C. Boyte, *The Backyard Revolution: Understanding the New Citizen Movement* (Philadelphia: Temple University Press, 1980).

4. The chapters in this book reflect the strengths and weaknesses of many community organizing efforts. For example, Staudt and Stone look at two groups in the El Paso–Ciudad Juárez border area. One, EPISO, is an affiliate of the Industrial Areas Foundation, a national network of local and regional organizing groups. The other, Coalition Against Violence, is a loose network of individuals, some of whom have good media and political connections, but not really a community organization in the sense of a grassroots organization that mobilizes people and develops leaders.

5. Most local community groups are not linked to any regional or national organizing or training networks. Those that are tied to such networks have been helped in various ways to improve the capacity of local groups to develop leaders, mobilize campaigns, and win local victories.

6. Kelly Candaele and Peter Dreier, "Housing: An LA Story," *Nation*, April 15, 2002, 22–23.

7. Karen Paget, "Citizen Organizing: Many Movements, No Majority," *American Prospect*, June 23, 1990, 115–128.

8. James Miller, *Democracy Is in the Streets* (Cambridge, MA: Harvard University Press, 1994).

9. Peter Dreier, "The Tenants Movement in the United States," *International Journal of Urban and Regional Research* 8 (1984): 255–279, reprinted in *Critical Perspectives on Housing, ed.* Rachel Bratt, Chester Hartman, and Ann Meyerson (Philadelphia: Temple University Press, 1986); Ron Lawson, ed., *The Tenant Movement in New York City, 1904–1984* (New Brunswick, NJ: Rutgers University Press, 1986); W. Dennis Keating, Adnrejs Skaburskis, and Michael Tietzs, eds., *Rent Control and the Rental Housing Market* (New Brunswick, NJ: Rutgers University Center for Urban Policy Research, 1998).

10. For a good discussion on CDCs, see Avis Vidal, *Rebuilding Communities: A National Study of Urban Community Development Corporations* (New York: Community Development Research Center, New School for Social Research, 1993).

11. See, for example, the research on "resource mobilization" by Doug McAdam, *Political Process and the Development of Black Insurgency* (Chicago: University of Chicago Press, 1982); and Peter Dreier, "Rosa Parks: Angry, Not Tired," *Dissent*, Winter 2006, 88–92.

12. Peter Dreier, John Mollenkopf, and Todd Swanstrom, *Place Matters: Metropolitics for the 21st Century*, 2nd ed. (Lawrence: University Press of Kansas, 2005).

13. The most fascinating factoid from the exit polls of the November 2004 election revealed that when voters' loyalties were divided between their economic interests and other so-called moral values concerns, union membership was a crucial determinant of their votes. For example, gun owners favored Bush by a 63 to 36 percent margin, but union members who owned guns supported Kerry 55 to 43 percent, according to an AFL-CIO survey. Bush carried all weekly churchgoers by a 61 to 39 percent margin, but Kerry won among union members who attend church weekly by a 55 to 43 percent margin. Bush won among white men by a 62 to 37 percent margin, but Kerry carried white men in unions by a 59 to 38 percent margin. Bush won among white women by 55 to 44 percent, but Kerry won among white women in unions by a 67 to 32 percent margin. In 2004, the labor movement poured enormous resources (money, staff, and members) into the election. The labor movement worked in coalition with community groups like ACORN and environmental, women's rights, consumer, and civil rights groups. But there were simply too few union members to overcome the Bush forces' edge. The long-term decline in union membership is perhaps the most important factor in explaining the gap between how well the Kerry and Bush forces did in mobilizing their respective bases. Union membership—35 percent of the

workforce in the 1950s, 25 percent in the 1970s—is down to 11 percent today. Had union membership been at its 1970s levels, Kerry would have won by a landslide.

14. Todd Swanstrom, Colleen Casey, Robert Flack, and Peter Dreier, *Pulling Apart: Economic Segregation among Suburbs and Central Cities in Major Metropolitan Areas* (Washington, DC: Brookings Institution, 2004).

15. See Timothy Egan, "'06 Race Focuses on the Suburbs, Inner and Outer," *New York Times,* June 16, 2006.

16. Theda Skocpol, *Diminished Democracy: From Membership to Management in American Civic Life* (Norman: University of Oklahoma Press, 2003).

17. Mara Sidney, *Unfair Housing: How National Policy Shapes Community Action* (Lawrence: University Press of Kansas, 2003); Gregory Squires, ed., *Organizing Access to Capital* (Philadelphia: Temple University Press, 2003).

18. Robert Gottlieb, *Forcing the Spring: The Transformation of the American Environmental Movement,* revised and updated edition (Washington, DC: Island Press, 2005).

19. Robert Bullard, *Dumping in Dixie: Race, Class, and Environmental Quality* (Boulder, CO: Westview Press, 1990).

20. Luke W. Cole and Sheila R. Foster, *From the Ground Up: Environmental Racism and the Rise of the Environmental Justice Movement* (New York: New York University Press, 2001); Rachel Stein, ed., *New Perspectives in Environmental Justice: Gender, Sexuality, and Activism* (New Brunswick, NJ: Rutgers University Press, 2004); J. M. Evans Adamson and Rachel Stein, eds., *The Environmental Justice Reader: Politics, Poetics, and Pedagogy* (Tucson: University of Arizona Press, 2002); Christopher Foreman Jr., "Winning Hand? The Uncertain Future of Environmental Justice," *Brookings Review* 14, no. 2 (1996): 22–25; Robert D. Bullard, ed., *Confronting Environmental Racism: Voices from the Grassroots* (Boston: South End Press, 1993).

21. Jeff Chang and Lucia Hwang, "It's a Survival Issue: The Environmental Justice Movement Faces the New Century," *Color Lines* 3, no. 2 (Summer 2000).

22. Isaac Martin, "Do Living Wage Policies Diffuse?" *Urban Affairs Review* 41 (May 2006): 710–719. In some cities, unions or union-sponsored organizations (such as the Los Angeles Alliance for a New Economy) initiated the living wage campaigns, then brought community, religious, and other groups into the coalition. Elsewhere, ACORN took the lead and (in most cities) recruited labor unions and religious and other community groups into the organizing effort.

23. John Atlas and Peter Dreier, "Waging Victory," *American Prospect,* November 10, 2006.

24. Cited in Robert Ross, *Slaves to Fashion: Poverty and Abuse in the New Sweatshops* (Ann Arbor: University of Michigan Press, 2004).

25. Alan Howard, "Labor, History, and Sweatshops in the New Global Economy," in *No Sweat: Fashion, Free Trade, and the Rights of Garment Workers,* ed. Andrew Ross (New York: Verso, 1997), 155.

26. Ross, *Slaves to Fashion;* Edna Bonacich and Richard Applebaum, *Behind the Label: Inequality in the Los Angeles Apparel Industry* (Berkeley: University of California Press, 2000).

27. See Janice Fine, *Worker Centers,* (Ithaca, NY: Cornell University Press, 2006).

28. Nancy Cleeland, "Migrant Amnesty Urged; Rally: About 20,000 Rally in Los Angeles to Demand Federal Legislation," *Los Angeles Times,* June 11, 2000.

29. Steven Greenhouse, "Immigrants Rally in City, Seeking Rights," *New York Times,* October 5, 2003.

30. John Broder, "Border War: Immigration from a Simmer to a Scream," *New York Times,* June 21, 2006.

31. John L. Allen Jr., "Mahony on Immigration," *National Catholic Reporter,* April 14, 2006.

32. Darryl Fears, "Immigrant Supporters to Counter Bush Speech," *Washington Post*, May 15, 2006.

33. Terese Watanabe and Nicole Gaouette, "The May Day Marches: Converting the Energy of Protest to Political Clout," *Los Angeles Times*, May 2, 2006, A1; Randal C. Archibold, "Immigrants Take to U.S. Streets in Show of Strength," *New York Times*, May 2, 2006.

34. Watanabe and Gaouette, "The May Day Marches."

10. Summing Up

Community Organizing and Political Change in the City

Marion Orr

This volume examines community organizing and its traditions, at different historical eras, across several regions of the United States, and through the lenses of different academic disciplines. The volume's approach provides a powerful vantage point from which to consider the strengths and challenges of community organizing within the current global political economy and public culture. While acknowledging the benefits of community organizing, the general theme of the chapters is that as an avenue for progressive politics, community organizing faces certain challenges. This chapter captures some of those themes and speculates about the implications for local policymaking, citizen input, and local democracy.

REPLENISHING DEMOCRACY: COMMUNITY ORGANIZING AND CIVIC ENGAGEMENT

The chapters in this book show the potential of community organizing for addressing concerns about Americans' disengagement from civic and political life. Although they approach their work within different "schools," models, or networks, the community organizations covered in this volume are all engaged in the practice of democratic politics. The members of the organizations learn the skills to negotiate and build relationships with people in power—leaders of institutions, corporations, and governmental bodies that make decisions that affect their families and communities. The deep, reflective, and deliberative process that Wood described in his chapter on PICO's national organizing effort is typical of many community organizing models. Political science research has shown that organizations like the ones covered in this volume facilitate civic and political engagement.[1] Because community organizing is largely associated with issues of social justice, organizing typically focuses on issues that impact poor, working-class, and lower-middle-income communities. In this sense, community organizing is replenishing democracy in communities not generally associated with civic engagement.

A group of scholars affiliated with the American Political Science Association concluded that organizations like the ones covered in the preceding chapters are reducing "the bias in civic engagement that stems from inequalities in material conditions, social status, and political privilege."[2] A recent article in the *New York Times* described these organizations as part of a broad "surge in populist organizing around the country" that are engaging poor communities of people of color around problems of crime, inadequate housing, wages, gentrification, environmental disputes, and immigrant rights.[3] As Fisher and Shragge observed, community organizing is "hot." This volume adds to the growing attention community organizing has gained as a strategy for engaging citizens in the democratic process.

The case study research in this volume also reveals that effective community organizing can improve urban residents' quality of life. This comes across clearly in Swarts's analysis of ACORN. For example, ACORN tax preparation centers expand the number of working families that claim the Earned Income Tax Credit (EITC), a federal antipoverty program. Taxpayers must file a tax return to claim the credit. However, nearly a quarter of eligible families fail to claim the tax credit, leaving an estimated $12 billion in unclaimed credits. ACORN provides direct EITC assistance. It also organized door-to-door campaigns and mass rallies to spread the word about EITC. Studies have shown that working families use the EITC to pay for home repairs, to purchase vehicles needed to commute to work, and to obtain additional education or training.[4] ACORN tax preparation centers provide direct EITC assistance and aggressively spread the word about the EITC through door-to-door outreach. In New Orleans, the community organizations covered in Burns's chapter joined with city hall to help reduce the city's crime rate, pressured local government to improve inner-city parks, forced the state legislature to change laws governing blighted housing, and worked to provide after-school and job training programs to their members. All the organizations covered in chapter 3 were active in helping Katrina survivors. In El Paso, Project Arriba, a job training and placement program and, according to Staudt and Stone, the city's "only viable living wage strategy" was started by EPISO. EPISO was also the initial spark behind the formation of the El Paso Collaborative for Academic Excellence, which joins business, government, and community representatives with key educational institutions to improve academic achievement. Shirley and Evans's case studies examine local organizations helping parents, educators, and community leaders make sense of a complex federal law. The varied responses of PACT, ACORN, and IAF to the No Child Left Behind act were driven by "street-level conversations" among parents, community leaders, teachers, and other local leaders. While acknowledging the limits of community organizing in "transforming broader institutional arrangements," the chapters in this volume nevertheless "demonstrate the powerful role of community organizing in strengthening democracy, building community capacity, and solving urban problems."[5]

GLOBALIZATION, PUBLIC CULTURE, AND
COMMUNITY ORGANIZING

The community organizing stories in this volume make clear that the scope of globalization has altered conditions of existence for many residents in the United States' central cities. Peter Burns shows how globalization rapidly transformed New Orleans' economy from a largely manufacturing to a service economy, shifting and weakening the city's governing regime. The impact of globalization is visible and magnified in El Paso, where free trade and economic restructuring have caused job instability in the garment and other industries. Shirley and Evans remind readers that economic restructuring and globalization have left many communities "mired in poverty," made superior skills and training essential in the information-era economy, and made the "achievement gap" between white children and black and Latino children more salient than ever. The mobility of global capital means that jobs—not only in manufacturing industries but also in management and services—are much more vulnerable. What is clear from many of the chapters in this volume is that globalization has made the social and economic environment of cities less predictable, more prone to sudden and drastic change. These shifts have altered the ecology of civic engagement, forcing community organizers to adjust their strategies and tactics.

Globalization's impact is not only economic. As discussed in the opening chapter, globalization raises many cultural questions about faith, family life, ethnicity, and community. In chapter 4, Staudt and Stone described men and women traveling long distances daily, moving within and between work zones, in search of better jobs and improved wages on the U.S.-Mexican border. Between 1993 and 2003, on the Mexican side of the border, nearly 400 girls and women were raped or killed. Meanwhile, in El Paso, women "scramble for a living when garment factories relocate to take advantage of the desperation of poorer countries." As Rinku Sen, a community organizer with CTWO, observed, the violence and family disintegration endured by low-wage workers living in the *maquiladora* zone provide a "compelling" example of the "cultural and social" results of globalization.[6] Families and communities in New Orleans, Miami, Chicago, and other cities are also impacted by globalization's market culture: "The market culture has a clear and powerful dynamic running through its center, like a unifying theme: the dynamic of buying and selling, trading and exchanging, moving money and moving goods. This dynamic defines the major roles within this culture—the roles of innovator, producer, seller, marketer, and consumer. The culture turns almost everything into a commodity—time, water, pleasure, and ideas; home mortgages, neighborhoods, downtowns, and entire cities."[7]

The pressures of the market culture and global economy are impacting public schools and local school politics. Education is conceived in mostly technical terms, as a means for people to obtain high-paying jobs and for schools and businesses to respond to the needs of the new economy. As Shirley and Evans explained in chapter 5, education is now seen as a means to succeed in the global market and knowledge society. The global economy requires much higher levels of training and education than was the case in the industrial past. In the new global economy, the stakes are high for the students trying to obtain the limited number of valued jobs. These challenges create tensions that community organizations must confront if they are to successfully build broad-based school reform coalitions.

For instance, Jeannie Oakes and John Rogers argue that "powerful cultural narratives" about merit, deficits, and scarcity shape education reform policy.[8] The "merit" narrative assumes that all children are competing on a level playing field and are rewarded for their talent and hard work. The "deficit" narrative presumes that minority students are incapable of educational success because of their race and social class. The merit and deficit narratives are not new. However, within the context of a highly individualist public culture and a competitive global economy, the scarcity narrative (the view that we can afford only limited outlays for public goods) compounds the inequality that results from the deficit and merit narratives and pushes parents, especially those in the upper-middle income strata, to view school reform as an individual concern and not as something requiring the kind of collective action embodied in community organizing. In the global economy, where workers are divided between highly valued knowledge workers and low-wage service workers, upper-middle-class Americans, "fearing their children will not attain their affluence," fight to have their children obtain the increasingly scarce seats in a high-quality school. Globalization exacerbates tensions in local communities over school reform, especially reforms that seek to equalize resources among schools and school systems. In a public culture shaped by hyperindividualism, community organizers must overcome the tendency for advantaged parents to use their power to resist equity and maintain the status quo.[9]

Santow's chapter on Chicago's housing struggle in the 1960s is a story about a community organization's attempts to address the attitudes, biases, and normative and cultural beliefs that undergird people's views on race and ethnicity. The premise behind the formation of the Organization for the Southwest Community (OSC) was to convince white homeowners that black neighbors were not a profound threat to their neighborhood. Community organizing creates a space that challenges the dominant cultural norms of consumerism, materialism, racial hierarchy, success at any price, and radically individualist identities. As Oakes and Rogers assert, "Strategies that challenge cultural norms and seek to alter power relationships are the stock and trade of social movements and grassroots organizations."[10] The community organizing stories in this volume are about challenging the larger set of norms and values that shape the contemporary public culture.

LOCAL ORGANIZING AND SOCIAL MOVEMENTS

There is a healthy dose of realism throughout this volume regarding the limitations of local organizing. Dreier's chapter captures this most directly, arguing that local organizing is "an essential but insufficient" foundation for addressing the powerful forces that impinge upon disadvantaged communities. Santow's study of Southside Chicago illustrates how the community's racialized context weakened the effectiveness of "place-based" organizing. Staudt and Stone's chapter on El Paso shows how the city's border location magnified the limited capacity of local organizing to address global issues such as immigration, border issues, and free trade. PICO's decision to launch statewide and later national organizing strategies is an acknowledgment that local organizing is inadequate for meeting the challenges facing its members.

ACORN's multilevel campaigns (local, state, and national) are recognition that forces beyond city hall also have to be addressed. ACORN's inability to win outcomes of consequence for its members at the city level has driven it to search for new venues at the state and national levels. For instance, the global pressures on wages and the pressures on cities to compete for scarce corporate investment, combined with a hostile national administration and Congress, have driven a search for successful venues to raise wages as well as win other economic reforms, such as in the financial industry. As Swarts explained, ACORN's structure as "one national organization" allowed it to be ahead of its time and other community organizations. As the ecology of civic engagement changed, ACORN's organizational structure allowed it to quickly develop national strategies. A national strategy enabled ACORN to survive and grow, helping the organization to ride out change, indeed, to integrate its efforts with change.

The contributors to this volume are not the first to point out the limits of local organizing. The philosophy behind the formation of National Welfare Rights Organization (NWRO), in 1966, had its roots in a critique of sectoral organizing. George Wiley, NWRO's founder, envisioned it as a vehicle for "an organized new majority" to be mobilized around common economic issues.[11] NWRO was composed of a national network of local organizations; ACORN, in turn, grew out of NWRO. In 1971, in *Rules for Radicals*, Alinsky acknowledged the weaknesses of place-based organizing.[12] As he remained committed to the view that local organizing was critical to poor communities' efforts to gain power, Alinsky also advocated concentrating the organizing task in suburban communities where the "middle-class majority" resided and "substantial sectors" were disillusioned and frightened about the impact the public culture had on their families and communities and felt powerless to do anything. In *Rules for Radicals*, Alinsky envisioned movement-style coalitions that would organize at regional and national levels on pollution, inflation, Vietnam, violence, race, taxes, and other issues that crossed local boundaries.

As one reads the chapters in this volume, one can almost feel the tension in the community organizing field that talk of a national movement can hamper the meticulous process of local organizing. Fisher and Shragge point out that short of a national social movement, grassroots organizing would lead to incremental change and modest victories. PICO's embryonic New Vision project is an effort to organize at the national level, a response to the view that many decisions affecting poor, working-class, and middle-class Americans occur beyond the city. The case studies from New Orleans and El Paso, however, show that there is still much to be done at the local level. The experiences in both cities reveal that community organizations could not take advantage of the "political opportunity structure" brought on by changing local political context. For example, EPISO was not in a position to shape a viable governing regime not dominated by local developers despite El Paso's fragmented ecology of civic engagement. The recently formed Westside Interfaith Action, IAF's second El Paso organization, was designed with a broader base of support. If EPISO and Westside Interfaith Action join forces, IAF hopes the organizations would have the capacity to push El Paso toward a more progressive urban agenda. IAF may have to collaborate with other El Paso organizations whose members also feel the impact of globalization and the dominant public culture. Whether or not developer interests will continue to control and shape El Paso's civic space is a substantial local issue.

The history of the U.S. civil rights movement suggests that tensions around local organizing and social movement are not insurmountable. Local organizations were the center of the civil rights movement.[13] Ella Baker, known for her crucial role in the black freedom struggle, was "a skilled grassroots organizer" and an "insurgent intellectual."[14] Baker was a strong believer in the need for a national social movement. She believed that "laws, structures, and institutions had to change in order to correct injustice and oppression,"[15] and that only a national social movement could bring about such a transformation. For Baker, local organizing was central to such a movement. The black freedom movement required that local people, even the poor, engage in collective action to improve their circumstances. Baker's organizing philosophy was influential in shifting the black freedom movement away from "high-profile events like the sit-ins and freedom rides to protracted day-to-day grassroots organizing in local communities."[16] Connecting with people through the problems and challenges they confront daily in their communities is the cornerstone of a transformative social movement. To be effective, organizers must "form relationships, build trust, and engage in a democratic process of decision making together with community members."[17] Peter Dreier is right—effective local organizing is hard work. In El Paso, New Orleans, and other urban centers, there is plenty of local work to be done.

The interrelationship between local organizing and higher-level/national advocacy is undeniable. As Dreier shows, local organizations have worked together at a national level on a number of significant issues, including environmental justice, living wage, and community reinvestment, with some success. The spring 2006 protests and boycotts over immigration were clearly national in scope. The successful mobilization of thousands of immigrants and their families, however, depended on the local organizing conducted by immigrant worker centers, labor unions, church groups, and community organizations. It remains to be seen if this national network of local organizations, allied with organizations of national scope (e.g., SEIU), can develop a national movement devoted to transforming immigration policy and related issues such as fare wages and workers' rights.

This is no easy task. As of this writing, the national "political opportunity structure" remains unfavorable for a wide swing to the political left. As long as the grain of national politics is against the issues pursued by community groups, they and their progressive allies will have the continuing challenge of confronting resistance to their issue agenda. Moreover, as discussed in the opening chapter, the public displays ambivalence and has mixed interests when it comes to such global phenomena as Wal-Mart. Reshaping the public culture from the top down may not be the most promising strategy. What is needed is "sustained infrastructure building" that "connects leaders and members to one another across places and institutions."[18] The civil rights movement provides an apt illustration of the relationship between local organizing and a national social movement. As Smock asserts, "The creation of such a broad-based movement is possible only if we start by organizing people at a local level around the issues of immediate concerns in their daily lives. . . . Community organizing not only provides an essential vehicle for combating the symptoms of unjust global systems, it may also offer the most realistic starting point for the formation of an inclusive movement for genuine social structural change."[19] In a metaphoric sense, community organizing can be likened to piles of kindling that can be used to ignite fires, fires that begin small but cumulate into something big.

NOTES

1. Sidney Verba, Kay Lehman Schlozman, and Henry E. Brady, *Voice and Equality: Civic Voluntarism in American Politics* (Cambridge, MA: Harvard University Press, 1995); Gregory B. Marcus, "Civic Participation in American Cities" (University of Michigan, Institute for Social Research, 2002).

2. Stephen Macedo et al., *Democracy at Risk* (Washington, DC: Brookings Institution, 2005), 99.

3. Erik Eckholm, "City by City, an Anti-poverty Group Plants Seeds of Change," *New York Times*, June 26, 2006, A17.

4. See Bruce D. Meyer and Dan T. Rosenbaum, "Making Single Mothers Work: Recent Tax and Welfare Policy and Its Effects," in *Making Work Pay: The Earned Income Tax Credit and Its Impact on America's Families,* ed. Bruce D. Meyer and Douglas Holtz-Eakin (New York: Russell Sage Foundation, 2001).

5. Kristina Smock, *Democracy in Action* (New York: Columbia University Press, 2003), 223.

6. Rinku Sen, *Stir It Up* (San Francisco: Jossey-Bass, 2003), 9.

7. Michael Gecan, *Going Public* (Boston: Beacon Press, 2002), 155.

8. Jeannie Oakes and John Rogers, *Learning Power: Organizing for Education and Justice* (New York: Teachers College Press, 2006).

9. Ibid.

10. Ibid., 17.

11. Gary Delgado, *Organizing the Movement: The Roots and Growth of ACORN* (Philadelphia: Temple University Press, 1986), 25.

12. Saul Alinsky, *Rules for Radicals* (New York: Vintage, 1971), 184–196.

13. Aldon D. Morris, *The Origins of the Civil Rights Movement: Black Communities Organizing for Change* (New York: Free Press, 1984).

14. Barbara Ransby, *Ella Baker and the Black Freedom Movement: A Radical Democratic Vision* (Chapel Hill: University of North Carolina Press, 2003).

15. Ibid., 1.

16. Ibid., 270.

17. Ibid., 270.

18. Theda Skocpol, *Diminished Democracy* (Norman: University of Oklahoma Press, 2003), 274.

19. Smock, *Democracy in Action,* 242–243.

ABOUT THE CONTRIBUTORS

Peter F. Burns is Associate Professor of Political Science at Loyola University, New Orleans. His teaching and research interests include American politics, urban politics, race and ethnicity, and public policy. He is the author of *Electoral Politics Is Not Enough: Racial and Ethnic Minorities and Urban Politics* (State University of New York Press, 2006). His research has appeared in *Political Science Quarterly, Urban Affairs Review, Journal of Urban Affairs, Social Science Quarterly,* and *Southeastern Political Review.*

Peter Dreier is the E. P. Clapp Distinguished Professor of Politics and Director of the Urban and Environmental Policy Program at Occidental College. He is coauthor of *Place Matters: Metropolitics for the Twenty-first Century,* 2nd ed. (University Press of Kansas, 2005); *The Next Los Angeles: The Struggle for a Livable City* (University of California Press, 2005); and *Regions That Work: How Cities and Suburbs Can Grow Together* (University of Minnesota Press, 2004); and coeditor of *Up against the Sprawl: Public Policy and the Making of Southern California* (University of Minnesota Press, 2004). He writes frequently for the *Los Angeles Times,* the *Nation,* and *American Prospect.* He served as senior policy aide to Boston mayor Ray Flynn from 1984 to 1992.

Michael Evans received degrees from the University of Notre Dame (M.Ed.) and Harvard Divinity School (M.Div.). He is currently a doctoral student in Curriculum and Instruction at the Lynch School of Education in Boston College. His research interests include family and community engagement, community organizing for school reform, and the role of religion in public education.

Robert Fisher is Professor of Social Work and Director of Urban and Community Studies at the University of Connecticut. He is the coauthor of *Settlement Houses under Siege: The Struggle to Sustain Community Organization in New York* (Columbia University Press, 2002) and *Social Work and Community in a Private World: Getting Out in Public* (Longman, 1997). He is the author of *Let the People Decide: Neighborhood Organizing in America,* 2nd ed. (Twayne, 1994), and he coedited *Mobilizing the Community: Local Politics in the Era of the Global City* (Sage, 1993) and *Community Organization for Urban Social Change* (Greenwood Press, 1981). Fisher is the recipient of two Fulbright fellowships to Austria.

261

Marion Orr is the Fred Lippitt Professor of Public Policy, Political Science, and Urban Studies at Brown University. His book *Black Social Capital: The Politics of School Reform in Baltimore* (University Press of Kansas, 1999) won the Policy Studies Organization's 2000 Aaron Wildavsky Best Book Award. He is coauthor of *The Color of School Reform: Race, Politics, and the Challenge of Urban Education* (Princeton University Press, 1999), which was named the best book in urban politics by the American Political Science Association in 2000. He is currently engaged in a study of the organizing experiences of the Industrial Areas Foundation (IAF) in various U.S. cities.

Mark Santow is Assistant Professor of American History at the University of Massachusetts–Dartmouth. He received his Ph.D. from the University of Pennsylvania in 2000. He has taught at the University of Pennsylvania, Fordham University, and Gonzaga University. Dr. Santow specializes in twentieth-century American urban history, politics, and social policy and has published numerous essays on racial segregation, community organizing, urban policy, and the War on Poverty. He is the coauthor of *Social Security and the Middle-Class Squeeze: Fact and Fiction about America's Entitlement Programs* (Praeger, 2005) and author of *Saul Alinsky and the Dilemmas of Race in the Post-war City* (University of Chicago Press, 2007).

Dennis Shirley is Professor of Education at the Lynch School of Education at Boston College. Shirley has a doctorate from the Harvard Graduate School of Education in Teaching, Curricula, and Learning Environments. He is the author of *The Politics of Progressive Education: The Odenwaldschule in Nazi Germany* (Harvard University Press, 1992), *Community Organizing for Urban School Reform* (University of Texas Press, 1997), and *Valley Interfaith and School Reform: Organizing for Power in South Texas* (University of Texas Press, 2002).

Eric Shragge is Associate Professor and Director of the Graduate Diploma Program in Community Economic Development in the School of Community and Public Affairs at Concordia University, Montreal. His most recent books include *Activism and Social Change: Lessons for Community and Local Organizing* (Broadview Press, 2003) and, as coeditor, *Community Economic Development: Building for Social Change* (University College Cape Breton Press, 2005).

Kathleen (Kathy) Staudt is Professor of Political Science and Director of the Center for Civic Engagement at the University of Texas, El Paso. She received her Ph.D. in political science from the University of Wisconsin–Madison. She teaches courses on public policy, women/gender, borders, and democracy. Her research interests include border politics and public policy; education, schools, and standardized testing; women and gender in international development and bureaucracy; domestic violence; and civic engagement and education. Professor Staudt has published more than sixty academic articles/chapters and twelve books, including four on the U.S.-Mexico border. She is currently writing *Violence at the Border: Gender, Fear, and Everyday Life* for the University of Texas Press. Staudt is active in community organizations and serves on four nonprofit boards.

Clarence N. Stone is Research Professor of public policy and political science at the George Washington University and Professor Emeritus at the University of Maryland. He is the author of *Regime Politics: Governing Atlanta, 1946–1988* (University Press of Kansas, 1989). His most recent book is a coauthored work, *Building Civic Capacity: The Politics of Reforming Urban Schools* (University Press of Kansas, 2001). His current research interests include local agenda setting, capacity building for local democracy, and continuing attention to urban school reform.

Heidi Swarts is Assistant Professor of Political Science at Rutgers University, Newark, New Jersey. She received her Ph.D. from Cornell University in 2002 and a a M.Div. from Harvard Divinity School in 1994. Her research interests include social movements in American politics, urban politics, American political culture, and religion and politics. Her book, *Invisible Actors: Grassroots Community Organizations in American Urban Politics,* forthcoming from the University of Minnesota Press, compares mobilization processes, civic engagement, and policy outcomes of grassroots mobilization by ACORN and by federations of churches in American cities.

Richard Wood is Associate Professor of sociology and Director of the Southwest Institute on Religion and Civil Society at the University of New Mexico. He earned his Ph.D. from the University of California at Berkeley. Wood's research focuses on the institutional, organizational, and cultural underpinnings of democratic life. He is the author of *Faith in Action: Religion, Race, and Democratic Organizing in America* (University of Chicago Press, 2002), winner of the 2003 award for the best book in the sociology of religion from the American Sociological Association. Most recently, he published "Religion, Faith-Based Organizing and the Struggle for Justice," in *The Cambridge Handbook of the Sociology of Religion* (Cambridge University Press, 2005); and "Religious Culture and Political Action," *Sociological Theory* 17 (1999): 307–332.

INDEX